IRELAND AND EMPIRE, 1692–1770

Empires in Perspective

Series Editors: Tony Ballantyne
                 Duncan Bell
                 Francisco Bethencourt
                 Caroline Elkins
                 Durba Ghosh
Advisory Editor: Masaie Matsumura

Titles in this Series

FORTHCOMING TITLES

IRELAND AND EMPIRE, 1692–1770

BY

Charles Ivar McGrath

Routledge
Taylor & Francis Group

LONDON AND NEW YORK

First published 2012 by Pickering & Chatto (Publishers) Limited

Published 2016 by Routledge
2 Park Square, Milton Park, Abingdon, Oxfordshire OX14 4RN
711 Third Avenue, New York, NY 10017

First issued in paperback 2015

Routledge is an imprint of the Taylor & Francis Group, an informa business

BRITISH LIBRARY CATALOGUING IN PUBLICATION DATA

McGrath, Charles Ivar.
Ireland and empire, 1692–1770. – (Empires in perspective)
1. Ireland – History – 18th century. 2. Ireland – Politics and government – 18th
century. 3. Great Britain – Colonies – History – 18th century.
I. Title II. Series
909'.0971241'00899162–dc23

ISBN-13: 978-1-138-66351-0 (pbk)
ISBN-13: 978-1-8519-6896-1 (hbk)

Typeset by Pickering & Chatto (Publishers) Limited

CONTENTS

In memory of Yvonne McGrath (Née Cherer)

LIST OF FIGURES AND TABLES

ABBREVIATIONS

BL	British Library
CJI (1st)	*The Journals of the House of Commons of the Kingdom of Ireland*, 1st edn, 11 vols (Dublin, 1753–63)
CJI	*The Journals of the House of Commons of the Kingdom of Ireland*, 3rd edn, 21 vols (Dublin, 1796–1800)
CHOP	*Calendar of Home Office Papers*
CSPD	*Calendar of State Papers, Domestic Series*
CTB	*Calendar of Treasury Books*
CTP	*Calendar of Treasury Papers*
DIB	*Dictionary of Irish Biography* (Cambridge: Cambridge University Press, 2009)
HMC	Historical Manuscripts Commission
Keightley papers	Inchiquin MSS, Keightley papers
NAI	National Archives of Ireland
NHI	*A New History of Ireland*, vols 2, 3, 4, 9 (Oxford: Oxford University Press, 1976, 1984, 1986, 1987)
NLI	National Library of Ireland
ODNB	*Oxford Dictionary of National Biography* (Oxford: Oxford University Press, 2004)
PRONI	Public Record Office of Northern Ireland
SHC	Surrey History Centre, Woking
Stat. Ire.	*The Statutes at Large Passed in the Parliaments Held in Ireland*, 21 vols (Dublin, 1765–1804)
TCD	Trinity College Dublin
TNA	The National Archives, London
UCD	University College Dublin

PREFACE

The aim of this book is to examine Ireland's place and role in the British Empire in the period 1692–1770. The subject emerged in 2004–5 from research I had undertaken between October 1999 and September 2003 on the related topics of money, politics and power in Ireland in the years 1714–61. I have published the results of that research during the past decade in various journal articles, essays and edited collections and I am indebted to both the National University of Ireland and the Irish Research Council for the Humanities and Social Sciences for providing the postdoctoral fellowships that facilitated all of that work. This book builds upon those foundations with further research undertaken since 2004–5, combined with a return to material first examined in the 1990s.

The completion of this book has been greatly assisted by a variety of people to whom I am deeply grateful. Marnie Hay, Eoin Magennis and Patrick Walsh have read and commented upon various chapters and have provided important corrections and improvements. All three have also discussed the work at length with me and patiently listened to lengthy discourses on the trials and tribulations associated with it. I am also much indebted to Catriona Magennis for her sage advice and assistance at a particularly difficult moment in the book's gestation. All of the participants at the biennial 'Money, Power and Print' Colloquia have helped me to form my ideas over the years, while my two co-convenors of those events, Chris Fauske and Rick Kleer, have been unstinting in their encouragement, support and intellectual stimulation. My colleagues in the School of History and Archives at UCD have all offered encouragement and support in a variety of ways and I could not have completed the writing of the book without a crucial research semester provided in the autumn of 2011, which was facilitated by the good graces of my co-workers. I am particularly indebted in this respect, and in many others, to my friend and Head of School, John McCafferty.

Over the years I have received advice, information, references, ideas and much more from a wide range of friends and colleagues. In particular, and in alphabetical order, I would like to thank John Bergin, Ciaran Brady, Maurice Bric, Andrew Carpenter, Catherine Cox, Louis Cullen, David Dickson, Linda Doran, Declan Downey, Mark Empey, Lindsey Earner-Byrne, Suzanne Forbes,

Patrick Geoghegan, David Hayton, Andreas Hess, Neil Johnston, James Kelly, Patrick Kelly, Michael Kennedy, Eoin Kinsella, Sylvie Kleinman, Patrick Leech, Marie Léoutre, Emma Lyons, Jason McElligott, James McGuire, Anthony Malcomson, John Miller, Sean Moore, William Mulligan, Eamon O'Flaherty, Tadhg Ó hAnnracháin, Martyn Powell and Susannah Riordan.

Everything in life is made easier by the love and support of family and friends. My thanks to Neville Scarlett, who has for many years kept me entertained and enlightened, and to Dee and Eoin Scarlett, Karen O'Brien, Gary Holohan and their boys Matthew and Andrew, Conor Deane, Ann Devlin, Katherine Breen (who sadly passed away in 2008), Sarah Kingston, Ann Jones, Tony Kinsella and Clare Doyle, Polli Kaminski, Steve Hollingshead and Kath Serkis, and to my brothers and sisters, Gráinne, Stephen, Siobhan, Shane, Donnie and Maria and their spouses, children and grandchildren. My mother, Yvonne, who passed away in September 2010, was always the most supportive and enthusiastic advocate of my work and this book is dedicated to her memory. My greatest debt of all is to my wife, Marnie, and our son, Ivar Will. Their love has sustained me throughout. They make it all worthwhile.

1 CONTEXTS

The maintaining a standing army in Ireland since the Revolution; the building of barracks for the ease of the country and the reception of the army; the supporting of those barracks. The increase of the civil list, and several other exigencies of the state, having exceeded the produce of the hereditary revenue of the crown, it became necessary to have frequent parliaments in this kingdom, in order to obtain aids by additional duties, which are generally granted for two years, and therefore the parliament assembles every second year.[1]

Published in London in 1754, the foregoing extract from a pamphlet on the revenue and national debt of Ireland offered a succinct summary of the complex constitutional, political, financial and military alterations that had occurred in Ireland since the Glorious Revolution of 1688. While not considered revolutionary, those changes were at times extraordinary. The advent of regular parliaments from 1692 onwards represented a dramatic break with the past. Politics was wholly altered as the executive arm of government had to deal with a much more forthright and influential legislature, which utilized its newly acquired control of the purse strings to good effect in extracting further concessions on constitutional, political, religious, economic and other issues.[2]

According to the author of the 1754 pamphlet, the maintenance of a standing army, including the provision of barracks, was the primary reason for these dramatically changed circumstances.[3] The permanent placement of a 12,000-strong standing army in Ireland in the aftermath of the war of 1689–91 required innovation in government, parliament and the country in general. It required new financial practices, new infrastructures and, in practical terms, a place for the soldiers to live – a place of residence. That army also needed to have a use, or uses, both at home and abroad. All of these considerations were recognized, engaged with and successfully facilitated during the following decades, culminating in 1770 with the official augmentation by act of the Irish parliament of the size of that standing army to 15,235 soldiers.[4]

In relation to Ireland, and Irish history in general, such events are significant enough in themselves. However, when viewed from a broader perspective, they take on even greater significance. Between the years 1689 and 1763 England and, after 1707, Britain fought four major international wars, on the back of which the empire greatly expanded. Fundamental to that success was Britain's ability to sustain warfare in both victory and defeat at a level beyond that sustainable by the countries with which it was at war. The British 'fiscal-military state', as portrayed by John Brewer, was the '*Wunderkind* of the age'.[5] Britain's ability to outfinance and outspend its enemies in maintaining its army and navy at war was the key reason for its overall success in those four international wars and the concomitant expansion of the empire.[6] There are questions that remain unanswered, however. What role, if any, did Ireland play in these revolutionary financial and military changes and, therefore, within the empire? And, given that Ireland commenced maintaining a standing army in the 1690s during the first of those four international wars and significantly altered its political, financial and constitutional structures in order to do so, was there a direct correlation between Irish developments and the more recognized and acknowledged changes in Britain and the empire in the period 1692–1770? It is the aim of this book to answer those two questions.

One of the foremost authorities on the British empire in the eighteenth century, P. J. Marshall, noted in 2005 that historians had

> long assumed ... that the eighteenth-century British state ... was a weak one by comparison with authoritarian continental states. This is now contested. In some areas at least, the eighteenth-century British state seems to have been a formidable one by contemporary standards. Recent historiography has above all focused on its highly developed capacity to make war. In the second half of the eighteenth century the British began to deploy more and more of their military and naval resources throughout the world in defence of their own colonies and to conquer those of their enemies. It was primarily through its capacity to wage successful war and the subsequent policies that it devised to defend its gains that the British state shaped the evolution of empire.[7]

While Marshall's emphasis is on the second half of the eighteenth century, the British state's capacity to wage successful war, to defend its gains, and for the empire to evolve as it did was not born ready-made in 1750. The financial capabilities for long-term international war were put in place in the seventeenth century, especially after the Glorious Revolution.[8] The military lessons necessary for successful, sustained international war were also commenced in the later seventeenth century with England's involvement in the Nine Years' War in 1689.[9] In the 1690s and early eighteenth century, the combined evolving developments in financial practice and military structures laid the foundations for the defence of colonies and conquering of others that enabled the British state to expand the empire. As a part of that empire and enterprise, though not officially a part of that state, the separate though dependent kingdom of Ireland played a key, if understated, role.

Marshall has also pointed out that it was a 'momentous decision' during the Seven Years' War for the British government to resolve upon maintaining a 'permanent garrison of regular British troops' in America.[10] Perceived as a key event on the road to the American Revolution, that decision sparked discontent over the age-old bugbear of standing armies and led to the disastrous attempts at direct taxation from Westminster. Both the military and financial implications of these events have been identified as central criteria in defining the separation or difference between the mother country and the colony, with the standing army as an army of occupation and direct taxation as an arbitrary or imperial imposition without the consent or consideration of the governed.[11]

Yet the decision seventy years earlier to station a standing army in Ireland and to build a countrywide network of barracks for those soldiers did not prompt the same reaction, primarily because that decision was not accompanied by attempts at direct taxation. On the very few occasions the idea was floated at Whitehall, it was quickly dismissed as fraught with too many difficulties and dangers.[12] It was also the case that the governing elite in Ireland were a Protestant minority of the population, divided from the Catholic majority by their confessional allegiance and linked by that same allegiance with the Protestant majority in Britain. For them, a standing army was in part a security against possible rebellion by Catholic Ireland.[13] In that light the army might well be construed as an army of occupation, defending the colonial settler against the dispossessed native, even though the colonial settler in America would ultimately reject that supposed security.

Yet in Ireland it was problematic to equate Protestant with colonial settler. If English or British was the adjective, then many Catholics had to be included in the same pigeonhole. Old English Catholics had preceded New English Protestants, intermarriage had mixed the Gaelic Irish with newer arrivals, plantations had been infiltrated by existing populaces and converts continued to cross the divide. Ultimately, Protestants in Ireland could be, and were, just as legitimately defined as Irish. Since before the arrival of the Norman English, the myriad patterns of settlement, migration, plantation, marriage, association and conversion, with the Reformation sandwiched in between, defied the simplistic description of any one grouping in Ireland as colonial or colonizer.[14] Thus the army was, when possible, as attractive a source of employment for Irish Catholics as it was for Irish Protestants. This was evidenced in particular in the 1680s, intermittently during the first seventy years of the eighteenth century, and then again more consistently after 1771.[15]

At the outset of his two-volume history of late medieval and early modern Ireland, Sean Connolly noted with reference to the various communities that made up Ireland that a 'history of changing notions of identity is also, inescapably, a history of changing alliances and oppositions. To redefine who one was, was also to accept a new relationship to other ethnic, social or religious groups.' For Connolly, the history of Ireland is one of 'multiple transformations' of people, their identities, loyalties and alliances.[16] Commencing with a 'society defined by the distinction between an indigenous Gaelic Irish population and the heirs of a partial English conquest some three centuries old', within two centuries

> in 1688–91, we find the descendants of both these groups, now united by a shared Catholicism, mobilized in defence of the ruling British dynasty, while the heirs of a more recent Scottish and English colonization support a rival claimant to the thrones of England, Scotland, and Ireland.[17]

Like those Irish Protestants whom they faced on the battlefields in Ireland in 1689–91, the Gaelic Irish and old English Catholics who fought for James II comprehended an early modern polity that was monarchical.[18]

At what point did the Saxon, Viking or Norman cease to be the invader, the colonizer, the settler – the other – and become English, Welsh, Scottish or Irish? When did the descendants of the colonizer and settler and conqueror become assimilated into the host society or subsume the pre-existing communities into a new distinct society? When did it cease to be a colonial endeavour and change into a new society of peoples, distinct from the original newcomers? When did those who arrived in different waves from England, Scotland and Wales become Irish? Were the Protestant community in Ireland in the eighteenth century still settlers or were they Irish? As Anthony Pagden has observed in a more general context,

> In the first instance, conquest and settlement created dependent communities which demanded massive and constant assistance from the metropolis if they were to survive. Later, when these had become strong (and potentially profitable), they obstinately insisted on going their own way like troublesome children grown to adulthood. Their inhabitants inevitably became new and different people.[19]

The Irish situation was complicated by waves of different patterns of arrival, settlement, plantation and conquest over many centuries, with a fundamental politically fraught divide created by the Reformation and Counter-Reformation, which continues to serve as a major hindrance to answering the previous questions. The Protestant–Catholic division and conflict in early modern Ireland was of such violent and traumatic impact that it remains unacceptable even today for many to acknowledge that the Protestant ruling elite in the eighteenth century could be anything other than English or British colonizers and foreigners – imperialists with no semblance of Irishness to their name. Yet the reality was very different.

The island of Ireland was witness over the centuries to significant movements of people within the wider British Isles and further afield. Some migrated for short periods, others settled permanently, either assimilating into the existing community or in small colonies defined by an earlier usage describing settlements of 'farmers or cultivators'.[20] The Vikings in particular made an indelible impact, but like others before and after, those who remained permanently also ultimately assimilated into the existing populations. There was no Irish nation or state of the kind we know in the twenty-first century, but rather there was a melting pot of numerous autonomous, overlapping and yet disparate individual kingdoms, petty kingdoms, lordships, tribes, septs and families of Gaelic Irish and other peoples. Violence, professional warriors and multifarious wars coexisted with a penchant for learning and literature, an endeavour at a type of uniform legal system, and an intellectually advanced, and in some respects unique, Christian church adherent to Rome.[21]

In 1169 the Norman English arrived into parts of this polymorphic polity. Like previous newcomers, many assimilated and acculturated through association, adaption, marriage and other means. But the retention of a clear political connection with and allegiance to the English Crown created a new polity of loyalty, law, culture and custom defined as the English lordship of Ireland, into which many Gaelic Irish in time assimilated or associated. Like all other separate polities in Ireland, the English lordship waxed and waned in size and influence as events within and outside Ireland affected the ability of those tasked with governance to resist the normal dynastic, military and territorial pressures of a frontier society defined by constantly shifting borders, allegiances and loyalties. At one point accounting for most of the province of Leinster and parts of Connaught and Munster, the lordship had shrunk to only a few counties surrounding Dublin before the Tudors began the process of extending English-style governance to the whole of Ireland in a piecemeal fashion in the sixteenth century through a hybrid policy of conquest and conciliation.[22]

Prior to that time, attempts had been made to strengthen that polity by trying to resist assimilation and prioritize difference.[23] A sense of ethnic otherness was retained, in that the descendants of the Norman English became known as the Old English, though within that number were descendants of the Gaelic Irish as well. The Old English themselves also developed a sense of autonomy and separateness from the mother country and, like the English lords of the Welsh and Scottish marches and elsewhere, were given to independence of action and rebellion on occasion, especially in reaction to dynastic uncertainty in England or Crown attempts to impose a new direction upon affairs in Ireland. By the end of the fifteenth century the newly established Tudor dynasty looked to impose a greater degree of control upon the Old English lords, most notably the House of Kildare which ultimately went into self-destructive rebellion. There was also a receptive audience among the gentry of the English lordship of Ireland for such an approach, though the introduction of the Henrician religious Reformation created a wholly new and massively complicating element in the process.[24] For many of the Old English, continued adherence to the Roman Catholic Church was ultimately to demonstrate that their sobriquet meant nothing in political, economic, social or ethnic terms as they came to be treated in the same fashion as Gaelic Irish Catholics. Those Gaelic Irish and Old English who embraced the new religion travelled in the other direction, becoming part of the new order alongside the Protestant newcomers arriving from England and Scotland as part of a new policy of coordinated state-sponsored plantation and settlement aimed at, from a Protestant English perspective, civilizing and anglicizing Ireland.[25]

It was under the Catholic rule of Mary I and Phillip II that the first attempt at dramatic state-sponsored plantation and settlement for the purposes of civilizing and anglicizing Ireland occurred in Laois and Offaly. Never as comprehensive, accepted, fully implemented or embraced as in theory planned, further large-scale state-sponsored plantations occurred in the 1580s in Munster following the Old English Desmond rebellion and in Ulster in the 1610s in the aftermath of the Gaelic Irish-led Nine Years' War of 1594–1603 and the flight of Hugh O'Neill, Earl of Tyrone, and other Gaelic lords in 1607. Following further encroachments in the 1620s and 1630s, the most ambitious attempt at a countrywide confiscation, plantation and transplantation occurred in the 1650s in the wake of the Cromwellian reconquest of Ireland in the aftermath of the 1641 Ulster rebellion and the Confederation of Kilkenny of 1642–9, in which Old English and Gaelic Irish had finally faced the realization of their shared identity and interest. The final large-scale transfer of land occurred between 1691 and 1703, following the war of 1689–91 between the Catholic James II and his Protestant nephew and son-in-law, William of Orange, and the ensuing Williamite confiscation of Jacobite lands.[26] Those who had lost out since the process had begun in the 1550s were the Gaelic Irish and Old English who above all other things shared one common trait – their Catholicism. In a world where church and state were indivisible and the state was monarchical, subjects of another religion, especially one which demanded spiritual and temporal loyalty to a foreign power, were not to be accommodated within the political, economic or social power structures of that polity regardless of their apparent ethnic or other connections to the ruling elite.[27]

In eighteenth-century Ireland the ruling elite came from the Protestant minority community. Committed ideologically and practically to maintaining the all-essential connection with England, Irish Protestants inherited a pre-existing governmental system which they looked to adapt to best suit their own sense of identity and purpose.[28] At the centre of that system was the executive arm of government which replicated in most facets the procedures, offices and institutions in England. The head of the government was the monarch, until 1541 as lord of those areas of Ireland under English governance and from then onwards as the crowned head of the kingdom of Ireland which was a separate though dependent sister kingdom to England. While the English lordship of Ireland had at times in reality only extended to a few counties, the 1541 Act for Kingly Title created a new entity that for the first time ever extended English government to the whole of the country, at first in theory and then after 1603 in reality. Given that the monarch of these two sister kingdoms was first and foremost the crowned head of England and, after 1603, of the separate kingdom of Scotland as well, it was not surprising or unusual that in practice the Crown sent a representative to govern in their place in Ireland.[29]

The holder of the office of viceroy or chief governor in Ireland was the Lord Lieutenant. In his absence, government devolved upon a lord deputy or a commission of lord justices, usually three in number. The chief governor was aided by a privy council made up of leading nobles, bishops and gentry of Ireland. The seat of this central government was Dublin Castle, from where the day-to-day running of the country occurred.[30] Law and order was overseen by the four courts of Chancery, Exchequer, King's or Queen's Bench and Common Pleas. Other national courts were more specialized, such as Admiralty, or had ceased to exist prior to the eighteenth century, such as Castle Chamber, High Commission and Wards and Liveries.[31] In the absence of the modern concept of a civil guard or police force, at a local level town corporations and justices of the peace from among the gentry were tasked with upholding law and order in tandem with sheriffs, constables, bailiffs and watchmen. Central and local government came together when the judges went on circuit around the country several times a year to preside at the assize courts.[32]

The other main arms of executive government comprised the revenue service and the army. The former was the most pervasive by the end of the seventeenth century in that everyone, by some means, paid taxes. With over 1,000 officials working in thirty-eight ports and districts collecting customs, excise, hearth tax and other impositions from every household, business, enterprise and trade and providing information and intelligence to Dublin Castle, it was little surprise that by the early eighteenth century the office of revenue commissioner, of whom there were seven to preside over the whole revenue bureaucracy, had become a coveted position among Ireland's leading politicians owing to the patronage opportunities and the potential political influence.[33] The army was also a visible presence and reminder of the rule of government, but it was less invasive especially when barracks were provided for accommodation.[34] Such a perception was also assisted by the government's disinclination to use soldiers for day-to-day policing activities. Instead soldiers were utilized for more specialist activities such as prisoner escorts, quelling riots, assisting revenue collection and countering smuggling and banditry.[35]

A final aid to executive government was the Established Church. As one half of the indivisible early modern entity of 'church and state', the Established Church in any state was expected to be 'a central part of the organization of society ... upholding ... both social order and the authority of government'. This was seen not least in the very practical role of Protestant clergymen serving as justices of the peace and by the inclusion of the bishops in the House of Lords and by their service as lords justices and on the privy council.[36] But the Church, like the revenue bureaucracy, was also a very visible countrywide institution and therefore could serve as a conduit both for the dissemination of central government policy and for gathering local information and intelligence. The main problem in Ireland was that the majority of the population were adherents of a different faith.[37]

Parliament served as a counterbalance to the executive. Like the courts and the other components of English government in Ireland, parliament had been transposed to Ireland in the wake of the arrival of the Norman English in the late twelfth century. The first record of an Irish parliament was in 1264. Thereafter the assembly of the leading nobles, gentry and clergy as a parliament with administrative, judicial and legislative functions became an accepted part of the governmental system in the following centuries. The location and regularity of assembly fluctuated erratically as in England, while the administrative and judicial functions decreased and the legislative increased in the sixteenth and seventeenth centuries. The numbers summoned to assemble also fluctuated as the area of English governance expanded or contracted. The removal of the representatives of the ordinary clergy as a result of their opposition to aspects of the Henrician Reformation left only the bishops in the upper House of Lords as representatives of the Church. The lower House of Commons evolved by 1692 into an assembly of 300 elected MPs representing 150 two-seat constituencies comprising thirty-two counties, 117 boroughs and Trinity College Dublin.[38]

It is in part because of this governmental system that, although on the surface similar, the different experience of Ireland and the other seventeenth-century component parts of the emerging British empire, in particular North America and the West Indies, are more pronounced. Ireland was the only sister kingdom, however dependent she was, and the only dominion with a legislature deemed worthy of the name parliament. Apart from Jamaica after the 1720s, none of the American colonies supported a sizeable permanent standing army or paid for it out of their own public revenues. There were also dramatic differences in terms of population density, geographical location, longevity of association, familial and political ties with the mother country, social, economic and political integration within settler communities and with the mother country and between natives and newcomers, and much more besides.[39]

The contribution of Ireland to the emerging British empire measured in this book has not been readily acknowledged in the past, in part because it is the contribution of a Protestant minority elite via the media of taxation and military administration. The role of individuals, especially Irish Catholics, tends to be viewed as more acceptable from an Irish nationalist historical perspective, even if they contributed as soldiers on the battlefield. Great achievements can be lauded and praised even if understood to be in support of the wrong cause.

However, the achievements of those who were victorious in the political, religious and economic struggles of the seventeenth century, who imposed the penal laws against Catholics, and who appeared to run Ireland in the eighteenth century as a minority Protestant oligarchy with a subclass majority of Catholics are less edifying within that historiographical tradition.[40] To dismiss those achievements as somehow less significant or important because they occurred as part of the actions of a non-representative administration in what some view as a colonial province is unhistorical. Just because what occurred did not have the apparent backing from or input of the vast majority of people in Ireland at the time does not diminish its significance for the empire. The French, Spanish and other soldiers who faced regiments that existed in the field because of the system developed and paid for in Ireland did not question the ability of those soldiers because they did not have the imprimatur of the whole people of Ireland. Nor when those soldiers were successful in the field of battle were their achievements diminished because Ireland was governed and administered by a non-representative, sectarian minority elite. That the people who made the decisions, voted the taxes, built the barracks and administered the military in Ireland were not representative of the 'Irish' people (whoever they might be) cannot obscure the fact that Ireland as it was then governed, administered and ruled, however different to its past or future, made a highly significant and, at the time, unique contribution to the British Empire in the period 1692–1770.

The origins of that empire, like other medieval and early modern imperial enterprises, has long being associated with preliminary adventures in exploration and trade followed later by colonization, exploitation and the establishment of dominion over a conquered people. The conundrum for many has been the apparent tardiness of the English in the sixteenth century in this respect, despite the voyages of discovery by Englishmen or those acting under English authority from the reign of Henry VII onwards. With the old medieval empire gone, the English were latecomers to the expansion into the newer worlds of the Americas, Asia and Africa in the early modern period. Despite the efforts of the likes of Sir Humphrey Gilbert in modern-day Canada and Sir Walter Raleigh in America in the later sixteenth century, it was not until the formation of the East India Company in 1600 and the first settlement at Jamestown, Virginia, in 1607 that the foundations for the emergence of the early modern and modern British Empire were truly laid.[41]

It has been argued that this apparent dilatoriness was owing to, at different times, an unwillingness on the part of both the government and merchant community to get involved in overseas expansion. However, the sixteenth-century investment of English and Scottish time, money and people in Ireland represented a significant commitment and drain of the various resources that might well have otherwise been utilized elsewhere. Hence Ireland has often been seen as the first English experiment in early modern empire-building, especially in the plantation policy pursued from the 1550s onwards, most noticeably in Munster in the 1580s and, in particular, in Ulster in the 1610s.[42] Yet such a perception does not sit comfortably with several hundred years of prior contact, settlement and interaction; with Ireland's constitutional relationship with England as it developed from the twelfth century; or with the role of religious division in affecting English policy towards Ireland from the 1530s onwards.[43]

Ireland's place and role within the emerging empire in the seventeenth and eighteenth centuries is therefore complex.[44] Aside from the viewpoint that Ireland served as a model for English colonization, plantation and settlement in the Americas in particular (an argument that has as many critics as advocates),[45] Ireland's contribution, like that of other countries subsumed within an empire, is often measured first and foremost in terms of the people who came to populate newly colonized territories. The Irish in America, Canada, Australia, New Zealand, Africa and elsewhere in former British colonies are thus seen as the true measurement of Ireland's role in the imperial enterprise, a role that is perceived as more acceptable than that of conquest, oppression and economic subjugation and exploitation, even if many of those Irish peoples served as soldiers within the imperial military machine and as colonial administrators.[46]

The involvement of the Irish in peopling the empire with labourers, servants, farmers, merchants, doctors, lawyers and other non-military or administrative personnel evolved over a long period of time and did not reach its peak until the famine years of the 1840s. Beyond the long-standing though changeable patterns of movement within Europe and the annual migrations for fishing and other work, the main focus for Irish emigration was North America. From the 1630s onwards Irish Catholics were moving to the West Indies in their hundreds on an annual basis in an emigration that included numerous indentured servants, convicts, prisoners of war and the younger sons of wealthy families looking to establish themselves as merchants and planters. Even more Irish Catholics and Protestants were drawn to the thirteen American colonies. The most conservative estimate for the total number that left for America in the seventeenth and eighteenth centuries up to the 1770s is 108,000. Not only does this pale in comparison to the 8 million who left for all parts of the world between 1800 and 1921, but it also defied the confessional demographic of nineteenth-century emigration given that at least 66,000 of those 108,000 were Irish (mostly Presbyterian) Protestants. In the nineteenth century the vast majority of emigrants were Catholic though Protestant Irish of all denominations also continued to leave for America as well as the newer destinations of Canada, Australia, New Zealand and elsewhere.[47]

The reasons for such movements of people were and are varied. Social, political, economic and religious motivations coupled with both internal and external factors were all enumerated. As Louis Cullen has stated, 'the mobility of the

Irish is a complex phenomenon, explained by a mix of elements of dynamism, persecution and poverty'.[48] Ultimately, Irish emigrants within the empire from the seventeenth through to the twentieth century were 'both subjects and agents of imperialism'.[49]

This much-studied movement of Irish people however only addresses one particular aspect of Ireland's contribution to the annexing and settling of newly acquired territory within the empire. Ireland's position in trading and commercial terms was in some respects more ambiguous because of the dichotomous nature of the relationship with England and Britain, but it was ultimately a profitable one. Trade was an essential precursor and staple of early modern imperial enterprise, but it was also a jealously guarded privilege.[50] English commercial restrictions upon Ireland were on paper and in theory prohibitive.[51] But loopholes were found, ambiguities abounded, restrictions were ignored or relaxed, and even when enforced the import trade via British ports was still profitable enough to warrant the ongoing growth in Ireland's trade with the emerging colonies of the empire around the world. In particular, Ireland's trade to the West Indies and mainland America grew significantly throughout the seventeenth and eighteenth centuries. Salted beef and other provisions for westward-bound fleets and for the populations of the Caribbean islands and mainland America were coupled with the importation of sugar, tobacco and other goods ultimately destined for Ireland. Whether based in the West Indies, mainland America, Ireland, England or the European continent, Irish Catholic and Protestant merchants and their families and, ultimately, Ireland's economy benefited from the British Empire's trading networks. It never constituted a completely free trade in the period 1692–1770 and the imperial restrictions certainly retarded certain developments within Ireland's mercantile and commercial communities and among those who provided the raw and manufactured goods and materials for commerce and economic activity, but such effects were neither as clear-cut nor as detrimental as was once believed. Rather, the economic and financial benefits for Ireland of having controlled access to the British empire's markets when many others were excluded has been more readily acknowledged as noticeable, significant and an economic opportunity that otherwise would not have come to pass.[52]

The most difficult question to answer, however, is the extent to which Ireland played a proactive role in the expansion of the British Empire. Did government policy and the actions and attitudes of the political nation and the general populace, whether wittingly or not, contribute in any significant way to the expansion of the empire in the period 1692–1770? And if so, does it have a bearing upon our understanding of Ireland's position within the empire, as either subject colony or agent of imperialism, or as an amalgam of both?[53] One area where answers have not really been sought before is that of Ireland's role in facilitating the expansion of empire from a financial and military perspective, within the context of John Brewer's eighteenth-century 'fiscal-military' state. Part II of this book examines the military establishment maintained in Ireland and its use in an Irish and imperial context both during peace and wartime in the period under study. Part III examines how that military establishment was paid for, from whence the necessary public funds arose, and the willingness of the public to fund such an undertaking. But in order to set such considerations within their proper context, it is first necessary to examine the religious and political circumstances prevalent in early modern Ireland and to assess how those matters help to locate Ireland within the emerging British Empire in the period 1692–1770.

2 RELIGION

Religion, and people's adherence to a particular confessional grouping, is central to understanding and locating Ireland in the early modern world and in relation to Britain and the empire. It is also the case that, because of the way in which the Reformations of the sixteenth century unfolded in Ireland, the history of religious division is also crucial for that understanding. In particular, it is a question of comprehending the relationship between Catholic and Protestant with regard to each other, the monarchy and the governments of both Ireland and England. It is less about theology, doctrine or faith and more about the consequences of different understandings of such matters.

As Ian McBride has asserted, Linda Colley's thesis in *Britons* of the centrality of Protestantism to 'the invention of Great Britain' has a resonance for Ireland in relation to those in the western kingdom who were adherents of the Established Protestant church.[1] However, if Protestantism was the 'primary cultural resource which united the peoples of England, Scotland and Wales' in terms of Britain and the empire 'despite the persistence of national, regional and local differences',[2] Ireland at first sight might appear to represent the black sheep of the family, given its predominantly Catholic demographic profile. Two issues are therefore paramount in assessing the impact of divided confessional allegiance in Ireland upon the country's place and role within the British Empire in the period 1692–1770: the first is the loyalty of the populace to, in the first instance, the monarchy and then to Irish and English or British governments; and the second is the relationship of the confessional grouping in power with those of other religious beliefs whom they governed.

The Reformation in Ireland, unlike in England, did not experience ultimate success in terms of demographic transfer of confessional allegiance. The reasons why for both England and Ireland are highly complex. The Reformation was not an overnight event, but rather a slow-burning fire that eventually caught hold for the majority in England but only a minority in Ireland. Geography, political will, provision of clergy, reforming zeal, societal structures, financial investment, local dynastic allegiances and conflicts, economic and political imperatives and a myriad of other reasons in one instance proved conducive to reformation and in the other proved a hindrance. Much has already been written on the subject, and need not be rehearsed here. Suffice to say that combined with the increasing efforts of the Counter-Reformation, by the early seventeenth century, if not earlier, Ireland was clearly no longer fertile ground for the sixteenth-century reforming instinct and was already demographically divided on religious grounds in a manner that England and most other early modern European countries were not.[3]

That is not to say that Ireland's religious status was exceptional. Indeed it was very much in keeping with other seventeenth- and eighteenth-century Post-Reformation European countries in that church and state were perceived as one indivisible entity, with failure to adhere to the religion of the state serving to marginalize, and alienate, those of different creeds and beliefs. As Protestants were marginalized in Catholic states, so Catholics in Ireland were marginalized because they lived in a Protestant state.[4] What was exceptional however was that in Ireland the marginalized populace made up the bulk of the population. Elsewhere in Europe, even in the Protestant United Provinces of the Dutch Republic where Catholics constituted almost 45 per cent of the population, they remained a minority community.[5] In Ireland however Roman Catholics accounted for 70–80 per cent of the people on the island. The remainder were Protestant, though made up from a mixture of adherents of the Established Church of Ireland, which accounted for the single largest minority grouping, and various nonconforming or dissenter communities, of whom the Presbyterians, most numerous in the north and closely connected with nearby Scotland, constituted the next largest minority grouping.

The difficulties both then and now in trying to understand Ireland's relationship with Britain and its empire in the eighteenth century were created not so much by the fact that religious-based coercion and exclusion of the kind common enough in Europe at the time was implemented in Ireland, but rather by the fact that it was the majority of the population who were on the receiving end of that treatment. Reflected to a degree in the actions and words of some in the seventeenth and eighteenth centuries, but even more in the imaginations of a significant number of nineteenth- and twentieth-century Irish people, eighteenth-century Irish Catholics were a colonized people who were the victims of an imperial power imposing its will through violent means. But Irish Catholics were by no means the same as the colonized and brutalized native populations of North or South America in the early modern period or the indigenous populations of Africa, Australia and New Zealand in the nineteenth century. The ethnic melting pot of Ireland had long since resulted in Gaelic Irish Protestants, Old English Protestants and New English Catholics muddying the validity of using religious adherence as a valid means of differentiating on ethnic grounds the colonizer from the colonized: it was not valid then, nor is it now, to oversimplify and thereby distort the complex reality by arguing that Protestant always

equated with English, British and oppressor, while Catholic always equated with
Irish and victim. To oversimplify in such a manner removes all but the Established
Church of Ireland Protestants from having any reason for playing a significant or
active role within the British Empire. The oversimplified response is that the victim can do little more than fulfil the roles designed for him or her by the imperial
power – indentured servant, slave, cannon fodder, emigrant, unskilled labourer.
However, eighteenth-century Ireland was a much more complex country than
that and, in terms of religion, the three main groupings were viewed differently,
viewed things differently, acted in different ways, and held different aims to
those personified by the oversimplified narrative outlined above. Examination
of Catholic, Dissenting and Protestant Ireland will thus help to clarify Ireland's
place and role within the British Empire in the period 1692–1770.

* * *

It was the Acts of Supremacy of 1536 and 1560 and the 1560 Act of Uniformity
that formed the initial basis for the religious division created by the Reformation
in Ireland and which placed Catholicism in a problematic position.[6] A wholly
Catholic community of Old English families who held the reins of power in those
parts of Ireland which gave allegiance to the English monarch as lord of Ireland
began to splinter as some turned Protestant and, joined by new arrivals from England, first political and later economic power began to shift in their direction. At
the same time, in the sixty or so separate political entities that made up the various
communities inhabiting the island, the dominant Gaelic Irish chieftains began to
see their own power rapidly diminish as the logic of Tudor policy, particularly
following the 1541 Act for Kingly Title, moved toward conquest of the whole of
Ireland. A policy of plantation, even though initiated under a Catholic Queen in
the 1550s and advocated for by Old English Catholics, in time became perceived
as a Protestant policy which defined an ethnic difference between Catholics and
Protestants, even though often there was little or no difference between those
who lost land and those who gained it – the Old English who converted to the
Established religion benefited while those who did not lost out. The Gaelic Irish
could be held up as an exception, yet there were those who converted to the
Established religion and survived in their estates unmolested.[7]

It was also the case that the vast majority of Irish Catholics, like the vast
majority of the other religious groupings in Ireland, understood that the normal
nature of government was monarchical. The obsession throughout the seventeenth century with the desire to find a formula by which they could demonstrate
their temporal loyalty to a Protestant monarch was the rule rather than the exception. Even the more extreme polemicists such as the Gaelic Irish Jesuit Conor
O'Mahoney who, while advocating the annihilation of the English in Ireland in

his *Disputatio Apologetica* in 1647, still advocated a monarchical form of government with a Gaelic Irish king. Likewise in the 1640s some advocated that the
monarch should be Catholic.[8] The majority however, even when unable to agree
upon a formula for expressing their loyalty to a Protestant monarch resident in
England, did not see the need to change the monarchical system of government or
the reigning monarch. And as Nicholas Canny has forcefully argued, that majority as measured by the leadership within a community, which in this case was the
landowners of both Gaelic Irish and Old English origins, 'were increasingly united
by allegiance to a common Catholicism, and out of fear of a Dublin administration that was bent on their destruction'. Therefore it was 'those who have been
identified in the literature as the representatives of the Old English interest [who]
were really negotiating on behalf of all Catholic landowners in Ireland'.[9]

Irish Catholics also understood that Ireland's monarchical system of government functioned within the early modern concept of a composite monarchy
or state, with different regions, communities and land masses being ruled over
by one monarch, with representatives appointed to govern in the localities,
and with the central institutions of government being replicated in the various
regions and localities in the manner that both Scotland and Ireland were governed for the most part in the seventeenth and early eighteenth century prior to
the Anglo-Scottish Union of 1707. Ireland continued to function within that
composite monarchy or state model until 1801.[10]

Thus for Irish Catholics, be they Gaelic Irish or Old English in origin, a Protestant monarch ruling from London via his or her representatives in Dublin
Castle was not overly problematic or alien. For Protestants, however, Catholic
loyalty was questionable because of their confessional allegiance to Rome and
the papacy. While Irish Catholics could readily argue that they were loyal in
temporal terms to their Protestant monarch, their inability because of their
Catholicism to take the required oath in accordance with the Act of Supremacy
undermined those arguments in the eyes of loyal Protestants. Such conflicting
views dogged Catholic attempts to come to an accommodation with an increasingly Protestant state in seventeenth-century Ireland and a wholly Protestant
state in the eighteenth century.[11]

The question of Catholic loyalty was central to the negotiation in 1626–8 of
the 'Graces', which were agreed between Charles I and his Catholic and Protestant Irish subjects and were aimed at addressing a range of grievances in return
for financial subsidies. Given the inherent confessional difficulty for Catholics
in taking the oath of supremacy, the ongoing desire to replace that oath with a
simpler oath of allegiance came to the fore in respect of 'entry into the possession
of estates, the holding of office and the practice of law'. In the end, article fifteen
of the Graces replaced the oath of supremacy with one of allegiance only for the
Court of Wards with regard to estates and the practice of law. But Charles I him-

self had realized the significance of allowing Catholics to express their loyalty to a Protestant monarch, and had even required an oath of fidelity to be taken throughout the Pale when the security threat to the British Isles was heightened by the Franco-Spanish treaty of Barcelona in 1626.[12]

Such declarations of allegiance seemed hollow if those making them were in actual rebellion. But in such instances, the perceived crucial difference was whether that loyalty was to the monarch or the government and institutions of the state. From its inception in 1642 the Catholic Confederation of Kilkenny, although the governing body for a rebellion that had commenced in October 1641, sought a variety of ways of declaring their loyalty to Charles I while also dismissing as 'malignant' the government and institutions of state in both Ireland and England.[13] As a precursor to the formal establishment of the Confederation, a national Catholic ecclesiastical congregation met in Kilkenny in May 1642 to discuss the various options for establishing a civil government in Ireland, when it was among other matters agreed that Catholic Ireland was engaged in a 'lawful and just' war

> against sectaries, and chiefly against Puritans, for the defence of the Catholic religion, for the maintenance of the prerogative and the royal rights of our gracious King Charles, for our gracious Queen so unworthily abused by the Puritans, for the honour, safety and health of their royal issue, for to avert and refrain the injuries done unto them.

Their enemies – the 'unlawful usurpers [and] oppressors' – were the English parliament, even though it was not yet in open conflict with the King, and the government in Dublin.[14]

The Catholic Confederation was formally established in Kilkenny in October, after civil war finally broke out in England between parliament and the King. From the outset, everyone in Ireland under the Confederation's authority had to

> bear faith and true allegiance, unto our sovereign lord King Charles, by the grace of God, King of Great Britain, France and Ireland, his heirs and lawful successors. And shall uphold and maintain his and their rights and lawful prerogatives ... against all manner of persons.

The necessity to take such a step was owing to the fact that government in Dublin was 'commanded by the malignant party, who are enemies to God and their King, and his majesty's well-affected subjects'.[15] Thereafter during the 1640s the various Confederate oaths required the swearing of 'true faith and allegiance' to Charles I and the promise to 'defend, uphold and maintain' his 'just prerogatives'. Even when the treaty negotiations in 1646 drove a divisive wedge through the Confederation, adherents still had to swear to advance and preserve 'his majesty's rights'.[16]

After the appointment of GianBattista Rinuccini as papal nuncio to Ireland in 1645 there was some support for the argument that the monarch should in fact be Catholic. Some countered by arguing that it was sufficient that Charles I's queen was a Catholic.[17] However, the adverse reaction in 1647 to O'Mahoney's *Disputatio Apologetica*, which was seen as an attempt to legitimize the idea of a Gaelic Irish king such as Owen Roe O'Neill, was indicative of the fact that the vast majority of Confederate Catholics, both Gaelic Irish and Old English, remained wedded for a variety of reasons to the Stuarts and the pre-existing monarchical system of government even if ultimately advocating significantly divergent proposals for a final political and economic settlement in the event of a royalist and Confederate military victory.[18]

With the Restoration of Charles II in 1660, Catholics again looked to find a solution to the loyalty conundrum, though the endeavour resulted in divisions within Catholic Ireland instead. In December 1661 a Franciscan priest, Peter Walsh, began promoting an 'Irish Remonstrance' penned by Richard Bellings and aimed at demonstrating Catholic loyalty to the Protestant Crown. In a lengthy document, those subscribing to it acknowledged Charles II as 'our true and lawful King, supreme lord, and rightful sovereign' and declared obedience in 'all civil and temporal affairs' regardless of any 'power or pretension of the pope or see of Rome'.[19] The remonstrance went further than any previous proposal in denying the temporal power and jurisdiction of the papacy in particular, and in so doing challenged previous papal actions, especially the bull *Regnans in Excelsis* issued in the reign of Elizabeth I.[20] It was unsurprising therefore that although signed by sixty-nine Irish Catholic clergy and 130 leading laity, the remonstrance was condemned by Rome and opposed by most of the clergy. Lord Lieutenant Ormond however still pressed Walsh to get as many signatures as possible as a means of distinguishing loyal from disloyal subjects and in 1666 agreed to summon a meeting of Catholic clergy in Dublin with a view to garnering further support.[21] Instead, the meeting rejected the remonstrance but came up with what appeared a reasonable alternative, though Walsh and Ormond rejected it in turn, an outcome that Rome celebrated because neither proposal was deemed to be in line with 'the truth of Catholic teaching'.[22] In 1670 another version of an oath was prepared by the Catholic Archbishop of Dublin, Peter Talbot, who had been one of the main opponents of the remonstrance when still a royal chaplain in London, though nothing came of his proposal either.[23]

In the 1680s Irish Catholic adherence to James II might easily be ascribed simply to the fact that he was their co-religionist. Since his accession in 1685 a Catholic Counter-Revolution had unfolded in Ireland offering the hope that the existing Protestant composite monarchy might eventually become a Catholic one. But it was also the case that Irish Catholics, especially after James was removed from the throne in November-December 1688, supported him because he was the *de jure* king of England, Scotland and Ireland. That such a stance was in fact the natural and normal order of things in seventeenth-century Britain and Ireland was seen in the manner in which so many English Protestants, despite their very clear self-interest in supporting William III, still struggled with their consciences in swearing allegiance to him. That many ultimately did so owed much to the fact that the new oath of allegiance to William and Mary was simplified into a *de facto* recognition of the new monarchs without the need for the overt acknowledgment of the legitimacy of their claim or the rejection of James. Even still, a significant minority of people could not bring themselves to subscribe to such an oath.[24]

The new oath, requiring a person to swear that they would 'be faithful and bear true allegiance to their majesties King William and Queen Mary' was also applied to Ireland by the end of 1691, following the conclusion of the war between the forces of William III and James II, which had lasted for almost three years from early 1689.[25] The Articles of Limerick, which brought the war to an end in October 1691, in theory revived the spirit of earlier attempts at finding an acceptable formula for Catholics to demonstrate their loyalty, as it was specified in Article IX that the new oath of allegiance was the only one to be administered to 'such Roman Catholics as submit to their majesties' government'.[26] Within a few weeks the English act for abrogating the oath of supremacy in Ireland and appointing other oaths stymied the apparent possibilities of the Limerick agreement. Although a saving clause was included for the beneficiaries of the Articles, the 1691 Oath Act included a new oath of supremacy, as it became known, which abjured the doctrine that princes excommunicated or deprived by the papacy could be deposed or murdered and denied the ecclesiastical and spiritual authority of the pope. The act also required a declaration against transubstantiation.[27]

The 1691 Oath Act ultimately ensured that no Catholic could sit in the Irish Commons and also resulted in the final exclusion of Catholic peers from the Lords.[28] It was apparent that the desire throughout the seventeenth century to find a formula for expressing loyalty had been driven in part by the hope that it would thereby prevent the coercion, alienation and marginalization of Catholics because of their confessional allegiance. The 1691 Oath Act not only demonstrated that little or no progress had been made in that respect, but it also confirmed, as a prerequisite to the introduction of the penal laws in Ireland, that throughout the seventeenth century Catholic Ireland had in reality fought a losing battle against the destruction of their political and economic power. The land confiscations, plantations and settlements between the 1550s and 1660s had dramatically reduced Catholic landholding in the country from *c.* 60 per cent in 1641 to *c.* 22 per cent in 1688, so that their concomitant political and economic power was reduced also.[29]

The reduction in Catholic political power was seen in many ways, including the loss of civil and military office, but was most readily evident in the decline in the number of Catholic MPs from an overwhelming majority in the later

sixteenth century to none in the 1660s. While Catholic peers had continued
in the Lords in the 1660s, the final collapse of Catholic political power was
poignantly signified, if primarily symbolically, by their exclusion from the 1690s
onwards.[30] The flight to the continent of about 12,000 Jacobite soldiers at the
end of 1691, commanded by leading Irish Catholic nobility and gentry, was in
reality an even more dramatic signifier of that collapse.[31]

The final resounding defeat of Catholic Ireland in 1691 ultimately paved
the way for the introduction of the penal laws in the 1690s and thereafter. Such
coercive measures were a central aspect of the second key question asked at the
outset of this chapter regarding the relationship of the confessional grouping in
power with those of other religious beliefs whom they governed. Such coercive
legislation was not exceptional in early modern Europe where the subjects of
confessional monarchical states were expected to be of the established religion.
If they were not, then for the primary reasons of loyalty and allegiance already
alluded to they were liable to be subject to legal disabilities in relation to political, civil and religious rights. Such was the situation for Protestants in France and
Spain and Catholics in England.[32] In that light, a more pertinent question might
be why the introduction of a body of laws imposing a series of penalties upon
Irish Catholics in relation to land, education, the franchise, weapons, horses and
religious worship did not occur in Ireland until 100 years after the same or similar had been imposed in England.[33]

The explanation lies in a number of areas. From the time of the Reformations in England and Ireland there had been laws affecting Catholics. The Acts
of Supremacy in 1536 and 1560 and the Act of Uniformity of 1560 comprised
the main legislation of the Irish parliament affecting Catholics and were wholly
modelled upon, and imposed because of, the English precedents of 1534, 1552
and 1559. The oath of supremacy required by the Acts of Supremacy applied to
all public office holders and clergy among others and required the subscriber to
acknowledge royal supremacy over the Church and to renounce the spiritual and
temporal jurisdiction and authority of the Pope. The Act of Uniformity provided
for conformity in religious practice, including the imposition of a fine of 12*d.* for
failure to attend Protestant religious service on Sundays or other appointed days.
These laws demonstrated in no uncertain terms the early modern concept of the
church and state as an indivisible single entity and the understanding that those
who were recusant in that respect were inherently problematic.[34]

In practice the Acts of Supremacy and Uniformity were not as rigorously
adhered to or enforced as might have been expected. Well into the seventeenth
century Irish Catholics continued to hold public office, while the recusancy
fines were not consistently imposed.[35] At the same time, in England the greatly
diminished number of adherents of Catholicism were legislated against in
a body of penal laws in the late sixteenth and early seventeenth centuries that

bore little resemblance to the acts for royal supremacy and conformity. A much more draconian body of legislation imposing truly coercive and fundamentally destructive economic, religious and political penalties upon English Catholics was enacted between the 1570s and 1620s in reaction to internal and external Catholic threats to the security of the Protestant state. Laws relating to Catholic education, office-holding, property, weapons and ammunition, place of residence, local and overseas travel, registration, religious worship and the clergy were enacted, if not always enforced.[36] Additional legislation was passed much later in 1673, 1678 and 1689 in response to renewed fears of the perceived threat from Catholicism at home and abroad.[37]

But although Catholic political power was diminishing in Ireland during the later sixteenth and early seventeenth centuries, it remained strong enough to prevent such English policies becoming permanent enactments in Ireland. There were still enough Catholic MPs to successfully oppose proposals in parliament and enough leading nobility and gentry to advocate against such measures when considered by government. For example, in 1569 Catholic MPs successfully opposed a proposal to introduce certain English legislation relating to Catholics into the Irish parliament, while in 1613 they successfully negotiated the dropping of proposed government penal legislation for banishing Jesuits and seminary priests, penalizing English Catholics in Ireland and banning foreign education.[38]

The norm therefore was for more fitful repression by temporary proclamations inspired by English statutes. In 1605 such rule by proclamation included the banishment of all Jesuits and other regular Catholic clergy from the country, the imprisonment of any who arrived in Ireland thereafter and the ordering of all subjects to attend Protestant service on Sundays and other holy days.[39] Similar orders were issued for the imprisonment of the more outspoken Catholic clergy, the seizure of Catholic clerical property held in trust by lay Catholics and the mandating of leading Catholic figures to attend Protestant services on penalty of monetary fines and removal from civil offices. Monarchical restraint however ensured that the policy was short-lived and less damaging than it could have been.[40] Similar restraint was shown from London on later occasions, as in 1613–14 when zealous officials in Dublin wished to pursue a harder line in the continued governance of Irish Catholics by proclamations covering matters such as foreign education and banishing clergy.[41]

Under Charles I sporadic and fitful repression continued alongside periods of quiet lassitude.[42] The 1641 rebellion turned the world right-side up for Catholics living within the areas controlled by the Confederation, but that experience was short-lived as the Cromwellian conquest from 1649 onwards was followed by the most oppressive regime yet. The Protectorate parliamentary union of 1653 meant that Irish Catholics were subject to the worst excesses, as was all too readily seen during that decade, of existing English penal legislation and new parliamentary ordinances. However, the dissolution of that union and the Restoration of the monarchy in 1660 meant that there were still no actual penal laws on the Irish statute books, a circumstance that the Irish Catholic interest proved powerful enough to maintain in the following three decades. Although no Catholic MPs sat in the Commons in 1661–6, there were enough Catholic peers in the Lords and sufficient influential Catholic members of society to constitute a significant and useful lobby. During the Restoration period Irish Catholics were able to ensure a degree of accommodation within the existing Protestant state owing to factors such as Charles II's pursuit of a policy of toleration, the conversion to Catholicism of his younger brother, the future James II, and the influence of individuals such as Richard Talbot, later earl of Tyrconnell and the last Catholic lord deputy of Ireland. Yet fitful penal repression remained the normal reaction to political or security crises, usually of English making, such as the adverse reaction in 1673 to Charles's 1672 Declaration of Indulgence and James's open acknowledgement of his earlier conversion to Catholicism, or in 1678 to the revelations of the wholly fabricated Popish Plot and the more real prospect of a Catholic succession to the crowns of England, Scotland and Ireland.[43]

Government in Ireland tended to follow the lead from England at such times. In both 1673 and 1678 proclamations were issued banishing all regular clergy, Catholic bishops and others exercising ecclesiastical authority, for suppressing all convents, friaries, seminaries, nunneries and Catholic schools, and for disarming Catholics.[44] The banishment and suppression proclamation was also reissued in 1674, 1679 and 1680.[45] The Popish Plot also resulted in a series of proclamations prohibiting Catholics from entering Dublin Castle or any other fort or citadel in Ireland, meeting in groups or at night-time, residing in any garrison towns unless already living there for more than a year, and for uncovering any converts to Catholicism in the army.[46] The need to reissue most proclamations from time to time demonstrated the inefficiency of rule by such temporary measures, as for example in 1678 when one was issued 'highly resenting the slackness of the justices … in executing the late proclamation' for disarming Catholics.[47] It was for such reasons that consideration was given in government in 1678–9 to the idea of enacting penal legislation in a proposed Irish parliament. Although it was ultimately decided not to summon the legislature at that time, it was indicative of the future that some of the proposed bills included the banishment of all Catholic bishops and regular clergy and the exclusion of Catholics and Protestant dissenters from the Commons.[48]

The reign of James II resulted in an about-turn for Irish Catholics. The changed circumstance was seen in 1689 when Tyrconnell, after war broke out, issued a proclamation for disarming all those who might be deemed to offer assistance to William III. Although Irish Protestants were not specifically mentioned, there was no doubt who was being targeted.[49] But the Catholic

Counter-Revolution was short-lived. The Williamite military victory at the end of 1691 not only meant the final defeat of Catholic Ireland; it also meant that after more than 100 years, the circumstances were now such that the enactment of Irish penal laws on a par with those of England was a realistic prospect. The 1691 Oath Act ensured a wholly Protestant parliament; the exile of over 12,000 Jacobite solders removed a large section of the leadership and voice of Catholic Ireland; the evidence in Protestant minds of past, present and future Catholic perfidy and treasonable behaviour was sufficiently abundant; and the ensuing regular assembly of parliament in the 1690s and thereafter provided the institutional continuity necessary for creating a body of penal legislation.[50]

The penal laws that were enacted between 1695 and 1709, with at least one measure passed in every session of the Irish parliament during that time, were more readily known to the legislators themselves and their contemporaries as popery laws.[51] From the outset, a very clear and evident concern for the security of the Protestant interest in Ireland against internal and external threat was evident. That interest was ultimately about economic and political power, while the threat was one of a Frenchified Catholic absolutism personified by the assistance Louis XIV had provided to James II in Ireland during the war of 1689–91 and the ensuing presence of the exiled James and his Irish Catholic army in French service after 1691. As long as the Nine Years' War of 1689–97 continued on the continent and England remained at war with France, Jacobite and French privateers harassing the Irish coast in league with Irish Catholic tory and rapparee outlaws constantly reminded Irish Protestants of the very real threat from which they had only recently been delivered by William III. It was little surprise that proclamations for disarming Irish Catholics and rounding up horses, clergy and prominent laity were issued in the same manner as they were in England at times of feared invasion during the first half of the 1690s.[52]

The first endeavour to engage with these issues in legislative terms came when the first post-Glorious Revolution Irish parliament was summoned in late 1692. Among the bills drafted by the government was a measure for settling the militia in Ireland, which included a clause for disarming Catholics. However, the bill was lost amid a constitutional crisis that resulted in the session being brought to an abrupt and precipitate end only four weeks after convening, though not before the Commons had signified their strong desire to draft their own legislation on the matter.[53] The political impasse that ensued was eventually broken in 1694–5, when as part of a negotiated compromise the government agreed to introduce two penal bills the next time the legislature convened. The first measure was for disarming and dismounting Irish Catholics and the second for prohibiting Catholic foreign education.[54] In reality, neither bill represented a concession on the part of the English or Irish governments. In the case of the disarming bill the policies to be enshrined in statute had been a constant part of Williamite government policy since 1690 and were modelled on antecedents in Ireland stretching back beyond the 1670s and in England to the late sixteenth and early seventeenth centuries.[55] As to that for prohibiting foreign education, the justification provided by Lord Deputy Henry, Baron Capell, that the bill would 'secure the Protestant religion' demonstrated how it also looked to address the same fears and concerns expressed by both government and Protestant Ireland in the preceding years.[56] The long-standing threat from European Counter-Reformation Catholicism and the more immediate danger of contact between Irish Catholics and Jacobite exiles in France in particular was in part responsible for the bill, while a sense of continuity existed with the restrictions placed upon Catholic education in the renewed Act of Uniformity in 1665 and the suppression of Catholic schools in the banishment proclamations of the 1670s.[57]

The two bills passed through the Irish parliament of 1695 without significant delay or opposition. Although a few MPs argued that they were 'ill drawn and of no great consequence',[58] the Commons chose to 'swallow them with their faults' rather than lose them.[59] The 'act for the better securing the government, by disarming papists' was self-evidently a security measure, aimed at removing the weapons from those whose allegiance to the monarchy and state was suspect. As the preamble stated, it was intended for 'preserving the public peace, and quieting the kingdom from all dangers of insurrection and rebellion for the future'. The act required Catholics to surrender 'all their arms, armour and ammunition' and prohibited them from possessing any in the future. It also restricted Catholics to owning horses of £5 value or less and allowed any Protestant on discovery of a horse of greater value to purchase it for £5 5s. If the offered price was refused in front of magistrates, the horse was deemed forfeit to the Protestant purchaser.[60] The value applied to horses was calculated from a wholly military perspective. While not wishing to prevent Catholics from owning horses for agricultural or transportation purposes which might otherwise have a detrimental effect upon the economy, the act aimed to remove all horses of a military capacity, the principle being that those between £5 and £8 value were good for dragoons and above that for cavalry.[61] The penalties for not adhering to the act with regard to weapons included fines of £100 for peers and £30 for everyone else with a year's imprisonment or longer until the fine was fully paid on first offence and *praemunire* on the second. The penalty for concealing a horse was three months in prison and a fine of three times the horse's real value.[62]

The 'act to restrain foreign education' was primarily aimed at preventing contact with Catholic absolutist Europe and the Counter-Reformation and, more pertinently, with exiled Irish Jacobites. It was 'designed to bring the Irish from their foreign correspondency and dependency and to incline them to affirm loyalty to the Crown' and was in theory intended to eventually 'bring them over to our [Protestant] Church'.[63] In reality, the more pressing and immediate concern about internal and external security was wholly evident in the preamble:

> many of the subjects of this kingdom have accustomed themselves to send their chil-
> dren ... into France, Spain, and other foreign parts ... to be educated, instructed, and
> brought up; by means and occasion whereof, the said children and other persons have
> in process of time engaged themselves in foreign interests, and been prevailed upon
> to forget the natural duty and allegiance due from them to the kings and queens of
> this realm, and the affection which they owe to the established religion and laws of
> this their native country, and returning so civilly disposed into this kingdom, have
> been, in all times past, the movers and promoters of many dangerous seditions, and
> oftentimes of open rebellion.

The penalties imposed upon anyone found guilty of sending, facilitating, assisting or supporting a person's Catholic education overseas included the inability
to hold public office and the forfeiture of all goods and lands for life. It was also
enacted that 'no person whatsoever of the popish religion shall publicly teach
school, or instruct youth in learning ... in private houses' in Ireland, on pain of a
£20 fine and three-month prison sentence for each offence. By way of compensa-
tion and for conversion purposes, the various acts for erecting Protestant schools
were to be more rigorously enforced.[64]

The two acts also clarified matters in relation to the oaths. Those who were
educated abroad could overturn their *in absentia* conviction under the Foreign
Education Act within six months of their return to Ireland by taking the two oaths
and subscribing the declaration in the 1691 Oath Act. The Disarming Act, which
actually recited both oaths and the declaration, required apprentices to the makers of firearms to do likewise, while it also stipulated more generally that anyone
who refused to take the two oaths and declaration were to be deemed Catholics
'within the meaning of this Act'.[65] It was therefore implicit that the taking of the
oaths and declaration were seen to be practical acts of conversion to the Established Church.[66] One of the first instances of the application of these dictates was
the confiscation by a group of dragoons of horses from William Penn and some
fellow non-oath taking Quakers on their travels around Ireland in 1698. However,
the intervention of local magistrates and the lords justices in Dublin on appeal
from Penn resulted in the soldiers being forced to drop their suit.[67]

The 1695 Commons had also endeavoured to draft a bill for banishing all
Catholic bishops and regular clergy. At the time, pressure from William III's
Catholic ally, the Holy Roman Emperor Leopold I, caused the bill to be put
aside, but when parliament reconvened in 1697 as the war drew to a close, there
was less reason for avoiding such a measure. The government therefore presented
an amended version of the 1695 bill which became law as an 'act for banishing
all papists exercising any ecclesiastical jurisdiction, and all regulars of the popish clergy out of this kingdom'.[68] Similar processes to those for the 1695 acts

can be identified for the 1697 Banishment Act. There were clear antecedents in
the proclamations issued in 1673, 1674, 1678, 1679 and 1680, in the proposed
legislation of 1678–9, and in the actions of the Irish government in 1692–3
by taking into custody more than eighty-seven regular priests and unsuccessfully pressing William III for permission to expel them.[69] Likewise, there were
precedents set by English legislation.[70] The revival of the issue in 1695 and its
successful completion in 1697 demonstrated the political will behind it and the
ultimately successful pressure exerted on the King.[71]

The 1697 Banishment Act was ostensibly aimed at undermining the Catholic
Church in Ireland by removing the hierarchy and regular clergy and therefore, in
theory at least, was intended to extirpate Catholicism. In reality, more immediate security concerns were evident once again. The preamble stated that

> it is notoriously known, that the late rebellions in this kingdom have been contrived,
> promoted, and carried on by popish archbishops, bishops, Jesuits, and other ecclesi-
> astical persons of the Romish clergy; and forasmuch as the peace and public safety of
> this kingdom is in danger, by the great number[s] ... now residing here, and settling
> in fraternities and societies, contrary to law, and to the great impoverishing of many
> of his majesty's subjects ... who are forced to maintain and support them; which said
> Romish clergy do not only endeavour to withdraw [them] ... from their obedience,
> but do daily stir up, and move sedition and rebellion, to the great hazard of the ruin
> and desolation of this kingdom.[72]

It was evident that the act was clearly concerned with the fact that because the
Catholic clergy were 'exercising a foreign jurisdiction' in Ireland they were therefore seen as a focal point for discontent and as the ringleaders of any resistance
to the Protestant Church and government in general.[73]

The clergy affected by the 1697 Banishment Act were expected to depart Ireland by May 1698. Any who returned were deemed guilty of high treason, while
any new Catholic bishops or regulars entering the country would be imprisoned
for a year and then deported. Anyone found harbouring a banished priest was
fined £20 for the first offence, £40 for the second, and suffered forfeiture of their
lands for life for the third. It was also enacted that no one was to be buried thereafter in any suppressed monastery, abbey or convent, unless it was now being
used for celebrating divine service according to the liturgy of the Church of Ireland as 'by Law Established'. Every person discovered at an illegal burial was to be
fined £10. The act also included authority to continue 'suppressing all monaster-
ies, friaries, nunneries, or other popish fraternities or societies'.[74]

A headcount was taken in late 1697 of the Catholic clergy calculated on
the basis of the 1695 poll tax which had included rates for such individuals.[75]
The initial results gave an estimate of 1,237 in total, comprising 838 secular
and 399 regular clergy, though late returns increased these figures eventually
to 892 seculars and 495 regulars.[76] Such statistics need to be treated with cau-

tion, as some priests, and possibly quite a substantial number, managed to avoid identification.[77] The known figures for priests transported in 1698 as a result of the act must be viewed in a similar light. A total of 444 were recorded as being transported to Portugal and France in the early months of 1698 from Dublin, Galway, Cork and Waterford, while at the end of the year 383 recently banished regulars were recorded in and around Paris.[78] The exiled Queen, Mary of Modena, thought that at least 700 regulars were transported, though if so it suggests that the 1697 poll figures were either very inaccurate or that the regulars had proved better at avoiding paying taxes than they had at being rounded up for transportation.[79] As a counterbalance, by 1700 there were apparently several hundred regulars in Ireland.[80]

The 1697 session had also enacted a law 'to prevent Protestants inter-marrying with papists', which was the first of four acts relating to that subject. In 1726 a law was passed for preventing marriages by degraded clergymen or Catholic priests, in 1746 another was enacted for annulling marriages performed by Catholic priests either between two Protestants or a Protestant and Catholic, and in 1750 an amending act was passed for making the 1726 law more effectual. This series of acts demonstrated two key aspects of the penal laws as a whole: first, amending legislation was common owing to loopholes or errors in earlier acts; and Catholics were evidently successful in circumventing the law.[81] This was seen even more readily in the legislation targeting Catholic practitioners of the law, not least because they represented the vanguard of opposition to the penal laws through legitimate legal channels in the courts.

The only penal law enacted in the 1699 session was 'to prevent papists being solicitors'. Based upon an earlier English statute, the stated reasons for the act were that Irish Catholic solicitors were 'the common disturbers of the peace and tranquility of his majesty's subjects in general' and that the 'great number' of them 'practicing within the several courts of law and equity' in Ireland at that time and the 'daily increase of them' was liable to 'great mischiefs and inconveniencies' ensuing to 'the prejudice and disquiet of his majesty's subjects'. The main purpose of the act was to require all practising solicitors to take the two oaths and declaration in the 1691 Oath Act, on pain of a £100 fine for each offence plus further related legal disabilities. The only exceptions were for people acting on their own behalf, for servants acting on behalf of their master and for all those comprehended within the Articles of Limerick.[82]

By 1707 it was felt an amending act was needed because since 1699 'several known' Irish Catholics 'have frequently and openly practised and acted as solicitors and agents ... contrary to and in contempt of' the 1699 act. The penalty of £100 was deemed insufficient 'in respect of the great gains they make by their practice, and the difficulties attending the prosecution thereof are such, that the mischief intended to be remedied ... remains unaddressed'. The fine was therefore

increased to £200 made payable to the discoverer of the offender, and all solicitors were now also required to take the new oath of abjuration, which had first
been introduced in England in 1702 and in Ireland in 1704. Catholics were also
no longer allowed to serve on juries unless there were not enough Protestants
for the purpose. Nor were Catholics allowed to be taken on as apprentices by
any law practitioners. While those covered by the Articles of Limerick were
still deemed exempt, it was a qualified exemption as they were now required to
have taken the oath of abjuration before 1 July 1707.[83] The legal requirement
for so doing seems to have been imposed at the time the abjuration oath was
introduced in Ireland.[84] It was certainly the case that Sir Toby Butler, one of the
leading practising Irish Catholic lawyers covered by the Limerick articles, was
understood to have taken the abjuration oath.[85]

Ongoing concern about Catholics working in the legal profession, especially
the increasing number of cases of nominal conversion or occasional conformity, resulted in an act in 1728 'for regulating the admissions of barristers at law'
and other legal practitioners 'into offices and employments; and for preventing
papists practising as solicitors; and for further strengthening the Protestant interest' in Ireland. The measure seems to have been intended to clarify doubts about
whether barristers in particular were covered by the previous acts, and therefore required every person working in any legal capacity to take the three oaths
and declaration. Also, any convert who wished to practise law in any capacity
had to prove, by the sworn testimony of other witnesses, that he had 'professed
himself and continued to be a Protestant for the space of two years'. Those serving as a sub-sheriff or sheriff's clerk had to have been Protestants for five years
before entering into such a post. Furthermore, all such converts then entering
into employment in the law had to educate all of their children as Protestants, a
stipulation that was then applied in general to all converts whatsoever their pro-
fessions or employments. The only exemption, unqualified on this occasion, was
for those covered by the articles of Limerick and, although overlooked in previous laws, of Galway.[86] Hugh Boulter, the Protestant Archbishop of Armagh, was
particularly keen on the act. In justification of it, he informed Thomas Pelham-
Holles, duke of Newcastle, that the legal profession in Ireland was dominated by
recent converts 'who give no farther security ... than producing a certificate of
their having received the Sacrament in the Church of England or Ireland, which
several of them who were papists at London, obtain on the road hither'. He had
even forlornly hoped that the five-year stipulation applied to a sub-sheriff and
sheriff's clerk might have been applied to everyone covered by the act.[87]

The final act relating to law practitioners, passed in 1734, was for amending
the 1699 law and 'remedying other mischiefs in relation to ... the several courts
of law and equity'. The reasons given in the preamble were that 'the laws now
in force against popish solicitors have been found ineffectual by reason of the

difficulty of convicting such solicitors' and that therefore 'the mischiefs thereby intended to be remedied still remain, to the great prejudice of the Protestant interest of this kingdom'. More pertinently, it was stated that because of such Catholic solicitors, 'the acts against the growth of popery have been and daily are greatly eluded and evaded'. No one was thereafter to be 'admitted an attorney, or licensed to be a solicitor ... who hath not been a Protestant from his age of fourteen years, or for two years before his being admitted an apprentice, and who shall not have served an apprenticeship for the space of five years at least'. As before, all practitioners were to take all three oaths and the declaration and a new specific oath against allowing disqualified people to practise the law and taking on Catholic apprentices. Any Protestant practitioner with a Catholic spouse or whose children were being brought up as Catholics was also disqualified and deemed a Catholic. Redemption was only possible for those who within a year of their marriage managed to convince their Catholic spouse to convert. The only exception was for those comprehended within the Limerick articles who had taken the oath of abjuration before 1 July 1707.[88]

Another law-related measure, also passed in 1734, aimed at ensuring that only people of 'known affection to the Protestant religion and our happy establishment' could serve as justices of the peace. Therefore all converts whose spouses or children were still Catholics were excluded from that office on pain of a year's imprisonment and £100 fine.[89] The 1734 act was also in keeping with two other earlier regulatory measures, one in 1716 for preventing Catholics 'from being high or petty constables, and for better regulating the parish watch', and one in 1728 'for the further regulating the election of members of parliament, and preventing the irregular proceedings of sheriffs and other officers in electing and returning such members'. The latter act finally excluded Catholics completely from both the national and local franchise.[90]

A third area of ongoing amendment and adjustment related to the Catholic clergy. In 1703 an act was passed to prevent Catholic regular clergy from coming into Ireland. The preamble claimed that 'great numbers' of bishops, Jesuits and other regulars were entering the country under the guise of being secular clergy and were doing so 'with intent to stir up her majesty's popish subjects to rebellion'. All such clergy were deemed liable to the penalties in the 1697 act, as were those harbouring or concealing them.[91] A follow-up act in 1704 'for registering the popish clergy' in Ireland was intended to facilitate the government in identifying the bishops and regulars. Any priest, including secular clergy, who failed to register would be banished in accordance with the 1697 act, while provision was also made for any priest 'convinced of the errors' of Rome to receive £20 a year income levied upon the population of the county in which he had officiated as a Catholic priest. He would continue to receive the stipend for as long as he remained in the same county and publicly adhered to the book of common prayer and liturgy of the Church of Ireland. The act was renewed in 1705 and made perpetual in 1709.[92]

While the acts relating to marriage, legal practitioners and Catholic clergy were very specific in focus, the two laws which are viewed as the main pillars of the penal code, passed in 1704 and 1709, were the exact opposite in that they covered a vast array of Catholic rights. The 1704 act to prevent the further growth of popery was a sweeping measure relating to rights to purchase and inherit land, education, guardianship, employment, the franchise and conversion, which latter consideration was to the forefront of the act because 'divers emissaries of the church of Rome, popish priests, and other[s] ... taking advantage of the weakness of some of her majesty's subjects ... do daily endeavour to persuade and pervert them from the Protestant religion'. The threat to 'the true religion' and 'peace and settlement' in Ireland also arose from the fact that many Catholics 'have it in their power to raise divisions among Protestants, by voting in elections for members of parliament, and ... to use other ways and means tending to the destruction of the Protestant interest'.[93] The penalty of *praemunire* was imposed on anyone who caused a Protestant to renounce their faith or reconciled a convert back to Rome, while protection and provision was made for convert children of Catholic parents, including the father becoming tenant for life to a converted eldest son. Orphans were to be placed in the care of their nearest Protestant relative, or if none existed then with another suitable Protestant. Children of mixed marriages were also to be educated as Protestants. Catholics were prohibited from purchasing land and property or associated rents and profits in their own or anyone else's name, in trust or otherwise, and were instead restricted to thirty-one year leases. Catholic inheritance was no longer to be by primogeniture but instead by gavelkind with the lands and property being divided equally among all sons, or if there was no male offspring then among all daughters, or if childless then among 'collateral kindred'. If an eldest son converted, however, he could inherit all by primogeniture. An unsuccessful attempt was made to exclude Catholics from the national franchise, while any advowson or right of preferment to a clerical benefice in Catholic hands was declared vested in the Crown. Catholic pilgrimages to holy wells and other religious sites were thereafter deemed to be riots and unlawful assemblies, and several loopholes in earlier legislation were also addressed, including the 1695 Foreign Education Act and the 1697 Inter-Marriage Act.[94]

A final component of the 1704 act related to the legal definition of a Protestant and the right to hold civil or military office. No one could benefit from the law as a Protestant 'within the intent and meaning hereof' unless they had conformed to the Church of Ireland and subscribed the declaration and taken the new oath of abjuration which was detailed in the act. Anyone in public office also had to take this new oath along with those of allegiance and new supremacy and the declaration. They also had to provide certified evidence that they had received the 'sacrament of the Lord's Supper according to the usage of the Church of Ireland'.[95] The inclusion of this Sacramental Test, in place in England since 1673, has been the subject of much debate primarily because it was introduced while the bill was under consideration at the English Privy Council, and because it was perceived primarily as an attack upon Ireland's Protestant dissenters or, more particularly, the Presbyterian community which represented the largest and most significant group of Protestant nonconformists in the country.[96]

Dissent within Protestantism had translated to Ireland from England and Scotland in the wake of the Reformation, and nonconformity had found some fertile ground particularly in the early seventeenth century in Ulster following the plantation of six of the nine counties after the flight of the earls in 1607. The presence of many Scottish settlers and their ministers helped to solidify an emerging Presbyterianism which was galvanized by the Scottish National Covenant, the attempts by Thomas, Viscount Wentworth, to impose the 'Black oath' against it, and the ensuing arrival of a Scottish army in Ireland under Robert Monro in April 1642 which began formally establishing Presbyterian organization in Ulster.[97] Thereafter, government policy towards Protestant dissenters was 'marked by the same anomalies and shifts as were seen with regard to Catholics'.[98] As with Catholics, the loyalty of Irish Presbyterians to church and state was problematic because their beliefs rendered them unable to adhere to the dictates of the Acts of Supremacy and Uniformity and they were presumed to hold radical and dangerous political principles owing to their close association with Scottish Presbyterianism. For those who conformed to the Established Church, Presbyterians in particular could be much more divisive than Catholics. Some believed that as fellow Protestants they should be shown greater toleration while others viewed them as the single most significant threat to church and state, even in comparison to Catholics. At a practical level, the sheer number of Presbyterians made some fear that if tolerated they would displace the members of the Established Church in the main positions of political, economic and social power. Others were more afraid of their religious principles and strict organizational structures. Such fears ultimately accounted for the ready acceptance of the Sacramental Test by the Irish parliament in 1704 and the lack of political will or desire thereafter to truly engage with the question of greater toleration until towards the end of the eighteenth century.[99] The only concession made before the repeal of the Sacramental Test in 1780 was the 1719 act 'for exempting Protestant dissenters ... from certain penalties, to which they are now subject', which in truth conceded little other than exempting them from the penalties under the Acts of Uniformity for non-attendance at divine service and ministering without authority, all of which had long since been in abeyance anyway. They were still however required to take the various oaths and declaration.[100]

Yet it should not be forgotten that the principal of a Sacramental Test also served a more mundane function in that it actually formed a central part of the practical process for conversion from Catholicism to the Church of Ireland, and was one that many converts undertook in the eighteenth century for that reason alone. In order to prove that a person had conformed themselves to the Church of Ireland, which process included receipt of the Sacrament of the Lord's Supper, it was necessary to receive a certificate from a Church of Ireland bishop to that effect and to enrol it in the Court of Chancery. The enrolling of these certificates resulted in the creation of what became known as the 'Convert Rolls', which listed all those who had so conformed and enrolled their certificate. In total, over 5,800 Catholics converted in this manner between 1704 and 1838, though only 380 of those were after 1789, by which time the repeal of the penal laws was well underway and the economic or political reasons for converting were less persuasive or relevant.[101]

While only a tiny fraction of the total Catholic population in Ireland, which has been estimated at 1.8 million by 1731,[102] the fact that over 5,000 converted in the first eighty years of the eighteenth century demonstrated that conformity did occur and did so for various reasons, though coordinated and constant missionary zeal on the part of the Church of Ireland was not high up that list. In the first twenty-seven years only 704 converts were enrolled, though thereafter the numbers increased as seen in ten-year totals of 600, 549, 864 and 1,347 between 1732 and 1771. A further 1,421 converted between 1772 and 1789. The converts included farmers, lawyers, merchants, doctors, soldiers, weavers, clerks, shopkeepers, innkeepers, schoolteachers, labourers and many more, including 1,500 women of whom 600 were described as married and more than 100 priests. It was evident that many enrolled their certificate for specific reasons such as holding public office, which accounted for at least 2,300 who also enrolled further certificates specifying that they had taken the oaths and declaration and received the Sacrament.[103] But not all conversions were entered into for purely practical or self-interested economic, political or social reasons. Many converted out of genuine religious conviction, some of whom may not have had sufficient economic, political or social justification for even enrolling their certificate and may well still elude the historians gaze.[104]

The 1704 Sacramental Test was, like many other aspects of the Irish penal laws, modelled upon prior English examples. However, in respect of the aspects relating to land, the 1704 act was noticeably different from previous English enactments. Elements of the measures introduced in 1704 had been considered in England, most notably in 1593, but had not made it to the statute book. The main threat to English Catholic landholding remained the penalty of *praemunire* which resulted in the confiscation of all lands if convicted, but in Ireland that was now superseded by measures that did not require a conviction but instead, as John Morrill has stated, appeared to be aimed at sinking Irish Catholic landownership 'in a sealed capsule within which oxygen would gradually run out', condemning it 'to a slow death'.[105]

If that was indeed the case, then by way of further facilitating that slow death, the second pillar of the penal laws was passed in 1709. The title of the act demonstrated that yet again it was concerned with rectifying loopholes and errors in earlier legislation, in this case 'explaining and amending' the 1704 act. In the intervening years Catholics had found ways of circumventing the 1704 act 'by making of settlements ... by granting annuities for lives, in tail, and fee-simple, and by perfecting collateral securities ... covenants ... private trusts' and other legal contrivances. All of these activities were explicitly prohibited in the 1709 act, along with further clarifications, confirmations and additions relating to the 1704 and earlier legislation, including those relating to Protestant children of Catholic parents, gavelkind, guardianship, advowsons, intermarriage, schools, education of children as Protestants, law practitioners, registration of clergy, banishment, horses and much more. One of the many amendments clarified that the Sacramental Test was understood to be a key component of defining what it meant to be a Protestant and therefore was a prerequisite part of the conversion process.[106]

A wholly new and notorious inclusion in the act was the Protestant 'discoverer'. Apparently borrowed from an English act of 1708 dealing with a specific case of land forfeiture in Ireland, the 1709 act empowered any Protestant 'to sue in respect of all property transactions forbidden to Catholics'. If they could establish such a 'discoverable interest' and prove in the courts that it was the result of a prohibited transaction, then they would be entitled to the purchased land or lease for the duration intended by the original transaction. Alongside the gavelkind enactment, the Protestant discoverer gave the Irish penal laws a uniqueness all of their own. Yet the discoverer's notoriety is not wholly justified. If the intention was to provide a further impetus to greater conformity among the landed community or to speed up the reduction of the percentage of land in Catholic hands, then it was not overly successful. The evidence of increased conformity after 1709 is complicated by the known instances of occasional conformity in families that remained otherwise Catholic, and even more so by the prevalence of collusive discoveries in which land was 'discovered' by a friendly Protestant and only nominally held on behalf of Catholic friends and relations or even conveyed back to the actual Catholic owner.[107]

In reality, the impact of the 1704 and 1709 acts on the percentage of land in Catholic hands was not overly dramatic, suggesting that the slow death was indeed very, very slow, and possibly misdiagnosed. Catholics proved very resourceful in purchasing land by collusive means through Protestant relatives or friends and complex legal instruments, with some estates actually increasing in size during the eighteenth century. Either by a natural quirk of nature, the misfortune of early deaths of younger siblings or strategic movement of younger siblings out of the country, other families managed to pass on estates wholly intact to a single inheriting son. Occasional conformity saw other estates return to Catholic ownership once the penal laws were repealed. Nor is there evidence of gavelkind being applied to Catholic estates.[108]

The figures for the percentage of land in Catholic hands from 1704 onwards are uncertain. It is probable that the figure of 14 per cent in 1703, at which point the last substantive land confiscation had been completed, was not greatly reduced by the 1770s. It is certainly the case that the 1770s figure of 5 per cent that held sway in Irish historiography for a time is incorrect. The 1770s also marked the start of the turnaround in Catholic landholding as the penal laws started to be repealed, with the provisions relating to leases, land purchase and inheritance being among the first to be rescinded.[109] It was therefore more likely the case that, as contemporaries claimed, the 1704 and 1709 acts were primarily concerned with preventing Catholics from regaining or advancing their economic or political position by preventing them from increasing their landholdings. Even gavelkind was not primarily about taking away Catholic land, but rather about breaking up existing large individual holdings into multiple-owned smaller holdings and thereby reducing the influence and authority that a person acquired through ownership of a larger estate.[110]

In part, the amelioration of the impact of the 1704 and 1709 acts could also be ascribed to the fact that as in England, the penal laws were not enforced in a rigorous or consistent manner. This was more evident in relation to matters not to do with land and where the political and economic imperative was not as pronounced.[111] The degree to which the laws were relaxed or overlooked was possibly most noticeable in respect of the Catholic clergy. Despite occasional fears and concerns being expressed by individual Protestants, the reality was that the Catholic Church quickly re-established its presence throughout Ireland in the early eighteenth century. On the basis of the 1704 Registration Act, 1,089 Catholic priests were accounted for in Ireland in that year. It was evident that within that number there were numerous regulars registered as secular parish priests, including Jesuits in Dublin, Meath and Waterford and two bishops in Thurles and Newry.[112] In 1709, when the abjuration oath was imposed upon Catholic clergy only thirty-three took it at a time when there were reportedly over 1,000 in the country. Despite a short-lived attempt thereafter to clamp down on the Catholic Church, there was 'no sustained attempt to put the laws into effect' thereafter.[113] By March 1728 the Church of Ireland Primate believed that there were at least 3,000 Catholic clergy in Ireland compared to 600 Church of Ireland clergymen.[114] Two years later however a report by the House of Lords put the figure at 1,445 secular and 254 regulars, though Connolly has argued convincingly that this is an underestimate owing to missing returns from the magistrates and Protestant clergy tasked with the enumeration and the ability of regulars in particular to go undetected.[115] By then, within Ireland and on the Continent, the Irish Catholic Church was in the process of firmly re-establishing itself, as was Catholic Ireland more generally.[116]

The body of laws enacted between 1695 and 1750 were the products of a variety of influences, ideologies and perceptions. Genuine fears for the security of the Protestant interest were juxtaposed with starker religious bigotry, missionary zeal was overshadowed by economic and political self-interest, and unrelated political agendas could readily affect legislative outcomes. In a parliament recently empowered by control of the public purse strings, meeting on a regular basis and comprising large and powerful political groupings with strong negotiating powers with the government, it came as little surprise that most legislation, including the penal laws, was the product of compromise, negotiation and accommodation. No matter how well-considered, the enactment of the penal laws was not a unilateral process and therefore required regular amendment and adjustment as new issues arose, loopholes were identified and errors discovered in earlier compromise enactments in the time-honoured fashion of legislative assemblies around the world.

As the eighteenth century progressed Catholic confidence grew and so the quest for a suitable oath of allegiance re-emerged as a means of demonstrating loyalty and as a preliminary step on the road to repeal of the penal laws. As early as 1724 in an anonymous pamphlet the author, who was apparently Cornelius Nary, the Catholic parish priest of St Michan's in Dublin, claimed that he 'was no ways concerned at taking the oath of allegiance, which is the law of nature and which the common practice of all nations allows me to take with a safe conscience to any prince who conquers me and the country of which I am a member'.[117] Nary also went to the trouble of composing what he believed to be an acceptable oath of allegiance for Catholics.[118] In 1727 a more focused endeavour was attempted by Christopher Nugent, Lord Delvin, which, as had happened before, divided Catholic opinion.[119] Further endeavours were made in the following decades, which accorded with more practical efforts to demonstrate loyalty through actions as well, especially in the military sphere of the empire,[120] though it was not until 1774 that a new and acceptable oath of allegiance was placed upon the statute book as a precursor to the commencement of the repeal of the penal laws from 1778 onwards.[121]

Ultimately, the imposition of the penal laws, and in time their repeal, was a central consideration of the Irish parliament and the political process surrounding that assembly, which was defined by the constitutional relationship between Ireland and England and, after 1707, Britain. In order to fully locate Ireland within the British Empire in the early modern period, it is therefore necessary to assess that constitutional and political relationship, which is the focus of Chapter 3.

3 POLITICS

Political activity in early modern Ireland was more often than not centred on the question of the constitutional relationship with England and, after 1707, Britain. That constitutional status in the period 1692–1770 is also central to understanding Ireland's place and role within the empire. This chapter aims to address the question by examining political ideology and activity in Ireland, England and Britain in relation to issues of government, parliament, authority and power in the early modern period.

Kingdom or Colony?

There are a number of fundamental considerations which help to address the vexed question of whether Ireland was a separate though dependant sister kingdom or more simply a province or colony of England and Britain. On the one hand, the plantations of the sixteenth and seventeenth centuries, the influx of new settlers from England and Scotland, the wars of conquest and reconquest in 1594–1603, 1641–53 and 1689–91, and the imposition of the penal laws against Catholics in the eighteenth century all bore the hallmarks of a colonizing endeavour. On the other hand, the institutions of state, the complex ethnic and religious mixed identities, the official status as a separate kingdom and the political ideology and practice suggested a different status.[1]

Stephen Conway has described the mid-eighteenth-century Irish parliament as 'a local institution, with severely limited powers, rather than part of the machinery of the British state'. That rather damning assessment is based upon considerations such as the fact that it 'met only for a few months every two years. In theory, at least, it could not even begin to debate proposed legislation until the subject had been sanctioned in London'. The device of heads of bills is acknowledged as a means of initiating legislation, but it is emphasized that even still such legislation 'remained subject to interference and ultimate approval from London'. Likewise, from 1720 the British parliament 'claimed the right to legislate for Ireland whenever it chose to do so'. While it is accepted that this right was little used thereafter and there was no attempt to tax Ireland directly from London, 'control of the army in Ireland was secured by the annual Mutiny Acts passed by the British parliament and Irish overseas trade was regulated by British Acts of parliament'.[2] As a British historian writing about the Irish parliament, or about the place and position of Ireland within the British Isles and the emerging empire more generally, this would not be an unusual or unexpected viewpoint.

On the surface, there is much to support arguments of this nature. In 1698 the Irish Lord Chancellor and English politician, John Methuen, made a proposal for erecting a mint in Ireland to coin silver specie as a means of advancing trade and productivity. It was not the first or last time such a proposal would be made in Ireland and rejected in London. On this occasion, the English treasury lords received a report from Sir Isaac Newton at the Royal Mint in September, which argued that such a proposition would be prejudicial to England as it would divert trade, money and bullion to Ireland. In this instance, it was argued, England could prevent such an occurrence because

> Ireland is one of the English plantations and though it has changed the title of lord-ship to that of kingdom yet it still continues annexed to the Crown of England like the other plantations is [sic], and ought to be inferior to this kingdom and subservient to its interests. And therefore we are unwilling that any opinion of ours should be made use of for promoting any design which may tend to draw thither the money and trade of this nation and to make them of equal dignity and dominion with ourselves and perhaps at length desirous to separate from this Crown upon some fit opportunity of joining in with its enemies.[3]

Newton's views are revealing of several issues. Ireland was perceived as the soft underbelly through which an international enemy could strike at the heart of England and the empire. Recent events in 1689–91 and those of the more distant past in the 1640s and 1601 had clearly demonstrated that fact. The establishment of a mint was seen to be a sovereign matter and could be perceived therefore as bestowing the authority to act as an independent state, so that it was understandable that English opposition to such a proposition for Ireland had been long-standing.[4] From an imperial perspective conquered lands were plantations rather than colonies and were subservient to the interest of the mother country. Ultimately, Newton expressed an underlying concern at the lack of certainty in the constitutional relationship between Britain and Ireland at the time.

Such a concern was not surprising in light of recent events. The publication of William Molyneux's *Case of Ireland* earlier that year had brought a long-standing constitutional discord between England and Ireland back into the limelight.[5] His arguments were not new, nor where they religiously exclusive.[6] The ambiguities within the constitutional relationship had resulted in contested interpretations which led to political conflict. Molyneux's attack upon the assumed right of the English parliament to legislate in a binding fashion for Ireland was one branch of such conflict. The other key area of disagreement, addressed in passing by Molyneux, was the status conferred by the 1494–5 statute known as Poynings' Law, which related to the authority for summoning an Irish parliament and the ensuing legislative activity of that parliament.

It was understandable that such areas of uncertainty existed. The piecemeal arrival of English common law and the associated trappings of English governance following the Norman incursion into parts of Ireland from the 1160s onwards resulted in a dichotomous understanding and interpretation of the authority that was thereby conferred.[7] As a lordship of the English monarch, those parts of Ireland under English modes of governance could readily be perceived as subservient or provincial. Yet the existence of a parliament representing the nobility, clergy and commoners of that lordship complicated matters. Ireland had its own high courts of justice including a Chancery and Lord Chancellor, an Exchequer and Lord Treasurer, a King's or Queen's Bench and a Common Pleas, all of which signified a separate state of being from England.[8] The 1541 Act for Kingly Title, in part aimed at clarifying the ambiguities in the constitutional relationship, actually served to give more strength to the arguments for a separate or sister kingdom status.[9]

Legislative Autonomy and Appellate Jurisdiction

The power conferred on parliament was a central consideration in the struggle to interpret the constitutional relationship to the best advantage of whichever side of the divide one stood on. If the English parliament had the right to legislate for Ireland without having to seek the approbation of the Irish parliament for such enactments, then it conferred a subservient status upon the Irish legislature. Hence such a perception or assumption was resisted at key points in time.[10] As early as 1460 the Irish parliament had taken a stance upon the issue, when a declaration was issued stating that

> whereas the land of Ireland is, and at all times has been corporate of itself by the ancient laws and customs used in the same, freed of the burden of any special law of the realm of England save only such laws as by the Lords spiritual and temporal and the Commons of the said land had been in great council or parliament there held, admitted, accepted, affirmed and proclaimed, according to sundry ancient statutes thereof made.[11]

Within this broader question there lay a more focused agenda that was to reoccur at key points which related to money and, more significantly, taxation. An inkling of this agenda was seen in the 1460 act for establishing an Irish coinage on the grounds that Ireland, although 'under the obedience of the realm of England, was separated from that realm and from all its statutes, except those that were freely accepted by Irish parliamentary assemblies'.[12] The existence of a separate Irish mint did not prove sustainable and was in fact a red herring. The truly pertinent fiscal consideration related to the power to tax or raise financial supplies. In 1441, in the English Court of Exchequer chamber, a king's serjeant, John Fortescue, had acknowledged that the English parliament could not tax Ireland without the consent of the Irish parliament.[13] Fortescue, having become chief justice of the King's Bench and later Lord Chancellor, was eventually to lay down that principle for posterity in his work on constitutional law *De Laudibus Legum Angliae*, the first of many printed editions of which over the centuries appeared in 1545–6.[14]

Although the referencing at that time of parliament and legislative authority was misleading, not least because the power to raise taxes still lay with a variety of individuals and bodies from the Crown down to local communities, the right of the people or their representatives to give their consent to taxation was recognized and undisputed since the thirteenth century in both Ireland and England. On one occasion in the fourteenth century an attempt was made to circumvent this understanding by summoning Irish parliamentary representatives to England in order to agree to raising new taxes, though it was made clear at that time that there was no obligation for Ireland to elect or send such representatives 'according to the rights, privileges, laws and customs of the land of Ireland, in use since the time of the conquest and before'.[15]

In time, the right to 'no taxation without consent' was to become closely identified with the broader question of legislative autonomy. This more general claim was engaged with again in 1494–5 when an act was passed in the Irish parliament for making all existing English legislation relating to Ireland binding. The passage of such an Irish act implied that the English parliament had incorrectly assumed it had a right to pass legislation for Ireland, an argument reiterated by Molyneux and others. However, the 1494–5 act was also flawed in that it only applied to existing legislation, making no allowance for the future either by explicitly denouncing or allowing the practice of the English parliament. It was therefore not surprising that the question arose again in future years.[16]

The re-emergence of a more assertive Irish parliament in the seventeenth century saw the subject revisited with renewed and sustained vigour. As part of the reaction against the 'infringing and violation of the laws, liberties, and freedom of the said subjects of this kingdom' under the government of Wentworth and linked to the concerns over the government of Charles I within the British Isles more generally, the Irish Commons in February 1641 drafted a series of twenty-one queries upon which they desired that the Lords require the judges 'to deliver their resolutions'. The preamble declared that 'inasmuch as the subjects of this kingdom are free, loyal, and dutiful subjects to ... their natural liege and king, and [are] to be governed only by the common laws of England and statutes of force in this kingdom, in the same manner and form as' the subjects of England, 'which of right the subjects of this kingdom do ... make their protestation to be their birth-right and best inheritance'.[17] The judges eventually gave a written response, which was deemed by the Commons to 'not merit the name of an answer'. An ensuing conference between the two houses formed the basis for the central component of a pamphlet entitled *An Argument Delivered by Patrick Darcy*, who was a Galway Catholic and MP appointed to present the case of the Commons. Darcy included in his arguments that the 1494–5 act had allowed for 'all general statutes' of England to apply in Ireland, 'but no other statute, or new introducing law, until the same be first received and enacted in parliament in this kingdom'. He also resurrected the question of consent to taxation, referencing Fortescue's *De Laudibus Legum Angliae* to argue that English monarchs had 'never assume[d] the power to change or alter the laws ... nor to take his people's goods, nor to lay tax ... other than by their free consent in parliament'.[18]

In the turmoil of the 1640–50s the issue resurfaced on several occasions. The English parliament's 1642 Adventurers' Act for financing the suppression of the Irish rebellion out of land to be forfeited in Ireland led to a remonstrance from the Confederate Catholics to Charles I stating that the act 'contravened the fundamental laws' of Ireland and undermined 'the rights and prerogatives' of the King.[19] In this, as in all other stances taken by the Confederates on the subject during the 1640s, the main argument for legislative autonomy was forcefully backed up by emphasizing that 'the subjects of Ireland are immediately subject' to the monarch 'in right of your Crown' as part of a separate and distinct kingdom, the parliament of which could not in any manner be construed as being subordinate or subject to the parliament of any other kingdom, even if they shared the same monarch. Ultimately, the Confederates desired the passage of an act in the Irish parliament declaring that assembly to be independent of its English counterpart.[20] The idea of a Declaratory Act which would once and for all state explicitly what the relationship was between the two parliaments made a lot of sense, but as was to become evident, such a declaration could be made by either parliament to the advantage or detriment of each other.

Despite the violent divisions within Ireland in the 1640s, the majority of Irish Protestants were still disinclined to fundamentally disagree with the Confederacy on the question of legislative autonomy. An anonymous 1644 manuscript on the subject, 'A Declaration Setting Forth', was attributed to the Protestant Lord Chancellor of Ireland, Sir Richard Bolton, and was intended to convince the Protestant rump of the Irish parliament in Dublin to support the Confederate stance and thus help to further the King's negotiations at Oxford with the latter grouping.[21] Among the arguments put forward were Fortescue's 1441 English Exchequer case on consent to taxation and the 1494–5 act.[22] Instead of serving its intended purposes, however, the 'Declaration' prompted a lengthy rejoinder from Sir Samuel Mayart, serjeant-at-law and second justice of the Common Pleas in Ireland,[23] and split the rump of the Irish Commons between Royalists and those sympathetic to the English parliament.[24] Ultimately, however, the idea of resolving the matter by means of a Declaratory Act was also perceived in Protestant quarters as the best solution to the problem, but at some unspecified point in the future.[25]

Following the Protectorate union of 1653, Irish Protestant MPs representing Ireland in parliament in London continued to restate the problems associated with the assumed right of that assembly to legislate for Ireland. In 1659, at the end of a decade when Ireland had been taxed directly, and excessively, from England, one of the Irish representatives argued that Ireland was overtaxed without means of redress while another argued that if Irish representation was to cease then so would the parliamentary power to tax Ireland. Both extrapolated that therefore Ireland should have its own parliament. Another Irish MP saw matters differently and seemed to put Ireland's overtaxation down to the fact that there were not enough Irish MPs allowed in the English parliament.[26]

With the collapse of the Protectorate in 1659–60, Protestants in Ireland took matters into their own hands. In February 1660 the council of officers, established at the time of the December 1659 *coup d'état* in Dublin, issued a declaration demanding that, among other things, no charge 'be laid upon any of the nations without their own free consent, given by their representatives in their several and respective parliaments'.[27] The convention assembly which met in Dublin in March 1660 followed suit when it reasserted 'the right of having parliaments in Ireland' and reiterated that the English parliament 'never charged Ireland in any age with any subsidies, or other public taxes or assessment' until after Pride's Purge in 1648 when the English rump and its descendants of the 1650s 'invaded the rights' of the Irish parliament.[28]

The matter was also focused upon in the summer of 1660 by the second-generation Irish Protestant and recently appointed Attorney General, William Domville, when he was directed by Ormond to draw up 'A Disquisition' on the subject. Domville's manuscript drew heavily upon Bolton's 'Declaration' and, like Bolton and others before, placed particular emphasis upon the right to legislative autonomy being based upon Ireland's status as a separate and distinct kingdom.[29] The 1494–5 act once again had a prominent place within the arguments advanced, while Fortescue's 1441 ruling on consent to taxation was also reiterated.[30]

The failure to resolve the issue through a Declaratory Act or by other means ensured that during the Restoration period the English parliament continued to legislate for Ireland when the perceived need arose. The acts that caused most political disquiet tended to be those that effected the Irish economy. The Navigation Acts of 1660, 1663, 1671 and 1685, and even more pointedly the Cattle Acts of 1663 and 1667, were particular examples.[31] All ensured that the issue would resurface on the Irish constitutional agenda when the opportunity to address the matter arose again as occurred in 1689, when the continuing absence of a confessional divide in relation to that agenda was also evident.

The Catholic Counter-Revolution witnessed under James II and Tyrconnell culminated in the arrival of the exiled king in Ireland on 24 March 1689. The following day writs were issued to summon a parliament, which on the basis of remodelled borough constituencies resulted in a predominantly Catholic Commons, with only about six Protestants among the 230 MPs returned out of a potential 300, which was a remarkable turnaround given that Catholic representation had previously dropped from a large majority in 1585 to zero in 1661–6. In the Lords there were only five Protestant peers and four bishops. The Catholic hierarchy were not present, while the remainder of the thirty or so peers were Catholic.[32]

Given that James II perceived it to impinge upon the Crown's prerogative powers, it was with some reluctance that he acceded to the passage of an act in the 1689 parliament for 'declaring, that the parliament of England cannot bind Ireland and against writs of error and appeals, to be brought for removing judgments, decrees, and sentences given in Ireland, into England'. The link with the past was evident in the provisions of the act, which stated at the outset that Ireland 'hath been always a distinct kingdom from that of his majesty's realm of England', and that

> the people of this kingdom did never send members to any parliament ever held in England, but had their laws continually made and established by their own parliaments: so no acts passed in any parliament held in England, were ever binding here, excepting such of them as by acts of parliament passed in this kingdom were made into laws here.[33]

As such, a Declaratory Act of the kind desired since the 1640s was finally enacted. The act also addressed the question of the appellate jurisdiction of the English and Irish upper houses, which was to become more of an issue from the 1690s onwards. However, as early as 1641 the Irish Commons had resolved that 'the court of parliament was the supreme court of judicature in Ireland'.[34] This perception had clearly not held sway thereafter though, as clause VII of the 1689 act stated that 'of late times several persons have brought appeals before the House of Lords in England, in order to reverse decrees granted ... in Ireland, which ... is an apparent new encroachment upon the fundamental constitutions of this realm' and which thereafter was prohibited.[35] The Jacobite parliament also addressed the issue of legislative autonomy in an act 'for the advance and improvement of trade, and for the encouragement and increase of shipping, and navigation', which was targeted directly at the English Navigation Acts and looked to overturn their restrictions on direct trade with 'his majesty's plantations, colonies and islands in Asia, Africa, and America'.[36]

Significant as these acts were for demonstrating the continued adherence of Irish Catholics to a constitutional agenda they had shared for a long time with Protestant Ireland, the circumstances of their enactment ensured that they did not receive the approbation of the vast majority of Irish Protestants. The 1689 parliament had met at a time when large numbers of Protestants had left the country and thrown in their lot with William of Orange. Others were openly defying James in strongholds in Ulster. Attitudes were hardened even further by the 1689 parliament's enactment of legislation attainting over 2,000 Irish Protestants of treason, confiscating their land and other goods and property, repealing the Acts of Settlement and Explanation and restoring land ownership to the same status pertaining in 1641 prior to the most significant Catholic land losses and Protestant gains. The only way that any of the Jacobite parliament's legislation could ever be of real effect was if James won the war and regained his Scottish and English crowns. The fact that he did not do so ensured that the 1689 Declaratory and Navigation Acts along with all other legislation from that parliament were declared null and void by Westminster in 1690 and the records destroyed on the orders of the wholly Protestant Irish parliament in 1695.[37] The direct association of the Declaratory and Navigation Acts with the less edifying legislation from 1689 ensured that they would not resurface as part of the continuing constitutional arguments for Irish legislative autonomy in the 1690s and eighteenth century.

The emergence of a political and economic Protestant hegemony in Ireland following the final defeat of the Jacobites in October 1691 ensured that the issue of legislative autonomy appeared thereafter to be a wholly Protestant concern. However, the war had also created extraordinary circumstances in which some Westminster legislation affecting Ireland was readily acceded to by Irish Protestants without any objections being raised. The 1691 Oath Act, which ensured that the Irish parliament from 1692 onwards was a wholly Protestant assembly, unsurprisingly did not provoke any discontent among Irish Protestants. Molyneux felt this was understandable and acceptable on the grounds that they submitted to the 1691 act and several others passed during the war at Westminster at a time when Irish Protestants were not in a position to legislate on such matters and their acceptance of those acts was 'purely voluntary'. He even suggested that the presence of so many Irish Protestants in London during the war could also be construed as a form of consent.[38]

Similarly, Westminster's annual Mutiny Act for regulation of the army was first enacted in 1689 at a time when Irish Protestants were in no position to take issue with it. A greatly watered-down three-year mutiny bill was presented to the Irish parliament in 1692 but was rejected because it did not in any useful way replicate the English version, not least in that the latter was an annual enactment which ensured annual parliaments. It was also the case that an all-out assault was being made at that time on all government-sponsored legislation as part of the constitutional conflict over Poynings' Law.[39] Thereafter, the ensuing renewals of the English and British Mutiny Acts and their application to Ireland did not prompt any discontent until the late 1770s, when it became a part of an Irish Protestant 'Patriot' agenda.[40]

Prior to that time, the absence of complaint about the Mutiny Act was owing to the same reasons why there was no overt or obvious objection to Westminster's 1699 Disbanding Act, which settled the number of soldiers to be maintained in

Ireland and to be paid by the Irish treasury.[41] While this may seem odd, a number of factors accounted for it. In the aftermath of the war of 1689–97, it was not surprising that Irish Protestants were happy to maintain the single largest part of Britain's peacetime standing army in Ireland for their own security. However, that in itself was not a wholly sufficient reason for the known constitutional question not to have been addressed. More significantly, it was understood that the authority for the Irish civil and military establishments, which formed the basis for the government's annual expenditure, came from the monarch and his or her ministers in London. These were concerns readily understood to be authorized by the great seal, royal patents, king's or queen's letters, the sign manual, English treasury warrants and the like.[42] The Irish parliament and the wider Irish communities did not have a role or place in such decisions and matters, and nor did they aspire to any in the 1690s and early eighteenth century. Parliament could address or petition the executive in Dublin Castle or the monarch in London over aspects of the establishment that were perceived as unfair, unnecessary or a burden, but it would not be till later in the eighteenth century that that assembly would actively start to try to subsume some of those powers to itself, in actions such as the money bill dispute of 1753 and the army augmentation of 1769.[43]

Parliament's emerging role in controlling public income was perceived as sufficient leverage in the late 1690s and early eighteenth century with regard to having an influence upon expenditure as authorized through the civil and military establishment.[44] The drafting of the annual establishment received input from the executive in Dublin Castle as the monarch's representatives on the ground, but there was no uncertainty about the fact that ultimate authority for making and legitimating the establishment came from the Crown via the offices of the treasury lords in London.[45] The significance of the vice-regal appointee in Ireland was particularly pertinent in this respect. The Lord Lieutenant was, in the absence of the monarch, the Crown's representative in the sister kingdom of Ireland, and therefore executive head of both civil and military government. Given that no monarch chose to visit their western kingdom after William III in 1690, throughout the eighteenth century monarchical prerogative and authority, including over the army, was administered and executed through the office of the Irish viceroy.[46] Thus it was known and accepted that the decision as to how many soldiers were to be kept upon that establishment rested with the monarch and, by extension, with his Irish viceroy. That William III had allowed his Westminster parliament to decide that figure in 1699 was his affair, but not a matter for the Irish legislature or political nation. For the Irish parliament, the primary concern in the future would be ensuring that that decision was upheld and not abused either by imposing too many more soldiers upon Ireland's treasury, or drawing too many out of the country along with ready cash from that self-same treasury.[47]

The Westminster parliament had only started to make inroads into these areas of control over the military since the Glorious Revolution. The first ever Mutiny Act was passed in 1689 and the assumption of responsibility for financing the army through voting supplies and stating the 'number and exact composition of the land forces' quickly evolved thereafter in the early 1690s.[48] This was readily seen in the decisions taken by the Westminster Commons in late 1691 and early 1692 on the size of the army in the British Isles and Flanders on conclusion of the war in Ireland, which included specifying amounts to be expended from the Irish treasury for the purpose of maintaining soldiers in Ireland.[49] The fact that the English parliament had assumed a right to decide upon the military expenditure of Irish money was not contested on any front, presumably once again because it was accepted that the annual cost of civil and military government in Ireland was controlled and regulated by an establishment drawn up by Crown government in England.[50]

The question of legislative autonomy had not gone away, however. Shortly before the Irish parliament convened in 1692, Anthony Dopping, Bishop of Meath, published a medieval manuscript of disputed provenance on the workings of that assembly, entitled *Modus tenendi Parliamenta*, which had formed part of the arguments put forward in 1660 by Domville who, as his uncle, had bequeathed the manuscript to Dopping.[51] Dopping's purpose in publishing the *Modus* was unclear, though his inclusion in the publication of a manual on parliamentary procedure written by Henry Scobell, clerk of the English Commons in the 1650s, 'suggests at the least that the exercise was an implied assertion of the Irish parliament's antiquity and comparability with the English parliament'.[52] Dopping was also married to Molyneux's elder sister, so it was not surprising that the *Case of Ireland* included arguments taken from the *Modus*, a manuscript version of which Molyneux acknowledged receiving from his nephew, Samuel Dopping.[53]

The 1698 *Case of Ireland* of course had a much more telling impact than the *Modus*, given that it was penned in response to pending English legislation prohibiting Irish woollen manufacture exports as well as concern at the intentions of the Westminster parliament in relation to forfeited Jacobite lands and an ongoing conflict over the appellate jurisdiction of the Irish Lords in a case between Bishop William King of Derry and the London Society over property rights.[54] In the latter instance, the decision of the English Lords to overturn a ruling of the Irish upper house on an appeal against an Irish Chancery Court injunction, on the grounds that it was *coram non judice*, was the initial spark in a lengthy battle between the two houses that would only conclude in 1720.[55] At the heart of that battle was the issue of appeals and jurisdiction previously addressed in the now defunct Jacobite parliament's 1689 Declaratory Act.

The *Case of Ireland* owed much to Bolton's 'Declaration' and Domville's 'Disquisition', a rare copy of which Molyneux, as Domville's son-in-law, had to hand. A further influence came from Molyneux's friend, John Locke, and his *Two Treatises of Government*.[56] Not surprisingly, therefore, Molyneux re-emphasized the importance of Ireland being a separate and distinct kingdom, pointing out that even in the 1690s while England and Ireland were

> both governed by the like forms of government under one and the same supreme head, the King of England; yet so, as both kingdoms remained separate and distinct in their several jurisdictions under the one head, as are the kingdoms of England and Scotland ... without any subordination of the one to the other.[57]

For these reasons Molyneux dismissed the arguments that Ireland was 'only ... a colony of England'.[58] He also applied the question of 'consent of the people ... or their chosen representatives' in the broadest terms with regard to the 'great law of parliaments, which England so justly challenges, and all mankind have a right to ... whereby all laws receive their sanction'.[59] The argument based on Fortescue's 1441 case was also later reiterated and developed further with the proposition that 'if one law may be imposed without consent, any other law whatever, may be imposed on us without our consent. This will naturally introduce taxing us without our consent', which to Molyneux was 'little better, if at all, than downright robbing me'.[60] A new argument about consent was introduced regarding whether Ireland had actually been conquered or instead had consented to the establishment of the English title to Ireland.[61] The 1494–5 statute was also once again invoked, while the question of Irish representatives sitting in the English parliament was engaged with at two levels. Molyneux acknowledged that it had occurred in the past during times of crisis, but advocated that it only served to confirm that the English parliament had no right to legislate for Ireland without the consent of the Irish people or their representatives:

> If ... it be concluded that the parliament of England may bind Ireland; it must also be allowed that the people of Ireland ought to have their representatives in the parliament of England. And this, I believe we should be willing enough to embrace; but this is an happiness we can hardly hope for.[62]

The *Case of Ireland* prompted a furore in England.[63] The Westminster parliament took particular umbrage, with the Commons condemning the book and resolving that it was 'of dangerous consequence to the Crown and people of England'. An ensuing address to William III suggested that there was a dangerous desire in Ireland 'to shake off subjection to, and dependence on this kingdom'.[64] If Molyneux had hoped to appeal to 'the English parliament's sense of fair play', then he would have been sorely disappointed had he not died later in 1698 from a kidney complaint.[65] In April 1699 the English parliament finally legislated to prohibit the exportation of Irish woollen manufactures and to limit the export of raw wool from Ireland to England, demonstrating once again that Irish constitutional

sensibilities could and would be ridden roughshod over when political or economic pressures in England dictated as much even when, as was the case in this
instance, the English government was opposed to such legislation.[66] A year later,
and again in opposition to the wishes of the English government, the Westminster parliament passed an act for resuming all the grants made by William III
out of the Irish Jacobite forfeitures and for appointing a board of trustees for
their sale, with the money going towards covering the cost incurred by England
in the 1689–91 war. To add insult to injury, the trustees held their proceedings
from 1700 to 1703 in Chichester House, the usual home of the Irish parliament which did not sit during that time. Despite significant opposition from
Irish Protestants in London and Ireland and alongside the even more significant endeavours of the English government in that respect, the reality was that
once again they were unable to prevent the English parliament from pushing the
measure through.[67]

   In spite of, or indeed possibly because of, the adverse reaction the *Case of Ireland* prompted, it was to become the seminal work on Irish legislative autonomy
and more generally a cornerstone of 'the demand for domestic self-government
within an imperial framework' in the eighteenth century in a manner that none
of the previous tracts achieved. The *Case of Ireland* became central to the assertion of the view that 'loyalty to the British Crown was compatible with a vigorous
assertion of the right traditionally enjoyed by British citizens to be governed
only by laws assented to by their own representatives'.[68] The regular republication
of the book demonstrated its abiding impact, with new editions being produced
in 1706, 1719, 1720, 1725, 1749, 1770, 1773, 1776 and 1782. Those produced
in the 1770s tied in with the book's appeal beyond Ireland's shores, in particular
'in the early stages of the American Revolution, for its relevance to the general
question of the relations between England and its dependencies'.[69]

   The 1719 and 1720 editions were produced as a result of the escalating conflict between the two upper houses over appellate jurisdiction.[70] The Bishop
King versus London Society case of the 1690s had been followed in 1703 with
the resurrection of a case from 1695 between Edward Brabazon, earl of Meath,
and an English peer, Edward, Baron Ward, over land in Tipperary. The Irish
Lords, taking the side of Meath, passed resolutions asserting their right to act as
the final court of appeal and supreme judicial body for Ireland, thereby creating
the potential for a problematic political showdown on the issue. On this occasion conflict was avoided, however, by the intervention of the Irish government,
with an accommodation being reached before the problem escalated. But the
willingness of the Irish Lords to take a stance on the issue meant that it was only
a matter of time before another case gave them an opportunity to embrace a constitutional contest with the English upper house. In 1709 the Irish Lords took
on Dublin Castle over an Irish Court of Exchequer decision, but Lord Lieuten-

ant Thomas, Lord Wharton, ultimately decided against an appeal to the British Lords for fear of how the fall-out might destroy the government's chances of securing financial supplies in parliament.[71]

No such discretion was evident however when the Sherlock versus Annesley case found its way to the Irish Lords in 1716. In another contest over land rights, the Irish Lords championed the case of a widow, Hester Sherlock, by overturning a decision of the Irish Exchequer Court in favour of Maurice Annesley. Annesley in turn appealed to the British Lords in 1717, setting in motion a series of events that included the arrest of the exchequer barons on the orders of the Irish Lords and culminated in the passage of the 1720 Declaratory Act in the British parliament, which proved much longer lasting than the Jacobite parliament's 1689 endeavour. The 1720 version was also the exact opposite of the 1689 act.[72] Entitled 'an act for the better securing the dependency of the kingdom of Ireland on the Crown of Great Britain', the 1720 measure

> declared ... that the said kingdom of Ireland hath been, is and of right ought to be, subordinate unto and dependent upon the imperial Crown of Great Britain, as being inseparably united and annexed thereunto, and that the King's majesty, by and with the advice and consent of the Lords spiritual and temporal, and Commons of Great Britain in parliament assembled, had, hath, and of right ought to have full power and authority to make laws and statutes of sufficient force and validity to bind the kingdom and the people of Ireland.

A second clause 'declared and enacted' that the Irish Lords 'have not, nor of right ought to have, any jurisdiction to judge of, affirm or reverse any judgment, sentence or decree, given or made in any court' in Ireland, and that all such proceedings before the Lords were null and void.[73]

Irish opposition to the act proved ineffectual. Alongside Irish lobbying in London and the objections raised by members of both houses of the British parliament, a number of pamphlets were published including one by the Irish deist and political hack writer John Toland.[74] But the reality was that more general and immediate 'tactical considerations at Westminster' along with other 'problems of political management in Ireland as well as Britain' meant that for the British government a Declaratory Act of the nature of the 1720 statute had much more attraction at that point in time than had been the case on any previous occasion when Anglo-Irish constitutional conflict might have suggested such a solution. Studiously avoided by previous English and British administrations, in 1720 the Declaratory Act offered immediate political gain on a variety of fronts, including the government's attempts to deal with the Whig schism of 1717 in England and a short-lived flirtation with the possibility of circumventing recent problems that had arisen in managing the leading political factions in Ireland by avoiding the meeting of an Irish parliament altogether, at least for a time during which

Ireland might be taxed from Westminster. The failure to come up with a realistic scheme to reduce Irish expenditure to a level that would remove the necessity for convening the Irish parliament, and the ensuing loss of nerve over the very drastic step of moving towards direct taxation from Westminster without the consent of the Irish people or their representatives ensured that the potential for the Declaratory Act to become a means for regular and invasive Westminster legislation relative to Ireland was not realized.[75] Instead, the act came to be more significant in theory than in reality, with little use being made of the declared power during the ensuing six decades. Even still, it did serve its purpose in putting an end to formal contestation of the matter of legislative autonomy and jurisdictional authority. Ultimately, however, it did not put an end to Irish Protestant aspirations in those regards, which instead became channelled in different directions before re-emerging revitalized in the 1760s and 1770s.

Poynings' Law and the Advent of Regular Parliaments

One reason for the lack of an overly dramatic negative response from Ireland to the 1720 Declaratory Act can be ascribed to the fact that it did not actually result in the demise of the Irish parliament. Indeed, normal service was resumed without interruption in 1721, the primary reason for which was the Irish government's continuing need for parliamentary taxes. In fact, the whole question of parliamentary financial supply, alluded to in aspects of the constitutional debate about legislative autonomy since the 1400s, was at the heart of the conflict over Poynings' Law, which was the other main source of constitutional contestation between Ireland and England in the early modern period. Unlike legislative autonomy, however, long before 1720 the issues relating to Poynings' Law had already advanced in a direction that was much more satisfactory and encouraging for the Irish parliament and political nation.

Enacted by the Irish parliament in 1494–5 alongside the act for making certain existing English statutes binding in Ireland, Poynings' Law was named after the English Lord Deputy at the time, Sir Edward Poynings. Ostensibly aimed at limiting the power of overly independent Irish chief governors of Norman or Old English descent such as Gerald FitzGerald, Earl of Kildare, who had among other things overseen the crowning of the pretender, Lambert Simnel, as Edward VI in Dublin in May 1487,[76] the law initially provided that parliament could not be summoned in Ireland thereafter without the 'causes and considerations' first being transmitted by the Irish chief governor and council to the monarch and council in England, along with any proposed bills. If the reasons for summoning parliament were deemed legitimate, the monarch's permission under the great seal of England for issuing writs for elections could then be authorized and a parliament summoned. The agreed bills were then presented, either to be passed or rejected.[77]

In its initial incarnation Poynings' Law was seen as a defence against overextended executive power including that of the English government, and therefore was viewed benignly by the Irish parliament. It was temporarily repealed in the 1530s and 1560s because it was perceived to restrict the English government's ability to present reforming religious and administrative legislation. Such a ploy was blocked by the Irish parliament when attempted again in the 1580s because it was seen to undermine the authority of that assembly.[78] In the interim, in 1557, Poynings' Law had been permanently amended in order to address a number of ambiguities in its interpretation, including making explicit the right of the monarch to alter and amend bills transmitted from Ireland, the right of the Irish executive to transmit further bills to England while parliament was actually sitting and the restricting of the consideration of legislation by parliament to only those bills transmitted to, and returned from, England.[79] It has also been suggested that the 1557 act made it legally possible for parliament thereafter to amend and initiate bills, if the executive and parliament 'saw eye to eye' on such matters, and that it appeared to empower the monarch to consider bills and transmit the licence for parliament without reference to his or her English council. In the latter instance, if this were true, it was never acted upon.[80]

It was however the question of parliament's role in amending and initiating legislation that turned the tables on Poynings' Law by the beginning of the seventeenth century. The first Irish parliament ever to have representatives from the whole country which was summoned in 1613 was faced with a variety of issues relating to the final completion of the Tudor conquest of Ireland in 1603, including potential penal legislation against Catholics. The Lord Deputy, Sir Arthur Chichester, initially proposed that another suspension of Poynings' Law would facilitate the smoother passage of various bills, but was refused permission by James I on the grounds that 'frequent dispensations' would 'weaken the authority of the law' which was there to protect the legislature.[81] When parliament convened, it became evident that there was a desire among MPs to interpret Poynings' Law in a manner that allowed an amending and initiating role to that assembly. The executive was presented with various addresses for amendments to bills and proposals for new ones, but despite the government's favourable response, few of either type made it into law. A later endeavour by the Commons to presented actual drafts of bills engrossed on parchment and to send a deputation to London to advocate on behalf of the proposed legislation was ultimately rebuffed by James I.[82] Parliament was shortly thereafter 'prematurely dissolved'.[83]

When parliament met again in 1634–5, a more problematic interpretation of Poynings' Law was propounded under Wentworth's lord deputyship. In the intervening period, in 1628, the usefulness of the law as a defensive measure for government was seen when an apparently inadvertent mistake made by Lord Deputy Henry Cary, Viscount Falkland, resulted in a proposed parliament having to be aborted. As part of the Graces agreed earlier that year, a parliament was to be summoned on 3 November to enact legislation aimed at making effective those agreements. But Falkland's issuing of the writs for election before transmitting the causes and considerations into England in accordance with Poynings' Law was deemed to contravene the legal requirements and therefore parliament could not be convened. The government soon realized that Falkland's error allowed them to avoid implementing those Graces which clashed with or might hinder future government policy in Ireland.[84]

When Wentworth arrived in Ireland he realized that Poynings' Law could not only be used to shield government from unpalatable policies advocated by the Irish, but could also be used as a more forceful weapon. In the 1634–5 parliament he interpreted the law in a 'revolutionary' manner that denied parliament any power to initiate legislation and allowed the government 'to regulate ... proceedings ... in minute detail'.[85] While wholly successful in achieving his intended aims in 1634–5, Wentworth was in reality creating a bigger problem for government in the future. In 1640 parliament had to be reconvened in order to vote money to assist the King in the Bishops' Wars in Scotland. With Wentworth, now Earl of Strafford, soon out of the country leading the King's army and then charged by the Westminster parliament with high treason, a viable Protestant and Catholic opposition emerged in Ireland united in their efforts to undo what had been done with regards to Poynings' Law. As had been seen with the issue of legislative autonomy, Anglo-Irish constitutional conflicts transcended confessional divides. In 1640–1 the Irish Commons pursued an agenda aimed at establishing a clear understanding of the procedural forms for certification of bills into England and parliament's right to initiate legislation within the parameters of Poynings' Law. By then the question of amending government bills seems to have dropped from the agenda. Despite such concerted efforts, however, nothing had been resolved by the time parliament was adjourned in August 1641. Before it could reconvene the outbreak of rebellion in October 1641 altered circumstances dramatically.[86]

As war engulfed the British Isles in 1641–2, Irish Catholics were the group who most actively took up the issue of Poynings' Law, in a similar manner to the way they advocated for legislative autonomy. It was evident that a desire existed for repeal of Poynings' Law from early on in the process which resulted in the formation of the Confederation.[87] While keen to protest their loyalty to Charles I at all times and to demonstrate that their unicameral assembly at Kilkenny was not a parliament and therefore not an attempt to usurp the prerogative power of the Crown in that regard,[88] the Confederates pushed for 'the immediate suspension and ultimate repeal of Poynings' Law' in the lengthy peace negotiations with Charles I and Ormond, the King's Lord Lieutenant and royalist commander in Ireland. As pressure mounted on Charles in 1644–5 with significant military defeats in England, he became more open to the idea of at least suspending Poynings' Law, but Ormond remained resolute in his opposition and the Confederates, not knowing of the King's changing views, wavered. Even when news of Charles's altered opinion leaked into the public domain after the royalist defeat at Naseby, the negotiations had already progressed to a point where Poynings' Law was no longer on the agenda and a settlement was agreed in March 1646 without any royal concessions on the matter. The Confederation however proved unable to avoid a spilt over the proposed treaty, their points of disagreement including the absence of a promise to suspend Poynings' Law.[89]

In the interim, the Protestant rump of the Irish parliament in Dublin had moved in a more conservative and reactionary direction. Having initially considered the possibility in 1642 of suspending Poynings' Law in order to facilitate bills such as an act of attainder against those in rebellion, by 1644 such an idea was long since abandoned and instead the Dublin rump had come to its defence as protector of the King's power and his Protestant subjects in Ireland.[90]

When peace negotiations were entered into again between the Confederates and Ormond in 1648, the repeal of Poynings' Law was back on the agenda. Yet news of Charles I's impending trial at the end of the year forced both sides to back down and to rapidly agree a peace treaty which only included the provision that once an Irish parliament was reconvened it would be allowed to consider the question of the suspension or repeal of Poynings' Law. However, the ensuing Cromwellian conquest in 1649–53 and the parliamentary union thereafter made all such agreements redundant.[91] By the time Charles II was restored in 1660, the altered political and religious balance of power in Ireland resulted in the issue being addressed in a more traditional manner by an overwhelmingly Protestant parliament and wholly Protestant Commons.

The restored Irish parliament of 1661–6 took up where the 1640–1 assembly had left off. In October 1640 the Commons had ordered a committee 'to draw up the heads of such acts' as they saw necessary.[92] This first reference to the idea of drafting heads of bills was to be given substance in the 1660s as the Irish parliament pressed forward with its belief in its right to a legislative initiative. During 1661 the Commons established select committees to prepare bills, used 'Declarations' along the lines of interregnum ordinances for the short-term continuation of customs and excise duties, and formally considered the 'manner and method of preparing and drawing of bills, in order to the transmission of them into England, according to Poynings' Act'.[93] On 27 July the lower house went so far as to order that the government be requested to draw up a bill in accordance with 'such heads as shall be propounded by both houses'.[94] The following year the Commons progressed from drafting mere headings to a procedure whereby they drew up the actual text of proposed legislation under the guise of heads of a bill, with the first substantive attempt being the 'heads and considerations' for an explanatory bill to address the many concerns that had arisen with the recently passed Act of Settlement. Although unsuccessful in this endeavour, the ideas propounded in the explanatory heads eventually fed into the Act of Explanation of 1665, while other heads of bills were drafted in proper form by the Irish Privy Council and transmitted to England in accordance with Poynings' Law, though few actually made it to the statute book.[95] It was still the case that the vast majority of legislation originated with the government, though the efforts of the 1660s parliament established a precedent which was to be of great importance when that assembly was eventually reconvened in the 1690s.[96]

In the intervening period, the Jacobite parliament of 1689 took up where the Confederates had left off, by reviving the idea of a more fundamental alteration of the constitutional framework with the complete repeal of Poynings' Law. While James II was at first apparently open to some modification of the law, he ultimately opposed the actual bill for repeal when introduced in the Commons and ensured its demise. The Jacobite parliament was also accused of failure to comply with Poynings' Law in that the causes and considerations, and related proposed legislation, was not certified into England. Yet it was wholly unrealistic to suggest that the Irish government would transmit such material for the approval of William III who was in their eyes a usurper of legitimate royal power and authority, while the actual presence of the usurped James II and his council in Dublin and their prior scrutiny of all bills put before the parliament offered a just as compelling counter-argument.[97] Ultimately, however, the legitimizing of either argument and more generally the validity of all of the parliamentary proceedings in Dublin in 1689 were wholly dependent upon who won the war. William's eventual victory ensured that thereafter engagement with the question of Poynings' Law was in accordance with the arguments advocated in 1640–1 and 1661–6 and not the starker approach taken in 1642–9 and 1689.

In the immediate aftermath of the Williamite victory in late 1691 it was uncertain as to whether or not an Irish parliament would be summoned. William had promised to do so on a number of occasions during the war, but there were those around him who advocated otherwise.[98] Yet the key and very practical question of the urgent and rapidly escalating government need for money in both England and Ireland demanded a quick decision.[99] Whatever the credence given to the arguments regarding consent to taxation, the English government and the Westminster parliament had never taken it upon themselves to tax Ireland directly, except when there were Irish representatives in the 1650s. There was no reason to believe that the political will existed in 1691–2 to change that understanding, especially given that neither the idea of a parliamentary union or that of the Westminster parliament continuing to legislate for Ireland as it had done during the war years without any Irish representation had garnered much support.[100] The arguments for an Irish parliament were looked upon more favourably. The 1691

Oath Act would ensure that any Irish parliament convened thereafter would be a wholly Protestant affair, peopled by individuals who were by necessity ardent supporters of the Glorious Revolution and therefore had a vested interest in the settlement of Ireland in a manner that reflected the outcome of the events of 1688–91. They would also convene in an assembly that received significant government oversight and control via the instrument of Poynings' Law.[101]

By early 1692 the decision to convene the Irish parliament had been taken, and the preparation of a legislative programme in accordance with Poynings' Law was underway.[102] The preliminary considerations for a proposed parliament in the 1670s appeared to inform the 1692 deliberations. Arthur Capell, Earl of Essex, and Ormond as Lord Lieutenants in the 1670s had made initial preparations for a legislative programme, and both had advised that the Irish parliament would not vote any more permanent revenues to the Crown as had been done in 1661–6. They both agreed that instead parliament would look more favourably upon bills for short-term taxation as had begun to be utilized in Westminster in the 1660s.[103] In 1692 the Dublin government prepared three supplies bills for imposing several taxes for one year only, with the Lord Lieutenant, Henry, Viscount Sydney, explaining to London that in one of the bills the original imposition for two years had been changed by the Irish council to one year out of fear that a two-year tax might 'beget a jealousy in [parliament], as though, after the ensuing session ended, they were not to meet again till after the expiration of two years'.[104] Such an acknowledgement would suggest that the full implication of agreeing to this approach was recognized in government circles in London and Dublin, in that as long as government expenditure remained in excess of its traditional non-parliamentary sources of income, then short-term taxation in the Irish parliament would result in the advent of regular sessions.[105] Prior to 1692, the Irish parliament, aside from the 1689 assembly, had only met on four occasions in the seventeenth century and had continued to be viewed as an irregular event. To countenance more regular assembly was to agree to it becoming a more central institution of the state, as had occurred since 1689 in England and had been witnessed first-hand by many future Irish MPs who quickly concluded that the same elevated status was the right of the Irish parliament as well.[106] To what extent Dopping's *Modus* was intended to fuel that fire is not evident, but it may well have encouraged MPs in 1692 in their search for precedents in the records of earlier assemblies.[107]

While the preparation of government supply bills of short duration may have been intended to gratify parliament, the decision of the executive to interpret Poynings' Law in a very traditional manner had the exact opposite effect. Having prepared a full legislative programme for presentation, it was evident that the government did not intend upon allowing parliament any initiative in the legislative process.[108] Having demonstrated in various ways their discontent on this and other matters and having scared Sydney into thinking they wanted to free themselves from 'the yoke of England' and to repeal Poynings' Law,[109] when the Commons were presented with the two supply bills returned to Ireland from London, a constitutional crisis unfolded which took several years to resolve.[110] On 27 October the Commons resolved 'that it was, and is, the undoubted right of the Commons of Ireland, in parliament assembled, to prepare and resolve the ways and means of raising money' and that 'it was, and is, the sole and undoubted right of the Commons to prepare heads of bills for raising money'. They then proceeded to take into consideration the first of the government supply bills, for imposing additional duties on beer, ale and other liquors for one year, which had been 'transmitted out of England', while at the same time emphasizing that they did so on exceptional grounds owing to the 'present exigencies of affairs, and the public necessity of speedily raising a supply'. To reinforce that point they thereafter resolved that 'the receiving or reading of the said bill, so transmitted as aforesaid, be not drawn into precedent hereafter'. If anyone remained in any doubt as to the Commons' stance on the matter, the following day they rejected the second government supply bill on the grounds that 'the same had not its rise in this house', which was then recorded for posterity and precedent in the Commons' Journal. The Commons then took the legislative initiative and commenced preparing heads of a supply bill for an equivalent amount to that lost with the rejected bill.[111]

The concept of a 'sole and undoubted right' seems to have been adapted from an English Commons' resolution of 1678 relating to supply legislation originating in the Westminster lower house.[112] In an Irish context, however, when combined with the stated reason for rejection of the second government supply bill, it served to deny the validity of Poynings' Law in relation to tax legislation. By insisting that only the Irish Commons had the authority to initiate such legislation, the 'sole right' claim, as it became known, forcefully implied that neither the Irish or English councils, or the monarch, had the right to prepare or present supply bills to the Irish parliament and thereby placed a limitation on the type of legislation that could be initiated by government. It also laid down the strongest claim yet to a clearly defined procedure for initiating legislation in parliament through the heads of bills procedure, which was presented as a long-standing right, though one without an explicitly defined date of origin. In all of this, the Commons were clearly endeavouring to significantly reinterpret Poynings' Law in parliament's favour.[113] More generally, as part of the attack on Poynings' Law, an all-out assault on the government's legislative programme had seen the rejection of six of the ten bills presented, with, in some cases, orders made for heads of bills to be drafted for the same or similar bills such as that for supply and, on the last day of the session, for a more satisfactory mutiny bill.[114]

Once the full significance of the actions of the Commons began to dawn upon Sydney, he gratefully accepted it as reason enough to bring a problematic session to an untimely halt. In his prorogation speech, he stated that the votes and resolutions on 27–8 October were contrary to Poynings' Law and 'continued practice ever since'. He was therefore 'obliged to assert their majesties' prerogative and the rights of the Crown of England, in these particulars, in such a manner as may be most public and permanent', by making 'in full parliament' his 'public protest against those votes, and the entries of them in the Journal of the ... Commons'. The protest was thereafter to be entered in the Lords' Journal, 'that it may remain as a vindication of their majesties' prerogative, and the right of the Crown of England, in these particulars, to future ages'.[115]

Sydney's grandiose reference to 'future ages' did not take account of the real practicalities of what had occurred. The political impasse that ensued into 1693 soon brought home the reality that if an Irish parliament was to be summoned again, agreement would have to be first reached on the thorny constitutional questions raised in 1692. The government's ever-worsening public finances demanded as much. For that reason, between late 1693 and early 1695 a compromise agreement was negotiated between the leading members of the 1692 opposition and the government, in particular with the English Whig, Baron Capell, one of three lords justices appointed to replace Sydney in the summer of 1693. The negotiations also saw the emergence of the Irish Whig, Alan Brodrick, one of the MPs imbued with the constitutional rhetoric of the Glorious Revolution, as a key figure in Irish politics. The compromise agreement, which included the lord deputyship for Capell and government office for Brodrick and others, centred upon the issue of the Crown's prerogative in initiating legislation, Poynings' Law and the rights of parliament. In return for the introduction by government of key legislation desired by parliament including penal laws against Catholics and explicit recognition of the right of the Commons both to decide upon the ways and means of raising taxes and to initiate supply legislation by means of the heads of bills procedure, the Commons agreed to receive and pass a token government supply bill of one year's duration at the start of a new parliament in recognition of the Crown's prerogative and Poynings' Law.[116]

Lord Deputy Capell's opening speech to the newly convened parliament in August 1695 was symbolic of the compromise. Having emphasized the government's great debts and difficulties in paying the army and having promised to deliver public accounts to that effect, he became the first viceroy ever to directly appeal to the Commons for supply:

> For raising some part of this money, his majesty has sent you a bill ... and he expects from you, gentlemen of the ... Commons, that you will consider of ways and means for raising such other sums as are requisite for his service, and prepare heads of bills to be passed into laws in due form.[117]

The Commons duly passed the token government supply bill, which as in 1692 imposed additional duties on beer, ale and other liquors for one year, and then proceeded to examine the public accounts, assess the ways and means and prepare and pass further supply legislation by means of the heads of bills procedure. The first penal laws against Catholics were also introduced by the government as part of an initial fourteen-bill legislative programme.[118]

The 1695 compromise was a success, but it had required concessions on both sides. The Commons conceded their sole-right claim in return for public acknowledgement of their right to assess the ways and means of raising taxes and to scrutinize the public accounts, and recognition for the heads of bill procedure. Because that recognition was explicitly for supply legislation, which quickly became the single most important and constant legislative process in the eighteenth-century Irish parliament,[119] it also ensured that the heads of bills procedure was not a peripheral or occasional occurrence but instead quickly became the normal, standard procedure for the vast majority of legislation.[120] The government in return secured recognition of the Crown's prerogative right to initiate supply legislation in accordance with Poynings' Law and got the all-important taxes voted. Yet in truth parliament had received the better deal, as they had achieved a significant reinterpretation of Poynings' Law that had eluded their predecessors in 1613–15, 1634–5, 1640–9, 1661–6 and 1689.

In the ensuing sessions of the 1695 parliament in 1697 and 1698–9 some confusion arose as to whether a token government supply bill was required at the beginning of second and ensuing sessions of the same parliament. The government's legislative programme in 1697 did not include a supply bill, and many of the bills that were prepared were versions of heads of bills that had not been enacted in 1695. In 1698–9 the government legislative programme was of similar composition while the matter of the token government money bill was also conceded in practical terms, with the only government tax bill, for imposing prohibitive duties on woollen exports, being presented late in the session for a variety of political considerations.[121]

After an interval of four years and eight months, which was to prove to be the longest of the eighteenth century, a new parliament was summoned in late 1703. In accordance with the 1695 compromise, a token supply bill of one year's duration was included in the government's much reduced five-bill legislative programme. The bill was passed by parliament and the Commons thereafter proceeded to draft heads of bills for raising the vast majority of the supply required. In the five ensuing sessions of that parliament in 1705, 1707, 1709, 1710 and 1711 no new token government supply bill was either introduced or even contemplated, while the Commons prepared further supply bills in each and every session. The government's general legislative programme also diminished in ensuing sessions. In 1705 only four bills were prepared before the session in accordance with Poynings' Law, in 1707 there were only three, and in the final three sessions between 1709 and 1711 there was no initial government legislative programme, though some bills were presented as the session progressed, though with an increasing level of rejection each session.[122] At the same time, the actual overall legislative output of the Irish parliament began to increase through the heads of bills procedure. During 1697–9, parliament had commenced drafting other non-supply bills without any objections being raised by government in Ireland or England. The number of such heads of bills increased further during 1703–11.[123]

Such increasing legislative output was also because parliament began meeting on a regular basis owing to the advent of regular short-term taxation from 1692 onwards and the continuing expenditure of more money than arose from non-parliamentary sources.[124] After some experimentation with one-year supply acts in the middle of Anne's reign as Irish Whigs tried to force annual parliaments along the lines of the English model, the preference for two-year duration taxation soon ensured that a system of biennial parliaments, meeting for about six months every two years, became the norm.[125] It was also the case that from the 1690s onwards a system of political management evolved centred upon leading Irish politicians who undertook to manage Irish political and parliamentary affairs in return for position, patronage and power. This 'Undertaker System' dominated Irish politics until the end of the 1760s, when permanent residency of the chief governor saw a move towards more direct management from Dublin Castle.[126]

As the century progressed, legislative output continued to increase while the divergence between the number of government and parliamentary bills became even more apparent. For a new short-lived parliament in 1713 only two government bills were prepared, while the first Hanoverian parliament of 1715–16 was summoned with only a five-bill legislative programme.[127] About twenty-four of the thirty-one acts passed thereafter in that session originated as heads of bills. There was no initial government programme in the ensuing five sessions between 1717 and 1726, while at least 100 of the 110 acts passed during that time originated as heads of bills.[128] For the new parliaments convened in 1727, 1761 and 1776, the constant practice was for three government bills to be prepared for presentation at the start of the first session, of which one was always a token supply bill.[129] For the new parliament of 1769 only two government bills were prepared, one of which was again a token supply bill.[130] In the intervening years, the biennial sessions were dominated by legislation originating as heads of bills. In the seventeen sessions of George II's Irish parliament held between 1727 and 1760, at least 259 of the 279 acts passed originated as heads of bills. In the four sessions of George III's first parliament from 1761 to 1768 at least 144 of the 148 acts passed were heads of bills, while in the five sessions of the second parliament of that reign from 1769 to 1776 at least 138 of the 140 acts passed originated as heads.[131]

The heads of bill procedure was by its nature more convoluted and time-consuming than the legislative process in Westminster, a fact that was in time to contribute to the agitation in the 1760s and 1770s for the complete repeal of Poynings' Law. Heads of a bill were first drafted and considered in a given house of parliament in a process that was not an exact science and which evolved and altered over time. The bill was then sent to the Irish Privy Council to be drawn up in form as a proper bill for transmission according to Poynings' Law to Whitehall for consideration by the monarch and English council. If deemed acceptable in London, it was then sent back to Ireland for presentation to parliament, where it had to journey through both houses before receiving the royal assent. This process allowed a lot of time for exposure to external interference, which could result in bills being amended, altered or wholly lost. But a balance also had to be struck. Too much interference via amendments, alterations or respiting of bills in Dublin Castle or Whitehall could provoke a backlash from parliament, with the threat of rejection of the all-important supply acts being readily used against such practices.[132]

The token government supply bill process evolved over time as well. For the short-lived parliament of 1713 the government had prepared a bill of only three months' duration but with a wider schedule of additional duties in order to ensure that none of the existing taxes lapsed before parliament had time to examine the public accounts and consider the ways and means. As such, the token bill became a bridging measure at the commencement of a new parliament, and was based upon precedents set by the Commons themselves in the 1709 and 1710 sessions.[133] In 1715 the government went with a variation on a theme for the first session of George I's parliament, presenting a bill for the wider schedule of duties for six months' duration, while in 1727 the first session of George II's new parliament was presented with a bill continuing the wider schedule of duties for three months. While this tinkering with the duration did not prompt opposition, on each occasion there was growing discontent with what was perceived as the precipitate nature of the presentation of the government bill before the Commons had fully examined the public accounts and assessed the need for a supply.[134] In 1716 it was made a standing order of the Commons that 'no money bill be read in this house until after the report from the committee of accounts be first made'. The failure to comply with that standing order in 1727 had resulted in some discussion in the Commons before the 1716 standing order was reconfirmed.[135] On the ensuing occasions when new parliaments were convened in 1761 and 1769, the government adhered to the dictates of these standing orders, which were renewed at the outset of the 1769 parliament. For the new parliament of 1776, failure to comply with the standing orders actually resulted in rejection of the government supply bill, though this in fact constituted an agreed part of the final compromise on the issue before legislative independence in 1782.[136]

It was evident that a significant reinterpretation of Poynings' Law in parliament's favour had been initiated in 1695. The Irish and English governments still had a very direct role in the legislative process, especially when heads of bills were processed in accordance with Poynings' Law in both Dublin Castle and at Whitehall, but on balance a dramatic alteration had occurred in the way in which Poynings' Law was interpreted and understood in relation to the government's initial legislative programme and the legislative initiative of parliament. This reinterpretation was ultimately to parliament's advantage, as control of the purse strings through the voting of short-duration taxation ensured that the legislature became a central and important apparatus of the Irish state in the eighteenth century.

As such, the Irish parliament between the 1690s and 1760s was much more successful in renegotiating the constitutional relationship with England and Britain in relation to Poynings' Law than with regard to legislative autonomy. Indeed, that success and the greater role allowed to parliament in the first six decades of the eighteenth century in large part helped to explain why those who advocated a third way of resolving the constitutional conundrums of the Anglo-Irish relationship via a parliamentary union were in a minority and were wholly unsuccessful.

Ideas of Union, Protestant Patriot Politics and Legislative Independence

From the earliest considerations of a possible union in 1690–2, there was a lack of sufficient support for the occasional proposals put forward.[137] In the *Case of Ireland* Molyneux had also raised the subject as part of the argument regarding the right of the people to be allowed to give their consent to taxation and other laws, describing union as something 'I believe we should be willing enough to embrace'.[138] Molyneux's strategy in this regard might be construed as proffering a less palatable alternative to his primary argument, a stance that was not unusual at the time not least because of William III's known antipathy to the idea of a union. The hope was that the primary argument would therefore win out, as was evident in a lengthy Commons' representation of October 1703 which rehearsed a multitude of grievances at the heart of which lay the fundamental belief that 'nothing but frequent parliaments, with a permission for them to sit and do the business of the nation, can reform so great and notorious abuses'. The less palatable alternative was rolled out at the end: that if Ireland was not restored 'to a full enjoyment of our constitution' then a 'more firm and strict union with your majesty's subjects of England' should be entered into.[139]

At the same time, the extent to which a parliamentary union was deemed unnecessary and superfluous was emphasized in an earlier address in September 1703 from the Commons on Queen Anne's 'happy accession'. On this occasion the Commons made clear that England and Ireland were already united by ancients bonds, ostensibly and pointedly ascribed to being of the Irish parliament's making, that were apparently unbreakable and were of the greatest importance to Irish Protestants: 'the kingdom of Ireland is annexed and united to the imperial Crown of England; and by the laws and statutes of this kingdom is declared to be justly and rightfully depending upon, and belonging, and for ever united to the same'.[140]

The Irish Country Whig Henry Maxwell's anonymous *An Essay upon an Union* was presumably written in advance of such activity in the Commons, but was apparently first published in London in November 1703.[141] Maxwell was part of the Whig grouping in the Irish Commons that had modelled and promoted the October 1703 representation in a manner best suited to their political agenda which included a desire for annual parliaments. But it was also evident that he was not just a creature of party politics, given that his pamphlet genuinely advocated for a union as a solution to existing constitutional anomalies. That said, it could also be construed as part of the Irish Whig policy of making life politically uncomfortable for the Tory Lord Lieutenant, Ormond, and his Dublin court party by creating the impression in English minds of political discontent and disorder in the western kingdom. Maxwell's decision to first publish in London and to assume the character of an author writing in England for the Queen and Westminster parliament added to such a view.[142]

The various activities around the idea of union in late 1703 stemmed in part from the early negotiations for the Anglo-Scottish Union of 1707, which had also attracted the attention of Jonathan Swift. Understood to have been written around the time of that union, the first publication date of *The Story of the Injured Lady* remains uncertain.[143] The piece itself contrasted the ill-treatment of Ireland, personified as an Anglican beauty, with the lavishing of attention and ultimately matrimony upon the Scottish Presbyterian harridan in a parody of the Anglo-Scottish Union itself. Swift's ultimate attitude towards union however remains unclear.[144]

Thereafter Irish political opinion tended to veer away from engagement with or advocacy for an Anglo-Irish union. Instead, the Irish parliament and its more central role within government and the state was looked to as the instrument for expressing and defending Irish constitutional rights and liberties and as the vehicle for proper government. The anti-union riots in Dublin in December 1759, sparked in reaction to a rumoured though non-existent plot to do away with the Irish parliament, demonstrated how strong opposition to such a proposal had grown in the intervening decades.[145]

Opposition to the idea of a union was also evident in the emergence of a Patriot grouping and agenda within Irish Protestant politics.[146] The occasions for the republication of Molyneux's *Case of Ireland* provided signposts along the way for the developing Patriot ideology centred eventually upon the idea of legislative independence. The 1725 edition coincided with the final stages of the Wood's Halfpence affair, which had also seen the emergence of Swift as the Patriot Dean or Hibernian Patriot via the instrument of the *Drapier's Letters*.[147] The affair had arisen because of the long-standing shortage of ready specie, in particular silver coinage, in Ireland. Ostensibly as a means of solving the problem, in 1722 George I's mistress, Melusine von der Schulenburg, Duchess of Kendal, received £10,000 from an English ironmonger, William Wood, for a patent she held for coining £100,800 worth of copper halfpence and farthings for Ireland over a period of fourteen years.[148] Concerted opposition to the patent commenced immediately in Ireland from within government and the wider community. In July, Archbishop King, then serving as one of the lords justices, informed the absent Lord Lieutenant that the 'generality of the people' in Ireland were greatly alarmed at, and dreaded the consequences of, the patent.[149] A month later the Irish revenue commissioners expressed their opposition to the patent in robust terms.[150]

The reasons for Irish opposition were both economic and political. On the economic front it was argued that an English ironmonger would export the profit arising from the coinage out of Ireland; that the real need was for silver and gold coinage; and that the economy would be ruined if flooded with debased coinage of no intrinsic value. The political arguments were of a Patriot hue: that the patent should have been issued to an Irish ironmonger; that the profit should stay in Ireland; that Irish economic concerns would always be second to English; and that Ireland was to be treated as a subordinate kingdom.[151]

The 1723–4 parliament made clear its opposition, as did the country at large with numerous addresses and representations during 1724.[152] Swift entered the fray in March 1724 with the first of his anonymous *Drapier's Letters*.[153] The fourth letter in October of that year, *To the Whole People of Ireland*, and the resulting *Seasonable Advice* addressed to the Dublin Grand Jury,[154] helped to bring the whole matter to a critical climax, with the newly appointed Lord Lieutenant, John, Lord Carteret, quickly coming to the conclusion that the patent had to be withdrawn.[155] It was no coincidence that the announcement of that decision was made when parliament convened in late 1725, because the really serious threat from the opposition to Wood's halfpence had always been that it would result in the loss of the supply bills.

Such concerted and broad-based patriotic action in Ireland was not the norm however. Thereafter, patriotic interest in civic duty and economic improvement coexisted with political patriotism in parliament which could be concerned as much with individual advancement as with core issues of opposition to British or Irish government policies perceived as damaging to Ireland's constitutional or economic position.[156] At the same time, a growing dissatisfaction with the fact that the Irish and British Privy Councils had a direct role in the Irish legislative process was central to the emergence of a more unified Patriot political or constitutional agenda from the 1730s through to the 1760s. Since the 1690s MPs had taken issue with amendments made in either Dublin Castle or London to Irish parliamentary bills, especially when made to supply bills.[157] As the eighteenth century progressed, that recurring concern evolved into a more focused agenda for repeal of Poynings' Law which became a central tenant of Protestant Patriot politics just as it had for the Confederates in the 1640s and the Jacobites in 1689. Likewise, the right of the British parliament to legislate for Ireland and the appellate jurisdiction of the Lords became key components of Patriot agitation. To a large extent, such policies were the logical culmination of the incremental gains made in relation to Poynings' Law in the previous decades. As one layer of restrictions was peeled away, another was revealed for attention.

In 1749 a new edition of the *Case of Ireland* appeared during the controversy provoked by the views being publicly propounded by the Dublin apothecary, Charles Lucas, about the rights and privileges of parliament and against arbitrary government.[158] However, the publication also coincided with the early stages of what became known as the money bill dispute of 1753. The build-up of a treasury surplus in the later 1740s resulted in the Irish parliament legislating for specified sums to be used to repay the principal of the national debt. The ensuing conflict arose over whether parliament required the Crown's previous consent to such action and whether the British Privy Council had the right to amend Irish bills.

The first bill for applying the surplus towards repayment of the national debt in 1749 was amended in the preamble by the Irish Privy Council with the inclusion of a phrase stating that the money was expended 'agreeably to your majesty's gracious intentions'.[159] The returned bill passed in parliament,[160] though in 1751 the attitude of the Commons was evident when they amended the preamble of the next debt repayment bill to the less authoritative phrasing that the King was 'graciously pleased to recommend' such expenditure.[161] London refused to accept such a diminution of the Crown's prerogative, and amended it to 'your majesty ... has been graciously pleased to signify that you would consent, and to recommend it'.[162] Despite significant opposition in the Commons, the amended bill passed through the efforts of the undertakers.[163] Two years later however a festering split within the highest echelons of Irish politics led to a showdown on the subject when the Commons' third debt repayment bill, which made no reference in the preamble to either the King's recommendation or consent, was amended once again at the British Privy Council in the same manner as 1751.[164] With the undertakers split asunder and the Speaker, Henry Boyle, breaking ranks and joining with the Patriot opposition, the returned amended bill was defeated on 17 December 1753 by five votes.[165]

The death of George II in October 1760 and the ensuing requirement for parliament to be dissolved and a new assembly elected brought the long-abated question of the token government supply bill back into focus. The changed attitude of the undertakers and the more apparent Patriot agenda on such matters ensured lengthy negotiations before a new compromise was agreed. The arguments from the undertakers for doing away completely with the token supply bill were successfully opposed in London, but it was agreed to make the bill even more peripheral by changing it from a three-month extension of the main taxes to an equivalent extension of the less substantial body of taxes voted for maintenance of the national debt.[166] Also, in accordance with resolutions of the Commons in 1716 and 1727, the bill was not presented until later than had occurred on all previous occasions since 1695.[167] Even still, a small but significant Patriot opposition forced a division on the first reading of the bill, which the government won 170 to 42. Although the bill passed through both houses successfully thereafter, it was evident that Poynings' Law was under attack once more.[168]

The 1760s saw further concessions to the Patriot agenda, including the Octennial Act in 1768 which meant that the dissolution and summoning of parliament was no longer dependent upon the monarch's prerogative (or in reality since 1714 their mortality) but that, as with Britain's long-standing Septennial Act, elections would now occur on a more regular basis in accordance with parliamentary statute.[169] The first parliament elected under that new statute in 1769 took the question of the token government bill one step further by rejecting it by ninety-four votes to seventy-one, and resolving thereafter without a formal division 'that the said bill is rejected, because it did not take its rise in this house'.[170] The process had gone full circle as the Patriots resurrected the 1692 'sole right' attack on Poynings' Law. The Lord Lieutenant, George, Viscount Townshend, recognized that fact as well, and actually used Sydney's 1692 protest when he himself protested and prorogued the 1769 session.[171] But unlike in 1692, he had waited until the usual heads of the supply bills had been drafted, processed and passed.[172] However much London and Dublin Castle might feel the actions of the Commons had truly entrenched 'upon the just rights' of the Crown, the very practical matter of getting taxes voted was more important than grandiose but pointless gestures.[173]

The Octennial Act ensured that the issue would arise soon enough again. Other occurrences helped to make the quest for a solution even more urgent. In 1770 another edition of the *Case of Ireland* was published in response to events in America such as the Stamp Act of 1765, the Declaratory Act of 1766 which asserted the rights of the British parliament to legislate for the colonies in a clear resurrection of the model used for Ireland in 1720, and the Townshend Acts of 1767. Further editions for similar reasons were published in 1773 and 1776.[174] Yet while Irish Patriots were sympathetic to the cause of the Americans, they were not ultimately in favour of breaking the British connection.[175] From the perspective of Irish Patriot politics, the 1770s were dominated by a desire for legislative independence for a sister kingdom remaining within, and ultimately remaining dependent upon, the British and imperial framework. In 1776 the final compromise on the token government bill saw a three-day prearranged charade in which a newly elected parliament convened only long enough to reject the government's proffered supply bill on the grounds that it had been presented precipitously in contravention of the standing orders of 1716, 1727 and 1769, with no mention of from whence it had been transmitted.[176] Matters had now reached a point where the Crown would accept a rejected bill as recognition of its prerogative, as long as the reason for rejection was anything other than the bill's place of origin. Six years later the final concessions were made as Yelverton's Act amended Poynings' Law by removing both Privy Councils from the legislative process. All that remained was the Crown's veto. The need for heads of bills was also done away with and for the final eighteen years of its life the Irish parliament processed bills in the same manner as its British counterpart. The logic of 1782 also required the repeal of the Declaratory Act of 1720 and, in 1783, the repudiation of any such declared right.[177]

In 1782 it appeared that the two key constitutional questions regarding the relationship between Britain and Ireland which had occupied the thoughts of so many since the medieval period had finally been resolved. In truth, the stripping away of these anomalies only seemed to allow for greater focus upon other even more fundamental paradoxes within that relationship which in an era of increasing national and international political radicalization, growing economic discontent and emerging sectarian conflict helped to convince a critical mass of leading politicians and others in Britain and Ireland that the long-avoided experiment with parliamentary union was a better solution. In 1800 that option was finally embraced and the Irish parliament officially ceased to exist on 1 January 1801.[178]

In the final analysis, it is evident that the Irish example of constitutional conflict and negotiation with the English and British parliament and government reflected and foreshadowed developments elsewhere in the empire in the seventeenth and eighteenth centuries. The right of the people to consent to taxation either themselves or through their representatives had been recognized in Ireland as early as the thirteenth century, and had been explicitly raised as an example of Irish legislative autonomy by Fortescue in 1441.[179] The continued reiteration of that argument over the centuries down to Molyneux's *Case of Ireland* in 1698 both predated and rehearsed the arguments that emerged in the 1760s in response to the Stamp Act and other measures of the British parliament aimed at taxing North America.[180]

It was also the case that, as the 1640s and 1689 had demonstrated, the Irish defence of legislative autonomy from the English parliament and desire to renegotiate or repeal Poynings' Law was not a constitutional agenda dictated by confessional allegiance. Catholics and Protestants alike supported that agenda, at times working in tandem as in 1641. From the 1690s onwards however it could easily be mistaken for a wholly Protestant constitutional concern, as Irish Catholics became sidelined from mainstream politics. Yet the adoption by Irish Protestant

Patriots of an agenda for repeal of Poynings' Law in the 1760s and 1770s created a new link to Irish Catholic agitation on that front in the 1640s and 1689.

Ultimately however, the areas of success in renegotiating the constitutional relationship in the period 1692–1770 had more often than not been connected with the increasing demands placed upon the government for more and more money. The question remains as to what that increased expenditure was for and to what extent it constituted a contribution by Ireland to the British Empire in the eighteenth century, answers to which are the focus of Parts II and III.

4 BARRACKS FOR A STANDING ARMY

In the last years of the seventeenth and first years of the eighteenth century a countrywide network of permanent residential army barracks were built in Ireland. Their purpose was to house the single largest part of Britain's peacetime standing army. Such an undertaking was unique within the British Isles, and represented the development of a military innovation that was still in its infancy in European terms. Even the word 'barracks' was 'still an unfamiliar term in this period'[1] and originated from the small temporary huts known as *barraques* (French) or *barracas* (Spanish) which soldiers constructed from wood and other materials gathered from the area surrounding their encampments.[2] Only Spain and, to a greater extent, France had engaged at any level with the idea,[3] France developing as extensive a countrywide network in the eighteenth century as that seen in Ireland. The scale of the French project was necessarily much larger, providing barracks in over 300 towns by 1742 and capacity for 200,000 soldiers by 1772.[4]

In Ireland accommodation was required for around 12,000 soldiers in normal peacetime circumstances. From an imperial perspective the importance of the barrack system was that it provided a home for a substantial part of the standing army, a first port of call for soldiers for service overseas, and a model for the introduction of this military innovation throughout the empire. The barracks that were to be built in Ireland in the late seventeenth and early eighteenth century also differed from the much smaller number built in the Scottish highlands in the first half of the eighteenth century, which were fortified structures placed at strategic points for pacification purposes, or those in England which, on the rare occasions such structures were built, were situated on the coast. The Irish barracks were to be, for the greater part, residential buildings.[5] Therefore many more could be built at a lesser cost with a greater spread throughout both rural and urban locations. The general populace would thereby be relieved of quartering the army, the movement of soldiers from place to place would be made easier, and a military presence would be retained throughout the country for security and policing purposes. As such, they presaged a new approach to army billeting which was to become a more integral and, at times, troubled part of the imperial enterprise as the eighteenth century progressed.

Early Modern Attitudes towards Barracks

To the modern eye, in most parts of the Western world at least, the permanent residential buildings defined as army barracks appear wholly functional and, for the most part, uncontroversial. They are far removed from the heavily fortified and defensive structures such as castles, garrisons, walls and towers associated with a semi-permanent or permanent state of war, whether on expanding or contracting medieval frontiers or along shifting early modern European borders. Yet in the seventeenth and eighteenth centuries, even the suggestion by government in London that it might consider constructing residential barracks was a political minefield. One senior British military official, General George Wade, a descendant of an Irish Cromwellian planter, a former commander of the forces in Ireland in 1714 and an advocate of barrack-building in the Scottish highlands in the 1720s,[6] noted in response to difficulties arising in England in 1739–40 over the billeting of soldiers that

> the people of this kingdom have been taught to associate the idea of barracks and slavery so closely together, that, like darkness and the devil, though there be no manner of connection between them, yet they cannot separate them, nor think of the one without thinking at the same time of the other.[7]

The English aversion to barracks was part of the long-standing opposition to a standing army, which was associated, among other things, with absolutism, tyranny, political corruption and Roman Catholicism.[8] Yet in the absence of residential barracks, the army in England had to be billeted among the general population. Not surprisingly, billeting created its own problems, as it was also closely associated in people's minds with martial law and arbitrary power.[9] Charles I's use, and abuse, of the system led to investigations in the English parliament and the representation in the 1628 Petition of Right of the fact that

> great companies of soldiers and mariners have been dispersed into divers counties of the realm, and the inhabitants, against their wills, have been compelled to receive them into their houses ... against the laws and customs of this realm, and to the great grievance and vexation of the people.[10]

Nor were the Stuarts alone in experiencing the ire of the populace on the subject. The victorious Parliamentarian side on conclusion of the Civil Wars was inundated with petitions from around the country protesting at the burden of billeting.[11] Discontent continued during the Restoration period,[12] culminating in the 1679 Disbanding Act which declared that 'by the laws and customs of this realm, the inhabitants thereof cannot be compelled against their wills to receive soldiers into their houses' without their consent, and that 'it shall and may be lawful for every such subject and inhabitant to refuse to sojourn or quarter any soldier or soldiers notwithstanding any command, order, or billeting whatever'.[13]

Despites such endeavours, under James II the problem was actually exacerbated by the growth in size of the army, first as a result of Monmouth's rebellion in 1685 and then as the threat of invasion escalated during 1688.[14] The mounting pressure over the issue resulted in a quick response from the new Williamite regime in January 1689, when a proclamation was issued prohibiting the quartering of soldiers in private houses without the owner's consent.[15] The following month the Declaration of Rights, enshrined in statute later that year in the Bill of Rights, included the assertion that soldiers should not be billeted upon private citizens, while the Mutiny Act of that and following years made it wholly illegal to quarter in private houses (though some billeting continued with the owner's consent).[16]

The greater security offered to private home owners against enforced billeting after 1689 meant that the burden fell even more heavily upon public houses such as taverns and inns.[17] During the eighteenth century that burden ruined many businesses, and prompted numerous objections and expressions of discontent from around the country.[18] Nor did the detrimental effect such billeting could have upon the army go unnoticed, a fact which was possibly best represented by William Hogarth in works such as *The March to Finchley* or *The Invasion*.[19] This potentially damaging effect that living in public houses could have on both the moral and corporeal well-being of the soldiers – the 'temptations of idleness and dissipation' – was recognized as a significant problem.[20]

There were a number of other serious problems associated with the billeting system. One was the issue of 'free quarter' – the refusal or inability of soldiers to pay for their accommodation and subsistence.[21] At times the government did not have the money to pay for soldiers' quarters,[22] while on other occasions, particularly in wartime, soldiers themselves refused to pay and instead took what they wanted for free.[23] At a more fundamental level, troops living in the type of unsanitary conditions arising from long-term placement in tents or makeshift huts were liable to be decimated by desertion, illness and death,[24] a fact that was vividly demonstrated in the Williamite winter encampment at Dundalk in 1689–90 when up to 7,000 soldiers were said to have died from disease arising from their living conditions.[25]

At the same time, the problems associated with quartering actually served as useful ammunition for those opposed to a standing army in the aftermath of the Nine Years' War of 1689–97.[26] Among the arguments put forward by John Trenchard was the enumeration of several 'lesser inconveniencies' of a standing army,

> such as frequent quarrels, murders and robberies; the destruction of all game in the country; the quartering upon the public, and sometimes private houses; the influencing elections of parliament by an artificial distribution of quarters ... the insolence of the officers, and the debaucheries that are committed both by them and their soldiers in all the towns they come in, to the ruin of multitudes of women, dishonour of their families, and ill example to others.[27]

Trenchard's fellow-polemicist, Walter Moyle, was even more forthright in arguing that a standing army would 'disenfranchise us of two of our native liberties, freedom from martial law, and [freedom from] billeting of soldiers', and later went on to raise the spectre of Richard II's 'life-guard' of 4,000 'profligate ... Cheshire-men' who 'plundered and lived upon free-quarter; beat, wounded, killed and ravished where-ever they came'.[28]

When the controversy over the standing army was renewed in late 1698, Trenchard borrowed almost word for word Moyle's example of the plundering, free-quartering Cheshire men as the first piece of evidence in his *Short History of Standing Armies in England*.[29] Trenchard also accused Charles I of approximately the same crimes, the Stuart king having 'raised many thousand men, who lived upon free quarter, and robbed and destroyed wherever they came'.[30]

The writers in defence of a standing army endeavoured to counter such arguments. Daniel Defoe challenged Moyle's primary argument in a significant engagement with the critical importance of parliament's 'power of raising money' as a balance to the monarch's power of raising an army: 'not a king ever yet attempted to raise money, by military execution, or billeting soldiers on the country'.[31] Matthew Prior was more mischievous, penning a poem which suggested that there were far worse things than the associated problems of billeted soldiers:

> Against the Souldiers Lusts and Gullets,
> Would they preserve their Wives and Pullets,
> And break our Guns to save our Bullets?
> *This is the time.*
>
> ...
>
> I pray then let 'em shew their Games,
> Fix us to one of their extreams;
> A Common-wealth, or else *K. James*?
> *This is the time.*[32]

Successful opposition to a standing army and to the building of barracks in England continued through the eighteenth century. Among the arguments put forward was the belief that the army was more likely to overthrow the government if the soldiers were withdrawn from contact with the civilian population.[33] Exposure to the general populace would, it was propounded, quash any potential within the army to gravitate towards absolutist, autocratic or tyrannical tendencies. In February 1741, in just one of the many debates in the Westminster Commons on the subject, it was argued that the building of barracks would result in 'a military government' and that it was essential to keep the army in the view of the people so that the general populace would always 'be sensible of the fetters, which are preparing for them' should there be any acceptance of a larger standing army.[34]

As late as the 1790s opposition to a standing army and barracks was still significant in England.[35] The establishment of an office of barrack-master-general in 1793 heralded an important shift in government policy, yet even though the ensuing investigations by the Westminster parliament in 1797 demonstrated that thirty-eight permanent barracks had been built since 1792 to complement the existing number of forty-three, the office was still building more temporary barracks than it was permanent constructions, and there was still some distance to travel before permanent residential barracks truly became an accepted part of the English built landscape and environment.[36]

The problems of billeting were also evident elsewhere in the British Empire in the seventeenth and eighteenth centuries. During the Restoration period the non-payment of soldiers in Jamaica left them 'uneasy in their quarters and occasion[ed] many of their deaths' because they were unable to pay for their subsistence from the innkeepers and private householders upon whom they were billeted. For the civilian population, the ensuing economic burden raised the question of whether the soldiers were there for 'their protection against a foreign foe or for their own suppression'.[37] In 1704 the council of trade and plantations recommended that barracks be constructed in Jamaica along the same lines as those already built in Ireland.[38] Two years later, troops sent from England were provided with quarters on the basis of a local ordinance, which, by its nature, was a temporary measure, and on its expiry the soldiers were turned out until the government 'could be prevailed upon to renew it' for a more lengthy period.[39] In light of such concerns, by the 1730s Jamaica had commenced building permanent residential barracks.[40] In Bermuda, one lieutenant governor in the early eighteenth century petitioned London on the sad state of the soldiers stationed on the islands, who had not received any bedding in fifteen years, and had 'no quarters allowed them by the country'. The associated sickness and ill-health was such that by the time a response came more than a year later, they had all supposedly died.[41] Complaints over quartering arose in Massachusetts and Connecticut in the 1670s during King Philip's war and again in New York in the 1680s while it was part of the short-lived Dominion of New England.[42] Similar complaints arose in Virginia,[43] South Carolina, and Nova Scotia in Canada.[44] The response of colonial legislatures was to endeavour to provide some form of legal protection from quartering, the ideological basis for which was that as freeborn Englishmen they were entitled to the same rights as their fellow countrymen living in England. In particular, the emphasis was placed upon the right of the individual to be protected against involuntary quartering, harking back to the Petition of Right in 1628. For the American colonists the problem was not, ostensibly at least, with the existence of a standing army, but rather with where that army was to reside.[45]

The British government's decision in 1763 to keep a permanent force of 10,000 troops in the thirteen American colonies, and to seek partial financial support for that purpose from within those colonies, served to bring the spotlight back onto the question of a standing army in peacetime.[46] Yet the focus for actual dispute remained the issue of quartering. The extension of certain provisions of the British Mutiny Act to the colonies in 1765 occurred in part because of the difficulties the military authorities were having in quartering the army, a problem that continued to worsen during the following years.[47]

The road to revolution in America was strewn with ideological debate and real conflict over the quartering question. The first Continental Congress in 1774 resolved that keeping a standing army in any colony, without its consent, was against the law and that the British Quartering Act was an infringement and violation of their rights.[48] Two years later, those sentiments were enshrined in the Declaration of Independence: George III was damned for having imposed a standing army upon them in peacetime without their consent, while the Quartering Act was foremost among the listed acts of 'jurisdiction foreign to our constitution'.[49] The leaders of the American Revolution, like many of the leading lights of the Glorious Revolution of 1688, soon found that with military success came the realization that a standing army had its uses, and was indeed a necessity for the newly independent United States. The quartering issue though remained significant enough to warrant becoming the focus of the third amendment to the American constitution in 1791, which provided that 'no soldier shall, in time of peace be quartered in any house, without the consent of the owner, nor in time of war, but in a manner to be prescribed by law'.[50]

It is therefore evident that permanent residential barracks were not part of the existing military infrastructure in the seventeenth- or early eighteenth-century empire, be it in England, Scotland, Wales, the West Indies or North America. Instead, the emphasis was placed upon forts and fortifications in towns, cities, along the coast, upon rivers and at other strategic locations. Occupied by small garrisons of soldiers whose primary purpose was defensive, none of these military complexes could provide the kind of residential facilities required for a permanent standing army. Nor were they intended to. Officially, only a small number of men, known as the 'guards and garrisons', were allowed in England in peacetime. The guards comprised the household cavalry and the horse and foot guards, all of which were for the monarch's protection, while the garrison establishment was made up of the gunners and other individuals appointed to maintain and care for the garrisons and other forts and fortifications around the country.[51]

While the guard regiments were fully functioning army units, the garrisons were far removed from the idea of a resident standing army. In 1700 the garrison in the Tower of London comprised fifty-seven individuals. At that time, the numbers elsewhere in England ranged from a low of three to a high of sixty-six. In Scotland the emphasis was slightly different, with an internal security dimension being added to the equation. The total number of men on the eve of the Anglo-Scottish Union in 1707 was greater than in England at 336, which rose to 642 following the union but thereafter decreased significantly to 182 in 1714.[52] The Jacobite rising in 1715–16, followed by ongoing internal instability, resulted in the building in the Highlands of fortified barracks which were primarily defensive structures able to house a small number of regular soldiers on a permanent basis.[53]

The guards and garrisons were in reality supplemented by large numbers of other soldiers stationed in England. In 1701 there was an additional 7,816 soldiers included on the estimates for guards and garrisons.[54] But the actual place of residence of these soldiers was a different matter. It was calculated in 1697 that there was sufficient accommodation in England to house 5,000 infantry, which was to be supplemented by tents for a further 6,000 infantry and 4,000 horse.[55] But what such accommodation entailed was unclear.

The contemporary understanding of a barracks, as given in a military dictionary in 1702, was a

> hut like a little cottage ... made, either when the soldiers have not tents, or when any army lies long in a place in bad weather ... They are generally made by fixing four strong forked poles in the ground, and laying four others across them; then they build the walls with wattles, or sods ... The top is either thatched, if there be straw to spare, or covered with planks, or sometimes with turf.[56]

Whether or not such barracks were part of the accommodation alluded to in 1697, it was evident that the provision of quarters in England at the end of the seventeenth century was far removed from the permanent residential buildings defined as 'barracks' and built in Ireland in the early eighteenth century.

The Building of the Barracks in Ireland

As the Dublin Castle undersecretary, Thomas Waite, pointed out in the late 1740s, 'before the [Glorious] Revolution the army in Ireland was quartered in public houses according to the method at present observed in England'.[57] Unfortunately, it was also the case that the problems associated with billeting in public houses, and among the general populace, were the same in Ireland as elsewhere.[58] A report sent at the time of the Popish Plot in 1678 to Lord Lieutenant Ormond demonstrated some of the problems prevalent in the system: 'Major Beversham's company in Kerry is quartered at Killarney and at Glaneroght, they all lie in cabins, they are much exposed, and as they now are quartered signify little'.[59]

Other problems were highlighted during the 1689–91 war. In December 1690, writing from County Cork, Thomas Brodrick complained of how 'our being forced to subsist the troops quartered with us makes this part yet poorer

than ever it has been in the worst of the late times'.[60] Brodrick's complaint was
made in the knowledge that those same troops were fighting to preserve his and
the rest of Protestant Ireland's interest in the country. Yet such an awareness did
not prevent his brother, Alan, from being even more critical almost a year later,
in the immediate aftermath of final victory over the forces of James II:

> Our part of the country is in the most miserable condition possible, the Danes quar-
> tered on us and the Irish to be shipped off ... we are infested by the worst of men
> and greatest of enemies. Several murders have been committed ... several robberies of
> houses, stripping and plundering in the highways ... some ... forced from their dwell-
> ings ...: the army pay nothing, the country calls it living on free quarter [but] we must
> give it a more gentle name.[61]

Irish Catholics were not immune either. An undated petition from the 1690s
detailed how Catholics throughout Ireland had been 'forced to maintain the
army upon free quarters for the winter season in 1691 and the following spring'.[62]
In 1692 Lord Lieutenant Sydney expressed how the problem genuinely affected
all of society in Ireland, 'where there is so great a scarcity, where the inhabitants
are so poor, and where there is not a public house in the kingdom able to give an
officer credit for a week, and where, if [the army] are allowed to live upon free
quarter, the country must be ruined'.[63]

The discontent expressed by the Brodricks and others was reflected in the
grievances enunciated by Irish politicians during the following years. It was an
emotive subject, and one which the government acknowledged was a genuine
problem. In January 1692 Lord Justice Sir Charles Porter wrote to Whitehall
for emergency funds to provide six months subsistence for the army: 'if we were
enabled to do this ... we shall ... make them live orderly in their quarters, and pay
for what they have, which will be of extraordinary advantage to the country'.[64]

At the same time, significant complaints were levelled against the government of Porter and his fellow lord justice, Thomas, Lord Coningsby, regarding
free quartering.[65] In February 1693 Francis Brewster informed the English Commons that the mismanagement of stores and money in 1690–1 had resulted in
the army having to live 'at discretion upon the country whereby the country
was destroyed more in one winter than it had been by King James' army'. Other
witnesses emphasized the failure to pay the army and the continuation of free
quarter after the war had ended.[66]

The issue resurfaced when the Irish parliament sat in late 1695 and the
Commons resolved 'that the free quartering of soldiers on any subject of this
kingdom, in time of peace, is arbitrary and illegal'.[67] The attempt however to
enshrine that resolution in statute failed with the loss of a proposed bill of
rights.[68] Alan Brodrick, having moved from the ranks of the opposition to that
of the government, had to temper his previous views and now believed that the

opposition's desire that the 'quartering on private houses and the right of it must be ... voted illegal' was absurd because it 'must starve and ruin the army especially on their marches where it is impossible to find public houses to receive them'.[69]

The reality was that a solution needed to be found. Although the Williamite commander, Godard van Ginkel, had asked for barracks to be built in Athlone and elsewhere as soon as the war ended in 1691,[70] the first formal acknowledgement of the need for a barrack-building project came from Dublin Castle in April 1693, when Lord Lieutenant Sydney suggested to Whitehall that part of £6,000 then being allotted for maintaining existing fortifications might be redirected towards building barracks and stables in an endeavour to ease the pressure placed upon towns by quartering.[71]

Initial tentative steps were taken in July 1693 when the Irish government entered into an agreement with Francis Burton, who received a lease for seven years of forfeited lands in return 'for building barracks for the soldiers at Limerick'. The new construction was to accommodate 1,400 'common men' and 'a proportionable number of officers' at a cost of £2,000. The deal was considered to be a good bargain for the government, 'because the inhabitants will be encouraged to repair and newly build their houses, being thus freed from quartering; the town will thus grow populous, and the trade and customs increase and the soldiers will be kept in better discipline, being continually under their officers eye'. The government hoped that similar arrangements could be made for Athlone, Galway and elsewhere, while the importance in general of building barracks was re-emphasized to Whitehall.[72] By 1694 barracks for six infantry companies had been completed in Limerick, though they remained empty as money had not been provided for the necessary furnishings and utensils, so that the local population was still 'over-burdened by quartering of soldiers'.[73] In 1695 the Protestant inhabitants petitioned their two MPs to request that more barracks be built in or close to the city with a fund provided for the necessary accoutrements and upkeep, and that in the meantime the army be quartered upon those Catholic inhabitants 'that have enriched themselves in the last war by spoil and with the goods of the English in the city'.[74] It has been suggested that these Limerick barracks were 'perhaps ... the prototype on which the envisaged network of barracks was based'.[75]

However, in order to undertake such a barrack-building scheme across the country the government needed more money than could be raised via the less than satisfactory source of Williamite forfeitures.[76] As the war on the continent started to draw to a close in 1697 and the possibility of a larger number of soldiers returning to the British Isles mounted,[77] the pressure to advance the barrack-building project increased. Overtures for peace had been made early in the year, and negotiations had commenced at Ryswick in May with the treaty eventually being signed in September.[78] When the Irish parliament convened in late July, in their opening speech the lords justices reminded the Commons of the 'debt due to the country for quarters' and went on to state that they believed it to be 'for the king's service, and the ease of the places where the soldiers are quartered, to build barracks to lodge them in'.[79] The appeal seemed well-targeted given the known concern of MPs over the debt for quarters and their desire to maintain an army sufficient to protect their interests amid a Catholic-dominated population which had demonstrated a bloody-minded dedication to the Jacobite cause a few years earlier. However, writing in 1715, a government official claimed that 'several officers in the army, and the country-gentlemen generally speaking' were initially 'violently opposed' to building barracks.[80] Although some difficulties were expected, the actual contemporary evidence for opposition in 1697, in parliament at any rate, was less dramatic: Wentworth Harman could not find anyone to second his motion that they 'should address the government that no foreign forces might be sent' to Ireland.[81] Although the government expressed some concern at the proceedings in the Commons on supply in general, there was a confidence that 'a considerable sum' would be given 'to pay the quarters, [and] to build barracks'.[82]

The supply act passed later that session included the appropriation of £25,000 for the building of barracks.[83] The preamble stated that

> it has been found to be absolutely necessary, as well for the good discipline and order of your majesty's army, as for the welfare of your majesty's liege people of this realm, that the said army should be disposed of, and lodged and quartered in barracks, whereby they will not only be kept together under the eye and care of their several officers, but your majesty's other subjects ... will thereby be eased of quartering in their houses, to which they have formerly, for the necessity of affairs, submitted.[84]

The barracks were to be erected 'in such convenient and necessary parts' of Ireland as was deemed 'most proper' for the purpose.[85] The money was to be spent 'according to the directions of the chief governor' and construction commenced 'as fast as any part' of the allotted sum 'shall come in'.[86] There was little delay. In February 1698 the lords justices requested particular direction from the King for issuing the £25,000 and a month later the necessary warrant was signed by William III and sent to Ireland.[87]

Construction had already commenced when parliament reconvened in September 1698. While the project would have required further funding anyway, the main reason for summoning another session was the government's need for even more money following the disbanding of William III's wartime army following the treaty of Ryswick,[88] so that from late 1697 new soldiers were arriving into Ireland which increased the demands for accommodation.[89] The lords justices confirmed to parliament that they had already advanced money for barrack-building and expressed the hope that the Commons would provide more for finishing the work.[90] The process was not to be as smooth as in 1697, however, as a threat to the supply arose when the Country opposition complained about the presence of five Huguenot regiments in Ireland and demanded that they be disbanded.[91] By the beginning of December the worst difficulties seemed to have been negotiated successfully and the Commons agreed to impose further taxes sufficient to provide £33,000 for barrack construction.[92]

The Irish government's task was however once again complicated by the English parliament's ensuing decision to actually disband the five Huguenot regiments.[93] The Country opposition now complained that they seemed to be expected to vote taxes for army pay and barracks when the actual demand for such additional income was in fact being reduced through disbanding, which caused Lord Justice Galway to fear that the relevant supply act would be rejected.[94] Such fears were misplaced, as the bill was in fact passed in January 1699, though a residual fear of barracks was addressed in ensuing resolutions that a subject could arrest, sue and prosecute an officer or soldier and that legal officials in the execution of justice should be allowed to enter barracks free from obstruction.[95]

As in early 1698, the lords justices did not dally over getting the relevant orders from England for spending the money. On 15 May 1699 they requested the King's warrant for that purpose, though permission for spending £33,633 10*d*. was not finally sent until November.[96] The amounts voted in 1697 and 1698–9 were not however sufficient to meet the full costs at that time. On 27 March 1700 another royal warrant was issued for applying a further £18,599 2*s*. 9*d*. towards construction, ironically made available out of money saved in the amounts voted in 1698–9 for army pay as a result of disbanding the Huguenot regiments.[97]

The increasing cost of construction was to a large extent dictated by the fact that the project rapidly evolved in scope and magnitude. In June 1701 some new foot barracks were considered necessary 'to entertain men in to prevent robbers and privateers'.[98] The following month another warrant was issued for a further £22,568 1*s*. 11*d*. for building four horse barracks, ten stables for dragoons, four foot barracks in Connaught and one each in the Newry and Kilworth mountains to secure passage through those places.[99] The evident concern in both these cases with security against outlaws and privateers had already been officially acknowledged in December 1700 as one of the reasons for building barracks.[100]

From 1700 onwards a barrack fund was added to the annual establishment for salaries, maintenance and repairs. From 1700 to 1703 it was set at £9,836 10*s*. per annum. In 1704 it was increased to £13,336 10*s*., which remained the official annual allowance through to the 1760s, despite continued and escalating overspending in the following decades which eventually prompted detailed and, for the government, problematic investigations into the matter in parliament in the 1740s, 1750s and early 1760s.[101]

The need for the annual barrack fund arose because people were needed to supervise and carry out the actual work and manage and maintain the finished buildings. In September 1699 the lords justices issued the first set of 'rules, orders and directions for quartering his majesty's army in Ireland in barracks, when fitted to receive them'. Central to this new undertaking was the appointment of barrack-masters who were given responsibility for the maintenance of both the buildings themselves and the furniture, utensils and other accoutrements necessary for the soldiers, their horses and their weapons.[102] Many of the first people employed in this respect were existing disbanded army officers on half-pay, who received an annual barrack-master salary of £36 10s. which increased to £50 in 1702.[103]

By 1703 there were twenty-five barrack-masters appointed around Ireland, excluding Dublin, all on twenty-one year contracts.[104] By that time however, they had come under the management of a new body ordered by royal warrant on 24 December 1700 and constituted on 12 February 1701, following the realization that someone needed to supervise the work of the barrack-masters.[105] The new body of 'overseers of all the barracks' in Ireland became known as the barrack board, and was made up from a quorum of any three from a wide range of people including the chief governor, senior law officers, senior army staff officers, other senior military and civil officials and the surveyor-general of 'buildings and for-tifications',[106] who had already been charged with 'the care and conduct ... [of] erecting' the barracks in March 1700.[107] The overseers were to carry out inspec-tions of the barracks to ensure they were 'kept in good condition and repair' and to do whatever else was necessary for the 'better ordering and regulating' of them.[108]

A second body, known as the 'trustees for the barracks', was incorporated by charter at the same time, which added further to the burgeoning bureaucracy surrounding the barracks. The trustees were a more select group, however, made up of five named individuals – Revenue Commissioners Sir Thomas Southwell and Christopher Carleton, Deputy Paymaster-General William Robinson, Brigadier Richard Ingoldesby, and Adjutant- and Quarter-Master-General Colonel Richard Gorges – who were empowered to take grants and leases of, or to purchase, houses and land up to a yearly value of £400 for the 'use of and in trust for the maintaining, upholding and supporting' the barracks.[109] The reason for appointing trustees was owing to difficulties that had arisen in 'pro-curing ground' on which to build barracks and in leasing land for hay for the horses.[110] While some assistance in this respect was provided by an English act of 1702 which conveyed any land included within the Williamite forfeitures upon which barracks were erected to the barrack trustees,[111] in time the procuring of ground would become a lot less difficult as the economic value of having a bar-rack within a locality resulted in increasing competition for the right to have one sited upon a person's lands.

Of the five trustees, Ingoldesby, Gorges and Robinson were all also overseers on the basis of their other offices. Robinson had also been surveyor-general until he resigned supposedly on health grounds in April 1700, in which year he was also recorded as being a barrack-master. The appointment of the same individuals to different but related offices could certainly lead to a conflict of interests or offer opportunities for corrupt practices, though such multiple appointments were not uncommon or unusual at the time. In the case of Robinson, his various connected offices did seem to lead to grave doubts in later years about his financial practices.[112]

The overseers or barrack board first met to establish their rules and orders for proceeding on 24 February 1701. As a result, a more detailed set of rules than those first devised in September 1699 were issued, along with more comprehensive inventories of the furniture, utensils and other accoutrements required by the soldiers, including candles and fuel.[113] The extent to which the whole process of building the barracks and organizing the management of them was proceeding at the same time was evident from the overseers' order that the barrack-masters were now to be put under the 'immediate care' of the army's quartermaster-general, given that he was responsible for the 'quarters of the army, who now are, or soon will be all placed in barracks' in Ireland.[114]

The culmination of all of these new arrangements from the perspective of the public was the issuing of a proclamation by the lords justices in March 1701 regarding the soldiers 'who now are and soon will be quartered in barracks'.[115] Instructions were laid down for commanding officers, barrack-masters, rank and file soldiery and the general public regarding the proper behaviour of all and sundry in the towns and localities in which barracks had been or were to be built, including directions that 'no women or children shall lodge within any of the said barracks', a concern that had also been addressed in the rules and orders issued by the overseers on 24 February.[116] Then, in light of all that had occurred, it was deemed sensible that all of these various rules, appointments, charter and instructions should be printed and published as the compiled *Rules, Orders, Powers, and Directions, for the Good Government and Preservation of the Barracks* ... (Dublin, 1701).[117]

This process of establishing a management system for the barracks between 1699 and 1701 was a wholly new and unique occurrence, not just within Ireland, but within the British Isles and the empire. The equivalent process did not occur in England until the end of the eighteenth century, with the establishment of the office of barrack-master-general in 1793 representing the most significant stage in formalizing barrack management structures at that time.[118] It also appears that the 'rules, orders, powers and directions' drawn up in 1795 for the management of those barracks drew upon, or at least bore close resemblance to, those developed in Ireland almost 100 years earlier.[119]

It was therefore the case that the lords justices governing Ireland between 1699 and 1701 did not have any precedents of note to rely upon, though it would appear that the presence among that body of Lord Galway was serendipitous. As a man with international military and diplomatic experience, as a close and loyal servant of William III, and as a Huguenot exile, he had a particular understanding of the international dimensions of England's, and by extension Ireland's, altered role in Europe and beyond in the aftermath of the Glorious Revolution, and of the central role that the army had to play within that changed circumstance. It was therefore not surprising that he had been a main instigator of the barrack building project in 1697–8, and was the driving force behind it in those early years. In 1715 one government official went so far as to claim that the barracks were in fact 'built by my Lord Galway', which would suggest that his name was very clearly and closely identified with the planning and execution of the initial project.[120]

Throughout 1700, the lords justices had engaged in detailed correspondence with the King and his ministers in London, putting forward the case for the appointment of both the trustees and the overseers. Their endeavours included arguing successfully for the incorporation of the trustees rather than their appointment by commission on the grounds that a body established by charter offered greater security for those conveying or leasing land for grazing and barracks. The overseers on the other hand could readily be appointed by commission and thereby be removable at the King's pleasure, a situation that William III was more comfortable with.[121]

In future years the barrack board or commission of overseers was renewed and updated. William III's death in March 1702 required the establishment of a new commission, formally constituted on 11 March.[122] Following Queen Anne's death in August 1714 a new commission was established on 5 July 1715.[123] By that time the barrack-masters, of whom there were now twenty-six, had come under the supervision of a barrack-master-general, with each individual having care of anywhere between two and seven barracks depending on their size. The only exception was the barracks in Dublin which had its own dedicated barrack-master who was paid the higher salary of £80 per annum and was provided with an assistant.[124]

Updated 'rules, orders and directions' for barrack-masters and commanding officers were issued by the overseers in 1725.[125] Included among the new stipulations was a ban on 'hounds, spaniels, or other dogs, hawks, or such like' being 'kept in any of the rooms of any barrack ... that may any way be a nuisance, or destructive to the same'.[126] It was also ordered that officers in Kinsale, Limerick, Galway, Derry and Carrickfergus could hire alternative lodgings if they swore upon oath to a magistrate that there was insufficient room in the barracks for them, demonstrating that even in 1725 there was still scope for further barrack construction.[127]

Concern at the damage been done by the soldiers, their dependents and animals to the barracks was clearly evident in a declaration issued by the Lord

Lieutenant Carteret in December 1725. An allowance was to be provided to the army for the purchase and issuing of barrack utensils in the hope that it would create a greater sense of responsibility for their upkeep and thereby reduce the abuse and spoilation of them. The soldiers were also to pay for any damage done to the furnishings or building itself. The declaration also tried to address the problem of damage being done during the times when barracks were unoccupied, thereby implying that the local inhabitants were likely to steal the furnishings and accoutrements or vandalize the building. Finally, it was ordered that barracks were not a haven for fleeing criminals, and such individuals were to be handed over to local magistrates.[128] At the same time, the rules and orders were reissued again with Carteret's declaration and extensive inventories of furnishings, utensils and allowances for candles and fuel included.[129] At the heart of such concerns was the fact that the wear and tear and damage evident in the barracks only resulted in increased public expenditure on repairs and rebuilding.

The ongoing building of barracks also meant that the general populace became even more resistant to quartering, though it did continue to some extent throughout the eighteenth century, especially when soldiers were on the march or patrolling in isolated areas.[130] The problem was exacerbated in wartime when more soldiers were required and were more regularly on the move. In August 1703 the chief secretary, Edward Southwell, went so far as to inform London that 'since the barracks were built here ... we cannot quarter anywhere else',[131] yet in January 1704 he reported that the Lord Lieutenant had 'long since filled the barracks, and there is not room for any more unless they are quartered on private houses, which at this time would not be convenient'.[132]

Such concerns kept pressure on government to continue building barracks, but at the same time the significantly increased cost of the project provoked public inquiry. In the new parliament convened in late 1703 the extra money expended since a supply had last been voted for that purpose in 1698–9 accounted for the subject being high on everyone's agenda.[133] Lord Lieutenant Ormond attempted to tackle the issue in his opening speech by informing the Commons that

> It is to be wished that you were in a condition to provide ... for the building barracks in [Dublin] ... and where else they are wanting; but that which her majesty expects at this time, is only, that the public debts be discharged, and the revenue made equal to the expense of the government, which is much increased by the charge of the barracks; and they are found so useful, and so great an ease to the country, that they ought not to be neglected.

He also acknowledged that the Commons would see from the accounts 'that the government has expended a very considerable sum ... more than was' voted for barrack construction, but hoped they would agree it was a justified expense.[134]

On 30 September Robinson presented details of the barrack expenditure to
the Commons in his capacity as deputy-paymaster-general. The accounts clarified
that on top of the £58,633 10s. previously voted by parliament, the 'chief governors have from time to time incurred ... other expenses' up to September 1703 of
£65,244 14s. 5d.[135] This excess was wholly accounted for by the two additional
sums warranted in 1700 and 1701 plus the annual barrack fund allowed on the
establishment since 1700,[136] but the public accounts committee were still 'ill-sat-
isfied with it' and readily 'found fault ... with the charges'.[137] Yet despite rumours
of 'mighty discoveries',[138] the eventual report into the matter, apart from stating
that several of the barrack-masters, especially in Ulster, lived far away from the
barracks and rarely visited them 'but superficially and in haste', was underwhelm-
ing.[139] The main point was that the annual barrack fund appeared to be more than
was needed for the purpose, which was a fairly standard response from parliament
with regard to most public expenditure.[140] However, although various other difficulties arose during proceedings on supply and Robinson was voted unfit for
public employment and ordered into the custody of the constable of Dublin Castle for having supposedly misrepresented the size of the government's debt,[141] the
accounts were eventually passed and a supply bill drafted which included, for the
purpose of 'building of barracks in Dublin', appropriation of the 6d. in the pound
fees to be 'taken by the treasury' on the taxes voted that session.[142] This latter decision was both contentious and in keeping with the mood in the Commons, as it
was perceived as an ultimately unsuccessful attempt by the opposition to get the
vice-treasurer or other officials whose income would thereby be reduced to get
the ensuing bill altered in London and thereby create a new conflict in parliament
over executive alterations to supply bills.[143]

The money provided by the 1704 supply act facilitated the commencement
of work on the jewel in the crown of Ireland's eighteenth-century barracks. The
Royal Barracks were begun in 1704, with the purchase of land 'lying near the
Bowling Green' in Dublin 'and belonging to' Lord Lieutenant Ormond.[144] The
work was undertaken by the surveyor-general, Thomas Burgh, who in 1706
claimed that it was at an advanced stage.[145]

However, although the source of the funds had gone unchallenged in 1703–
4, prior to parliament reconvening in 1705 Ormond made it clear in public that a
renewal of the imposition upon the vice-treasurer's fees would not be acceptable.
As desired, the ensuing supply bill did not include the levy on the 6d. fees, nor
did it make any other provision for building the Dublin barracks.[146] Instead, later
in the session the Commons drew up an address of thanks to Ormond expressing
their concern for the security of Ireland and the Protestant religion and promising to make good in the next session any necessary money spent in the interim
on fortifications, arms, ammunition and other defensive measures, as had been
advocated by Ormond in his opening speech.[147] Although the opposition were

incensed that the address had been forced through in a depleted house,[148] the Court party readily justified it on the grounds that everyone was agreed upon the need to keep building barracks, but that their failure to replace the *6d.* levy with any other fund meant that they needed 'to declare that those necessary things should be done and that they would provide to answer those payments'.[149]

The Royal Barracks were still incomplete in March 1707, at which time the Lord Chancellor, Sir Richard Cox, pressed that the Queen send orders for the remaining sum to be paid out of the public revenue at large, given that the 1705 address had committed parliament to reimbursing the cost in future supply acts. Otherwise, the work would remain unfinished 'and then the city will clamour, and others will join in the cry'.[150] Pressure to complete construction also came from the passage of the 1707 act 'to prevent the disorders that may happen by marching of soldiers, and for providing carriages for the baggage of soldiers in their march', which required that all soldiers in Dublin after 29 September 1708 had to be lodged in the new barracks.[151] Yet the final payments for completing construction were not made until 1709–10.[152] Despite the delays, however, the completed military complex was reckoned to be the largest and best example of army barracks in the empire until the completion in 1855 of Aldershot.[153]

Of course, the 1707 Marching of Soldiers Act was not only concerned with Dublin, and in reality represented, in conjunction with the barrack-building enterprise, the finalization of the greater regulation of billeting in Ireland. From that time onwards soldiers could only be quartered among the populace when on the march, awaiting transport overseas in a port, or 'during such time as there shall be any commotion in any part of Ireland, by reason of which emergency [the] ... army ... shall be commanded to march from one part ... to another'.[154]

The political focus on barracks waxed and waned in the following years,[155] though with the conclusion of the War of the Spanish Succession in 1713 there was renewed focus upon the accommodation of soldiers. In September the new Lord Lieutenant, Charles Talbot, Duke of Shrewsbury, was instructed to ensure that the army was quartered according to the rules and with as little burden to the people as possible.[156] By that time, there were 102 barracks throughout Ireland. In the province of Leinster there were twenty-five spread over the twelve counties, with accommodation for fourteen horse troops and fifty-nine infantry companies. The smallest concentration, of one barrack each, was in Dublin and Athy in Kildare. Of course, the Royal Barracks could accommodate two troops of horse and thirty companies of infantry, which was by far the largest capacity in the country, while Athy catered for only one horse troop. County Wexford had the largest concentration in Leinster, with one each in Wexford town, Enniscorthy, Duncannon and New Ross, which together could accommodate seven infantry companies and one horse troop.[157] The latter cavalry barracks was in New Ross and was one of the first tranche to be built. The site known as St Michael's church or chapel and burial grounds on Michael Street, which in time was to be renamed Barrack Lane, was purchased in 1699 and construction was carried out in 1700. Further work was required in 1706 and 1710, with some of the soldiers at one point being temporarily quartered in the courthouse. A new barracks was built in 1718, though it was 'out of repair' by 1730. It was still in use in the 1750s, and there was still a cavalry barracks on the site in the nineteenth century.[158]

A barracks existed in Athlone in 1691 with temporary accommodation for 1,500 infantry and 1,000 cavalry. A more permanent structure was built around 1697, capable of accommodating one horse troop and four infantry companies. New cavalry barracks were built in 1766–71, while a new infantry barracks was built in 1798.[159] In Bray an infantry barracks for one company had been completed by the time the land was leased to the government in 1700 and was not closed until 1818.[160] In Kilkenny city a horse barracks for one troop was built around 1700 and extended in 1758, but it was closed in 1800 following the construction of a new infantry barracks. Another infantry barracks for four companies already existed on part of the site of St John's Abbey, and had been built around 1700 as well. It was replaced by an asylum in 1818.[161] There were a number of barracks in Longford town, including a horse barracks for one troop built by 1708 and another by 1774 which incorporated Longford Castle.[162] The barracks at Navan and Drogheda were constructed around 1702,[163] while in Dublin, aside from the Royal Barracks, there were two shorter-lived buildings, one dated to 1711 and sited on Cork Hill and the other on Dame Street in 1721.[164] Later in the century a barracks was built for the Royal Irish Artillery.[165]

In Munster there were thirty-five barracks spread throughout all six counties by 1714 with accommodation for nine horse troops and ninety infantry companies, which represented the greatest concentration of barracks and soldiers in the four provinces. The largest number was eleven in County Cork, followed by ten in County Tipperary. The greatest capacity however was in Limerick, where twenty-two infantry companies could be accommodated.[166] The concentration of barracks and soldiers in Munster indicates that in the first stages of the countrywide barrack-building project the question of internal and external security concerns was given significant consideration.[167] The number of infantry in Limerick clearly related to the historic importance placed upon that city as a bastion of resistance to conquering armies in 1651, 1690 and 1691, and its geographical location at 'the lowest fording point of the River Shannon, at the head of the 113 km-long Shannon estuary' which flows out into the Atlantic Ocean.[168] The earliest barrack was noted on the former site of St Saviour's Priory in 1679 on what is now, and by 1719 had become known as, Barrack Street, in which latter year a 'new barracks' was recorded there. This may have been the construction commenced in 1694–5 by Francis Burton.[169] By the 1750s eight or nine barrack blocks with accommodation for twenty companies supposedly existed on the site, which was referred to as the Lower Barracks. By 1767 it was referred to as the Old Barracks, and was in a ruinous condition. Castle Barracks, in King John's Castle, was built in 1751, John's Barrack in Barrack Lane was first noted in 1752, while another new barracks built in 1798 remains in existence today.[170]

In County Cork the security agenda was again very evident. The highest concentration of infantry was in Kinsale town where twelve infantry companies could be accommodated with a further ten on the eastern shore of the bay at Charles Fort. Next was Cork city where eleven companies could be stationed. Historically, and most recently in the war of 1689–91,[171] these two closely connected coastal locations were of significant strategic importance, particularly from an imperial perspective, be it the threat of foreign invasion, the need for naval provisions or bases from which to transport soldiers overseas, or to facilitate the navy in offering protection to shipping going to and from the West Indies and North America.

In County Tipperary security concerns were also to the fore. Two of the first barracks in the county were completed at Nenagh in 1699 and Clonmel in 1700 in keeping with the desire to end quartering upon civilians, but other barracks were built to counter tory and rapparee activity in the hinterland. Tipperary contained six of Ireland's thirty-five redoubts (there were fourteen in total in Munster and only two in the whole of Leinster), which were smaller defensible barracks built for purpose 'in response to banditry which followed' the war of 1689–91. With those in the 'adjoining districts of Limerick and Waterford', they 'constituted the largest concentration of redoubts in the country'. Their purpose was to 'eradicate' the hideaways of outlaws in problem areas such as the uplands of South Tipperary and to protect 'arteries of communication' to key locations such as Dublin, Cork, Limerick and Waterford. In both respects the redoubts were successful.[172]

With twenty-seven barracks spread throughout nine counties in 1714, Ulster had two more than Leinster but eight less than Munster.[173] However, thirteen of those were redoubts, highlighting the fact that outlaw activity continued to be an issue in the early eighteenth century.[174] The real difference however was the fact that the Ulster barracks could only accommodate seven horse troops and thirty-eight infantry companies, which was less than half the number stationed throughout Munster and just under two-thirds of the Leinster capacity. The barracks were also quite evenly spread out, with four a piece in Counties Cavan, Fermanagh, Londonderry and Armagh, three in Monaghan and two a piece in the remaining counties. The individual barracks in Derry and Carrickfergus had the largest capacity, both providing accommodation for six infantry companies.[175] Carrickfergus also had a horse barrack built around 1703 which accommodated two troops by 1740 but was destroyed by fire nine years later and rebuilt after 1754.[176]

The first barracks in Derry was built by 1700, but was already 'too small' by 1706. It was closed by 1800, as was a second barracks from the 1730s. New barracks for infantry and horse were built in 1799–1801.[177] The site of the first barracks in Armagh in 1703 is unknown, though that of 1737 was partly on the site of the County Gaol. It closed in 1773 and transferred to a new site.[178] The first Belfast barracks was recorded on Castle Street in 1685, while another had been built by 1715 and rebuilt in 1735 on Barrack Street. By 1764 it was in need of repair and extension. There was also an artillery barracks in Cooney's Court by 1797 and Victoria Barracks on North Queen's Street was under construction by 1790.[179] In Downpatrick a horse barracks had been built by 1708, and remained in existence until converted into Down infirmary around 1774. The infantry barracks, which was opened in 1797, was located in the former lunatic asylum.[180] Ballyshannon lays claim to the 'earliest surviving barrack of note in the country', which was built for infantry in 1700 with eight rooms for officers to the front, eighteen for enlisted men to the back, and a central passage through the middle.[181]

The smallest number of barracks in 1714 was the fifteen spread across the five counties of Connacht, which could accommodate seven horse troops and twenty-three infantry companies. County Galway had the highest concentration, with one a piece in Galway, Portumna, Headford, Athenry and Loughrea. Galway city, as a key port on the western seaboard, had the biggest capacity, accommodating ten companies. Portumna housed one horse troop and two companies and Athenry three companies. The rest of the barracks in the province housed either one troop or one or two companies.[182]

It is therefore apparent that a number of barracks had existed in some form or other before the barrack-building project got under way in 1697–8, and also that very significant construction was carried out in the decade following. The official establishments during that decade listed all of the places were soldiers were quartered and where barracks were already built, under construction or intended for construction. In 1700 it was recorded that there were 105 places in which thirty-two horse troops and 229 infantry companies were quartered,[183] in 1702 the figure stood at thirty-six horse troops and 231 infantry companies,[184] while in 1704 the number of locations was 101 with accommodation for thirty-six horse troops and 227 infantry companies.[185] By 1714 the number had settled at 102 completed barracks with accommodation for 210 infantry companies and thirty-seven horse troops. The decrease in capacity was explained by reduced accommodation in the completed facilities in Galway city, Dublin and Athlone.[186]

The variation between 101 and 102 barracks was explained by Kinsale and Charles Fort being counted as one location in 1700 and 1704 and as two separate locations in 1714. The four extra places in the 105 locations listed in 1700 were Dundalk, Barnesmore Gap, 'Burroughs Ossa' (probably Borris in Ossory) and 'Sharkin' (probably Sherkin Island).[187] None of these locations recurred on any of the later lists or maps created during the eighteenth century, so they probably had short-lived existences as barracks.[188] However, in the case of Barnesmore Gap, the remains of the redoubt still existed in the twentieth century.[189]

At the beginning of George I's reign it was decided that more barracks were needed, so a new wave of construction was undertaken. It was initially proposed that eight horse barracks be built. In January 1715 William Conolly, recently reappointed to the revenue commission and quickly becoming the most important commoner in Ireland,[190] wrote to London to advise the Lord Lieutenant, Charles Spencer, Earl of Sunderland, that the decision as to where these barracks were to be located should be deferred until after the first session of the new parliament to be summoned later that year. His reasoning was that 'a great many [probable] members of the ... Commons ... and others' had already submitted proposals for siting barracks on their lands, 'and there can be but eight of them obliged' and many, many more 'disobliged'. Strategically it made sense to keep as many MPs as possible on their best behaviour during the session in hopes of their proposals being successful, and likewise to avoid pushing others into opposition because their proposals had been turned down.[191] The commander-in-chief of the army in Ireland, Charles O'Hara, Baron Tyrawley, expressed the same view to Sunderland in early February.[192]

A Dublin Castle undersecretary, Eustace Budgell, elaborated on the subject. Describing the existing barracks as 'so many little military-colleges scattered up and down the country', he claimed they were the reason 'Ireland [is] so fond of an army. The officers by this means keep the soldiers all together, and the country gentlemen find that a barrack built on their estates considerably raises the rent of them.' It was for this latter reason that whenever there were new barracks required and public funds available for the purpose, 'everyone is trying who shall get them'. Supposedly the news that the eight horse barracks were to be built had resulted in about 150 people offering 'ground on their estates' and sending 'in their proposals' to the barrack overseers.[193] Archbishop King believed there were in fact at least 200 people who had put forward proposals.[194] And it was not only MPs – there was even one from John Vesey, Archbishop of Tuam.[195]

In light of the advice from Conolly, Tyrawley and Budgell, the eight barracks were put on hold.[196] It was not surprising though that the return of Lord Galway as lord justice in 1715–16 should coincide with the plans being revived after the session of parliament. In the interim, however, the government had been advised by Tyrawley that infantry barracks were more necessary, and so the scheme was altered to build ten foot barracks, which were all under construction by the second half of 1716. Only one, at Elizabeth Fort in Cork, was being constructed on government land, the rest being sited on the private estates of three peers, including Tyrawley, and six members of the gentry, all at a cost of £14,021 18*s*. 5*d*.[197]

The apparent self-interest on Tyrawley's part in securing a barracks on his own estate was in keeping with the increased public awareness of the benefits of having a barracks sited in the locality. The infantry barracks in Ballyshannon built in 1700 and a later cavalry barracks in the town were supposedly built at the expense of Conolly and were then leased to the government, an arrangement that was made official at a national level with the appointment of the barrack trustees in 1701, though as Conolly's case demonstrates, it was clear that such agreements were entered into on an individual basis prior to that time. The rush to procure barrack-building projects in 1715 was indicative of the phenomenon. Some landowners offered to share the cost of construction or to shoulder the whole expense and rent them to the government. As Conolly had also pointed out, many had to be disappointed as well, some of whom might readily in future years take their revenge by promoting parliamentary investigations into the barracks. It certainly was the case in the 1740s and later that people complained that barracks had been located on private estates for the landowner's benefit without consideration of strategic concerns.[198]

For the successful landowner, the benefits were indeed many. Nicholas Price of Hollymount in County Down was commended after his death in 1734 for having turned Saintfield into a town through his industry and care, which had included having 'a barrack fixed for a troop of horse'. As a career soldier who rose to the rank of lieutenant-general by 1710 and sat as an MP from 1692 until 1714, Price was well placed to take advantage of the economic and other possibilities that could arise from locating a barracks close to his own estate and local area of influence.[199] At the same time, in 1706 Lord Chancellor Cox highlighted the potentially parochial nature of such arrangements when, in the search for billets, he suggested that 'We will mind the troops at Down unless Col. Price keeps it for his own regiment'.[200]

The benefits of having a barracks in the locality was not just confined to the landowner, however. Many others profited as well through trade, provisioning, the circulation of ready specie, which otherwise was usually problematic, and leasing grazing land among other activities. An English visitor in 1732 noted that the army 'far from being thought a nuisance is adored by the tradesmen, as their chief support in many places'.[201] In the 1750s Sligo town's principal merchant was providing the cavalry barracks with 'several hundred tons of hay and oats'. The locals in general benefited as well. In 1733 it was reckoned that in Sligo town most of the £7,000 paid to the soldiers in the cavalry barracks was spent there. Not everyone felt that way, however. In 1738 a Sligo resident complained that 'the army consume only the produce of the country, but the profit if any to the farmer and contribute little to the wealth of the town'.[202] But the subtext was the same: the army in barracks was a profitable business for the locality.

As for the ten new barracks commissioned in 1716, an official establishment for 1717 recorded all of them among a total of 108 in Ireland, although there is no evidence that they had all been completed by that point in time. Given that the new barracks at Elizabeth Fort was included as an increase in capacity for the existing barracks at Cork city rather than a new location, it meant that nine totally new locations had been added since 1714, although the overall recorded increase was only six. However, the numbers still correlated given that in the interim four pre-existing barracks had been decommissioned and one new one constructed.[203]

Similar types of fluctuations in numbers and locations occurred in future years for similar reasons.[204] In 1725 the total number was given as 112, a figure which reoccurred in government correspondence in the late 1740s, while in 1759 it stood at 110, although thirty-five of those were said to be not in use.[205] Some barracks were decommissioned owing to the need to station less soldiers in a given area.[206] At other times, and probably more commonly, barracks were condemned owing to poor construction or irreparable damage, while others deteriorated over time and required either minor or substantial repairs. In 1729 the barracks at Belturbet and Castle Dawson were both deemed to be 'almost irreparable'. At Dungannon the barracks was 'neither wind nor watertight', while Clonmel was 'in very bad repair' and those in Carlow and Athy needed roof repairs. In 1769 the Mallow barracks was deemed 'not habitable', Clonmel was once again in need of repair with rain 'penetrating' the walls, while in Thurles the problems were such that the soldiers were being 'billeted on the inhabitants'. Charleville was in a 'ruinous state', while Kinsale needed minor repairs. Charles Fort was said to be 'very old and decayed and barely habitable', while the barracks in Cork city were in a 'ruinous condition' and uninhabitable owing to 'natural decay, length of time and original defects'. However, in both 1729 and 1769 the majority of the other barracks were deemed to be in 'good order' or 'good repair'.[207]

As barracks were decommissioned, new ones were built either at the same or new locations.[208] Wartime also resulted in new demands for barracks. In 1759 the Lord Lieutenant, John Russell, Duke of Bedford, had ordered three new barracks at locations already or previously in use at Philipstown, Enniscorthy, and Athenry. All three new constructions were on private estates.[209] The permanent increase in the size of the army in Ireland agreed in 1769 also required new barracks.[210] Examples of later constructions included two at Tuam, one of which eventually became the site of a saw mill, and the other which had by 1816 become the Tuam Free School.[211] In Bandon, the first recorded barrack was commissioned in 1748 and completed in 1752. It was refurbished and enlarged in 1798, but having been partly burnt was closed in 1922.[212]

The barrack-building project also contributed to the development of eighteenth-century maps of Ireland. The countrywide spread of barracks naturally lent itself to the recording of those locations in cartographic form, both for military and civilian uses. The first two known maps of the barracks, in manuscript form from 1700, were signed by Robinson in his capacity as surveyor-general and in fact appear to be, as noted by Lord Justice Galway, an itemization of the sites chosen for construction throughout Ireland.[213] They also included the first of two known endeavours to represent the 'spheres of influence' for groups of barracks through colour shading.[214] Printed maps were produced in *c*. 1707, 1708, 1711, 1714, 1728, and 1759, the latter of which was used in 1770 to make manuscript additions denoting spheres of influence for the infantry, stained red, and cavalry, stained blue. Another map was undated, but completed before 1762.[215]

Politics and the Barracks

In the 1717 session of parliament the barracks re-emerged on the agenda of the Commons with the passage of an act for vesting in the Crown lands upon which barracks were 'built or being built or contracted for', and for amending the 1707 Marching Soldiers Act.[216] More ominous though was the report from the committee of public accounts which identified an overrun of £6,745 5*s*. 9*d*. in two years on the annual barrack fund, which was deemed an overcharge upon the public and should therefore be deducted from the agreed 'debt of the nation'.[217] It was not until late 1724 however that an inquiry into the barrack management was ordered, the results of which gave Lord Lieutenant Carteret cause for concern at the actions, or lack thereof, of some of the barrack-masters, and led to the updating and reissuing of the rules, orders and directions for both the barrack-masters and the overseers.[218] Carteret's decisive actions ensured that when parliament convened in late 1725, he was publicly thanked for the 'strict examination into the ... barracks, and the rules prescribed by you for their future regulation'. Indeed, the public accounts committee were apparently so mollified that they were prepared to overlook an overspend of £4,200 on barrack building even though it had not been approved by royal warrant.[219]

By the end of 1731 the overrun on the barrack fund for the previous two years had risen to £12,607 8*s*. 6*d*. At that time, the Commons resolved 'that the number of barracks already built, and contracted to be built, are sufficient to contain the army upon the establishment of Ireland'.[220] However, the main issue to animate the Commons in the following years was the continual overruns. At the end of 1733 it stood at £10,399 10*s*. 8*d*. for the previous two years, prompting the recently sidelined parliamentary undertaker, Marmaduke Coghill, to comment that 'the old topics of the overdrawings' had, as usual, been 'animadverted upon'.[221] In 1735 it stood at £13,731 14*s*. 10*d*. and in 1737 at £15,530 17*s*. 11*d*., prompting the public accounts committee to enquire further into the matter. Having examined various papers, the committee resolved that 'not obliging barrack-masters to perform their contracts, and not suing them, or their securities for the breach thereof' was a significant cause of the overrun. It was also the reason for the 'buying and selling' of the office at exorbitant prices', which was 'prejudicial to the public'. Finally, the constant overruns were identified as 'one great cause of the debt of the nation', prompting the Commons to resolve 'that the great overdrawings ... if continued, must ... tend to the impoverishment of this kingdom'.[222]

Such proceedings were warnings of potential problems down the line, though the outbreak of war in 1739 probably accounted for the less rigorous engagement with the issue in the next three sessions, in which the usual warranted biennial overruns were noted as £17,234 10s. 8d. in 1739, £11,640 8s. 2d. in 1741, and £16,136 4s. 11d. in 1743.[223] However, in the 1745–6 session the barrack establishment came under closer scrutiny that ever before. Although the biennial overrun had decreased to £10,623 14s. 6d., a much more detailed investigation was entered into with one of the Dublin Castle undersecretaries, John Potter, reporting that the Commons were likely to 'come to some very strong resolutions as to the conduct of some concerned in' the barrack management.[224]

The end result was thirty-eight resolutions. The initial focus was on the overruns which amounted to £136,841 11s. 3d. in total between 1723 and 1745, which was declared to be part of the national debt. The supposed reasons for the overruns included accusations that the barrack trustees had exceed their limit for leases and purchases and the overseers had condemned barracks without sufficient reason, apparently in order to facilitate making new contracts at higher costs and rents, and this despite the Commons' resolution of 1731 that there was already a sufficient number of barracks in existence. The inspectors and overseers were also upbraided for failing to ensure that the barrack-masters performed their duties correctly and for allowing repair costs to be paid out of the public purse rather than from the contracted allowance for that purpose. Acting by deputy was also condemned, as was sale of the office of inspector and barrack-master, while it was also resolved that the salaries and allowances of the barrack-masters should be stopped and applied to the cost of repairs. To reduce corruption, it was recommended that the inspectors should no longer receive a fee, reward or gratuity from barrack-masters and that all accounts should be vouched and sworn before a baron of the Exchequer or master in Chancery. A reconstitution of the overseers was also desired, not least because of their application to the King for an increased annual allowance of £18,652 12s. 10d., which was deemed a 'presumptuous attempt to impose on the government' to the great injury of the nation. It was also resolved that 'the persons who advised the government to contract for new barracks since 1731 acted presumptuously and in violation of the right of this house to advise in any case which may create a new expense to the public'.[225]

The Lord Lieutenant, Philip Dormer Stanhope, Earl of Chesterfield, responded that he would 'endeavour to do what is practicable to put the barracks in a proper method for the future'.[226] In private however he was more sceptical, noting that the resolution to stop all salaries of barrack-masters was, 'as everybody else' had already perceived, 'absolutely impracticable', and he wondered 'how it ever came to pass that house'.[227] However, he agreed it was 'a thing of absolute necessity' that the barrack board, which had clearly been unregulated for quite some time and lacked the timely oversight and renewal of the early years, be reconstituted, which occurred in March 1746.[228] The new board immediately ordered inspectors to carry out surveys of all the barracks and to itemize those in need of repair or rebuilding, while in April Chesterfield ordered the surveyor-general to appoint individuals to accompany the inspectors. Everyone involved was to make separate returns of their findings on oath.[229]

In reality, however, the resolutions were in many respects based upon unrealistic expectations, ill-informed opinion and a degree of malice. The most substantive response came from Henry Brooke, the writer and playwright, who was also barrack-master at Mullingar.[230] While clearly having a vested interest in undermining the validity of the resolutions, Brooke still managed to provide a detailed and convincing riposte to what had been alleged.[231] Interest in Brooke's argument was evident by the fact that his pamphlet, *The Secret History and Memoirs of the Barracks of Ireland*, went through three editions in 1747. Presenting his arguments through the character of a farmer, a mode he first utilized in his *Farmer's Letters* of 1745–6 which were written in response to the Jacobite threat at that time,[232] Brooke outlined that the investigations had been wholly one-sided without any attempt to understand why certain actions had been taken or practices had developed.[233] He pointed out that between 1697 and 1703 over £132,000 had been allowed for building and maintaining barracks, yet

> For all the buildings whereon those mighty sums were expended, there is scarce a single barrack whose duration we can promise for any considerable time. Walls cemented with clay mortar, clay plaistrings and renderings, wattle partitions, and slight scantling of sapling timber, could not seriously be intended for the use of the next century.[234]

The reasons for using less enduring building techniques he imputed in part to the insufficient amounts allowed for the original buildings and in part to the guile of the original overseers 'who making a most judicious and exact calculation of the term for which many of their buildings would endure, proportioned the contracts of the barrack-masters and the leases of ground accordingly, that is to say, they struck off the whole at the term of twenty-one years'.[235]

As a result, the cost of maintaining the buildings increased dramatically for later overseers and barrack-masters because rebuilding work was required or buildings were deemed unfit and new ones had to be provided. Such building or rebuilding costs were not envisaged as part of the requirements to be covered by the annual barrack fund, which was rendered even less effectual by the inflation in prices of both commodities and labour. Likewise new expenses had been added for the upkeep of other buildings and salaries for new officials, though without any additional allowance being made to the annual fund. The increased numbers of soldiers at various times explained legitimate overruns for extra wear and tear, while the increased rental charge was owing to higher rents on renewal of leases. Further additional costs arose because, in the absence of sufficient funds to build all the necessary barracks at public expense, the overseers had contracted with private individuals for both ground and building rents for barracks constructed at private expense.[236]

Brooke concluded by emphasizing the importance of the barrack system to Ireland, and by implication, for the empire:

> The long experience of fifty years hath demonstrated, that this our institution of barracks hath been effectual to the preservation of peace, to our protection from invasion, to the prevention of intestine riots and rebellions, to the suppression of robberies and thefts, to the encouragement of commerce, the insurance of property, and to the confirmation of our liberties in every branch. There is therefore no farmer, no stockmaster, no tradesman, no proprietor of house or holding, there is no lover of his country, no lover of his own interests in this kingdom, who grudges his proportion of any tax which he pays, to the support of an establishment so necessary to the support of our constitution itself.[237]

The barracks were also of course significant for the army, as the 'men are kept apart from the people, in the eye of and in obedience to their respective officers, and are thereby withheld from insulting and being insulted'. Brooke went so far as to claim that because of the barracks, the army in Ireland was 'actually reputed the best disciplined army upon earth'.[238] He concluded by reminding his readers that the barracks were instituted in the 'wisdom' of 'that glorious deliverer', William III, in order to save their constitution, Protestant religion and 'peace, property and liberty'.[239]

When parliament reconvened in late 1747, the matter arose once again. However, on this occasion the government seemed better prepared. The resolutions of the previous session having 'rendered it impracticable to proceed' with any work on the barracks 'without the advice and concurrence of parliament', a Commons committee was appointed for that purpose.[240] Edward Weston, chief secretary to the new Lord Lieutenant, William Stanhope, Earl of Harrington, reported that they were 'at work … to get rid of the difficulties under which we were left by the barracks committee of last session. It is no easy matter but I hope will be compassed to general satisfaction.'[241] At least the warranted overrun was dramatically reduced to £1,304 1s. 10d.[242]

The select committee finally reported on 9 December on the surveys carried out between April 1746 and October 1747. The committee acknowledged that there were many barracks in need of repair and rebuilding owing to the use of substandard materials when first constructed and the work needed to be carried out urgently in order to avoid a greater expense at a later date. It was noted however that there was great discrepancy 'between the returns made by the inspectors, and those made by the persons appointed by the surveyor-general'.[243] The Commons thereafter resolved to address the Lord Lieutenant 'to give directions for repairing ... and ... rebuilding or building such barracks as he shall judge necessary'. About thirty MPs tried unsuccessfully to prevent the address being made, in part 'upon account of what passed in the last session' but also because the address gave an 'unlimited power ... to the chief governor, both in regard to the situation of barracks, and to the sums to be expended', and was, as such, perceived to be 'an absolute vote of credit'.[244]

Overall this was a better result for the government. Harrington lost no time in notifying London of his plans, explaining that the work was essential given that 'the barracks ... are generally in a most ruinous condition', with many of them 'situated in places where they are of no signification towards the defence of the kingdom'.[245] Parliament also prepared an act for amending the 1717 statute for vesting land in the Crown upon which the barracks were built so as to allow the Lord Lieutenant to contract for new ground.[246]

Harrington duly completed a 'scheme and estimates' for the work, but the man ultimately tasked with carrying out the project with a budget of just under £39,000 was the surveyor-general, Arthur Jones Nevill.[247] Originally, the surveyor-general had sole responsibility for contracting for barracks and the related architectural work, though once the first tranche were completed by 1710 the barrack board took on those responsibilities.[248] Nevill was however part of the reconstituted board in 1746 and so was involved in the barracks at two levels: as an overseer he had ordered the inspectors' survey; and as surveyor-general he had been responsible for appointing individuals tasked with accompanying the inspectors.[249]

When parliament reconvened in 1749 Nevill presented accounts of all barracks built, repaired or under construction since 1 January 1747 and their expense. In total, thirty-four barracks had been built or repaired for foot regiments which were intended to eventually house 630 officers and 8,190 men. A further twenty-nine barracks had been built or repaired for dragoons and cavalry which would in time house 252 officers and 1,555 men. At the same time a possible source of future conflict was seen in the increased overrun of £16,264 8s. 5d.[250]

Two events transpired during the next two years that were to alter Nevill's fate dramatically. The first was the return of Lionel Cranfield Sackville, Duke of Dorset, as Lord Lieutenant in the autumn of 1750 with his son, Lord George Sackville, in tow as chief secretary, which within in a year was to result in a major split within the highest reaches of Irish political circles between Speaker Henry Boyle on the one hand and Archbishop George Stone, the Ponsonbys and Lord Sackville on the other, and an ensuing prolonged factional battle in parliament over power, position and patronage. The second was the successful return of Nevill as MP in the 1751 by-election for County Wexford where he had received the backing of Archbishop Stone. Nevill's clear connection with Stone and the Castle administration eventually resulted in his becoming the target for the disgruntled but powerful Boyle faction in the Commons.[251] The barracks provided the opportunity but in truth were neither the real prize nor the real concern.

Dorset was not unaware that the barracks would be on the Commons' agenda. In his opening speech in October 1751 he informed the Commons directly that he had ordered them 'a particular account of the money expended in repairing, rebuilding, or building barracks, pursuant to your address in a former session'.[252] Following notification of an increased overrun of £21,276 3s. 3d., Nevill presented the barrack accounts and the Commons ordered further evidence from the barrack-masters, including alternative costings for the work with a view to demonstrating that it could have been carried out for less, and documentation relating to army complaints, all of which prompted Waite to express the view that there 'never was a man so unjustly and hardly treated as Nevill has been'.[253]

During their investigations the Commons discovered that the original estimate that had formed the basis for allocating money to the project was not the same as the last version agreed by Harrington and upon which Nevill had proceeded to base his contracts and other work. It was also the case that as work progressed, apparently practical adjustments had been made to the scheme.[254] But such justifications for a discrepancy in the estimates or practical alterations in details of the scheme were of no weight when it came to trying to convince MPs that no wrong had been committed, particularly when the real purpose of the investigations was evident in the fact that 'the Speaker and his friends threaten to show their influence and weight upon this occasion at Mr Nevill's expense, who unfortunately does not belong to their party'. Sackville claimed that in that respect, 'as far as evidence and justice will warrant them in their proceedings, my Lord Lieutenant will not interpose, but if any violences are offered they must carry their point in defiance of the government'.[255]

Unfortunately, Boyle's party did intend more than the evidence would warrant. It was rumoured that 'the Speaker's forces are all summoned with an intention to expel' Nevill from the Commons 'and to vote him incapable of executing the office of surveyor-general'. The government's forces were 'likewise mustering' to his defence.[256] Such an all-out rupture was apparently prevented by Dorset, who, according to a later account, asked Boyle to intervene directly on the promise that Nevill would be punished 'if, upon enquiry, it should appear he deserved it'.[257] As a result, Sackville was convinced that the final resolutions would stop short of expulsion or a vote of corruption. Instead, the government was 'to be chastised' through Nevill, who at worst would be censured 'in respect to economy in making contracts and to his care in enforcing the ... performance of them'. Certainly his integrity and 'intention of doing right' could not be impeached.[258]

In March 1752 the committee finally submitted its report along with eight-een resolutions to the Commons.[259] Nevill was accused of inflating the prices of materials and work, acting without judgement, care or economy, showing unjus-tifiable favour to certain contractors to the 'great detriment of the public', being unwarranted in departing from Harrington's original scheme and estimates, and causing the public to be defrauded and the barracks to be badly built and incomplete so that ultimately many of them remained unsuitable and unfit for the purposes 'proposed by the ... Commons'. Direct accusations of corruption were levelled against Nevill's clerk, George Ensor, who was said to have taken bribes. It was further resolved that Nevill should be obliged at his own expense to get the contractors to complete their work to acceptable standard. The Com-mons then requested that £24,000 from supplies voted that session be allocated for completing the repair and construction work.[260] Such a request at the end of a lengthy investigation demonstrated the ongoing belief in, and commitment of, parliament to the overall barrack project and the associated military system developed in Ireland since the 1690s.

The investigations had gathered a momentum against the government as and when other avenues of opposition had proved fruitless.[261] While much of what occurred could be attributed to an unfortunate awkwardness of character on Nevill's part, Speaker Boyle's party had the ability to 'make any man unpopular'. Even still, the majority of MPs appeared to be convinced of Nevill's 'honesty and integrity'. Of the resolutions themselves, the only ones that Waite felt were substantiated by the evidence were those relating to the use of a different scheme and that many of the barracks were 'ill-executed, which was by no means brought home to any want of economy, care or judgement' on Nevill's part. Ultimately, Waite was convinced the resolutions were simply the result of 'violent power and of a party that meant to wound my lord primate [Stone] through the sides'.[262]

Archbishop Stone must have felt the wound, for he clearly was disenchanted with Nevill, despite being fully aware that the real target was himself and the Dor-set administration. He blamed Nevill for having 'not succeeded in his work to the satisfaction of the army officers' and for making 'himself disagreeable to members of the country gentlemen, and amongst others to Lord Kildare [James Fitzgerald, earl of Kildare], which has been a principal ingredient in this prosecution'.[263] There is a suggestion here that some of Nevill's unpopularity may have stemmed simply from his failure to gratify those who wished to have barracks sited on their own lands, and it may well have been significant that his estate at Furness near Naas in County Kildare was connected to that of Lord Kildare, though the issue of 'the ill-accommodations complained of by the [army] officers' was also certainly relevant and had resulted in Dorset being 'not over partial' towards Nevill.[264]

Dorset certainly seemed more concerned with his own reputation and administration. He acknowledged that Nevill 'stands greatly censured' but as the inquiry related to 'a transaction that happened before' he was made chief governor, his primary concern had been to ensure that money was voted for the necessary repairs, which was 'effectually secured' by the address for £24,000, the very amount he had desired at the outset.[265]

As the session drew to a close, one fact remained uncommented upon. The estimated cost for the repairs, as detailed by Harrington in June 1748, had been £38,993 10*s*. 2*d*. The actual amount expended was not significantly more, totalling £40,921 7*s*. 4*d*.[266] Under a different administration, without a split in the higher echelons of Irish political circles, and with a more wily surveyor-general, such a small overrun might have prompted no debate at all.

As it was, the rift in Irish politics widened and the Nevill affair gathered momentum. Lord Kildare, who was Ireland's most senior peer, travelled to London in June 1753 to present a memorial to George II detailing the 'discontents and divisions' in Ireland and 'ascribing the causes thereof to the conduct of the Lord Lieutenant, and ... those, in whom his excellency ... places a confidence'.[267] The Nevill affair was at the heart of the memorial. According to Kildare, Nevill was rewarded rather than punished by being allowed to sell his office (which was true) and by supposedly being freed from the expense of carrying out the repairs despite the Commons' directions to the contrary, while Boyle's supporters were penalized, with two of them having their pensions stopped for a time.[268]

One of the most immediate consequences of the memorial seemed to be a general resolve that when parliament reconvened in late 1753 Nevill would be 'expelled whether he has fulfilled the resolution of the ... Commons or not'.[269] Ultimately, however, the memorial was, like all that had gone before it, intended to be a damaging attack upon Dorset and his administration rather than a reflection upon the barrack system.[270] Archbishop Stone was the most animated by it. Regarding the cost, he claimed the 'fact is notoriously otherwise' and that Nevill was 'now actually employed in making good the deficiencies at his own expense'.[271] This was true, but the fact that the work had not commenced until the summer of 1753 was to play into the hands of Boyle and Kildare.[272]

Prior to commencing work, Nevill had requested a detailed breakdown from the lords justices of what repairs were incumbent upon him as distinct from those that lay within the remit of the barrack-masters, on the grounds that the Commons had not provided him with that information. The lords justices instructed the new surveyor-general, Thomas Eyre, to whom Nevill had been allowed to sell the office in August 1752, to provide such a report, with which Nevill in turn complied, but only after work had been further delayed by his contesting, with Eyre's agreement, two other reports on the work.[273] Nevill's actions created two problems. First, the long delay to work meant that repairs were still ongoing when parliament convened in October 1753. Second, however reasonable Nevill's request to the lords justices might have been, it was seized upon by the opposition as a means of expelling him because he had shown contempt for the resolutions of the Commons. When the time came, Nevill's actions were deemed an 'affront and indignity to the house, and said to be calculated for delay and with a design to do nothing'.[274]

The summer of 1753 also saw the commencement of pamphlet campaigns by both sides that lasted until 1756 and resulted in well over 150 publications.[275] One of the earliest works, published anonymously though attributed to Brooke, made passing reference to Nevill as 'a mason' about to be immured 'in his own rotten bricks and mortar', though its primary focus was upon the split within Irish politics and Ireland's constitutional relationship with Britain.[276] More direct and detailed attacks upon Nevill occurred during the first weeks of the new parliamentary session in October. The anonymous *Groans of Ireland* replicated much of Kildare's memorial in a damning attack upon Nevill (the '*misapplyer general*, and *general compiler*') and the Dorset administration, and appealed to parliament to rectify the itemized wrongs.[277] Shortly thereafter the same author published a satirical play, *Court and no Country*, which again attacked Nevill ('Sir Arthur Vantrype') and the administration and glorified Kildare.[278]

The intention in the Commons of inquiring as to whether Nevill had complied with the resolutions of 1752 was evident early on in the session.[279] Waite even believed that Nevill had 'so well executed their orders about the defects, that they will be disappointed in their aim upon him'.[280] But it was also generally acknowledged that the Nevill affair was first and foremost about providing an opportunity for 'the Speaker and his party ... to show their strength in points not so immediately relating to government'.[281] As a vast array of documentation was ordered and witnesses summoned, including evidence from the commanding officers in the relevant barracks, it became clear that even if Nevill could prove he had done 'everything in his power to comply', it was still required that 'he must be expelled to prevent my Lord Kildare separating from the Speaker'.[282] To compound matters, the biennial warranted overrun had increased to £29,177 3s. 11d.[283]

In mid-November the fourth in a series of printed handbills published under the title *The Patriot* was dedicated to an all-out assault on, and character-assassination of, Nevill ('Sir Arthur Van Tripe'),[284] the timing of which seemed stage-managed, as the first open division on the issue occurred the next day, on 16 November, when, as Sackville described it, 'Nevill ... is to be hunted'.[285] Incongruously, the division arose over a motion proposed by Thomas Le Hunt for widening the scope of the inquiry in Nevill's favour. Although 'a trifling question', the government pushed it to a division to test their strength, and all were taken by surprise as they won by 118 to 115.[286]

The government's pleasure soon turned to concern however as it quickly became apparent that the defeat had only served to galvanize Boyle and his party. During the next three days the government lost two divisions, by 123 to

119 and 122 to 120, which demonstrated how evenly divided the house was on the issue. Unfortunately for Nevill, however, the tide had turned sufficiently against him, not least because Boyle had now sworn to quit the Speakership if Nevill was not expelled, a stance aimed at keeping Kildare and his supporters onside.[287] It was of little consolation to Nevill that supposedly 'the very people who are outrageous against [him] ... say they believe him as honest a man as ever lived, but he must be sacrificed'.[288] It was now being advocated that, regardless of his defence, in order to be victorious in the struggle with the administration over the second supply bill, 'these assertors of ... [Ireland's] liberties', as Archbishop Stone derogatorily referred to the opposition, had to demonstrate their power 'by expelling this unfortunate man'.[289]

The end came on 23 November, with two resolutions, the first of which stated that Nevill had not carried out the required repairs at his own expense in accordance with the order of the Commons, and the second that he had not used 'reasonable and proper endeavours' to carry out those repairs. Following his withdrawal, the house divided 124 to 116 in favour of a motion that 'in not complying with the resolution of the ... Commons, [Nevill] has acted in manifest contempt of the authority thereof'. The debate was said to have lasted until ten o'clock that night. Thereafter, a motion to expel him was passed by 123 to 116.[290] To rub salt into the wounds, the Commons then proceeded to draft the heads of a bill to oblige Nevill to make good the remaining repairs at his own expense. It was a particularly galling action, given that during the earlier proceedings he had offered his whole estate or any sum of money as security for the completion of the work, to be held by any person the Commons wished to appoint for that purpose. The bill stalled at the Irish Privy Council and, like many other pieces of proposed legislation that session, would have been lost anyway in light of the early prorogation in the new year as a result of the rejection of the second supply bill in late December.[291]

Nevill's expulsion was ultimately about preventing a split between Boyle and Kildare, an alliance that was required for the more dramatic events relating to the second supply bill.[292] As such, Nevill was sacrificed in order to maintain an opposition alliance aimed at defeating the government on a much more significant constitutional issue centred around the control of expenditure and the repayment of the national debt. The proof was in the speed with which the barracks receded into the background as attention turned to the second supply bill. Newcastle was quick to admonish Archbishop Stone over the government's defence of Nevill, stating that it was better to have sacrificed him and 'reserved yourselves for the great question ... Whereas now, you have suffered yourselves to be beat upon an insignificant point; and are less able by that means to stand the great question when it comes. Popular runs must sometimes be yielded to.'[293]

Newcastle proved prophetic, and also showed how callous and cold the world of realpolitik could be for the unwary individual.

Nevill and the barracks quickly faded from view, with little attention being paid to either in the rash of pamphlets published during the following three years regarding the second supply bill. The one exception, published with two editions in 1754, endeavoured to deflect attention away from the second supply bill by arguing that the Nevill affair in actual fact proved the loyalty and fidelity of Boyle, Kildare and their supporters to George II and Britain because they had a genuine desire to see the army housed properly. Despite significant inaccuracies in the details of the affair, the idea that MPs were primarily concerned with 'providing for his majesty's troops, after their gallant behaviour against the enemy in the field abroad, a safe retreat at home, and beds of comfort for limbs wearied out in their country's service' was wholly valid and suggested a very real sense of understanding in Ireland about the importance of the barracks for the military system that was essential to the growing empire.[294] As for Nevill, his own public career was rehabilitated in time, with his election as MP for Wexford town in 1761, a borough he represented thereafter until his death in 1771. He also served as sheriff of Kildare and mayor of Waterford.[295]

With the affair a thing of the past, the ongoing necessary repair, maintenance and building of the barracks continued. As far back as March 1753 some initial thought had been given to the idea of reforming the barrack management, while in April the King had given consent for the issuing of the £24,000 requested by the Commons in 1752.[296] The reports from the various commanding officers around the country in both 1752 and 1753 provided some insight into the kind of problems arising with the barracks in general, and not just those for which Nevill was deemed responsible. The barrack design from the outset had been based upon cost and basic utility rather than comfort. Hence the complaint in 1753 about 'the general want of room' was not new, nor was it a fault that originated with Nevill. Indeed he had been overruled when he proposed a greater allowance of space.[297] Most, if not all, of the reports 'made most heavy complaints'. Some reported 'that the walls and coverings of their several barracks were not sufficient to protect their men or themselves from the inclemencies of the weather, and that few or none would keep out the rain entirely'.[298] At Cobh the rain came 'through the walls and windows' so that 'there is no living in the lower and middle rooms', at Rosse Castle the rain 'has a free passage from the top of the barrack to the bottom', while at Tullamore a marquee tent had been erected in one room to keep off the water.[299] One barrack-master compared his barrack 'to an old whore, who was painted on the outside, and looked showy, but was rotten within'. As to the repairs carried out, he said they were 'so slight, that a force sufficient to pull an old woman's tooth out of her head would pull his barrack down about his ears'.[300] Such complaints had contributed to Nevill being satirized as an Italian engineer who could 'demonstrate the utility of building forts and barracks without furnishing them with water ... by supplying the troops with the rain water which passes through the walls'.[301]

Escalating conflict in North America in 1755 served as backdrop to the much more circumspect consideration of the barracks in the 1755–6 session. The new Lord Lieutenant, William Cavendish, Marquis of Hartington, who had been sent to resolve the divisions in Irish politics, had, on taking office, undertaken a review of Irish matters, including defence and the barracks. The usual warranted overspend, on this occasion of £12,685 18*s.* 7*d.*, was reported upon, but thereafter nothing of account occurred.[302]

The official outbreak of the Seven Years' War in May 1756 brought the disposition of the military into the public view once more in Britain.[303] In Ireland, focus in parliament in 1757–8 turned to the barrack board and its proceedings since reconstituted in 1746. The new administration of Lord Lieutenant Bedford was unconcerned, and rightly so, as even the attempt to revive the bill for forcing Nevill to make good the repairs at his own expense was ultimately unsuccessful, as it was blocked in Whitehall.[304]

The focus upon the barrack board was not lost on the government, however. During the summer of 1758 a plan of reform was drafted, including tighter controls on money and restrictions on the power of the lords justices to make appointments to the board. Although Bedford was keen on the proposal, it was opposed by his lords justices, Archbishop Stone, Boyle (now Earl of Shannon), and John Ponsonby. Stone argued that the plan needed to be 'thoroughly digested' before being implemented, not least because 'the proceedings of the present board' had been 'so cramped and entangled by various resolutions of the ... Commons framed from dislikes differently pointed in different periods of time'. He also believed that 'some help from the legislature will be wanted before that machine can be put rightly in motion'. However, he was not slow to recommend two MPs for appointment to the current board.[305] While the fear of how parliament might react was perceived as a legitimate concern, Stone's actions gave some credence to the view expressed by the Irish resident secretary in London, Sir Robert Wilmot, that the lords justices were primarily concerned with losing a source of patronage.[306]

A plan was finally agreed in early 1759 and a patent issued for a 'new board of seven "salaried commissioners and overseers"' of the barracks and forts and fortifications.[307] This new body, to whom the surveyor-general was now answerable much to the consternation of the incumbent, Thomas Eyre,[308] was clearly a response to the problems arising since 1746, yet was also in part an attempt to address more recent concerns expressed over the fortifications, by placing responsibility for both in the hands of one body.

In 1759–60 the Commons included the barracks in the reasons for a government loan of up to £300,000,[309] while in late 1761 the notification to the lower house by the new Lord Lieutenant, George Montague-Dunk, Earl of Halifax, that among the extra military expenditure 'a large sum will be wanted for the effectual repair of the barracks, a work which cannot be delayed', did not prompt discussion.[310] In the meantime, the barrack board was reformed once again at the prompting of Lord Kildare, who had been appointed master of the ordnance in October 1758 in an attempt to keep him onside with the government.[311] Kildare was keen to bring the fortifications completely under his control, a point he argued successfully when the barrack commission came up for renewal in March 1761. At the same time, the office of surveyor-general as far as it related to fortifications was discontinued. The end was in sight for Eyre and came in August 1762 when orders were issued for reappointing the barrack commissioners along with new staff to carry out the work previously performed by the surveyor-general. These new officials were formally constituted as part of the new 'Barrack Board and Board of Works' in September. The new arrangements were to last until the end of the eighteenth century.[312]

In the 1763–4 session the Commons cast a close eye over the new commission.[313] The Lord Lieutenant, Hugh Percy, Duke of Northumberland, was initially concerned that 'there was an intention not only to censure the general powers given to the Lord Lieutenant in the late patent for the board of works, [and] of creating new officers', but also to vote the new posts of treasurer, comptroller and architect 'to be useless and unnecessary'.[314] In the end, however, few MPs were prepared to support a motion for an address to that effect, which was easily defeated by 102 votes to 29. The defeat appeared to kill off any further desire to target the new commission.[315] However, it was instructive that despite previous attacks upon the old office of surveyor-general, it was evident that the Commons were not convinced that the new arrangements were any better. It was also the case that the detailed nature of the 1763–4 investigations, even if not overly contentious in the end, served to remind all and sundry for future years that the Commons continued to have a vested and keen interest in the management and maintenance of the barracks.

A single episode from 1760 offers significant insight into this tortured history of the barracks and their construction in the period. In that year Eyre had found it necessary to publish a detailed reply to issues raised by the new barrack commissioners in relation to recent repairs carried out on the Royal Barracks. In a wider ranging report offering their observations on the barracks throughout the country, the commissioners expressed their concerns about various aspects of the Royal Barracks, including that the 'front walls of Palatine square "are in so ruinous a state ... they must necessarily be rebuilt"'.[316] Eyre pointed out that the commissioners had acknowledged that the problem was a result of the original construction work and materials used in 1704–8, but that they were incorrect in ascribing the warping of those walls to the weight of stone used by Eyre in his repairs, as that problem had also originated with 'the slightness of the original construction'. In fact, Eyre had carried out his repairs on the basis of several professional assessments of the load-bearing capacity of the pre-existing warped walls.[317] Eyre countered the issues raised by the commissioners in detailed arguments that were accompanied by affidavits from various construction professionals such as masons, carpenters and bricklayers. He also pointed out that most of the commissioners who signed the report had not actually been in attendance when the barracks was inspected, that the two master builders who also signed it were aggrieved because Eyre had previously refused to employ either of them, and that the remaining master builder who had refused to sign the report had done so on the grounds that he felt it was 'partial'.[318]

By contrast, various public responses to the barracks in general, and the Royal Barracks in particular, were much more flattering. In the 1730s a visitor to Ireland described the barracks as 'the finest largest and most sumptuous edifices'. In the same year another visitor described them as often being the finest buildings in the towns.[319] In a 1766 publication about Dublin the Royal Barracks was described as 'the largest and most completest building of the kind in Europe',[320] while in 1787 Richard Lewis described it as 'the largest building of that nature in the British dominions, being capable of containing 3,000 foot and 1,000 horse'. It was 'pleasantly situated' with 'a fine prospect over the Wicklow mountains' and had had some 'additions lately made, particularly one of the old squares, rebuilt with Portland stone in an elegant manner', which exhibited 'fine proofs of architecture'.[321]

Lewis's recording of recent repairs to the Royal Barracks in 1787 resonates with a key point made in 1760 by Eyre which encapsulated one of the main causes for the abiding sense of dissatisfaction with barrack construction and also the reason why such dissatisfaction was for the most part misguided. To the accusation that the roof repairs carried out with timber scantling 'ordinarily used in private houses' were 'not sufficient to ensure that permanency required in all public buildings', Eyre responded that it was foolish to consider that private gentlemen used inferior materials for their own houses and, more significantly, that materials did not exist that could ensure 'this extraordinary permanency' which was unknown in any other public building in Ireland, including Dublin Castle.[322] At the heart of his argument was the basic fact that standard eighteenth-century building materials and practices in Ireland were such that running repairs, and the associated ongoing expense and opportunities for corruption, were a necessity of life: that the most permanent of buildings required regular maintenance and repair, especially those that were used and abused in the manner that army barracks were.[323]

More generally, what is evident in all of the lengthy investigations into the barracks was that at no point did anyone advocate that the purpose of the buildings themselves or the military system they supported was in any way unnecessary or problematic. It was indeed very much the opposite. No one disagreed that the barracks provided a new and important contribution to their own and the Crown's security both in Ireland and abroad. Such understanding of the utility of the barracks was evident in 1758, when the Commons resolved that some new barracks should be built in parts of Connaught to assist the civil authorities in making the local inhabitants more amenable to the law of the country.[324] It was evident that the sentiments expressed about the usefulness of barracks were genuine. Similarly, the particular interest taken by the Commons in the project was at one level owing to the fact the lower house viewed the whole undertaking since the 1690s as a parliamentary innovation and therefore requiring their oversight and protection.[325]

That oversight and protection related to possible corruption within the pricing, costing and expense of what were essential public works; the misuse of public funds; the undermining of the project through substandard building materials and poor workmanship; flawed or poor management; and the use of such works as a means of giving patronage and favour to friends of the government. The overt use of these various concerns for factional point-scoring in political conflicts that had absolutely nothing to do with the utility of the barracks or the military system they supported simply served to obscure the real attitude towards the barracks, and created a false impression of a military system under attack when in fact the opposite was the truth.

In 1737 Lord Lieutenant Devonshire had informed London that the regiments in Ireland were 'in as good order as troops can be' and that there was 'a good deal of emulation in the colonels here to keep their regiments so, and the barracks contribute not a little to it'.[326] A more detailed exposition on the benefits of barracks for the soldiers was provided by Waite in the late 1740s:

> By being united as one body, they become more active and more powerful to the suppression of riots in others; they also become more formidable to the lovers of sedition, and the peace is thereby preserved throughout the nation, they further become more convenient and apt to the voice of their commanders, and by use and frequency are easy and expert in their sword exercises ... Nor is this the language of one man only. It is the sense of every Protestant in this kingdom, that they are not otherwise secure of their lives, liberties and religion, than by the continuance of the military force.[327]

While he was clearly being overenthusiastic, Waite's sentiments were indicative of the unique nature of what had occurred in Ireland during the previous fifty years. The ultimate purpose of the barracks however was to house an army. It is therefore necessary to examine that army in greater detail so as to understand the extent to which this new military innovation in Ireland truly contributed to the British Empire in the period 1692–1770.

5 A STANDING ARMY FOR IRELAND

Ireland's major contribution towards the empire in the period 1692–1770 was the financing, housing and general maintenance of a peacetime standing army that was capable of going to war in Britain's interest at short notice. The central focus in practical terms for facilitating that contribution was the general maintenance of the army in Ireland on an annual basis, and it was this activity that was reflected in the government's annual military establishment and the regular debates and considerations of the Irish parliament. This chapter is concerned with the size and regulation of the army and its logistical and financial administration, and the centrality of these concerns within Irish political life. It provides an assessment of the strength and readiness of the army in Ireland and the cost. It also includes a consideration of recruitment policies.

In discussing the British military in the eighteenth century, John Brewer pointed out that no country 'could afford to sustain the expense of continuous fulltime mobilization'. Instead, in peacetime the army needed to be reduced in size. For the first half of the century the British peacetime army numbered 'about 35,000', and after the Seven Years' War it increased to 45,000. This army was stationed in

> mainland Britain, in those outposts of the empire such as Gibraltar, which required constant protection and, above all, in Ireland. This had the advantage ... that a large proportion of the peacetime force was kept on the Irish establishment, funded by the Irish taxpayer and kept out of view of the English parliament. But they could be transferred quickly to England if the need arose. In short ... England, like the other great powers of Europe, had a standing army – a body of professional 'effectives' which was in a constant state of readiness and which provided the core around which a wartime army was built.[1]

This assessment highlights the central importance of Ireland, which provided a home for, and covered the cost of maintaining, the single largest part of the British peacetime professional army and the core of the wartime army. Because the regiments on the Irish military establishment 'were trained soldiers rather than raw recruits',[2] they were able to provide the backbone of the British military machine in the period 1692–1770. Ultimately, the importance of the peacetime army in Ireland was greater than the actual proportion it eventually constituted among the overall number of soldiers required during wartime, and hence it was a central reason why Britain was able to go to war successfully in the eighteenth century.

The relationship between the actual number of soldiers and the number of regiments in Ireland was complex. The crux of the matter was a policy of reducing the size of those regiments which were not disbanded following the conclusion of a war. A reduced regiment had a smaller number of officers and men, with reduced officers moving onto the half-pay list and reduced rank and file being disbanded. Also, there was usually a higher ratio of officers and NCOs to rank and file than in regiments with a full complement. Those who remained in the reduced regiment formed the core body of soldiers around whom full-sized functioning regiments could be quickly put in the field, either on renewal of war or for other active service in some part of the empire, by bringing the officer corps up to strength from the half-pay list and doing the same for the rank and file with soldiers from other reduced regiments or by raising new levies. The remaining regiments in Ireland if overly depleted could in time be strengthened with new recruits or drafts of serving soldiers from regiments returning from overseas. Two criteria – a legislative limit of 12,000 on the number of soldiers allowed in Ireland and the varying number of regiments sent in and out of the country over time – meant that the actual size of any reduced regiment could fluctuate quite substantially from year to year as could the overall number of regiments, while the actual number of soldiers might remain about the same most of the time.[3]

This cadre system of reduced regiments in Ireland was almost unique. Only Scotland experienced anything similar, and on a much smaller scale.[4] The system has been alluded to enthusiastically as a strategic reserve, but it was certainly much more.[5] Its attractiveness was evident in 1762 when, as the Seven Years' War drew to a close, George III and his leading minster, John Stuart, Earl of Bute, in the face of impending demands for the army to be disbanded, drafted plans for applying the same principle to all of the regiments to be kept in peacetime in Britain and the Americas as well as continuing the practice in Ireland, so as to save on costs while still having a larger number of regiments to hand than any time before in peacetime. Thus the needs of both 'security and economy', of so much importance to the Westminster parliament, would be served.[6] The only problem with their plans was the decision to station a standing army in North America supported by colonial taxes imposed by Westminster, which of course sparked the events that led to the American War of Independence.[7]

Historians traditionally have a fairly negative opinion of the efficiency and capability of the army in Ireland in the eighteenth century. It has been portrayed as being particularly – indeed at times almost uniquely – corrupt, venal, nepotistic, debauched, drunken, decadent, undisciplined and pox-ridden, generally unfit for service and a waste of public money.[8] Similar terminology and sentiments have in the past been applied to the eighteenth-century Irish parliament, resulting in an unflattering assessment of both the institution and the community from which its members came.[9] One reason for such stereotyping in both instances is a tendency among some historians to lean toward an insular interpretation of Irish history in which the nation is taken for granted 'as the proper unit of analysis' within a broader 'nationalist tradition ... strongly imbued with religious currents'.[10] Within such a paradigm, the problems identified with the army appear to be just symptoms of a greater evil, which is implied by the presentation of these problems as being apparently unique, either in occurrence or outcome, to Ireland. The greater evil is the unnatural and unacceptable presence of, and power held by, the Protestant English, or British, in Catholic Ireland.

In reality, the army in Ireland was a fair reflection of the British army as a whole and of armies in the eighteenth century in general. A myriad of factors from low or at times non-existent pay to ill-suited gentleman officers to harsh environments and discipline which led to common problems such as corruption, theft, desertion, drunkenness and the like. Yet not all officers were inefficient, including even those appointed on the grounds of having powerful patrons rather than recognized military ability. Throughout the British Empire soldiers were left without pay at times, some of whom took to crime as a result.[11] Plunder and theft were common at other times as well, especially during war.[12] Similarly, drunkenness and debauchery were part and parcel of the perception, and often the reality, of military life throughout Europe and the British Empire, as readily depicted by William Hogarth among others.[13] As for desertion, despite suggestions to the contrary,[14] it was no greater in Ireland, and indeed was often a smaller percentage of the whole than the rates experienced elsewhere in the British Isles or in other countries and armies.[15]

Regulation and Discipline

The Lord Lieutenant was head of both the civil government and the army, in which latter capacity he was assisted by a board of general officers.[16] However, from 1689 until 1800 there was always a separate military appointee who served as commander-in-chief.[17] There were also logistical officers: the quartermaster-general; a master, lieutenant, comptroller, and clerk of the ordnance and major of the train; and a muster-master-general for auditing the army's accounts. The secretary-at-war in England was responsible for issuing army commissions and warrants.[18]

The importance of the Lord Lieutenant was highlighted in June 1693 when Lord Chancellor Porter expressed his concern at the departure of the outgoing viceroy:

> we find how difficult it is for him to keep the army in tolerable order in their quarters [though] their subsistence is paid. How then can it be hoped for when the officers will not be under that deference they now are to him and when in all probability money will be wanting.[19]

Porter was admittedly prone to being overly pessimistic about Ireland in general. In time, better discipline, the provision of permanent barracks, and more regular pay ameliorated such concerns.

The government of the army in Ireland was regulated by the British parliament's annual 'act ... against mutiny and desertion, and the articles of war' which were 'calculated to extend equally to the two kingdoms'. However, the fact that circumstances in Ireland were 'very different, particularly in ... quartering ... soldiers' resulted in the Irish government being allowed 'to make orders for ourselves, as occasions may require'.[20] Also, as the eighteenth century progressed, the Irish Patriot agenda grew to include the desire for an Irish mutiny act, though this was successfully resisted in London until 1780.[21]

A 1749 report described how at the end of every month the adjutant-general was required to lay before the government 'a return of the state of every regiment on the establishment'. Four times a year the army was mustered and the quarterly returns transmitted to England. All officers below the rank of regimental colonel were obliged to seek a licence if they wished to leave Ireland, 'under a penalty of forfeiting three months' pay'. No one was 'allowed upon the muster rolls' unless 'actually present at the time' of the muster or 'absent with licence'. It was Waite's opinion that because of 'these regulations we are seldom deficient in numbers, and I must do the officers the justice to say that there are no troops more orderly or disciplined'.[22] Overall, the report described an extraordinarily well-organized and disciplined army by eighteenth-century standards. At other times, the evidence suggested otherwise, and it was certainly the case that these admirable arrangements had evolved over the first fifty years of the century, rather than arisen phoenix-like whole and complete from the war of 1689–91.

Concern over the potential for fraud and corruption was as common in Ireland as it was elsewhere. It was not unique to Ireland to find evidence of false musters and non-existent soldiers on the payroll. In January 1692 the lords justices advised London that 'some severe penalty should be laid upon those [officers] who do not keep their troops and companies full'.[23] In 1705 Francis Flood, MP for Callan, County Kilkenny, was expelled from the Commons after he was found guilty of abusing his authority as an officer, including making false enlistment returns. He was also found guilty of illegal methods of recruitment, which had involved forcing people to enlist against their will through intimidation and violence, and with unlawfully billeting soldiers on the tenants of his neighbours.[24] In 1713 the instructions to Lord Lieutenant Shrewsbury included orders for ensuring an exact muster of the army to clarify that the numbers were as they ought to be and that they tallied with the numbers on the payroll. He was also instructed to ensure that the officers actually paid the men when the warrants and money were issued to them for that purpose.[25]

A variation on a theme occurred in 1756 when full subsistence was being paid to twelve regiments for new recruits from 1 April onwards, although by 15 August they were still 1,320 men short. Waite was horrified that these regiments 'are ... to put into their pockets the subsistence of so many men who appear never to have been raised'.[26] However it does not seem to have been looked upon by others as anything to worry about.

As was the case throughout the British army, the imposition of discipline was a regular and, occasionally, worrying topic. During the 1689–91 war William III and his commanders had acted regularly to curb pillaging, desertion and absenteeism,[27] and the King himself had had two soldiers hanged who were caught plundering in Kilcullen.[28] In 1693, owing to 'great excesses committed by several officers in the army', William issued orders for breaking five or six of them by way of example.[29] Later that year the lords justices requested they be given similar powers 'upon great emergencies'.[30] In 1695 the Commons ordered into custody Lieutenant-Colonel Richard Gorges, a Lieutenant Collop, a Cornet Montgomery and nine enlisted soldiers for a 'notorious breach of privilege' against an MP at the County Kilkenny election poll in Callan earlier that year. It was also requested that the army units stationed at Callan be removed while the investigation was ongoing. Gorges was found guilty of a violation of the privilege of the Commons, reprimanded and fined. Montgomery received the censure of the house on his knees.[31] Duelling was also a problem; in 1713 the instructions to Shrewsbury included orders for the suspension and trial of soldiers and officers who broke military discipline, with particular emphasis on cashiering officers involved in duels.[32]

A variety of incidents through the century demonstrated the kind of discipline problems that a society might expect to encounter from soldiers living among them, but once again, these were not unique to Ireland; they were endemic to all countries in which the military were stationed, be it in England, Scotland, Wales, France, Spain, Austria, Russia or further afield.[33] The relationship between soldiers and the locals, both Protestant and Catholic, could be at times 'fraught and antagonistic'.[34] In 1711 the Protestant inhabitants of Limerick complained of a riot caused by army officers,[35] while in Dublin in 1765 soldiers rioted and broke open Newgate jail.[36] Injury and death also occurred. In Dublin in 1711 an officer was demoted for shooting a civilian who had been taunting him over his drilling of soldiers, while in 1736 the city saw a fight between soldiers and apprentices which resulted in several fatalities.[37] However, in 1750 three soldiers who had previously mutinied in Dublin were actually saved from death by having 500 of the 1,000 lashes they were to receive remitted, because of the likelihood they would not survive the remainder of their punishment.[38] The large garrison in Limerick also meant that that city featured heavily in reported incidents. Thomas Smyth, Bishop of Limerick, ran into trouble with the garrison in 1718;[39] in 1750 a regiment leaving the city consumed so much alcohol on the eve of departure that the following morning the commanding officer had to be carried on a cart while drummers could hardly play;[40] and in 1753 an army wife reported that the city was 'governed quite by the military, all the gates are shut at ten o'clock and no body admitted to pass after that hour but with leave of the commanding officer'.[41] Elsewhere in 1721, Bishop William Nicolson and the corporation ran into trouble with the Derry garrison.[42]

One means of addressing the question of false musters and discipline at the same time was the developing practice of annual summer encampments.[43] When the army was mustered together in encampment in 1696, one side effect was that the tories in outlying areas were bolder than usual, which served to demonstrate how the army successfully functioned as a form of policing in Ireland.[44] However, despite such concerns, the practice of summer encampment continued and developed as part of the routine and regulation of the standing army. In May 1698 £2,000 was issued for purchasing tents to facilitate the lords justices in bringing the horse, dragoon and foot regiments together in a summer camp.[45] In June 1703 it was reported that Lord Lieutenant Ormond wished to review the army at the Curragh, County Kildare; in August 1704 the army was brought together near Kilkenny; and in March 1707 the lords justices desired instructions about whether a camp was planned for that summer.[46] More significantly, at the time of the Jacobite rebellion in Scotland in late 1715 and early 1716 the horse and dragoon regiments were all sent initially to Athlone for encampment. However, a rumoured invasion to be led by the then exiled Ormond caused the government to move the encampment to the heartland of his old patrimony in Kilkenny.[47]

The usefulness of such encampments was also seen during the War of the Austrian Succession and the Seven Years' War. In 1746 Lord Lieutenant Chesterfield ordered an encampment at Kilkenny for ten companies each from four foot regiments which 'consist chiefly, if not entirely, of raw undisciplined men (not to say officers, too)'. His purpose was 'to teach these regiments a little of their business'. He planned upon exchanging the encamped companies after two months with the remainder on garrison duty so that all would benefit from the experience 'with regard to discipline'.[48] Almost a decade later, on the eve of renewed conflict, ten regiments were encamped around Thurles in 1755,[49] while in August 1759 the government agreed that the summer encampment had served to prevent the cavalry from becoming useless, which would have occurred if they had been allowed to go to grass. Instead, they were now 'in readiness to act' should any invasion occur. The encampment had also ensured that the new recruits were now used to camp duty and the infantry 'ready to be counted upon for real service'.[50] The following summer, with new regiments raised in the interim, the same process of encampment for training purposes was put in place.[51]

The presence of the military in towns and surrounding areas could not pass without notice or effect. Soldiers brought their wives, children, servants and other attendants and hangers-on with them, all of whom became 'a part of the social fabric, socializing with locals in both public and private'. Yet they were also 'set apart ... their martial appearance alone provided a vivid contrast with locals'. In the 1730s in Limerick and Galway 'soldiers marched to their respective churches for divine service each day, with drum beating and arms shouldered'. In the Cathedral in Limerick army officers 'were provided with separate seating in galleries', a practice replicated in nearby St Munchin's church. In 1757 'Major-General Murray's regiment marched into Cork preceded by French horns, hautboys and bassoon players'.[52]

It is difficult to assess how the army was perceived. The army's role in policing and security was well understood, and certainly served as a boon to Protestant Ireland. However, it should not be assumed that all Catholics favoured anarchy and riot. The maintenance of law and order mattered to all religious denominations. Hence policing activities covered the same areas of concern elsewhere in the British Isles and Europe, including escorting prisoners, assisting revenue collectors around the country, quelling riots and other socio-economic and political disturbances, counteracting smuggling and illegal distilleries, and protecting communities and individuals from outlaws and bandits in more secluded parts of the country.[53] At the same time, individual and general Protestant perceptions of Catholics were not generally favourable, with many believing Catholic Ireland was innately disloyal which in itself provided ample justification for maintaining a standing army.[54] Agrarian unrest from the early 1760s onwards, although not solely confined to Catholics, fuelled such concerns, and resulted in increased demands for the assistance of the army in various localities.[55] But while it may have been presumed that Catholics viewed the army with malice, the reality is that even when supposedly banned in the eighteenth century, Catholic recruitment in Ireland and especially overseas in imperial outposts and warzones was constant and significant.[56] Such activity was significant in considerations about recruitment policies for the regiments on the Irish establishment.

Recruitment

The question of confessional allegiance was a key factor in relation to recruitment for the army in Ireland from the 1690s through to the 1760s. Irish Catholics serving in the army was a particular issue. Memories of Catholic armies in the 1630–40s and in the 1680s haunted Protestant Ireland, so that at the end of the war of 1689–91 disposing of the defeated Irish Catholic Jacobite army was of paramount concern. In accordance with the Articles of Limerick agreed on 3 October 1691, Jacobite soldiers who wished to go to France were assisted in doing so. Eventually, more than 12,000 men went, but the great fear was that the remaining force would turn outlaw.[57] William III was keen to make use of any willing ex-Jacobite soldier in his own cause and at least 3,000 were supposedly keen to do so. However, William needed to decide quickly how to employ them, as 'men who have been used to a soldier's manner of living will not easily return to the plough'.[58]

The government had some success in sending ex-Jacobite soldiers to serve with William's allies,[59] but the King's endeavours to recruit them into his army in Ireland were more problematic.[60] In January 1692 the lords justices recommended that officers 'be positively ordered hereafter to recruit in England' owing to the fact that 'several officers' were known to be recruiting 'the Irish, which may prove of very ill consequence'.[61] The practice was persisted with however, to the extent that in October 1692 the Irish Commons resolved that it was endangering 'their majesties' government and the English and Protestant interest' in Ireland 'and the peace and security thereof'.[62] Such sentiments were reinforced in February 1693 when a number of Irish MPs gave evidence to the English Commons on the state of affairs in Ireland, including the allegation that many Irish Catholics were permitted 'to be in the now standing army there' which it was believed 'did endanger the peace at home and might encourage the French to return'.[63] As a result, in March the English Commons addressed William on the issue, warning that the recruiting of Irish Catholics would lead to the 'great endangering and discouragement of your majesty's good and loyal Protestant subjects'.[64] When the address was forwarded to Lord Lieutenant Sydney, he acknowledged that there were some Catholics in the army, but that 'all imaginable care [was] taken to prevent it'.[65]

To that end, in May 1693 the Irish government issued a warrant for the discharge of all Irish Catholics out of the army. It stated that 'many of the private soldiers in most of the regiments' in Ireland were 'mere Irish', who had been 'brought up in the customs, manners, and religion of their ancestors, in a natural aversion to the laws, government and religion of the English', which was dangerous to the Crown, the government and peace in Ireland. Therefore, the background of every private soldier was to be examined and all who were 'descended from mere Irish' were to be discharged. For the future, only 'persons duly qualified ... and known Protestants' were to be recruited.[66] Officers were also instructed to tender the oaths according to the 1691 English Oath Act and soldiers were encouraged to tell on each other. Any Catholics who were discovered where liable to physical punishment as well, as happened to Private Robert Gill of Brigadier Stuart's regiment, who was whipped before being discharged.[67]

Despite such endeavours, however, complaints still occurred. Part of the problem related to practical considerations such as the ease of recruiting soldiers in Ireland in comparison to England or Scotland, where higher rates for levy money were required on the grounds that 'any less would make it impossible to get English levies'.[68] Kinship or other relationships also facilitated the flaunting of official policy. In late 1693 the perpetrator of a murder in County Londonderry, James Hamilton, was described as 'a papist officer of the late King James's army and very lately returned from France, but now entertained as a solider in Capt. John Hamilton's company' in the Derry garrison. Yet Hamilton continued to receive the protection of his commanding officer after the event, to the frustration of the local authorities.[69] The following year, a warrant was issued for his arrest 'for uttering treasonable and seditious words against their majesties'.[70] In 1695 the Protestants of Limerick petitioned their representatives in parliament that a 'more exact scrutiny be made into the soldiers of the garrison at musters ... whereby Irish papists may not wear the King's livery and be trained in feats of arms'.[71]

The problem also transposed itself to England when regiments were moved off the Irish and onto the English establishment. In 1697 the London government instigated an inquiry into the number of Catholics who 'had crept into the army', which uncovered sixty-four Catholics in one battalion and a remarkable 400 Irish Catholics in Colonel Richard Coote's regiment.[72] One of the Catholic rank and file claimed that he had never had the oaths tendered to him.[73] On questioning, Coote expressed great surprise, assuring the English lords justices that his family were not favourers of Catholics and that he had purged his regiment before leaving Ireland. He also highlighted another of the problems for officers recruiting in Ireland, in that it was difficult to distinguish between Protestant and Catholic among the lower orders: 'There might be some, who had the brogue on their tongue, but the Protestants in Ireland are most averse to the papists'.[74] Such recruitment continued despite the fact that from 1695 onwards the Irish parliament's act for disarming Catholics offered an apparently watertight legal impediment to Catholic enlistment.[75] In reality, there appeared to be many Irish Catholics at the lower levels of society who were not worried about breaking man-made laws in order to be able to serve in the army.

Despite orders of late 1701 prohibiting Catholic recruitment in Ireland,[76] the problem continued to exist in Anne's reign. From mid-1701 onwards preparations for pending war with France saw regiments being sent overseas and new ones raised in Ireland, with a total of eighteen foot, two dragoon and one horse regiment being recruited between 1701 and 1709, though it would seem that this was done for the most part with a view to sending them overseas as well.[77] The dramatic impact of such activity was seen in June 1703 when it was reported that 'They are beating up here [in Ireland] for ... [two] foot [regiments] ... and it is said there will be commissions for raising six more'.[78] The problems arising from such large-scale recruitment was also quickly demonstrated. In December 1703 the chief secretary, Edward Southwell, expressed his surprise at complaints from England that two regiments sent over from Ireland had included Catholics, and claimed the government had done all in its power to prevent such an occurrence.[79] More significantly, when the army was encamped near Kilkenny in August 1704 it was discovered that 'about sixty private sentinels ... had combined to desert with their arms ... and ... £1,200 ... and having perfected that they designed to repair to the bog of Allen and turn rapparees'. The field officers reacted by taking out parties of soldiers to secure the passes in the area, 'which the deserters perceiving dispersed save six which were taken'. It was again highlighted that 'men raised here ... are generally papists', for which reason had 'this design ... not been discovered it is a query whether a great part of the army had not joined'. Ultimately, 'whatever the papists may pretend to [be] ... not one of them can be reckoned a good subject to the Queen, their behaviour plainly showing they are the French King's creatures'.[80]

Continuing concern resulted in occasional clampdowns. In September 1713 Shrewsbury was ordered to ensure that the various oaths were administered to every soldier and that any who refused were cashiered, while in January 1716, following the Jacobite rebellion in Scotland and the north-east of England, the Commons requested that the government issue a proclamation for a reward to anyone discovering any Catholics in the army.[81] Thirteen new regiments were to be recruited in Ireland at that time, but as the joint chief secretary, Martin Bladen, pointed out, it was not an easy task:

> The greatest care imaginable has been taken to prevent any papists from getting into these levies, and yet I fear there are some amongst them, but ... the chaplains are directed to examine every man very strictly in his principles of religion, that such as are not found to be true Protestants may be immediately punished according to law, and dismissed the service. However I believe the best method for the future will be, to reduce things to the same foot they were upon when my Lord Galway was formerly in the government here, and oblige the army to raise all their recruits in England.[82]

As noted by Bladen, there had been a policy for a time of only recruiting in England and Scotland, which had coincided with a period of peace between 1697 and 1701, when the demand for new recruits was less onerous. Some historians have intimated that this blanket ban on recruiting Irishmen of any religious denomination, including the Church of Ireland, among the rank and file was more pervasive and permanent from the 1690s through to at least the 1770s.[83] The evidence suggests however that such a policy only coincided at best with periods of peace. It was evident that during wartime or other critical junctures recruitment in Ireland was returned to as a viable option, even with the associated dangers of Catholic infiltration of the rank and file.

The legal basis for excluding Protestant dissenters from the army rested upon the 1704 Sacramental Test. During the Jacobite rebellion of 1715, however, Protestant dissenters served in the militia and on the commissions of array, prompting a failed attempt to pass a bill for relaxing the restrictions regarding militia and military service. One anonymous writer ascribed the vigorous opposition to the measure in some quarters to a hope that more Catholics would end up as rank and file: 'that unless four parts in six [of the thirteen new regiments] be dissenting common soldiers then men won't be Protestants'.[84] Unintentionally, the writer also highlighted a fundamental problem revealed by this rudimentary confessional demography: there did not appear to be sufficient numbers of Church of Ireland Protestants willing and able to populate all of the higher public and military offices while also sustaining rank and file recruitment.

The lengthy period of peace from 1716 to 1739 witnessed the reinvigoration of attempts to halt Irish rank and file recruitment. Yet significant examples still arose. As detailed in Table 5.1, an abstract from 1724 listed 25 per cent of the effective rank and file in the twenty-one foot regiments in Ireland as 'Irish'. In one regiment, 144 were Irish in comparison to only 137 British.[85] At a review a year later the figure had dropped to 23 per cent Irish in nineteen foot regiments. However, there were actually fifteen more Irish than in 1724, but the percentage difference was owing to a larger overall increase in the number of effective British soldiers in the interim.[86] Although the abstracts did not give the number of Irish in the mounted regiments or any intimation of the origins of any of the officers, individual abstracts recorded two squadrons of cavalry with over 50 per cent Irish rank and file, while the Royal Irish Dragoons had 131 Irish rank and file out of a total of 137 men.[87] Given that at all other times the highest percentage of Irishmen in the army in Ireland were to be found in the mounted regiments, for which potential Irish officers and rank and file always showed a preference, it is probable that the overall percentage of Irish in 1724–5 was even higher than 25 per cent. This was even more probable given that Church of Ireland Protestants were always allowed to serve as commissioned officers in Ireland, and did so in significant numbers. It was also understood that most of the men listed in 1724–5 as Irish were Protestant, given that of eighty discharged in 1724 only three were Catholics.[88] These dismissals were undertaken 'pursuant to a regulation for reform of the army approved by' George I.[89] At the same time it was ordered that two Irish per foot company were to be replaced each year with British recruits.[90]

Table 5.1: Total effective soldiers in Ireland, 1724–5.

	Infantry		Cavalry	Dragoons	Total men	Inc. NCO + officers
	Irish	British	N/A	N/A	N/A	N/A
1724	1,464	4,387	470	742	7,063	8,301
1725	1,479	4,784	491	791	7,545	8,645

The pressure on army officers to find new recruits resulted in occasional requests for the policy to be relaxed, as in 1727 when Primate Boulter, acting as lord justice, appealed that 'leave [be] … given to raise men in this country', but only those 'as can have good certificates' that they and their parents were Protestants.[91] Such permission was not forthcoming, though clearly the officers had gone ahead with their plans anyway, as a year later it was discovered that eleven regiments had tried to pass off Irish recruits as British-born. Despite their claim that all the men were Protestant, the recruiting officers were dismissed. By 1732 it was reported that only 641 of the 4,794 rank and file infantry were Irish,[92] while in 1737 there appeared to be even less, with only one regiment returning thirty-four Irish on the muster roll. There had been 108 more, but they had been discharged because they had been recruited after the reimposition of the ban. Those who were retained were 'old ... Irish, by old they mean men that have served a long while, before the regulation'.[93]

The war of 1739–48 resulted in the regulations being relaxed once again. Initially unofficial recruitment was overlooked by the authorities rather than condoned as recruiting officers took the initiative themselves.[94] But the Jacobite rebellion in 1745 forced an official recognition of the need. In September George II agreed to allow Protestants to be raised in northern Ireland with a view to bringing the rank and file in six foot regiments up to strength and adding an additional four companies to each. The estimated maximum number of men to be enlisted by this means was 5,600.[95] By April 1747 the Irish government believed that the security situation was sufficiently improved to require a reinstatement of the ban, which was complied with, though by October Lord Lieutenant Harrington successfully requested that it be overturned once again.[96]

With the conclusion of the war in 1748 the ban was officially reimposed, but in reality the presence of Church of Ireland rank and file seems to have been condoned from that point onwards.[97] Protestant dissenters and Catholics were still officially excluded. In 1756 a bill was enacted to make it legal for Protestant dissenters to hold commissions in the militia and to act on commissions of array,[98] though it was not until 1780 that they were officially allowed to enlist in the army. Catholics had to wait until the 1790s for official licence to enlist, although their numbers were increasing dramatically long before that time.[99] However, as far as such Catholic recruitment was concerned, until the 1790s it was primarily advocated for service abroad.[100]

As detailed in Table 5.2, an account on the eve of the outbreak of the Seven Years' War highlighted the country of origin for all soldiers in Ireland. By that time, soldiers described as Irish dominated both the rank and file and officer classes of the cavalry and dragoon units, comprising 75 per cent and 79 per cent respectively of the officers and 96 per cent and 95 per cent of the rank and file. In the infantry however the Irish comprised only 36 per cent of the officers and 7 per cent of the rank and file. Overall, 51 per cent of officers and 26 per cent of rank and file were from Ireland, combining to form just over 28 per cent of all ranks.[101]

Table 5.2: Account of the Army in Ireland, July 1755.

Nationality:	Irish		English		Scottish		'Foreign'		Total	
Rank:	Men	Officers	Men	Officers	Men	Officers	Men	Officers	Men	Officers
Horse:	534	80	13	21	4	5	5	1	556	107
Dragoon:	889	138	36	29	11	6	0	0	936	173
Foot:	383	165	3096	168	2020	134	23	2	5522	469
Total:	1806	383	3145	218	2035	145	28	3	7014	749

The number of Irish officers was not surprising, as it had always been allowed for Irish Protestants to be commissioned in the army in Ireland. Indeed such commissions were an important part of the patronage that viceroys and their political undertakers could utilize for keeping Irish politicians onside.[102] Army careers for younger sons were often an attractive proposition, to the extent that one historian has argued that the Irish military tradition should be seen to commence under Marlborough rather than under Wellington a hundred years later.[103] The disproportion between the numbers of Irish in the mounted regiments and the infantry was best explained by the inclination, as William Pitt put it, 'to engage in the horse, which is known among that better sort of people, in Ireland, who will not list in the foot, or dragoons'.[104] He was wrong about the dragoons, but correct in everything else. But given that dragoons were mounted, they were probably viewed as the next best thing to the cavalry.

The 1755 figures are higher than might be expected, and the reality was that from that point onwards the number of Irish throughout the army increased further. A plan in 1755–6 for augmenting the size of the army in Ireland was based upon the premise that the extra men could be 'raise[d] ... in the north of Ireland', while at the end of 1756 the continuing demand for soldiers was such that recruiting parties from British-based regiments were also active in Ireland.[105] In early 1757 orders were issued for completing a new regiment with recruits in the north, where it was to be barracked.[106] It was claimed that this regiment, consisting of two battalions of 600 men each, had been raised 'under the strongest restrictions that could possibly be given that none but Protestants should be enlisted'.[107] Another regiment was also recruiting in the north at that time, also with strict guidelines regarding the religion of the new levies. The idea was also put forward of painting the Irish harp on the regimental colours in order to facilitate recruiting throughout the whole country, the logic being that many more might join regiments that were perceived as 'English Irish', in imitation of the sense of national identity promoted in the Irish regiments in the French service.[108] At the same time, the competition from British recruiters was starting to become an issue of complaint.[109]

The demographic difficulty associated with the official policy of only allowing Church of Ireland Protestants to enlist began to prove burdensome as well. In April 1757 orders were issued for allowing open recruitment, excluding Catholics, which presumably allowed Protestant dissenters to enlist,[110] while in November the government requested that further recruitment in Ireland by British-based regiments be prohibited because

> this country has within these two years past, been so drained of men by the numbers raised to augment the battalions of foot from fifty to seventy per company, by the twenty-four additional companies that were raised in 1756; by ... two battalions which were raised here last spring; and by the battalions of foot recruiting in this kingdom at large, that more of the Protestant hands cannot be taken off, without very great detriment to their trade and manufactures.[111]

Thereafter it was forbidden for British-based regiments to recruit without prior consent from the Irish government.[112] The demands of the war also resulted in the minimum size of recruits being decreased from 5 foot 6 inches to 5 foot 3 inches in both England and Ireland.[113]

In 1758 Lord Lieutenant Bedford complained that the number of foot regiments 'composed entirely of English and Scotch' had been greatly depleted in Ireland. He claimed he would rather trust one such

> battalion ... than ... two of those ... which have of late been wholly recruited here, and consequently are liable to a suspicion of being full of Irish papists. But let their religion be what it will, though they are doubtless excellent soldiers in foreign countries, they are not to be depended upon in their own.

Apparently the horse and dragoons were 'entirely under this predicament'.[114]

However, the apparent pressure upon Irish Protestants was not always believed or accepted. In November 1759 Bedford complained again of the difficulties he had in completing the infantry regiments in Ireland. Recruiting in Ulster had gone very slowly, and had received little assistance from the nobility and gentry. He expected even greater difficulties in Dublin and the south: 'I have no adequate succedaneum left, the southern parts of this kingdom being very bare of Protestants'.[115] The King was not amused: Pitt expressed George II's disappointment at the failure of the promised efforts of the Irish Protestant nobility and gentlemen to raise men at a time of great danger when the city of London had raised more at its own expense. The dismay in England was coupled with a suspicion that Irish Protestants were happy to rely upon Great Britain to come to the rescue if an invasion occurred.[116]

A response to such criticism was not long in coming. In November proposals were put forward by several individuals to raise new regiments at their own expense and time, and to be under their own command. Lieutenant Colonel Hugh Morgan proposed raising 500 Irish Protestants in five companies of light infantry; Charles Moore, Earl of Drogheda, offered to raise a regiment of light dragoons of six troops of seventy men each; Sir James Caldwell of County Fermanagh proposed raising an independent troop of light horse or hussars, eventually comprised of 200 men plus officers; and Lieutenant Colonel Blayney offered to raise a regiment of ten companies of seventy privates each plus NCOs and officers in Ulster. In December Sir Ralph Gore proposed raising a regiment of light infantry comprising 900 Protestants in Counties Donegal and Fermanagh, Lord Kildare offered to establish a regiment of royal Irish artillery, and Lieutenant Colonel Samuel Bagshawe proposed raising a foot regiment of Protestants, with nine companies of seventy-eight men each.[117] All of the proposals were agreed to and put into immediate effect, though the various requests for personal promotions and commissions for family and friends were refused.[118]

In November–December 1761 similar proposals were made and accepted. On this occasion, seven lieutenant colonels offered to each raise a foot regiment of 700 privates plus NCOs and officers, to a total of 818 men, from among Irish Protestants. Five of the proposals were accepted and acted upon, while the idea of creating a sense of Irishness as a means of assisting the recruiting process was seen in the suggestion that the regiments be given names such as the King's Irish Volunteers, the Queen's Irish Volunteers, the Queen's Royal Irish Regiment and the Queen's Royal Irish Fusiliers. As before, the regiments were to be raised at the officers' own expense.[119]

As Terence Denman has argued, from the end of the Seven Years' War onwards the 'Irish presence in the army, Catholic or Protestant, was now substantial'.[120] The increasing imperial demand for soldiers around the globe ensured that there would be no return to the more restricted policies of earlier periods of peace. The evolving crisis in North America quickly ensured that the demand for recruits from Ireland, to serve both at home and abroad, continued to grow, while the French Revolutionary and Napoleonic Wars altered the landscape of recruitment completely, especially with regard to Irish Catholic enlistment.[121] These developments after the 1760s also affected the size, composition and nature of the army in Ireland in relation to how it had been settled in the 1690s and had thereafter evolved and to its place within the political considerations of government and parliament. At the heart of such issues was the question of numbers.

Numbers, 1692–1753

The size of the army in seventeenth-century Ireland had fluctuated over time. On the eve of the 1641 rebellion it comprised only 3,240 men, yet by the 1650s the numbers had risen to 30,000. Such a figure was exceptional however for both Ireland and the British Isles as a whole and was a product of the unique circumstances of the interregnum period. A more traditional pattern re-emerged following the Restoration. In 1661 the number was 7,500, which was 'the largest military concentration in the British Isles' at the time.[122] By the 1670s Irish finances were sufficient to maintain 'a very considerable army' and to allow for a regular contribution to the cost of the imperial army through the maintenance of the Tangiers garrison.[123] By 1683 the figure had decreased slightly to 7,000, though it was still larger 'than its English counterpart'.[124] A year later it was estimated at 7,800.[125] On occasion enlarging that number even further was considered, especially under Lord Lieutenant Ormond, who placed a particular emphasis on his role as commander-in-chief.[126]

The Restoration experience might well have served as a model for developing Ireland's role in the empire as it was to unfold in the eighteenth century had it not been interrupted by the reign of James II, which clouded any sense of continuity of practice from the early 1680s to the 1690s. In 1685 James II found himself with a ready-made military machine in Ireland which contributed to his power at home and abroad. The radical overhaul of that machine which he allowed Tyrconnell to undertake as part of a policy of Catholicization might well be considered a reason for the break in continuity, though events in England, the United Provinces and France were in truth more significant in that respect.[127]

Following James's removal from England at the end of 1688, the influx of soldiers into Ireland during the war of 1689–91 marked a dramatic break with previous practice. James's Irish army dropped from an initial high of 36,000 to about 28,400 by late 1690 and thereafter averaged about 30,500 during 1691, while that of William III rose from an initial 9,030 to 34,884 by September 1689 and to over 36,000 by mid-1690, remaining at that level thereafter.[128]

The machinations entered into in 1691–2 in order to agree upon the size of the army to be retained in Ireland revolved around finding a balance between the needs for internal security against Jacobite unrest or French invasion and external demands for the continuing war on the continent. However, both considerations were essential precursors to the re-establishment and further development of a military role for Ireland in the empire. Although, like many Englishmen, Edward Harley was more concerned that the cost to England of the reconquest of Ireland should be recouped from forfeited Irish lands, he still acknowledged in late October 1691 that 'if in Ireland the quarters, musters, and discipline of the armies be not well regulated, great must be the mischief'.[129] On 17 November it was reported in the Westminster parliament that all but 10,000 of the army were to be shipped to England and then onwards to Flanders. Two days later it was clarified that of the 65,000 land force the Commons had agreed to maintain for the coming year, 8,000 were to be stationed in Scotland, 10,000 in England, 32,000 in Flanders and elsewhere, and 12,000 in Ireland inclusive of officers and NCOs, with a further 2,000 unallocated.[130]

The decision to station 12,000 soldiers in Ireland also included a financial commitment. In January 1692 it was recorded that the English parliament had 'allotted that the [Irish] revenue ... shall contribute' £165,000 'towards the charge of the army'.[131] However, in reality, the annual cost of the 12,000-strong army was in excess of that amount. As it was also evident that, unlike in the past, subventions from England would not be forthcoming, Irish finances would in fact have to provide for the full cost of the army whatever the amount required.

In the end, the military establishment for 1692 consisted of one horse regiment with six troops of fifty men each plus officers, two dragoon regiments with eight troops of sixty men each plus officers and fifteen foot regiments with thirteen companies of fifty men each plus officers.[132] The total number of soldiers estimated to be in Ireland in that year was 12,960, as compared with 17,133 in England and Wales, 32,402 in Flanders, 2,718 in Scotland and 1,160 in the

West Indies and North America.[133] The numbers in Ireland fluctuated thereafter during the remainder of the Nine Years' War. By July there was one less foot regiment, while by the end of the year the threat of a French invasion led to further military movements in and out of Ireland.[134] Lord Chancellor Porter hoped that 'the regiments that are designed [for Ireland] will not be long ... because though we have sent all we can towards Cork and Kinsale yet they are but few'. Yet even amid heightened security concerns, he also noted that 'the country say they had rather have no more, than that the French regiments should make three of the four which are intended'.[135]

With the continuing fear of an invasion at the beginning of January 1693, all officers in England were ordered to return 'forthwith' to their commands.[136] More generally in response to the overall decrease in numbers, a new dragoon and foot regiment were raised with Colonel Henry Cunningham and Arthur Chichester, Earl of Donegal, in command. Only known Protestants were to be enlisted, with arms and clothes provided from England. The two new regiments increased the overall number to three dragoons and eleven foot.[137] During 1694 four new regiments were stationed in Ireland to replace four or five that had been transferred out.[138] By 1695 the overall number had increased to one horse regiment, three dragoons and fifteen foot, though a decrease during 1696 by one dragoon regiment and four foot saw the regimental strength finally reach a settled level for the remainder of the war.[139]

From 1692 until the conclusion of the war in 1697 the numbers in Ireland had fluctuated between 12,000 and 15,000.[140] But the English parliament's desire to reduce the size of William's army in 1697–9 meant further readjustments in Ireland. The pamphlet debate on the matter was revealing of the perception of Ireland within Britain's military strategy. Writing in 1698, one advocate of a standing army went so far as to suggest that Ireland was an example that England should follow:

> Has not Ireland more cause to complain? A country which though for some years it was the seat of war, yet has not requested to be released: the Irish keep forces in their own country without murmuring; and we who have so precious a King's life to preserve, would hazard all that is dear to us, to save a little charges.[141]

The usefulness of a separate military establishment in Ireland was also evident to those in favour of disbanding the army. Trenchard suggested that 'no invasion can be so sudden upon us, but we shall have time to ... bring some forces from Scotland and Ireland'.[142] He seemed to contradict himself a year later however, when he claimed that ever since James I, English monarchs had looked to encourage Irish Catholics in their disloyalty in order to have 'a pretence to keep up standing armies there to awe the natives'.[143]

These considerations culminated in the English parliament's 1699 Disbanding Act in which the standing forces in England were settled at 7,000 men and

those in Ireland at 12,000.[144] A number of much smaller units were to be stationed in the Channel Islands, the West Indies, Newfoundland and New York.
Although Scotland was not mentioned, a troop of guards, two dragoon regiments and seven foot were stationed there post-disbandment in March 1699.
This compared to the intended three troops of guards, a troop of grenadier
guards, seven horse regiments, one dragoon and seven foot in England and two
horse regiments, one dragoon and eighteen foot in Ireland.[145] Although the
actual size of each regiment remains unclear, the implication is that the number
of soldiers in Scotland was well below that of England and Ireland. Certainly by
1701–2 the number in Scotland was only 2,934.[146] The reality was that beyond
times of serious disturbance such as 1715–16 and 1745–6, Scotland was not
home to a significant part of the British standing army, a situation which has
been attributed to topographic and demographic considerations.[147]

The army restructuring in 1697–9 had political repercussions in Ireland. The
government's need for more money to pay the increased costs associated with
the new military establishment was the primary reason for summoning another
session of parliament in 1698–9.[148] In their opening speech the lords justices
acknowledged what was occurring:

> The King hath, since the peace, thought fit to send hither a part of those forces who
> served abroad during all the war, having disbanded the greatest part of those who
> served here [in Ireland], with a resolution notwithstanding to continue the subsist-
> ence to the officers until they can otherwise be provided for. His majesty expects that
> you will enable him to support the charge of the present establishment.[149]

The main threat to the supply arising from these arrangements related to the
inclusion of five French Huguenot regiments in the troops sent to Ireland. Following a heated debate, a motion for disbanding these regiments was defeated
by 101 votes to 72, while the government prevented an ensuing attempt to delay
the supply by 105 to 55. The desired quantum of £138,978 was finally agreed
upon a split of 94 to 64, though the succession of divisions had been unusual
and was representative of a discontented house.[150] A second threat arose following the Westminster parliament's decision to actually include the five Huguenot
regiments among those to be disbanded in 1699. Irish MPs were quick to point
out that 'we make provision for these very men ... here, which [the English par-
liament] ... have voted shall be forthwith disbanded'.[151] The government's fears
went unrealized, however, and the relevant supply bills passed successfully,
though with unusual delay and amid contentious related debates.[152]

Unlike England, however, there had been no objection in Ireland to the reality of a standing army supported by Irish money. Rather, the focus of opposition
had been upon excluding any soldiers who were not from the British Isles. Clearly
xenophobia was alive and well in Ireland and carried useful political advantage.
Alan Brodrick expressed his annoyance that he and others were represented 'as

men ... in opposition to the true interest of our country' because they had been 'against the address to break the five French regiments'.[153]

The Huguenot regiments were broken in March 1699.[154] However, because of the negative attitude in both England and Ireland towards foreigners in the military, 'it was thought prudent not to put the [French] officers ... upon half-pay but to give them pensions on the civil list'. Hence the French pension list came into existence on the Irish civil establishment at an initial cost of about £25,000 a year, which was less than it would have cost to include them all on military half-pay. Also, unlike the half-pay list, the French pension list was meant to be finite in its existence. However, although it did decrease in cost over the years, at times widows and other officers were 'substituted in the room of those that died' so that the charge reduced more slowly than might have been expected. The French pensions were to occasionally resurface as a focus for discontent in parliament when financial costs increased, but many MPs were also appreciative of the military service these refugees had performed in preserving the Protestant interest in Ireland during 1689–91 and more generally thereafter in William III's service on the continent.[155]

The breaking of regiments and reduction of the overall size of the army in 1697–9 was a time of great uncertainty and insecurity for many. Some feared that France, along with Jacobites in Ireland and elsewhere, would see it as an opportunity to restore the Stuarts.[156] The actual process also took a long time. The complexities of the movements and alterations included the clearing of pay on the English establishment and the commencement of the same on the Irish, alongside the clearings for disbanded soldiers and the transfer of hundreds of officers to the half-pay list.[157] By the time all of these changes had taken place in mid-1699, the settled establishment comprised two horse regiments, three dragoons, twenty foot and a half-pay list of 373 officers. Given that the half-pay served as a reserve of experienced commissioned officers for active service as and when the need arose, the military potential of the establishment was greater than the legislative limits in theory allowed.[158] A year later an additional two horse and one dragoon regiment had been added, though by 1702 the foot had reduced to thirteen regiments.[159]

As in the 1690s, during the 1702–13 War of the Spanish Succession the Irish establishment fluctuated with demand. The immediate impact of war was a greatly reduced military presence in Ireland. On 13 July 1702 the Tory MP, Edward Singleton, recorded how

> the money the public revenue brings in, lies in the exchequer, there being not now an army here to be paid out of it, so that it is said there is now near £100,000 lies there which goes a great way in the current cash of this kingdom, and much occasions the scarcity of money, for while there was an army here constantly paid, the money did circulate which now lies dead.[160]

Apart from the obvious security issue, Singleton's observations highlighted the extent to which the army had already become a central part of the Irish economy, ensuring a regular circulation of ready specie through general trade and commerce as well as provisioning and maintenance. In that same month however two regiments were sent to Ireland, while in August it was reported that four more were on their way, amid the usual concerns that the French would look upon Ireland as a means 'to stir up trouble' for Queen Anne.[161]

Not surprisingly, the army was again central to political considerations in the early years of Anne's reign. In late 1702 discussions were held with a view to summoning a new parliament as money was needed to pay for the military establishment. Complaints from leading politicians about trade restrictions and other grievances were countered by Lord Justice Thomas Keightley who argued that if money was not provided the army would have to be disbanded or allowed 'to live on free quarter'. Alan Brodrick simply responded that 'a parliament was the best place to think of an expedient in, were the mischief is so great'.[162] When parliament did eventually convene in late 1703, the main focus was actually on paying overseas regiments and barrack building, though the presence of agents for English half-pay officers looking for commissions in new regiments being raised in Ireland led to a proposal that the Irish half-pay officers be provided for first with a view to diminishing the overall increase in costs.[163]

The raising of new regiments to replace those sent overseas was an ongoing process during the war. In March 1703 it was noted that Lord Lieutenant Ormond, to his political and personal advantage, was 'to raise a regiment of horse in Ireland of which he is to be colonel himself, [and] will give him an opportunity of obliging a great many gentlemen that went over with him'.[164] By June two new foot regiments were being recruited in Ireland, while in early 1704 five more foot and one dragoon regiment were recruiting.[165] Ormond had actually delayed naming the new officers to these regiments until after the parliament of 1703–4, in order to ensure the good behaviour of any MPs wishing to secure such positions for themselves, family or friends.[166] The continued movement of regiments overseas ensured that in November 1704 more new levies had to be recruited, while in 1706 another new dragoon regiment was recruited, and in 1708 four more foot regiments were raised. In 1709 yet another foot regiment was raised, which was the last home-grown unit of the war.[167] By that time the establishment comprised three horse regiments, three dragoons, fourteen foot and a much reduced half-pay list owing to the number of regiments raised in the preceding years.[168]

The demand for soldiers abroad resulted in the regiments left in Ireland in 1711 being noticeably understrength, with numerous vacancies which translated into financial savings for the government. While this might have seemed an attractive outcome for the 1711 parliament, in fact it was identified as a grievance because of the potential security threat and concern that the money voted in 1710 for such payments was being diverted to other uses. The government therefore expected trouble but hoped that the Queen's declared intention of bringing the military establishment back to full strength would 'be a sufficient answer to this objection'.[169] To that end, the government endeavoured to demonstrate that all of the financial savings had been applied to clearing army pay arrears and that any extra money would be used to bring all of the regiments up to strength.[170]

As the war began to wind down the movement of soldiers started to be reversed, while its conclusion in 1713 brought the British army in for renewed scrutiny, redeployment, reduction and relocation. At least six regiments were moved to Ireland in 1713. In March 1714 orders were issued to break two dragoon regiments and four foot. The first was broken on 13 April without any difficulty. However, the two dragoon regiments refused to lay down their arms, causing the government to send other regiments to force them to do so. Thereafter one regiment quickly complied, but the other refused on the grounds that the promise made at the time of their embarkation at Dunkirk of replacement horses in Ireland had yet to be fulfilled. They were also due pay arrears. However, the threat of being accorded the status and treatment of rebels finally forced the recalcitrant soldiers to disband. Five foot companies had also initially stood to arms and only the threat of dragoons forced them to disband.[171]

While the regiments were being disbanded, Shrewsbury was instructed by London to transmit proposals for further reductions. The ensuing report returned an establishment of five horse regiments, four dragoons and fifteen foot. Disbanding had also resulted in a dramatic increase to the half-pay list, which now comprised 654 officers from forty-three regiments.[172] After Queen Anne's death in August 1714, however, the renewed possibility of a Jacobite rebellion resulted in a change of focus, as evidenced by the removal from the army in Ireland of five potentially disloyal general staff officers and eight regimental commanding officers who were also 'ordered to dispose of their regiments'.[173] At the same time, concern was expressed that there were insufficient forces to defend the country from either a Catholic uprising or a Jacobite invasion.[174]

More significantly, in the early months of George I's reign London sought advice from Dublin about the possibility of stationing 15,000 soldiers in Ireland, though this suggestion was dismissed with the warning that it would prove difficult enough to maintain the existing limit.[175] Lord Chancellor Brodrick, Revenue Commissioner Conolly, Commander-in-Chief Lord Tyrawley and the three chief justices, William Whitshed, John Forster and Joseph Deane, were all agreed that, at best, 12,000 'may be subsisted till a parliament may meet' and that thereafter the legislature would continue to support that number as long as they were only paid from Irish funds while actually in Ireland.[176]

When parliament finally convened in late 1715, the number of general staff officers came under scrutiny as part of a wider concern about parliamentary supplies being 'draw[n] away ... by king's letters for bounty and pensions' to 'undeserving people' and to 'persons that live out of this kingdom'.[177] The number of staff officers had doubled since the 1690s to about two dozen, which led MPs to believe that the position was being used as a form of peacetime pension for unemployed senior officers who might never set foot in Ireland and caused the lords justices to request that 'those who have commands here may be hastened to their posts, and that the commissions of such as cannot attend the service ... may be disposed of to those that will not make sinecures of them'.[178] Attention was also drawn once again to officer vacancies, all of which it was believed should be filled by men on the Irish half-pay.[179] Such a request cut across the important patronage value attached to the granting of army commissions, which may account for the fact that there was no response on the matter from London.[180] In the end, an increased demand placed upon the army by the Jacobite rebellion of late 1715 rescued the government from a potentially difficult situation.

Information regarding an intended Jacobite rebellion somewhere in the British Isles started to come to light during the summer of 1715. In reaction, the Irish government sent soldiers into Galway, Limerick, Cork and Kinsale, 'to prevent any sudden attempt on those places of consequence, either from the inhabitants, or others, in favour of the Pretender'.[181] Rebellion finally broke out in Scotland and north-east England in September.[182] In November the lords justices encouraged parliament to put itself 'in the best posture of defence' because, although the King had 'ordered an addition to be made to each company' in Ireland, the reality was that the standing army was understrength.[183]

News of the Pretender's landing in Scotland in December 1715 filtered into Ireland in January 1716, prompting the Irish government to request permission to raise an extra two companies per foot regiment given 'how far the present number of forces here falls short of the establishment'.[184] A monthly return from early 1716 demonstrated the problem: there was a total of 5,573 effective men and 762 NCOs in the eighteen regiments in Ireland, which represented a deficiency of 958 private soldiers for those units alone, not to mention the absence of sufficient other regiments to bring the numbers up to 12,000. At the same time, sixty-eight officers were absent, including eight colonels and five lieutenant-colonels.[185]

For their part, the Commons reacted by resolving to make good any expense thought 'necessary for the defence of the kingdom in raising troops'.[186] Although 'not within the rules prescribed by the establishment', the lords justices felt that the Commons had thereby 'warranted' them to make the necessary military preparations for any invasion or rebellion. Senior army officers were despatched to key strategic points around the country, as were half-pay officers and French pensioners who were to serve with and assist in modelling the militia. All of these men were put on full salaries 'while they are thus employed'. A final group of half-pay officers were put on active service and full pay in the horse and dragoon regiments which were placed in encampment.[187]

These measures all represented actions that could be undertaken immediately, but the raising of new levies required permission from the Crown and a degree of time. In late January rumour of a possible Jacobite landing in Ireland prompted London to issue orders for such new forces, in response to which the Irish Commons promised to make good whatever amount was expended in bringing the establishment back to full strength and for 'as many more [soldiers] as they shall think necessary for the further security of the kingdom at this critical juncture'.[188] The lords justices immediately commenced raising eight foot and five dragoon regiments, accounting for about an additional 6,000 men on top of the number already allowed on the existing establishment. Coupled with the militia, they believed this would represent a sufficient force to repel an invasion or quash a rebellion. The raising of the new regiments also offered employment opportunities for enough of the half-pay officers to mollify parliament, while also giving the lords justices greater patronage opportunities.[189]

Even when news of the defeat of the rebellion reached Ireland in late February, the recruitment process continued, although it did not go as smoothly as might have been hoped. In late March and again in April the lords justices expressed their concern that the new levies were in much confusion owing to the lack of field officers, and desired that the King issue orders for all relevant officers to attend to that service in Ireland. At the beginning of April arms from Holland and ammunition from England finally arrived, though it was discovered that the arms were useless and where therefore returned. The process was still ongoing in May.[190] However, despite such difficulties, the raising of the regiments had offered reassurance at a time of Protestant insecurity in Ireland. At the conclusion of the session, the Commons saw fit to pass a vote of thanks to the lords justices, mentioning specifically the employment of so many of the half-pay officers.[191]

One unforeseen circumstance of the employment of so many half-pay officers was a temporary reduction in the effectiveness of the list as an active reserve. Most of those remaining on half-pay were either too old to serve or were Irish Protestants who had served in the 1689–91 war and were in reality only ever considered of value in the militia. Their half-pay was seen as a pension and they had all long-since returned to their previous lives. The remainder were either minors, absent or of 'dubious principles'.[192] Likewise it had been discovered that the French pensioners, of whom there were still 372 in 1714, were no longer of much use. Most were now 'old and not fit for service'.[193] The suggestion that they might be moved onto the half-pay list was dismissed because the increased cost of about £4,000 a year would be blamed on Lord Galway and would cause a public outcry because there was no evidence that such an alteration would be of any practical use.[194] Politically, it would

> give a very plausible handle to those who from Tory principles, from disappointments of preferments ... or from a natural peevish disposition, do not like the present administration, to clamour against the court [and] ... the ministry ... for loading them with the pensions and creating a necessity of new taxes to be lavished away upon foreigners.

The financial evidence suggested as much: since 1701 the cost of pensions on the civil and military lists had increased from £29,518 to £43,739.[195]

In reality, once the Jacobite threat was seen to be removed in 1716 the increased cost of the enlarged army had to be addressed. With regiments returning from Britain, the government's income was insufficient for the purpose.[196] By the beginning of 1717 it was clear that the intention was to reduce the army back to more manageable peacetime proportions.[197] Parliament was notified of the government's plan in August, which involved disbanding the thirteen new regiments. The resultant new establishment comprised four horse regiments, six dragoon and twenty foot.[198]

The various military adjustments made in 1715–16 were a focus for opposition in the 1717 session, as some MPs looked to undermine the reputation of the previous government, though Speaker Conolly believed 'they will get little by that'.[199] Attention was focused on an additional pay allowance for the horse and dragoon regiments, the importation of the 10,000 non-functioning muskets and the half-pay and French pension lists. In the end, however, when it emerged that not all French pensioners and half-pay officers on active duty had received full pay, the Commons actually resolved in their favour. Nothing more came of the other rumblings.[200]

In the following years the number of regiments in Ireland fluctuated in accordance with supply and demand. A general overview of the following decades suggests that Ireland maintained on average twenty-two infantry battalions in the 1720s and 1730s and twenty-five in the later 1740s and early 1750s and again in the 1760s and 1770s. On average, a further four horse and six dragoon regiments were included as well on all occasions.[201]

The lengthy peace from the end of the War of the Spanish Succession to the outbreak of the War of the Austrian Succession in 1739–40 was particularly revealing of how the military arrangements in Ireland functioned over time. It was also the case that the total regiments recorded on the Irish establishment in these years did not always equate with the actual number in Ireland because some were often overseas though still paid by the Irish treasury.[202] In 1719 the public accounts committee noted that the main reason for the increasing cost of the army was the varying number of reduced regiments on the establishment over time: more regiments meant more officers, which meant a higher percentage of the 12,000 men were on higher salaries. Increased numbers of horse and dragoon regiments also increased costs, as did higher numbers of half-pay officers.[203] These calculations once again demonstrated the flexibility of the Irish establishment and its value to Britain and the empire, as in peacetime the purpose changed as regiments were reduced in size but the actual number of army units and half-pay officers increased.[204]

Between 1721 and 1734 the government's biennial reports to parliament recorded a constant presence on the establishment of four horse, six dragoon and twenty foot regiments.[205] However, as two army reviews from 1724–5 demonstrated, there were fluctuations between reporting periods. In 1724 there were actually twenty-one foot regiments, while a year later there were nineteen.[206] In 1734 eight foot regiments were removed from the establishment, though new rank and file were recruited to the remaining twelve foot regiments in order to bring the numbers back up to 12,000. The resulting overall percentage increase in private soldiers actually resulted in financial savings because the number of officers decreased along with the half-pay. By 1739 the number of foot regiments had increased back to twenty.[207]

With Britain's return to war in 1739, troop movement in and out of Ireland escalated in rapidity and volume once again. Ten foot regiments were removed in June 1739 with the remaining ten being doubled in size with new levies.[208] The following years saw the Irish government struggle to maintain the army at anything near the 12,000 limit.[209] In 1745 the number of regiments stood at three horse, three dragoons and six foot, with a total of 7,941 rank and file. The board of general officers made proposals in September to bring the total up to 11,725 men, NCOs and officers, by raising a new foot regiment and additional companies for other units.[210] However, the need for soldiers in Britain following the Jacobite rebellion further reduced the number of foot regiments to four and the dragoons to two.[211] As a result, parliament briefly discussed the idea of facilitating the raising of 4,000 men, though nothing more came of it.[212] At the other end of the spectrum, by the beginning of 1747 Lord Lieutenant Harrington was expressing his concern that the pending arrival of a horse and dragoon regiment into Ireland would push the number of soldiers above the 12,000 limit by 331 men. Even though three of the Irish establishment regiments were not actually in the country at the time, he pointed out that the 1699 limit had never been exceeded and that it was preferable to reduce the numbers to either 11,991 or 11,994.[213] But continuing fluctuations meant that towards the end of the year he was expressing concern at 'the regular troops in this kingdom being reduced ... to a number, which cannot but appear small and insufficient, in case of any foreign invasion'.[214] That summer the rank and file in four horse, four dragoon and four foot regiments had numbered only 6,425 effective men, with a further 828 absent.[215]

The conclusion of the war in 1648 resulted in another realignment of the British military, with the disbanding of regiments and the return of the Irish establishment to its peacetime role of maintaining a large proportion of the standing army. Before that occurred however, and in imitation of considerations entered into at the conclusion of war in 1713–14, the idea of increasing the size of the army was discussed, on this occasion to 16,000–18,000 men. A key stumbling block was whether or not such an action could be carried out in light of the legal limit set in 1699. That aside, the Irish lords justices were initially tentatively favourable, though their primary concern was the reaction of parliament to the increased cost, particularly in relation to guarantees that the additional soldiers, and more importantly their pay, would remain in Ireland. They also recommended that the ratio of officers to rank and file should be readjusted in favour of the latter so as to reduce the overall cost and advocated other cuts, especially on the pension list. Ultimately, however, Harrington could not get consensus on the matter and it was allowed to drop.[216]

A new establishment was transmitted from London in October 1748 for four horse and six dragoon regiments and twenty-six infantry battalions, comprising a total of 11,850 men, NCOs and officers. At the request of the Irish lords justices the number of battalions was changed to twenty-seven, with an overall increase in the total number to 11,946.[217] These alterations involved an additional dragoon regiment and twenty-one infantry battalions being sent to Ireland and the existing four horse regiments, five dragoon and four foot being reduced and two foot disbanded. Accordingly, the half-pay list more than doubled in size.[218] The reduction in numbers within units was therefore quite dramatic. There had been thirty troopers in each horse troop, fifty-nine in each dragoon troop and either ninety-five or ninety-six privates in each foot company on the old establishment, whereas the new establishment had only twenty-one men in each horse and dragoon troop and twenty-nine in each foot company.[219] Such significant reductions vividly demonstrated how the Irish establishment adapted to accommodate the needs of Britain's army and how the relationship between the number of regiments or battalions and the actual number of soldiers was very flexible. As Figure 5.1 demonstrates, these alterations also resulted in the cost of the army increasing, not least because of the much higher number of officers on the establishment, which reflected the fact that, because of the transfer of soldiers back to Ireland following the conclusion of war, the overall cost during the first half of the eighteenth century could on occasion be higher in peacetime than wartime.[220]

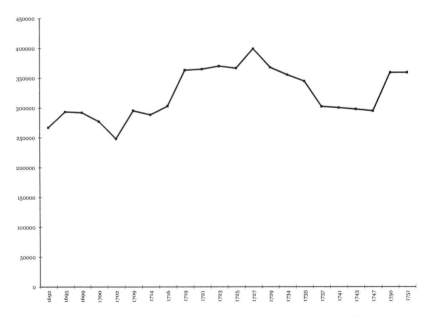

Figure 5.1: **The annual cost of the army in Ireland, 1692–1751.**[221]

Augmenting the Size of the Army, 1754–70

Imperial concerns in 1754–5 once more highlighted Ireland's role within the empire. Although officially still at peace, fighting between Britain and France in India and North America required regiments from Ireland, with the usual associated demands placed upon those that remained behind. In March 1755 the Irish government was instructed to ensure that the army was brought back up to strength with new recruits.[222] Yet by July the ongoing fluctuations in the number of units in Ireland meant that there were only 7,763 officers and men in total in the country, in four horse, six dragoon and fourteen foot regiments.[223] A month later the number of effective men had risen to 8,624, though draughts overseas continued to undermine such efforts. Recruitment of a further 1,880 men, coupled with four Irish establishment regiments overseas, would make up the 12,000 limit.[224] The new levies included six men per infantry company and five per horse and dragoon troop. In one month alone 3,740 men were added to the infantry regiments.[225] However, continued fighting in North America and the threat of a French invasion of England led to further removals. In October Lord Lieutenant Hartington warned parliament that the 'present critical state of affairs abroad demands a more than ordinary attention for the defence and security of this kingdom', to which end the King had ordered 'a proper augmentation … in the remaining regiments of foot'.[226]

The augmentation process had clearly been ongoing since March 1755, though the increasing demands from overseas led the Irish government by the end of the year to actively consider the practicality of increasing the establishment beyond the 12,000 limit. In December, the government intimated to London that Irish politicians were agreeable to maintaining the army in Ireland at 12,000 men while also supporting additional numbers overseas. The crux of the matter was whether the 1699 Disbanding Act was 'binding as to the number in times of danger'.[227] The British government was of the view that the 1699 act did not impede such a move, but that the consent of the Irish parliament should be sought.[228] The Commons duly complied with only one dissenting voice at the end of January 1756, addressing the King 'to increase the number of forces in this kingdom to 12,000 men complete'.[229]

By March 1756 the army stationed in Ireland comprised four horse regiments, six dragoons and eleven foot, with a combined total of 11,646 men and officers. A further 748 men overseas were paid from Ireland, which meant that the establishment had finally exceeded the 1699 limit.[230] However, the continuing demand for soldiers saw the government's thoughts turn simultaneously towards raising a further 3,000 men in order to bring the total to 15,000. Concern over the cost of such activity meant that parliamentary approval was desired first.[231] Also, despite the earlier exceeding of the limit by 394 men, it was now felt that the addition of 3,000 men would be best facilitated by following the letter of the law, which meant that it would have to be carried out under the authority of the Westminster parliament as the enacting assembly for the 1699 act. To that end, a timely and tactical message from the King on 23 March 1756 to the British parliament stating that he had carried out a general augmentation of his forces in light of the threat of a French invasion, resulted in both houses providing the necessary authority by addresses requesting that the army in Ireland be augmented.[232] A request to that effect was laid before the Irish Commons on 31 March, as a result of which the house promised to concur in any necessary security measures.[233] Orders were immediately issued for raising an additional eight men for every troop in the six dragoons regiments and two new companies for each of the twelve infantry battalions in Ireland.[234]

The complex movements of soldiers during 1755 and into 1756 presaged the formal outbreak of war between France and Britain. The ongoing war thereafter resulted in continued utilization of the Irish establishment in the manner of previous wars since the 1690s, but with one added difference: the 12,000 limit would be exceeded with increasing regularity as the logic of a permanent augmentation of the army started to become a *sine qua non* for the government at any rate. Such a development served to differentiate the Seven Years' War from those that had gone before, as Ireland's military role was accelerated further with the increasing demand for soldiers overseas requiring that the army was almost constantly involved in significant ongoing recruitment in order to ensure a sufficient supply of men abroad. While in the wars of 1689–97 and 1702–13 the number of soldiers stationed in Ireland had occasionally and briefly exceeded the limit, in the 1740s the number had regularly dropped significantly below that limit. From 1755 onwards however, the exceeding of the limit was more constant and dramatic than ever before.

At the time when parliament agreed to the augmentation to 15,000 men there were 10,571 soldiers in total in Ireland, comprising 479 cavalry, 1,149 dragoons, and 8,943 foot. Of these, 9,565 were considered fit for duty, the remainder either sick (454 with a further eighty-seven in hospital), on leave or otherwise occupied.[235] Thereafter throughout 1756 and 1757 the regimental agents were busy raising new levies. Alongside the 312 new men for the six dragoon regiments and the further twenty-four infantry companies ordered in April 1756, an additional 120 each of sergeants, corporals and drummers and 2,010 men required for twelve infantry battalions and three wholly new foot regiments were raised for Ireland.[236] As seen in Table 5.3, a series of accounts laid before the Commons in January 1760 demonstrated how this new reality had evolved since 1756. On only two out of twelve reported occasions, in March 1756 and May 1757, was the total number below the 12,000 limit. On all other occasions it was exceeded, rising as high as 17,372 in October 1756. Even when at its lowest in May 1757, it had risen above 12,000 later that same month. The degree of rapid fluctuation in numbers was also evident by the fact that in three instances, October 1756, May 1757 and March 1758, two sets of figures were given demonstrating that significant movement or recruitment had occurred at those times. None of the figures included the overseas soldiers paid from Ireland, which would have raised the numbers for March 1756 and May 1757 over the 12,000 limit as well.[237]

Table 5.3: Army numbers in Ireland, 1756–60

March 1756:	11,646	May 1757:	12,986
October 1756:	17,372	October 1758:	13,800
October 1756:	14,158	March 1758:	12,172
March 1757:	14,614	March 1758:	13,108
April 1757:	16,242	March 1759:	12,294
May 1757:	10,544	January 1760:	14,360

Such apparently healthy figures were not always the full story, however. The fear was almost ever-present that the balance would shift in favour of overseas demands. In January 1758 Lord Lieutenant Bedford claimed that, taking into consideration the numbers of soldiers always required in Dublin and other major locations, if any more infantry regiments were sent abroad he would struggle to get 'a body of above 4,000 infantry' to muster 'in any one place'.[238] In August he claimed the whole number of effective infantry 'amounts upon paper' to only 7,000,[239] while invasion fears in 1759 provoked him to claim that only 5,000 soldiers could be put in the field in the south-west given the need to retain others in the 'great towns for the security of the Protestants'.[240] By October the effective strength was 10,439 men in four horse, six dragoon and fourteen foot regiments.[241]

Parliament also continued to play a direct role in the process, passing a vote of credit in November 1759 for £150,000 for the 'necessary defence of Ireland'.[242] At the same time, however, a sense of discord in England at the apparent lack of enthusiasm within Protestant Ireland for defending the empire at a time of great danger, resulted in the Irish government agreeing to offers from eight individuals in Ireland to raise at their own expense army units ranging from troop to regimental strength.[243] Some opposition arose ostensibly on the grounds that the country could not afford to pay for more soldiers, though one Patriot MP, Edmond Sexton Pery, was less diplomatic when he asserted that 'it was greediness of rank and expectation of being continued after the peace, and not the service of the public, which had induced these many offers'.[244] In reality however all of the individuals involved had been informed that they would not be promoted above their current rank and had been refused permission to grant commissions to friends, family or others of their choosing.[245]

The raising of these new units saved the government money and time at first, but ultimately created an increased expense which Bedford feared would prompt complaints in parliament.[246] However, despite a degree of wrangling on the subject with two related divisions going in the government's favour by 109 to 37 and 114 to 28, in reality the objections of a minority made no difference to a done deal. Another vote of credit for the purpose, for £300,000, passed without a division at a time when Francois Thurot's landing at Carrickfergus served to focus minds once again upon the threat from France. This latest augmentation resulted in 5,108 men in one horse, one dragoon and five foot regiments and an artillery company being added to the establishment.[247]

Further offers to raise army units in Ireland were forthcoming while the war continued. In July 1760 permission was granted for raising an independent foot company, while in late 1761 Lord Lieutenant Halifax, who was tasked with augmenting the size of the army once again, accepted five of eight proposals for raising regiments.[248] However, in light of the number of augmentations already undertaken, careful management of parliament was required if voting of the necessary money was to be achieved. Demonstrating the opportunistic nature of politics, Halifax proposed that, on the basis of previous successes in this respect especially under Bedford's government, a message from the King

> expressing, or at least very strongly suggesting, that the French armaments (or the Spanish, if circumstances should admit) have, or probably will have this kingdom for one of their principal objects, would here, I am persuaded, have a very powerful and a very desirable effect.[249]

The suspicious movements of the French Brest squadron and the formal declaration of war with Spain at the beginning of 1762 provided the propaganda Halifax needed.[250] At that time the army in Ireland comprised two horse and seven dragoon regiments and sixteen foot battalions, plus an artillery regiment and four invalid companies, with an effective rank and file strength of 11,752, of whom 559 were sick. At the end of January Halifax ordered all absent officers, including recruiting parties, to return to Ireland, and all officers to return to their regiments. Orders were also issued for the new corps to be completed as soon as possible. Deficiencies of about 2,000 rank and file in the existing regiments were expected to be resolved by March, at which time the total number of horse, dragoons and foot, exclusive of the five new regiments of 3,900 men and the artillery regiment of 435 men, would amount to 16,065, inclusive of NCOs and officers.[251] Such figures indicated that the Irish establishment, both within and without Ireland, was about to top the 20,000 mark, which demonstrated how dramatically the system had been developed in light of the demands of the Seven Years' War.

All of this activity still had to be paid for. To that end, and in accordance with Halifax's earlier advice, a message was delivered at the end of January from the King to the Commons, expressing the dangers Ireland lay under by the 'unhappy, though ... inevitable rupture with ... Spain', the ensuing need for 'an immediate augmentation of five battalions to his forces', and the consequent 'unavoidable necessity' of asking for more money. After some debate, the Commons agreed to provide for the additional expense.[252] To make that promise effectual, in early February a vote of credit was passed for £200,000, which, as Halifax noted, occurred 'without a negative, or a single word of objection'.[253]

The 1759–60 and 1761–2 augmentations ensured that a higher number of regiments could thereafter be maintained in Ireland for the remainder of the war while also continuing to provide for the military requirements of the empire overseas. As demonstrated by Table 5.4, the plan was seen to work in that the absolute number of regiments stationed in Ireland from 1760 to 1763 remained higher than at any time since the first significant movements out of the country in 1755. The number on the Irish payroll overseas was also higher in those final war years.[254]

Table 5.4: The total number of regiments on the Irish establishment, 1755–63.

Year	Ireland	Overseas
1755	24	4
1756	22	4
1757	25	4
1758	22	5
1759	22	5
1760	30	5
1761	26	6
1762	31	6
1763	32	6

But as William III had discovered in 1697–9, it was difficult to maintain an augmented army in peacetime, and following the end of the war the Irish establishment was returned to its limit of 12,000.[255] Such an occurrence had not been in accordance with the government's wishes. As the war approached a conclusion in late 1762, attention had turned yet again towards ideas for maintaining a larger army in Ireland in peacetime. For Irish officials, MPs and other public figures the main focus was on the potential increased cost, while for government in London the primary concern was with the broader agenda of maintaining a larger peacetime army than ever before, including in America.[256] Archbishop Stone felt that a potential increase to 18,000 or 20,000 was not unobtainable if the question of cost was addressed.[257] At the end of the year the British attorney-general, Charles Yorke, delivered an official legal opinion that the 1699 Disbanding Act was still in force and that the army 'cannot be increased in time of peace without the authority of an act of parliament'. More pertinently, such an act would have to be passed in the Westminster parliament, as the 1699 act 'could not be controlled by any law passed in' Ireland 'nor by the royal authority alone'. As Yorke pointed out, the actual authority for the augmentations carried out during the Seven Years' War had been the addresses from the Westminster Lords and Commons in March 1756.[258] Although a bill was drafted to that end, objections from within government itself and the potential for more significant opposition from the Westminster and Irish parliaments resulted in the quiet dropping of the scheme in early 1763.[259] Although the plans for stationing a 10,000-strong army in America were already underway at that time, it has been suggested that the dropping of the Irish scheme gave added impetus to the American one and, thereby, to the imperial crisis which evolved over the following two decades.[260]

By the end of March 1763 the reduction of the army in Ireland to the 1699 limit was underway. With the notable exception of Lord Drogheda's regiment, most of those disbanded were the ones raised in Ireland as part of the two augmentations in 1759–60 and 1761–2. The reduction of the remainder involved disbanding six rank and file from each of four horse regiments, eighty-one from the royal regiment of dragoons and fifty-four from each of the five other dragoon regiments, 325 of various ranks from Drogheda's light dragoons, 486 of various ranks from each of eleven infantry battalions and a total of 1,185 from four more infantry regiments of which three were still abroad.[261]

The alterations undertaken for peacetime did not escape the scrutiny of parliament when it reconvened in late 1763. As detailed in Figure 5.2, a key issue was the fact that although the military establishment had been reduced to the limit in place in 1756, the cost and overall number of regiments had increased. In 1756 there had been four horse, six dragoons, and fifteen foot, while in November 1763 the dragoons had increased to eight and the foot to thirty.[262] Lord Lieutenant Northumberland feared that MPs would 'be more readily struck with the weight of the expense, than with the utility of the service'.[263] However, there were sufficient government supporters in parliament to ensure that the issue did not become a mainstay of a successful opposition campaign. On three occasions motions to address the King on the matter were readily defeated, with four divisions being decided 112 to 73, 124 to 58, 139 to 43, and 126 to 52.[264] One of the attempted addresses was intended to assert that the number of officers on the establishment had increased to such an extent that, in an echo of English anti-army ideology, it must 'raise just apprehensions for the constitution, not only of this kingdom, but of Great Britain'.[265] Such rhetoric was, in Irish terms, a new occurrence and also started to appear in the *Freeman's Journal*, a public mouthpiece for the Patriot opposition in the 1760s.[266] The proposed address was also intended to attack the increased number of regiments and the cost of the ordnance and the mostly absent general officers.[267]

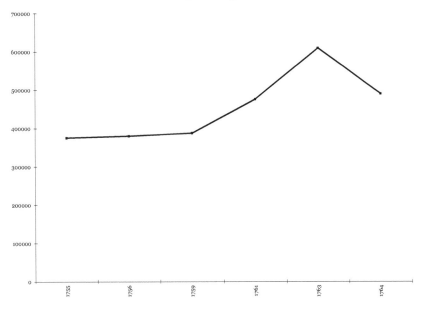

Figure 5.2: The annual cost of the army in Ireland, 1755–64.[268]

The example of the temporary augmentations of 1759–60 and 1761–2 and the failed endeavour at a permanent augmentation in 1763 served as precursors to a more sustained and eventually successful government campaign on the issue. That campaign was part of the wider British considerations for empire in the aftermath of the Seven Years' War, with the perceived need for greater centralization of power in London and increased financial contribution from the colonies towards the imperial war machine. Initial considerations regarding Ireland were entered into as early as 1765–6, though the need in the first instance for Westminster to legislate on the matter required a degree of coordination that was not yet evident in government circles.[269]

Throughout the years 1763–1767 the actual number of horse and dragoon regiments based in Ireland remained static at four and eight respectively. The foot regiments fluctuated between twenty and twenty-five. As detailed in Table 5.5, the number of officers, NCOs and effective men varied a bit more, ranging from a high of 11,357 in October 1763 to a low of 7,730 in July 1764. The fluctuation in numbers was owing to the system of troop rotation adopted for the empire in 1764 which had highlighted the fact that the reduced regiments on the Irish establishment were not compatible with regular rotation, having served their purpose more readily when such a requirement occurred in time of emergency only. It was therefore necessary to bring those regiments up to the same rank and file strength as all other regiments in the empire, a task entrusted to Lord Lieutenant Townshend who arrived in Ireland in October 1767 with instructions for a permanent augmentation.[270]

Table 5.5: Number of officers, NCOs and effective men in Ireland, 1763–7.

October 1763:	11,357	January 1766:	8,522
January 1764:	10,234	April 1766:	9,220
April 1764:	8,400	July 1766:	8,859
July 1764:	7,730	October 1766:	9,021
October 1764:	8,867	January 1767:	8,983
January 1765:	8,639	April 1767:	9,547
April 1765:	9,172	July 1767:	7,486
July 1765:	8,935	October 1767:	8,230
October 1765:	8,666		

Townshend's task was complicated by a variety of political factors centred around London's refusal to countenance the demands of the undertakers for getting an augmentation through parliament and the increasingly important public profile of the Patriot opposition.[271] For the first time since the permanent stationing of a standing army in Ireland in the 1690s, a rhetoric had emerged in political and public circles that replicated aspects of the much older anti-standing army ideology prevalent in England. By way of example, in January 1768 the *Freeman's Journal* made the grandiose assertion that 'it is universally confessed, that keeping up a standing army in times of peace is contrary to law, and dangerous to the liberties of the subject', a claim backed up by a printed resolution of the Dublin guild of merchants 'that a standing army is in its nature opposite and dangerous to civil government'.[272] Inspiration for such rhetoric came in part from a sense of Patriot solidarity with American opposition to the imposition of taxes by Westminster for support of a standing army, but at the same time was also utilized as a practical tool for advancing a home-grown agenda for political and constitutional reform that did not in fact comprise any real opposition to the army.[273] However, while these ideological arguments were propounded by those who openly opposed the augmentation, it was evident that in reality the primary concerns of most were the additional expense and the long-standing fear motivated by security and economic concerns that, even with the augmentation, 12,000 soldiers would still not be kept in Ireland.[274] While all of these arguments were contested by those who favoured the augmentation, the most salient point seemed to be that the opposition was the work of 'emissaries of faction'.[275]

The opposition of the parliamentary undertakers, the Patriots and independent country gentleman scuppered the first attempt to get the augmentation through parliament in early 1768. Townshend had addressed the Commons on the subject in April 1768, though an ensuing motion to address the King on the matter was defeated by 108 to 104 and was followed by a vote that Ireland could not afford the increased expense.[276] Yet as one proponent of the scheme pointed out, the plan for augmentation itself had not been rejected; instead, the Commons had 'declared their inability to lay any further burden on the establishment, so near the close of the present session, not having had sufficient time to consider the state of the country, and its resources'. At the same time, the Lords had given their full approbation to the scheme.[277] Such sentiments suggested that the augmentation could be successful if better managed. Likewise, the fact that the Westminster parliament had legislated in early 1768 to amend the 1699 act ensured that the proposal could be readily revived again when the opportunity arose.[278] In the summer of 1769 Townshend was empowered by the King to engage in negotiations on that score and to accept 'any modification which will not defeat its purpose'.[279] As a result, Townshend was confident that with strategic modifications, the most significant of which was an assurance that 12,000 men would be kept in Ireland at all times, the augmentation could be carried without the assistance of the undertakers.[280]

A new parliament was summoned in late 1769. Townshend did not refer directly to the augmentation in his opening speech, but raised the matter a few weeks later in mid-November when he informed the Commons that the King desired that 12,000 men should be constantly kept in Ireland except in cases of invasion or rebellion in Great Britain, and that in order to do so that army needed to be augmented to 15,235. Savings were then promised in other areas, including a reduction of the general staff officers.[281] Efforts were also made to counter the view put forward that 'the real object of this measure was against the Americans'.[282]

It was evident that the Patriots and others were not going to let the augmentation through without a fight. Two divisions regarding subsidiary motions went against the government by 83 to 90 and 77 to 93, though these defeats did not come as a surprise given that the Patriots had already been successful in divisions by 73 to 102 and 72 to 104 during the passage of their motion for consideration of 'what number of forces are necessary to be maintained within Ireland for its defence'.[283] Yet at the end of November the Commons agreed to grant £71,923 5s. for the payment of the extra 3,235 men for two years. Continuing Patriot opposition was seen in an ensuing defeated motion that the money was voted 'notwithstanding that we have reason to believe that the aforesaid sum is intended to be drawn out of this kingdom'.[284] However, support for the Patriots had evidently dwindled significantly as the government won two votes on the augmentation by 175 to 51 and 168 to 53.[285]

Despite continued opposition in the *Freeman's Journal*, the promised modifications had clearly helped in achieving such a turnaround.[286] More important however was the manner in which the augmentation was to be implemented, as Townshend had finally conceded that it was necessary to agree to 'the security of an Irish Act' in order to convince MPs of the government's sincerity.[287] Such a step represented a significant constitutional concession, as it gave the Irish parliament 'a certain power over the army which it had not possessed before'.[288] To that end, the heads of a bill were drafted for a new loan of £100,000 which included clauses for augmenting the army to 15,235 men and stating that 12,815 would always be kept in Ireland except in time of rebellion or invasion in Britain. The bill passed without difficulty and thereby Irish MPs got their coveted promise on the numbers stationed in Ireland enshrined in statute. The act also meant that for the first time ever the Irish parliament became an active player in controlling the size of the army, most particularly with respect to the additional men whose continued financial support was dependent upon biennial Irish parliamentary legislation.[289]

Prior to the 1769 augmentation, the establishment maintained four horse regiments, five heavy dragoons, three light dragoons, and twenty-five foot stationed in Ireland and five foot regiments overseas, comprising a total of 11,998 men. The augmentation brought the number up to 15,235 by moving three foot regiments to the British establishment and adding 126 privates, a quartermaster, nine sergeants, corporals and drummers, six mates and two fifers to each of the remaining twenty-seven foot regiments, thereby constituting a total addition of 4,218 men.[290] In 1773 it was revised to 15,046 as part of a scheme to equalize the number of men in cavalry regiments throughout the empire, which among other alterations required a minor reduction in the number of infantry in Ireland. It remained officially at that latter figure through the 1770s and into the 1780s.[291]

In theory, the augmentation was meant to ensure that 12,815 soldiers, made up of four horse, eight dragoon and twenty-two foot regiments (minus four companies for the Isle of Man) would be stationed in Ireland, with the remaining five foot regiments, comprising 2,420 men, serving overseas.[292] In reality however increasing demands meant larger and larger draughts of soldiers from Ireland, first with the outbreak of the American war of Independence in 1775–6 and the ensuing involvement of France in 1778, Spain in 1779 and the Netherlands in 1780, and thereafter with the even more demanding French Revolutionary and Napoleonic wars from 1793 to 1815. As the British Empire entered into a period of dramatic alterations and challenges, and ultimately consolidation and further growth, the role of the Irish establishment also changed. As more and more soldiers were required overseas, new solutions to home defence were needed as it became less realistic to even attempt to maintain anywhere near the 12,815 soldiers that were in theory legally obliged to be stationed in Ireland. In time of emergency the Irish parliament proved willing, however reluctantly, to consent to the withdrawal of more soldiers than was officially allowed.[293] But it also meant that new means of finding men were required. The Volunteers of the late 1770s represented a practical solution, but they were political, unofficial and potentially subversive. The government's preferred options were a reinvigorated and functioning militia, home-based 'fencible' regiments and, ultimately, the yeomanry.[294] However, the most dramatic change and conclusive alteration following the 1798 rebellion was the 1800 Act of Union, which finally did away with the separate Irish military establishment altogether.[295]

6 AN ARMY FOR EMPIRE

The Irish military establishment served a number of purposes. It provided a barracks for the single largest part of Britain's standing army in peacetime. It provided an army in Ireland for internal defence and policing and security from external threats. Last but not least, it provided soldiers for different European and colonial conflicts and concerns – an army for empire. This latter function however has either been overlooked or misunderstood by historians. It is therefore necessary to enter into a consideration of the draughts of soldiers and number of regiments sent abroad from Ireland, the number paid for out of Irish revenues, the locations to which they were sent, their purpose abroad, and their contribution to the British Empire and its expansion during the period 1692–1770.

It has been argued that the 'priorities of the eighteenth-century British army were at home or in Europe. It was only slowly turned into an instrument for protecting Britain's colonies or subjugating those of other powers.' For the first half of the century, colonial wars were 'limited ones largely waged by colonial forces ... or the troops of the East India Company'. However, from the middle of the century onwards 'there was a marked increase in the deployment of the army overseas'.[1] During the Seven Years' War, 20,000 British regular soldiers served in North America, while that number had increased to 50,000 by the time of the American War of Independence.[2] This level of commitment was not overly significant when considered in relation to the number of men voted by parliament for the army each year: the average figure was 76,404 during the Nine Years' War; 92,708 during the War of the Spanish Succession; 62,373 during the War of the Austrian Succession; 92,676 during the Seven Years' War; and 108,484 during the American War.[3] Peacetime figures were significantly less, though from the 1760s onwards the costs 'rose sharply with the augmentation of the garrisons kept permanently in the West Indies and North America'.[4]

Broadly speaking, Ireland's contribution to the British army overseas fits comfortably within such an assessment, and the importance of the Irish military establishment for overseas activities was prioritized in relation to these foregoing perspectives. First, when necessary, Ireland provided trained regular soldiers for service in the British Isles or on the Continent, with regiments sent overseas to areas of conflict in England, Scotland and mainland Europe, or to Britain's allies such as the United Provinces or Portugal, or to significant British possessions in or close to Europe such as Tangiers in the 1670–80s or Gibraltar after 1713. Second, soldiers from Ireland were dispatched to serve in the colonies, in particular in the West Indies and North America. However, this second role was proportionally more important in the first sixty years of the eighteenth century than it was to be thereafter when other British resources began to be turned to the same purpose, though the movement of soldiers out of Ireland also altered in emphasis because of the increasing demands for a military presence in the colonies after the Seven Years' War. Third, Ireland's peacetime establishment was at face value numerically more significant to the empire than its wartime establishment. However, the provision of a core of trained soldiers for an expanded army on the outbreak of war, the ongoing recruitment and training of new levies thereafter, the continuous draughts of such soldiers during the war, and the continued financing of a number of regiments while overseas can be less readily quantified in solely numerical terms, though by the time of the Seven Years' War a clearer and very significant picture began to emerge in that respect. Ultimately, the Irish military establishment in the period 1692–1770 served the purpose of filling a gap in military provision until such time as British government practice caught up with the British state's theory on the expansion of empire.

The usefulness of a separate Irish military establishment for British interests overseas was evident from the Restoration period onwards. The financial and manpower provision for the Tangiers garrison in the 1670s until its evacuation in 1684 was the first noticeable case in hand,[5] with the Irish treasury contributing £44,000–£62,000 per annum during those years, while at the same time a further £36,000 was apparently being sent to England for 'shipping to secure the Irish coast'.[6] The healthy state of Irish finances under James II was such that £30,000 per annum was being sent to England towards the pay of the army there as well.[7] In 1697, Trenchard argued against a standing army in England in part on the grounds that the army in Scotland and Ireland could be quickly brought to England's defence.[8]

But there was a balance to be struck with regard to sending Irish establishment soldiers overseas. The emphasis might shift over time, but the basic premise remained the same: the views of the Irish political nation had to be taken into account, for whom the main complaints were that the withdrawal of such soldiers undermined the security of the Irish Protestant interest and that the continuance of overseas regiments on Irish pay was an unsustainable drain of ready specie from the country. In the Restoration period Lord Lieutenant Ormond had complained that the withdrawal of soldiers 'undermined the regime and betrayed the loyalists they were there to defend',[9] reflecting a view that would be expressed on a regular basis during the eighteenth century and which served to remind all and sundry of the need to find the right balance between supply and demand in order for the system to work. Examination of the practical administrative and military logistics, alongside the politics, of sending soldiers overseas provides the necessary insight into the working of the system, but before so doing, it is necessary to assess the related issue of recruitment of Irish men into the army for overseas service.

Irish Recruitment for Service Abroad[10]

As was the case with recruitment for service at home, the question of Irish recruitment for service overseas was fraught with difficulties. The constant concern expressed by the government and leading Irish politicians that the recruitment of Church of Ireland Protestants denuded the country of the most loyal subjects was more pertinent if the regiments in which they served were actually sent overseas.[11] However, the question of Catholic recruitment for service overseas was often viewed differently. Even when Protestants could not bring themselves to trust armed Catholics within Ireland, there were enough individuals in government and elsewhere who could readily see the utility for Britain and the empire of facilitating the service of Irish Catholics overseas. Such practical approaches were evident from the 1690s onwards.[12]

In the aftermath of the 1689–91 war, overseas service with William III's allies was seen as an option for dealing with the numerous ex-Jacobite soldiers who had chosen not to go to France. While some had been sent in piecemeal fashion since June 1691 if not earlier,[13] between January and May 1692 a total of 2,150 such men were transported to Germany to serve with the Holy Roman Emperor.[14] Following a general rounding-up of Catholic priests and ex-Jacobite army officers owing to fears of a French invasion in late 1692,[15] in January 1693 Lord Lieutenant Sydney informed London that he was inclined towards sending some regiments of Irish soldiers 'into the Venetian service ... for I find a great number of officers who, without doubt, will be ready to do some mischief whenever it is in their power'.[16] In April a warrant was issued for the infamous ex-Jacobite officer, Colonel Henry Luttrell, to recruit 1,500 Irish Catholics for 'the service of the Republic of Venice', including any who were hiding 'out in the mountains'.[17] These troops were also successfully recruited and transported.[18]

The issue of recruitment for service overseas remained on the agenda whenever war, or the threat of war, was around. In 1702 William O'Brien, Earl of Inchiquin, proposed to the government that he raise a regiment for Jamaica, 'admitting Irish among them which may from time [to time] be recruited better from Ireland by one of the kingdom than any other'.[19] While it is unclear if Inchiquin was referring to Irish Catholics or Protestants in this instance,[20] there was no uncertainty as to the confessional allegiance of Thomas Dungan, the Catholic Earl of

Limerick who in August 1703 was sounded out by Secretary of State Nottingham about taking a commission as lieutenant-general in the army of Portugal, Britain's Catholic ally.[21] Limerick's positive response resulted in Queen Anne giving him permission to go to Lisbon in October,[22] by which time he had been joined by 'other Irish [Catholic] gentlemen', including Colonel Nicholas Purcell and Nicholas Browne, Viscount Kenmare, who all 'kissed her majesty's hand' before their departure.[23] At the other end of the Irish Catholic social hierarchy, in September 1704 a number of rapparees proposed an end to their outlaw activities if allowed to serve overseas.[24]

Irish Protestants were permitted in 1705 to enlist for marine service, while overseas regiments were allowed to recruit Ulster Protestants.[25] The idea of enlisting Irish Catholics into the navy was considered in 1706. It was believed there were 'able papists enough ... for the fleet, if an encouragement by proclamation were given them, but sure it is of dangerous consequence to do so'.[26] In December considerations were still ongoing. Lord Chancellor Cox believed that Irish Catholic recruits would serve best under their own commanders, with a 'colonel ... of the same gang' such as Henry, Viscount Dillon, who was 'the fittest in the world for it. He has a good estate but encumbered, his lady is the Duchess of Marlborough's niece. He has wit and vigour, and is the idol of the papists.' Cox also recommended Lieutenant Colonel John Bodkin from County Galway, 'one of the best officers they had, and doubtless would go'. Others included Cox's own favourite, Captain Florence McCarthy, a convert who had brought in a company of Irish soldiers just before the surrender of Limerick. Cox felt that if the matter was made public, there would be no shortage of able ex-officers offering themselves.[27]

In early 1707 Cox presented further options. He recommended Colonel William Burke and Lieutenant-Colonel Richard Burke, 'a man of more courage and military skill than of morality or estate as I hear'. However, he warned that 'the Irish formerly suffered too much in Spain for want of meat or money, that it must be known that England will pay them, else they won't stir, also the colonel must be known to the regiment, else few will enlist but with design to desert'.[28] In early 1708 Thomas Nylan wrote to the Catholic peer, Peter Plunkett, Earl of Fingal, 'about a commission in your lordship's regiment for the use of the Duke of Savoy', which was to consist of 1,200 Catholics.[29] It was rumoured at the time that Viscount Kenmare was also to raise a regiment for that service, though it was over a year later before an official request by him for permission to do so was acknowledged by Lord Lieutenant Wharton.[30]

One of the fears expressed in opposition to such schemes was that Irish Catholics would desert to the armies of Britain's Catholic enemies. The presence of the Irish brigades in French and Spanish service and their ongoing recruitment of Irish Catholics certainly made such a fear seem justified,[31] though the evidence was not as damning as might be expected.[32] Indeed, while the French formed army units from Irish deserters, so did the British both on the Iberian Peninsula and in Flanders.[33]

The advent of peace in 1713 saw the end of all such schemes.[34] Thereafter, while the surreptitious recruitment of both Irish Protestant and Catholic rank and file continued during the following two decades, especially when regiments were ordered overseas and needed to fill up their numbers quickly, it was not until war broke out again in 1739 that the subject was officially back on the agenda.[35] Protestant recruitment was allowed once more, though the idea of those soldiers serving abroad was still resisted, while that of Catholic recruitment for overseas was even less in evidence than during 1702–13.[36] This was particularly evident when, towards the end of the war in early 1748, Britain's Dutch ally requested permission to raise a regiment in Ireland for the service of the United Provinces. The proposal raised serious concerns, as it was believed that the intention was to raise the regiment

> in the most popish counties [and] ... that the private men should consist of papists; and indeed it would be highly prejudicial to the manufactures, as well as to the general interest of this country, to take such a number of ... Protestant subjects from hence, where the papists are so numerous, as to be generally computed, in the proportion of four to one.

Despite a list of potential Protestant officers being drawn up, fears about 'a great number of papists ... well disciplined, and inured to the military service' returning to Ireland after peace or joining the French service following disbandment ensured that the scheme ultimately came to nothing.[37]

Such opposition to Catholic recruitment continued through to the Seven Years' War. By then, Irish Protestant recruitment had become much more common, though again initially on the premise that those soldiers would serve only in Ireland.[38] Yet the pressures of war in time led to whole newly raised regiments of Irish Protestants serving overseas.[39] At the same time, unofficial Catholic recruitment continued and increased.[40] In 1758 Lord Lieutenant Bedford had no scruples in recommending that the marine officers be permitted

> to recruit in Munster and Connaught ... with directions not to be over nice in their enquiries as to the religion of the persons enlisted, by which means, not only a fine body of men would be obtained for the service ... but likewise great numbers, who on account of their religion, are not capable of entering into his land service, would be prevented from seeking their bread in the service of the enemies to their King and country.[41]

This scheme was agreed to in London later that year and by the end of 1759 between 1,100 and 1,200 men in various parts of Ireland had enlisted as marines.[42] In light of this success, Bedford proposed in 1760 that even more marines should be recruited from Catholic parts of Ireland as long as the war continued, a policy that was again pursued successfully.[43]

A more official endeavour at recruiting Catholics for overseas service was instigated in early 1762. Leading members of the Catholic community had been trying for some time, through loyal addresses and offers 'to assist in supporting his majesty's government against all hostile attempts whatsoever', to facilitate the repeal of the penal laws and enable Irish Catholics to demonstrate their loyalty to the Hanoverian regime in practical ways including serving in the army.[44] While such approaches were often fraught with difficulties within the Catholic community itself, especially in relation to clerical opposition,[45] in February a proposal was put to Lord Lieutenant Halifax by a leading Catholic peer, Robert Barnewall, Baron Trimleston, that genuinely appeared to have a broad base of Catholic support. Trimleston had informed Halifax that the 'great consumption of men' in the war had 'suggested to his majesty's Roman Catholic subjects … that means may possibly now be struck out, whereby they may give public proof of the sincerity of that loyalty they have long ineffectually professed'. He proposed that Irish Catholics, 'as they could not by law serve under his majesty', might instead be 'taken into his service, as elector of Hanover', or in whatever other manner the King might order. Trimleston's offer was supported by an address signed by four peers and sixty-one gentlemen, described by Halifax as the 'principal Roman Catholic noblemen and gentlemen of fortune in and near Dublin, and by one principal merchant, who signs for himself and the other merchants'.[46] At the same time a letter was circulated by the Catholic bishops to the clergy in every parish, which reminded Irish Catholics that 'the law of God, and your religion command you, in the strongest and most explicit terms, to be faithful, dutiful, and obedient to the powers, and governors, and vice-regents, which the omnipotent has placed over you'.[47]

While the idea of recruiting Irish Catholics for the service of Hanover was quickly dismissed on legal grounds, the fears of a pending Spanish invasion of Britain's Catholic ally, Portugal, led to a counterproposal for service on the Iberian peninsula.[48] In March 1762 a core group among the signatories of the Catholic address produced detailed proposals for raising seven wholly Catholic regiments for that purpose,[49] while in April the defeat by 26 votes to 9 and 113 to 64 in the Lords and Commons respectively of motions to examine the proposal led Halifax to believe that the 'doubts and objections' that had arisen 'from ancient prejudice' had been dispelled.[50] However, those opposed to the idea then chose to link the outbreak of agrarian disturbances in Tipperary, Cork, Waterford and Limerick with the Portuguese proposal.[51] The linking of this 'Whiteboy' unrest to Catholic recruitment served to heighten Protestant anxiety and, coupled with a declining demand for soldiers as the war began to come to an end, resulted in the scheme being dropped.[52] Instead, the Portuguese themselves were to be allowed to enlist men in Ireland 'without enquiring what religion they are'.[53] As for the 'outrages of the levellers', as Halifax described it, he recommended that, aside from hanging 'some of the ring leaders', there were 150 of the 'villains' in jail who would be good for the marine service.[54]

Despite such apparent setbacks, ultimately the relaxation of the regulation against Catholic recruitment came about as the demands for soldiers overseas increased.[55] As P. J. Marshall has pointed out, by the time of the Seven Years' War 'Irish Catholics ... were ... being recruited in large numbers' for overseas service, even if still 'unofficially'.[56] At the end of 1770 Townshend advocated such recruitment as a means of avoiding draining Ireland of Protestants. Although officially Catholics were still not to be enlisted, British-based regiments were now allowed to recruit throughout the predominantly Catholic provinces of Leinster, Munster and Connaught without needing to inquire into the religion of the new levies. This latter approach was helped by the replacement of the various religious-based oaths with a basic oath of allegiance in 1774, and a year later permission was given to recruit 'at large' in Ireland, resulting in further dramatic increases in Catholic numbers.[57] By 1776, sixteen out of the forty-four battalions serving in North America 'had originated in the Irish establishment and had been augmented to combat strength with Roman Catholics'.[58] However, the status of Catholic soldiers remained ambiguous until 1793, when it finally became legal for Catholics to take commissions in the army.[59]

Sending the Army Overseas

The question of Irish recruitment aside, the argument that Ireland contributed to the empire in the period 1692–1770 is predicated in large part upon the degree to which the standing army in Ireland genuinely provided a first port of call for soldiers, regardless of their individual ethnicity, to serve overseas. The evidence for such service is first and foremost to be found in the movement of soldiers in and out of Ireland and the reasons for such movements.

The logistics for the transfer or regiments in and out of Ireland were complex, and a process evolved over time. In the immediate aftermath of the 1689–91 war it was a priority to move regiments to new areas of conflict on the Continent. In November 1691 it was reported that all but 10,000 of the Williamite army in Ireland were to be shipped to England and then onwards to Flanders, though the number remaining was soon readjusted to 12,000.[60] By December the excess soldiers were on the move, with three regiments departing for Chester. Similar troop movements continued during the first half of 1692.[61] Such major military activity created pressing demands on the Irish government. In April, the lords justices bemoaned the lack of provisions, especially wheat and rye, in the major centres of departure at Cork and Kinsale where 'so many of the forces appointed for foreign service are shipping off'.[62] The financial accounts for all of these regiments were still being made up in March 1693.[63]

The demands on government in 1691–2 had been created primarily by the need to transport the army from a concluded war to a continuing one, and might therefore be perceived as a unique, once-off requirement. Developments in the following years were more pertinent for demonstrating the commencement of a process whereby Ireland began to function as an integral part of the empire as the provider of soldiers on an ongoing and structured basis. In August 1692 two regiments were ordered to the West Indies, while in July 1693 four new regiments were being raised in Britain in order to replace four others sent overseas from Ireland.[64] In February 1694 William III planned to move five foot regiments and one of dragoons to Flanders.[65] Although the lords justices requested that he reconsider, as such action would render Ireland exposed 'to any attempts from abroad or at home',[66] at least four foot regiments were sent overseas at that time.[67] In 1695 another new regiment was being raised for service in Ireland to replace others sent overseas.[68] More regiments were sent overseas during the remaining war years.[69] It was also the case that in all instances the regiments sent overseas were removed from the Irish establishment at the time of their departure, thereby ensuring that the Irish treasury did not have to pay for troops serving abroad at a time when Irish government finances were still in a process of recovery in the aftermath of the devastation wrought by the war of 1689–91.[70]

The advent of peace in 1697 saw a reversal of movement, with regiments returning to Ireland as part of the wider process of reducing the size of the peacetime army.[71] However, by 1701 the possibility of renewed war with France heralded a new phase in the overseas service of regiments on the Irish establishment.[72] In June twelve foot battalions comprising 5,000 men were despatched to Holland and removed from the Irish establishment, causing a serious reduction in the size of the army and resulting in four new regiments being immediately recruited in Ireland, apparently, as seems to have often been the case during the ensuing war, ultimately with a view to future overseas service as well. At the same time, one or two more regiments were raised in England for Irish service.[73]

A month later two foot regiments were ordered from Ireland to the West Indies. Initially it was intended that they be brought up to full strength with draughts from other regiments in Ireland. However, with twelve battalions already gone, Lord Chancellor Methuen warned that the remaining foot would be only 1,000 strong and that 'it is hard to imagine what effect this hath in the minds of the English here, who are always used to carry the consequences of things even further than there is reason'.[74] Instead, it was decided to recruit the extra men elsewhere, though as a destination the West Indies was much disliked and was known to result in significant desertion before departure.[75] The full extent of the problem was seen in October, when William III 'struck fifty-nine officers of the Irish establishment off the half-pay list when they refused to go to the West Indies'.[76]

With war now a certainty, in March 1702 levy money was issued to bring four foot regiments up to strength so that they could be put on board the fleet for a summer expedition to Cadiz being undertaken by Ormond. At the same time a horse regiment and a number of dragoon troops were sent to England, while at the end of the month a fifth foot regiment was ordered for embarkation.[77]

Although these various regiments were removed from the Irish establishment on departure, the two sent to the West Indies in 1701 were not. The decision to continue to pay them from the Irish treasury represented the commencement of a more regular practice only previously entertained in the 1670–80s and one that served on occasion to irritate and animate the Irish political community. In 1702 it was noted that £36,000 a year was being exported in cash from Ireland to pay these soldiers. In theory this money was meant to be repaid from England, but the reality was different.[78] Of four regiments going to the West Indies in mid-1702, three were on the Irish establishment, two of which had only been raised in Ireland the year before.[79] All three continued to be paid from Ireland while in the West Indies, with the English treasury making up the difference between the slightly lower Irish rates of pay and those on the English establishment.[80] At the same time Lord Inchiquin proposed to the Irish government that he raise a regiment for Jamaica,[81] were his father had served and died as governor in 1692.[82] By 1704 he was raising a foot regiment in Ireland.[83]

The question of financing the army while overseas was a recurring theme in parliament. Over time the practice became tolerated, if not wholly accepted, but it always required careful management and monitoring. At the end of 1702 when the lords justices sought the opinion of leading Irish politicians on the subject of convening a parliament, they had already identified that not paying for the three regiments in the West Indies would be welcomed by the Commons, and Lord Lieutenant Laurence Hyde, Earl of Rochester, had resolved to address that issue in London. However, the lords justices suggested that it was surely reasonable that Ireland should bear a part of the cost of the war, and that the expense of the West Indies regiments bore no proportion to what England paid. Solicitor-General Brodrick could not resist the opportunity to discomfort the Tory-dominated administration by suggesting that the state of the Irish economy was such that it was impossible to continue such payments anyway, particularly given that exporting ready specie overseas for army pay was draining off Ireland's running cash. He also argued that Ireland had 'borne more than double, nay treble … [its] proportion of what hath been spent since the revolution by means of it and the war with France, regard being had to the trade and wealth and sufferings of both kingdoms'.[84]

When parliament finally convened in September 1703, the issue was still central to considerations. Placing emphasis in his opening speech on his desire to serve his 'native country', Lord Lieutenant Ormond stated that he had 'all the assurances that can be given, that the regiments in the West Indies ... shall soon return, and I will use my utmost endeavour, that the whole revenue may be expended in this kingdom'.[85] In October, the government's negotiations with Speaker Brodrick over supply included the latter's expressed desire, which remained unfulfilled, that 'England ought to pay back the £40,000 the West India regiments have cost this country'.[86] Nor did it help the government's case when it was reported that a further £15,606 7s. 5d. had been paid in subsistence to the three regiments in the West Indies, though they still had to be cleared for their full pay from 31 April 1703.[87] In the end, the government's request for a supply of £170,000 for two years was rejected in favour of £150,000, and while many factors had contributed to that decision, the focusing of attention on the regiments in the West Indies had certainly assisted the opposition's cause.[88]

However it was still evident that imperial demands outweighed political ones, given that by January 1704 four other regiments were being sent to the West Indies, apparently to replace those sent in 1702, in what appeared to be an embryonic phase of the later official policy of rotating regiments from place to place within the empire. As usual, the process was drawn out by the need to fill up the regiments to active service strength. This included issuing £1,000 per regiment for new levies, though the cost of new recruits and transportation ultimately was to be paid from England. Even then, the Irish government's cash-flow problems were still evident as it struggled to clear the pay of five or six regiments going overseas at that time.[89] Nor did the matter go away as a political issue. In the 1705 session some of the opposition 'pretended the demand for clearing the West India regiments ... might not be allowed'.[90]

The more traditional pattern of regiments being removed from the Irish establishment upon going overseas continued for those sent to the continent, as the war placed increased demands on Ireland. For example, in April 1703 two regiments were embarked for Holland.[91] However, the real focus of attention was on the Iberian Peninsula. In June the review of the army by the Lord Lieutenant at the Curragh in County Kildare was followed by the embarkation of three regiments for Portugal, which involved raising new levies, including recruitment in England, and the sale of dragoon horses with a view to purchasing new mounts overseas. At the same time several other regiments had been transported to England.[92]

The transfer of soldiers from Ireland required complex logistical as well as military preparations. In June 1704 plans for an expeditionary force for Portugal included victualling of recruits raised in Ireland. By the end of the month the government reported that if the convoy arrived soon and the winds were fair, they could embark them all by the middle of July. However, by late July there was still no word of the convoy, and the preparation of the transport ships which were to gather at Kinsale was still at least three weeks from completion, with particular problems arising over the arrangements for horses. There were claims that Irish horses were unfit for dragoons, though it was also the case that fitting out ships for transporting horses was a costly business, requiring slings, water vessels, racks and stalls among other things. The cost of horses, levy money and transportation was to be reimbursed from the English treasury.[93] Thus, while all of the work was done in Ireland to put together the expeditionary force, the cost was ultimately shouldered by England.

Lord Donegal's regiment, which had previously been in the West Indies in 1702–4, was among those being sent to Portugal, though the need to clear their pay arrears had reached a critical point, as soldiers were deserting and a mutiny was feared. By late August the transports were ready though there was still no convoy, which was essential given the reports of four French frigates waiting off Cape Clear. As a result, the transports were moved from the open harbour in Cork to the safer location of Kinsale under the protection of Charles Fort. In November the transports finally sailed. A total of 1,600 men had been recruited for the expedition from ten regiments, though two of those were soon to be sent overseas as well, depleting the army in Ireland even further. It was unsurprising that Ormond warned of the dangers of always taking draughts from the army.[94]

In January 1705 attention was briefly directed elsewhere when three regiments, including another returned from the West Indies, were ordered 'to go on board the fleet, pursuant to directions' from London.[95] However, the organizing of expeditionary forces for Portugal was soon back on the agenda with the adoption of plans to 'succour Catalonia'.[96] On this occasion, the lords justices expressed their concern for security in Ireland with a depleted army.[97] The preparations went ahead regardless, though the process was slow and drawn out, commencing as early as May though still incomplete in December. The transport ships had still not arrived in Kinsale by January 1706. In late March it was reported that the fleet had finally sailed for Cadiz.[98] At the same time, plans to raise six foot regiments and one of dragoons in England for service on the continent facilitated the removal of large numbers of French pensioners from Ireland. These men had been looked to before in 1703–4 to serve in Portugal and Savoy with at least 113 leaving the country at that time. In 1706 they proved very willing once again, as too many went over for that purpose, 107 of them returning in October with orders for the reinstatement of their pensions.[99]

Plans for a further expedition in late 1706 appear not to have been fully implemented. The transport ships that had returned in October from Spain were discharged rather than put to further use, but by February 1707 another expedition was being prepared, with four regiments being sent on this occasion.[100] The desire for sea clothing for the soldiers was dependent on whether the items could be ordered and paid for by the English treasury.[101] The Irish government claimed to be doing 'all that is possible to make the officers complete their regiments', with recruiting officers at work in England and Scotland and new recruits arriving daily.[102] As before, these preparations were tempered by government concerns at the impact upon home security.[103]

Yet the demand for soldiers still had to be met. By 1707 about 29,000 'British or British-paid troops were serving in the Iberian peninsula', and would continue to do so until the war ended.[104] Hence in October 1708 at least two more foot regiments were ordered to Portugal. A group of thirty-eight French pensioners ordered to Kinsale in August may have been intended for these regiments, though they were still waiting for transport at the end of November.[105] In early 1709 another three regiments were required, including Inchiquin's raised in 1704, which had until then functioned as support for his governorship of the fort and town of Kinsale. Despite his offer to serve overseas in 1702, by 1709 he believed such service would ruin him and requested that his regiment remain where it was.[106]

The security concerns raised by all of these movements were recognized in England. As instructed from London in March 1709, Lord Lieutenant Wharton offered reassurance to the Irish parliament 'that the troops which have been or shall be drawn from thence shall be forthwith replaced'.[107] In part that promise was aimed at alleviating concerns in the aftermath of the Franco-Jacobite invasion threat of the previous year.[108] Yet despite the evident uneasiness in Ireland over the depleted army, in June 1709 a dragoon regiment was dispatched abroad as were three more foot regiments which continued to be paid from Ireland while overseas, much to the dissatisfaction of Irish MPs in 1711 when it was noted that £20,000 had already been sent abroad for pay and more was still owing.[109] At the same time London raised the idea that five regiments in Spain that had survived the defeat at Brihuega in December 1710 should be placed on the Irish establishment while continuing overseas, but the Irish government successfully resisted the plan on the grounds that it would be too disruptive in the Irish parliament.[110]

As the war began to wind down during 1712, the movement of soldiers started to be reversed. In August orders were issued in London for three regiments stationed in England to march to Ireland.[111] Following the war's conclusion in 1713 Lord Lieutenant Shrewsbury assured the Commons that any supplies voted would, 'as much as possible, be spent among yourselves'. To that end, the Queen had 'ordered the two regiments of foot, which being upon the Irish establishment are yet in Great Britain, to be sent over' as soon as possible.[112]

However, the end of the war also brought significant change in the requirements for overseas service. Gibraltar, captured by an Anglo-Dutch fleet in 1704, was in accordance with the Treaty of Utrecht to remain in British hands. A garrison was needed, and Ireland was turned to for a regiment in early 1714, which marked the beginning of decades of continuous provision of regiments on the Irish payroll for the garrisoning of what was to become, along with Minorca which soon thereafter was also manned by Irish-paid soldiers, Britain's key strategic location in the Mediterranean.[113]

Gibraltar and Minorca aside, in peacetime the expectation was that the amount of movement in and out of Ireland would reduce alongside the disbanding of large parts of the British army elsewhere. Yet the succession of George I in August 1714 impacted upon the overseas use of the Irish establishment with the re-emergence of a significant Jacobite threat in Britain. In August and early September 1714 the half-pay officers in Ireland were put on standby to go to Scotland on active service.[114] Although leading Irish politicians and members of the government continued to warn that political discontent was best avoided by ensuring that the soldiers 'remain in Ireland while they are paid by it',[115] by the summer of 1715 the mounting evidence of an intended rebellion resulted in more troop movements to Britain. At the end of July three regiments were sent to County Down in order to embark for Portpatrick in Scotland.[116] By the end of August all three had been transported, and three more had been ordered to England. The lords justices claimed a lack of financial resources for transportation and the fact that Irish Catholics were 'vastly superior to the Protestants and are at all times ready to rise upon us if an occasion offers' as reasons against sending the further three regiments but were undermined by the fact that one of the regiments offered to pay their own transport costs and set off for Chester for that purpose and, more generally, because the Irish treasury would actually save the salary costs of the three regiments once they left Ireland.[117]

Following the outbreak of rebellion in September, more regiments were required in Britain.[118] In early October five more regiments were sent to Scotland, raising the number sent there to eight.[119] In total, twelve regiments were sent to Britain during this period, a fourth having been dispatched to England in the interim.[120] Yet even in the midst of rebellion, the Irish government remained wary of any attempt to get the Irish parliament to agree to subsist those regiments while in Britain.[121] That said, Ireland's military contribution to the defeat of the Jacobite rebellion and the securing of the new Hanoverian regime, and with it the empire, was still very significant. Several years later, in a discourse aimed at highlighting Ireland's financial contribution to Britain since the Glorious Revolution, Archbishop King noted that the regiments were dispatched to Scotland in 1715

> before any could be sent from England, and four regiments to Preston and this was done with all expedition and cheerfulness imaginable, and if circumstances had required it all the rest would have been sent in the same manner, for the Protestants were aware that England is the head and if that be secured the members will certainly in time be taken care of.[122]

The removal of the Jacobite threat and the commencement of a lengthy period of peace to 1739 saw a significant reduction in the demand for soldiers overseas.

Occasionally the threat of war resulted in plans for significant movements, such as in 1717 when the possibility of an invasion by Sweden of Hanover resulted in a number of Irish establishment regiments being put on standby for embarkation.[123] The short-lived hostilities with Spain in 1718–20 and again in 1727–9 also resulted in greater concern for security in Ireland and the need for soldiers overseas.[124] In 1719 four regiments were sent to England for a planned expedition but were continued on the Irish establishment while abroad, while in 1722 six regiments were sent to England.[125]

The most significant exceptions to the peacetime rule, however, were the Irish establishment regiments which were rotated in and out of Gibraltar and Minorca during the 1720s and 1730s.[126] The demands of maintaining this permanent presence were seen in 1719 when seven regiments paid from Ireland were already overseas at those locations and in 1725 when a foot regiment sent back to Ireland had only seventy-seven men owing to draughts taken before embarkation in order to maintain the regiments remaining behind. As usual, the difference was made up from draughts from other regiments in Ireland and the raising of new levies.[127] In 1727 it was recorded that there were six regiments stationed in Gibraltar that were on the Irish establishment.[128] All of this activity was summarized in an account from 1728, detailed in Table 6.1, which demonstrated that a total of thirty regiments and one battalion had been supported overseas at one point or another between May 1718 and late 1728.[129]

Table 6.1: The regiments on the Irish establishment employed in England and abroad, 1718–28.

Number of Regiments	Embarkation	Return
3	May 1718	July 1718
1	July 1718	July 1719
1	July 1718	November 1719
1	July 1718	December 1720
2	March 1719	December 1719
2	March 1719	September 1721
4	August 1719	December 1719
1	June 1722	December 1722
4	August 1722	December 1722
2	July 1725	August 1725
1	August 1725	October 1725
1	August 1725	May 1728
1 [battalion]	May 1726	July 1726
2	June 1726	July 1726
2	June 1726	May 1728
1	June 1726	still abroad
2	February 1727	still abroad

The sending of regiments overseas in general, and especially the maintaining of some of them thereafter on the Irish establishment, remained a point of contention for the Irish parliament. In reality, MPs were happy enough if those sent overseas were replaced with new levies or regiments to bring numbers back up to strength in Ireland, and there was also a begrudging acceptance that some degree of contribution to overseas costs was a reasonable expectation on the part of the Crown. However, it was important to MPs to make it clear that such contribution should not be taken for granted or escalated in size and cost. Complaining about it helped to keep government cautious in its actions, as in the 1719 session when the view was expressed that they were 'ready to provide for the establishment while they are enabled to do it by the monies circulating among themselves at home'.[130]

By 1729 Lord Lieutenant Carteret was able to point out to parliament that three of the six regiments overseas in 1727 had been sent back in the interim and offered his assurance that 'the rest shall be ordered back, as soon as the circumstances of affairs will permit'.[131] Such a promise was not sufficient to placate the Commons. The continued presence of Irish establishment regiments in Gibraltar was included among the complaints about expenditure, while little heed was given to the government argument that such expenditure contributed to 'the common defence of England and Ireland'.[132] As a result, it proved difficult to get the Commons 'to state the whole debt, and to take it upon them, ... specially when near £70,000 of the money to be raised is to be remitted to England; being an arrear on the account of absent regiments', which simply served to further increase the pressure to get the supply bill and associated loan passed in parliament.[133] Once the bill passed, however, at the beginning of 1730 the deputy vice-treasurer was able to remit £40,000 in ready specie to the pay office in England as part of that arrear.[134]

The three regiments overseas in 1729 were still abroad when parliament reconvened in late 1731. At that time, Lord Lieutenant Dorset offered his assurance that the supplies to be voted 'shall not only be most frugally applied to the purposes for which they are intended, but that they shall, as much as possible, be spent amongst yourselves', and that towards that end 'two of the regiments ... in service abroad, [are] to be immediately brought back ... and from the happy circumstances of affairs in Europe, I have the greatest reason to hope, that the other will be soon recalled'.[135] On the back of another loan voted in the 1731–2 session, further money was remitted to pay the overseas soldiers.[136]

When parliament reconvened in late 1733 only one regiment remained overseas in Gibraltar.[137] In early 1734 the sum of £6,020 was still owed to the British treasury for the regiments that had been abroad until 1732 and £9,079 for the one remaining in Gibraltar.[138] That paled in significance though when a further six regiments were sent to England and two to Scotland in April–May. The cause of such significant movement was the French preparations of a fleet and transport ships at Brest for a possible descent on Danzig (Gdansk). The eight regiments were brought up to full strength with draughts from those remaining in Ireland.[139] Such activity did not go unnoticed. Even 'upon the close of a session, [it] has put us in no little hurry, and would alarm the people here very much, if they did not comfort themselves with the hopes, that the kingdom may in a little time expect the troops back again to protect them'. More significantly however was 'the money, which they, with great sorrows apprehend, must follow the men'.[140]

All eight overseas regiments were still being bankrolled by the Irish treasury over a year later. In July 1735 the lords justices expressed their concern that the general discontent about paying for soldiers overseas was significantly heightened by the current situation, as people were now calculating that 'near a fifth part of the whole revenue of Ireland which used to circulate among them is now to be remitted into England', which would have detrimental effects upon trade and commerce in general. They also feared that the issue might threaten the supply in parliament unless the pay due to the overseas regiments was respited until the end of the year.[141] However, by the time parliament did convene in late 1735 the eight regiments had actually been removed from the Irish establishment, with new levies being raised to strengthen the remaining units which resulted in an overall financial saving.[142] In early 1736 all eight were ordered back to Ireland, thereby necessitating the reduction of all regiments to the normal peacetime strength. The hazards of early modern travel were seen in the fact that part of one regiment perished at sea on the return journey.[143] The regiment in Gibraltar since 1726–7 was still there in 1738 and was owed three years pay of £27,263, but it was expected back in Ireland soon.[144]

It was not until the outbreak of war in 1739 that significant movement overseas commenced once again. The pattern of departed regiments being removed from the establishment was also reintroduced in most instances, as in June 1739 when ten regiments embarked for England and April 1742 when a horse regiment, two dragoon and four foot were sent to the West Indies.[145] In September 1745 two foot regiments were sent to Scotland to assist in putting down the Jacobite rebellion and likewise were transferred to the English establishment.[146] One of the regiments, the Royal Scotch, broke and retreated without fighting at Falkirk, an occurrence that Chesterfield had warned might happen given that they were so 'absolutely a Scotch corps'.[147]

Other overseas regiments however remained on the Irish establishment. A dragoon regiment and two foot sent to England in March 1744 continued on Irish pay up to the end of 1747 at least, costing £132,737 7s. 4d. plus a further £10,993 15s. 9d. for the rate of exchange.[148] Speaker Boyle was very keen to emphasize that this cost was something that 'Ireland does not complain of, though it feels [it], since the necessity of the war requires it'.[149] At other times draughts were taken from regiments instead, which did ensure at least that they ceased to be a burden to the Irish treasury after departure, such as in late 1741 when 720 draughts embarked for America, December 1743 when 474 draughts were taken from the cavalry and dragoon regiments, and January 1744 when 1,400 men were taken from the foot regiments for Flanders.[150] In February further draughts were briefly delayed when the movements of the Brest fleet and the Young Pretender suggested a possible invasion of Ireland, though within a month calm had been restored and the men were shipped out.[151] In May 1745 draughts were made of 1,200 men from the six remaining foot regiments in Ireland in order to replace those lost at the battle of Fontenoy, while in June 1747 a further 660 soldiers were taken out of the four remaining foot regiments.[152] At the end of 1746 another regiment had been sent overseas, but a cavalry and dragoon regiment were sent back to Ireland which suggested a lessening of the demand during the final year of the war.[153]

All of the regiments and draughts of soldiers sent overseas during the war demonstrated once again the importance of the Irish establishment for Britain. When war first broke out, a large number of full-strength regiments were quickly transported from Ireland, followed by more in ensuing years. The constant raising and training of new levies to fill up the remaining regiments thereafter facilitated the shipping of thousands more men abroad on a regular basis as well. The crises of Fontenoy and Scotland in 1745 were also addressed with significant military aid from Ireland.

As before, the conclusion of war required a realignment for the British army with the disbanding of regiments and the return of the Irish establishment to its peacetime role.[154] The brief and unsuccessful toying in government with the idea of permanently increasing the size of the army to between 16,000 and 18,000 soldiers resurrected the traditional concern about the detrimental economic effects of money leaving the country to pay overseas soldiers. As one government official put it, the 'nation would be better pleased to maintain an additional quantity of troops' only if they were all to 'spend the money that was to be raised in the kingdom', with the only exception being in time of national emergency.[155] Even the deputy vice-treasurer, Luke Gardiner, 'began to be uneasy for want of some authority' to pay the regiments abroad.[156]

Despite such concerns, the 1750s were to witness an escalation in both the number of overseas regiments paid from Ireland and the number of regiments and soldiers provided for the British establishment. In 1749 a battalion was sent to America,[157] while at the end of March 1750 it was decided in London that the necessity of supporting the settlements in Nova Scotia required that a foot regiment be sent from Ireland. Three regiments were to cast lots to decide which would go, the loser making the journey. While the cost of victualling and transport was to be paid by Britain, the regiment 'when arrived there, will be on the Irish establishment'. The King did not feel this was too much of a hardship, especially as the one regiment already in Nova Scotia, although ostensibly paid from Ireland was actually funded by Britain.[158] Although not usually countenanced, in this instance the wives and children of the soldiers were allowed to go as well. To that end, in a regiment of ten companies, 116 women and fifty-two children were willing to go. By May 1750 the losing regiment was on its way to Halifax, Nova Scotia.[159]

Officially the Irish establishment continued to support one overseas regiment during 1751–3.[160] However, at the end of 1751 it was noted in the Commons that £82,574 9s. 6d. plus £7,997 12s. 1d. for exchange rates had been sent to England on account of regiments abroad in the previous two years. These figures would suggest that more than one overseas regiment was still on the Irish payroll, or that significant arrears were owed to the British treasury.[161] Even with a degree of inflation in costs over the first six decades of the eighteenth century, the number of regiments that might be paid out of about £41,000 in one year could be anywhere between two and four, depending on the type of regiment, its manpower and whether in peacetime or wartime.[162] In 1753 however only £19,652 19s. 1d. was sent to England for overseas regiments in the previous two years, while in 1755 that figure was £27,962 12s. 10d., suggesting that only one regiment was indeed being paid overseas until 1754 at any rate.[163]

From 1754 onwards the demands placed upon Ireland started to increase remorselessly as conflict escalated in India and North America and renewed war with France in Europe became more likely.[164] In January a foot regiment was ordered to augment its numbers to full strength with draughts from other regiments in order to go to India. It then spent four years in India, during which time its numbers were decimated.[165] In October 1754 two regiments were ordered to North America, but both first required draughts of fifty men each owing to men having been taken from them to facilitate the regiment sent to India.[166] All three regiments were removed from the Irish establishment.[167] In March 1755 increased numbers were on the move with preparations underway for two regiments to go to Scotland and four to England, all of which were also to go onto the British establishment. Eventually a total of eight regiments were removed from the Irish establishment in that month alone.[168] However, even with such significant movement off the Irish establishment, in August Ireland was still able to send four regiments to the West Indies which all remained on the Irish payroll and by early 1756 accounted for a total of 1,496 Irish establishment soldiers serving abroad.[169] By that time, three more regiments had been ordered to America and onto the British establishment.[170]

These increasing demands from London caused Lord Lieutenant Hartington to negotiate the first of several augmentations of the size of the army in Ireland, though he warned London 'against sending any more troops from hence. ... I have represented the jealousy of having the money spent out of the kingdom, and that I could not answer for the consequences'.[171] However, the continuing rapid movement of soldiers in and out of Ireland prompted the Commons in March 1756 to request an up-to-date account of affairs. The ensuing report noted that there were two foot regiments out of Ireland with 374 men and officers in each, giving a total of 748. Combined with those in Ireland, it brought the number over the 12,000 limit by 394 men, as had been agreed by parliament in January.[172] However, a degree of obfuscation may have been employed in the report, as more than one government official had already committed to paper the fact that double that number of regiments and men were overseas at that time.[173] By July 1756 it was noted that of six Irish regiments serving in the Americas and India, four were still on the Irish establishment even though they should have been removed at the time of their departure. It took several months to resolve the problem.[174]

The movement of soldiers overseas continued unabated, forcing the government to quickly negotiate a further augmentation of the army.[175] Once again, the Lord Lieutenant warned about not sending the extra soldiers overseas 'without absolute necessity'.[176] Yet the demands of the war were such that the pressure for soldiers abroad only increased. In September 1756 another regiment and twenty-four additional companies of about 1,100 men were sent overseas,[177] while in January 1757 six more regiments totalling about 5,200 men were ordered to America, taking with them a large number of men that had already been raised in Ireland when they had been completed to 700 privates per unit as well as an additional 587 draughts each from the remaining Irish regiments in order to increase them to the correct size for the American establishment.[178] In July two highland battalions were sent to North America along with apprehended deserters from other regiments already sent overseas. The following month another draught was made from the foot regiments in Ireland of 520 men who were embarked for America also.[179]

With such significant movement overseas it was not surprising that in late 1757 the Commons requested another detailed account of affairs. The resulting report demonstrated that between March 1755 and May 1757 eighteen foot regiments plus twenty-four additional companies had been sent overseas and removed from the Irish establishment, accounting in total for 13,482 soldiers. A further four overseas foot regiments still paid from Ireland accounted for 1,496 soldiers.[180] At that time, there were also a further 12,986 soldiers in Ireland, thereby demonstrating that in a three-year period, the Irish establishment had been able to accommodate over 27,964 men, furnishing 14,978 of them for overseas imperial service.

Such successful provision of soldiers served only to ensure continuing demand and increasing pressure on government in Ireland. In January 1758 a regiment which had recently been transferred from England was sent to America with draughts of 100 men from Irish units.[181] The same regiment had previously been in Ireland in 1749, having been stationed in Minorca before that.[182] It was now to continue on the Irish establishment while in America, suggesting that despite its peregrinations since the 1740s, it is possible that it was constantly paid from Ireland throughout that time. The regiment's transfer to America prompted Lord Lieutenant Bedford to take issue with London on the matter:

> This kingdom has been so drained within this twelve month past ... that I think it absolutely incumbent on me ... to represent to [the King] ... that I think, (in concert I believe with all his Protestant subjects in Ireland) that no further diminution of the infantry here can be made without the utmost hazard of the peace and safety of this kingdom in the present critical circumstances of affairs.[183]

Despite Bedford's concerns, however, in June three dragoon regiments were ordered overseas. Again, Bedford protested and warned of a growing sense of insecurity in Ireland and the concomitant need to raise new levies for home service.[184]

Following a relative lull in troop movements during the remainder of 1758 and first half of 1759, the process picked up once again in September when orders were issued for draughts of two men from each infantry company remaining in Ireland in order to fill up the British regiments in Germany.[185] Although the orders were carried out, with draughts of nine officers and 278 NCOs and men, Bedford still felt it necessary to point out that such demands were undermining Ireland's ability to restore to working order regiments decimated overseas, which constituted another aspect of Ireland's military purpose. Three such units had been transferred to Ireland in 1758–9, one of which landed from India with only seventy-six men, and two others with only 102 and 189 men respectively. In part the reason for their small numbers was that they had already had draughts taken from them before they came to Ireland, which raised concern that the men left in the regiments were not the most useful anyway.[186]

In late 1759 the Commons once again asked for an update on affairs. The resulting account showed that since the last reported movements up to May 1757 a further three regiments had left the country and been taken off the establishment along with a further draught of 287 soldiers from various regiments, comprising in total 2,607 soldiers. During the same time, five overseas regiments with 2,280 soldiers had been continued on the Irish establishment until October 1758, when one had returned to Ireland thereby reducing the number paid overseas to 1,936.[187]

Such activity was an ongoing process. At the time of the report, orders were issued to draught one man per dragoon troop in Ireland, to a total of thirty-nine men, to complete the Enniskillen regiment which was serving in Germany, while two cavalry regiments were ordered to the same country. Both regiments were first brought up to a strength of forty-nine private men per troop with draughts from other Irish mounted regiments which thereafter recruited new levies as replacements. Although the expense of recruiting, new clothing and horses was paid from Britain, Ireland continued to contribute the amount it had previously paid for salaries for those two regiments during the whole of their time abroad. The difference in pay was made up by Britain. In May five foot regiments were also sent overseas.[188]

During 1761 the main activity seems to having been the taking of draughts from various regiments, though in February 1762 orders were issued for two regiments to go to Portugal, both of which were from among the most recently raised units in Ireland. They were augmented to a strength of 1,000 soldiers each from other newly raised Irish regiments. Care was to be taken that 'those two corps so completed, shall consist, as much as possible of such men, as, from their suspected religious principles, are least to be trusted with the defence of Ireland, in case of actual danger'. Two Scottish regiments were sent to Ireland at the same time.[189]

When the Seven Years' War had commenced the British government's policy for the North American theatre of war appeared to have been for local colonial forces to provide the bulk of the military requirements. Any regular regiments sent from the British Isles were to be brought up to full strength with recruits from America. However, the reality had quickly proved very different and the commitment of regular soldiers from the British Isles had become much more substantial than originally intended.[190] In this respect Ireland had clearly played a significant part, including paying for an increasing number of those regiments while in North America and providing ever-increasing numbers of soldiers for the war on the Continent. Indeed, the Irish establishment had sustained more regiments overseas during the last years of the war than it had ever done before.[191]

With the conclusion of the war in early 1763 the Irish establishment was returned to its original limit of 12,000 men, but with two important differences: the reintroduction in 1764 of regular troop rotation in the empire, first experimented with in the period 1749–55,[192] was now to include Ireland and therefore meant that unlike before there would now be continual pressure during peacetime for draughts to fill up regiments rotating out of the country; and Ireland was to sustain a permanent and increasingly expensive commitment to paying for regiments while overseas. The latter element was apparent in the figures for Irish treasury expenditure on overseas regiments between June 1750 and December 1778, as detailed in Table 6.2. In that period the total amount spent was £1,297,526 10s. 6d. From a low of one regiment in the early 1750s costing around £7,000–£9,000 a year, the significant increases commenced from 1755 onwards with costs escalating from £22,500 for four foot regiments to over £63,500 per annum for 1761–3 when two horse and four foot regiments were serving overseas. These war years were the most expensive, even though more regiments were actually supported abroad in the later 1760s when the costs dropped below £50,000 per annum. Such fluctuations were also caused by factors such as whether they were horse or foot regiments, reductions in size and returning to Ireland during a given year. The expenditure highs of the early 1760s were not exceeded until after war broke out again in 1775–6. In 1777 one dragoon and twelve foot regiments cost the Irish treasury £73,415 9s. 10d.[193]

Table 6.2: Regiments on the Irish establishment serving overseas, 1751–78.

Year	Number	Cost	Year	Number	Cost
1751	1F	£ 7,118 13s. 4d.	1760	5F	£42,700 19s. 8d.
1752	1F	£ 8,569 10s. —	1761	2H 4F	£63,977 1s. —
1753	1F	£ 8,547 1s. 8d.	1762	2H 4F	£63,516 1s. 8d.
1754	2F	£ 8,928 9s. 2d.	1763	2H 4F	£63,516 1s. 8d.
1755	4F	£22,437 6s. 8d.	1764	2H 7F	£42,452 18s. 22d.
1756	4F	£36,657 — —	1765	5F	£40,292 4s. 2d.
1757	4F	£36,560 16s. 8d.	1766	1D 6F	£49,269 10s. 10d.
1758	5F	£38,179 3s. 4d.	1767	1D 6F	£49,241 10s. —
1759	5F	£47,346 10s. —			
1772	6F	£56,785 9s. 6d.	1776	1D 8F	£61,868 14s. —
1773	7F	£59,343 14s. 4d.	1777	1D 12F	£73,415 9s. 10d.
1775	7F	£38,020 11s. 6d.	1779	1D 6F	£53,193 10s. 8d.

Ireland was included in the reintroduced system of troop rotation for the empire from the outset. At the end of February 1764 Lord Lieutenant Northumberland was informed that the King 'thought proper to establish a general plan of rotation for the relief of his troops in his American dominions'.[194] In accordance with that plan, in March four regiments were ordered to embark from Ireland for the West Indies. Although the Irish government had expressed the usual concern about the army being thereafter understrength in Ireland, they were informed that it would only 'be but temporary, and of short duration' because the 'plan established for relieving the troops in America' involved the three regiments being moved onto the British establishment on arrival in the Caribbean and the three they relieved going to Ireland and onto the Irish establishment. The fourth regiment, numbered the 62nd in a numerical system of identification which was starting to replace the more traditional and proprietorial naming of units after their commanding officers, continued on the Irish establishment though all new draughts for increasing it to full strength were thereafter paid from Britain.[195] This latter regiment was sent to Dominica, St Vincent and Tobago to relieve several detachments of the 4th regiment, which returned to Britain. The other three Irish regiments – the 66th, 68th and 70th – went to Jamaica, Antigua and Grenada to relieve the 49th, 38th and 63rd respectively, all of which went to Ireland.[196]

These arrangements were not without their difficulties. The colonels of the four regiments destined for the West Indies submitted a memorial expressing their concern at the fact that only six women per company were being allowed to travel with them. They feared 'many desertions' unless the number was increased to 200 for the whole regiment, as many of the men were now married.[197] The request was dismissed in London on the grounds that the allowance was a long-established norm, and to deviate from it would create a precedent which would 'be productive of great expense and inconvenience'.[198] As for the three regiments from the West Indies, it was found upon their arrival in Ireland that they had 'hardly brought over one man fit for service'. The intention had been that these units would be reduced down to the size of the Irish establishment, with the excess soldiers being used to fill up the other Irish regiments from whom draughts had been taken in order to bring up to strength those sent overseas. But given their abysmal state, they had 'not furnished a man towards replacing the draughts'.[199]

A year later the 29th, 52nd and 59th foot regiments were augmented to the size of the American establishment for further troop rotation. As the Irish establishment maintained reduced regiments of 328 soldiers, a further 252 had to be drawn from the other Irish regiments before departure. The destinations this time were Nova Scotia, Quebec, Newfoundland and Louisbourg on Cape Breton Island respectively, where the 40th, 44th and 45th foot were relieved and sent to Ireland.[200] That Quebec and Louisbourg had only recently become part of the empire following the conclusion of the Seven Years' War highlighted the importance of the system of rotation for manning Britain's overseas garrisons.[201] In 1767 another four regiments were rotated to North America.[202]

The regular application of the system of rotation during 1764–7 brought into stark relief the main limitation of the older system of reduced regiments on the Irish establishment. Devised as a means of keeping a large number of regiments in existence in one place during peacetime when the political imperative was to decrease the overall number of men in the army, the reduced regiment system depended upon being able, upon emergency, to fill up a number of regiments quickly with draughts from other regiments which would then raise new levies to replace those taken away. However, the system was not able to take the strain of a permanent state of emergency, as was evident during the Seven Years' War when the wartime strength of the army in Ireland had to be augmented in size on several occasions in order to handle the constant demand for draughts of men in particular. The newer system of rotation, by introducing the regular need for draughts of men even in peacetime, simply served to emphasize that limitation. The solution was the permanent augmentation of the army in Ireland which was undertaken in 1769.[203]

As already seen, the 1769 augmentation brought the number of soldiers on the Irish establishment up to 15,235. In theory 12,815 soldiers would always thereafter be stationed in Ireland with the remaining 2,420 serving overseas. Immediately prior to the augmentation there were five regiments overseas within which, in keeping with the approach commenced in 1764, the Irish treasury supported the 1,639 soldiers that had been in those regiments when first ordered out of Ireland and the British establishment sustained the additional 780 draughts raised at the time of embarkation. But the 1769 augmentation now committed Ireland to providing financial support for all 2,420 soldiers in those five overseas regiments and, more significantly, to doing so on a permanent basis. As such, the principle of making a financial contribution to overseas imperial military service, regularly fought over in the past even though usually begrudgingly acceded to, had now been formally conceded. Just as important, the augmentation permanently increased the number of men in all Irish foot regiments to the same strength as those serving overseas and finally did away with the need for draughts when regiments were rotated onto other establishments and reductions when others were rotated into Ireland.[204] In 1773 the augmentation scheme was amended slightly in order to equalize the number of men in cavalry regiments throughout the empire as well.[205]

As Kenneth Ferguson has pointed out, 'in the final analysis [the army in Ireland] ... did not exist to mount the guard in Dublin or to ensure that the loyal lived peacefully in their habitations, but to defend the British Isles and to serve their King overseas'.[206] The rotation system of the 1760s and the augmentation of 1769 demonstrated that real commitment on Ireland's part to the wider British considerations for empire in the aftermath of the Seven Years' War, with the perceived need for greater centralization of power in London and increased financial and manpower contributions from the dominions towards the imperial war machine. While ultimately resulting in the loss of the thirteen colonies by the early 1780s as the Americans violently rejected the ill-conceived efforts to initiate such a policy in North America, no such crisis arose in Ireland because the country had already been making a very significant contribution to imperial manpower since the 1690s through the barracking of the standing army, the maintenance of the single largest part of the British standing army in peacetime, and the provision of soldiers for overseas service. In 1769 Ireland simply agreed to increase the level of commitment and amend some of the logistical detail relating to that contribution within the parameters of an existing framework that had developed and evolved since the 1690s. Such increased commitment also meant growing expenditure, but again, it was a further expense made within an existing and successful system of public finance which had been ensuring an Irish financial contribution to the empire since the 1690s, which forms the focus of part three.

7 INCOME, EXPENDITURE AND TAXATION

Ireland's contribution to empire in the period 1692–1770 has been examined thus far in terms of the sustaining of the army both at home and abroad and in the innovative undertaking to build and maintain a countrywide network of barracks. But that contribution would not have been possible without a more immediate and fundamental commitment of money to the public purse for the purposes of covering the expense of the army and barracks. To fully measure that military contribution, it is necessary to assess exactly how much money was spent on that enterprise, what percentage of Ireland's public funds that expenditure represented, where the money came from in the first place, and the degree of innovation, experimentation and political and public commitment evident therein towards making that financial contribution. This chapter examines these matters in relation to public income and expenditure in general and to taxation in particular.

Income and Expenditure

Annual income and expenditure in Ireland rose steadily during the period 1692–1770. In the early seventeenth century, government income from Irish revenue sources fluctuated between £15,000 and £27,000. With expenditure always being greater, constant subventions of between £8,000 and £67,000 were required from England.[1] The revolutionary circumstances of the 1650s saw wholly exceptional income levels attained with internal sources producing on average £264,900 per annum with a further £213,758 provided from England.[2] The collapse of the Protectorate in 1659 saw the internal annual yield from the existing permanent or hereditary revenues drop to somewhere between £35,000 and £70,000. In the short-term further subventions were received from England, but the continuation of such a situation was no longer acceptable in the long term. The solution was provided in a Restoration financial settlement voted to the Crown in the 1660s which established the foundations for a secure tax base able to sustain improving public income yields in the following decades.[3]

The Restoration settlement led eventually to the highs of the 1650s being exceeded by the 1680s in both gross and net annual yields, which peaked at £325,228 and £286,516 respectively in 1686.[4] The net yield was what remained in the treasury following deduction of the cost of collection and associated remittances, and represented the real income available to cover the cost of the annual establishment for the civil and military lists. During the Restoration period, overall government expenditure on the establishment remained well within the limits of the net yield, so that there was no debt and instead substantial amounts of money, rising in the late 1670s to at least £98,000 per annum, were sent abroad to pay for soldiers in Tangiers, to contribute to the cost of the navy and to line Charles II's pockets.[5] Such peak payments represented the removal from Ireland of just under 42.5 per cent of the average annual net yield of £230,702 for the years 1676–80.[6] Under James II, additional sums, up to £30,000 or more, were sent to England to contribute to the pay of the army there.[7]

The war of 1689–91 created a crisis in public income and expenditure, with the recorded net yield in 1689 being only £4,038. With increasing expenditure owing to the presence of a standing army in Ireland outstripping the slower recovery in income as demonstrated in part by the rapid growth in collection arrears, a significant debt of pay arrears developed very quickly in the early 1690s, which was only brought under control with new parliamentary taxes which facilitated a significant recovery and eventual improvement in overall yield, with the highest gross and net Restoration figures being exceeded in 1697 with returns of £335,911 and £299,335 respectively. Ongoing recovery in the yield from the existing hereditary revenues saw the figures from that source alone improve beyond the best levels of the 1680s by 1698 with continued improvement thereafter, but with the enlarged army demanding that expenditure remain above the pre-Glorious Revolution figures, parliament had to continue to provide the extra income required to facilitate payment of the permanently increased establishment.[8]

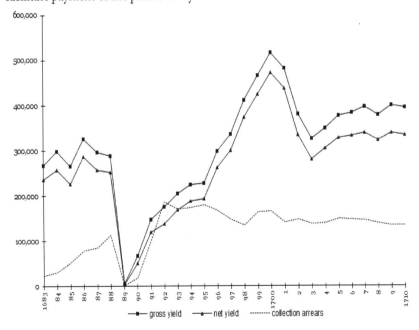

Figure 7.1: Annual gross and net yields and collection arrears, 1683–1710.[9]

On average, more than four-fifths of the government's core annual expenditure went on the army and associated costs of the military list, including the annual barrack management fund. The remainder was spent on the civil list, which covered the chief governors, the judges and other legal officials and costs, the ancient customs officers, the French and other civil pensions, the *regium donum* to the nonconformist ministers, and sundry other incidental expenses of day-to-day government.[10] Together, the two lists constituted the annual establishment, which comprised the annual charge to, or costs for which, the government was liable. The charge of the establishment and actual annual expenditure always differed in the period 1692–1770 because of pay arrears from previous and current years. In the 1680s the highest annual charge on the establishment had stood at £243,663 yet by 1698 it had peaked at £390,627 at an exceptional time when large numbers of soldiers were being transferred to Ireland following the peace of Ryswick. A more consistent pattern of an annual charge of between £325,000 and £350,000 was seen in the first two decades of the eighteenth century.[11]

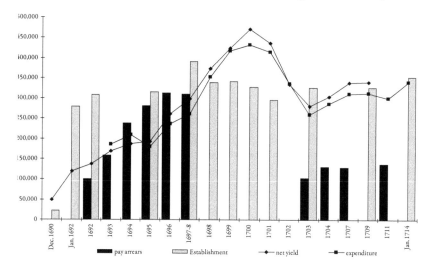

Figure 7.2: The establishment, expenditure, net yield and pay arrears, 1690–1714.[12]

Actual expenditure provided the clearest overview of the government's financial commitments. For the first ten years in which the newly settled military establishment was in existence in Ireland, between 1699 and 1708, the average overall annual expenditure towards clearing the establishment was £336,913, of which 16.7 per cent, or £56,314, was paid toward the civil list and 83.3 per cent, or £280,599, to the military.[13] As demonstrated in Table 7.1, in later years a similar pattern was evident. For ten years from March 1719 to March 1729 just above

82.7 per cent of income was spent on the military list and just below 17.3 per cent on the civil list, with the annual averages increased to £350,915 and £73,366 respectively. Similar percentages were evident in the following three decades up to March 1759, while a thirty-year overview of the charge of the establishment as a comparator from March 1729 to March 1759 resulted in a close correlation whereby 17.6 per cent of the overall charge was accounted for on the civil list and 82.4 per cent on the military.[14] As a percentage commitment of public revenue these figures compare very favourably with those for Britain during the major wars of the eighteenth century which have been estimated at between 75–85 per cent if the servicing of the national debt is included or 61–74 per cent if it is not, which is the situation in the Irish example.[15]

Table 7.1: Ten yearly amounts for civil and military list expenditure, 1719–59.

Years	Civil list	Military list	Total expenditure
1719–29	£733,661 (17.3%)	£3,509,150 (82.7%)	£4,242,811
1729–39	£765,178 (17.1%)	£3,704,119 (82.9%)	£4,469,297
1739–49	£764,742 (19.5%)	£3,162,677 (80.5%)	£3,927,419
1749–59	£786,094 (16.5%)	£3,979,155 (83.5%)	£4,765,249
Totals:	£3,049,675 (17.5%)	£14,355,101 (82.5%)	£17,404,776

Both the annual charge of the establishment and actual expenditure passed the £400,000 mark in 1718. Thereafter both remained either steady or increased slowly in the ensuing decades, apart from the mid-1740s when slight dips occurred owing to unexpected savings on the military list during the War of the Austrian Succession because so many regiments were sent overseas and not wholly replaced in Ireland. Expenditure breached £500,000 in 1748, rose to over £600,000 in 1751, dropped back briefly to the £500,000 level in the mid-1750s and then escalated to over £700,000 by 1759. Despite continuing fluctuations, there was a relatively steady increase thereafter to over £800,000 by the mid-1760s, £900,000 by 1775 and over £1 million by 1777, which level became the norm after 1781–3.[16]

The charge of the establishment lagged behind expenditure from the late 1740s owing to increasing non-establishment, or extraordinary, costs such as loan interest, principal repayments and parliamentary bounties, grants and other such awards of appropriated public income.[17] Even still, the establishment had risen to over £500,000 a year by 1759, surpassed the £600,000 level in the early 1760s and continued to grow thereafter.[18] As was to be expected, both the cost of the civil and military lists increased accordingly. By 1761 the payments on the civil list had finally crept above £100,000 a year and those for the military to over £570,000, while the £200,000 and £600,000 marks respectively were breached in 1777.[19]

In order to service such payments, income also had to grow in line with expenditure. Net income surpassed £400,000 in 1718, rose above £500,000 in

1749 and leapt above £600,000 in 1750, thereafter remaining at similar levels until the early 1760s when the £700,000 mark was permanently surpassed. In 1777 it rose beyond £800,000 and eventually breached £1 million in 1783.[20] On the occasions when net income was less than expenditure, the difference was made up either from surpluses from previous years retained in the treasury or through public loans.[21]

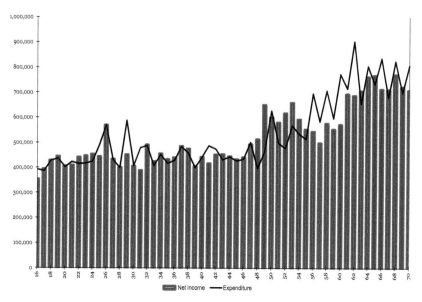

Figure 7.3: Net income and expenditure, 1716–70.[22]

The question remains as to where all of this money came from in the first place and what role did parliament play in its procurement?

Government Sources of Income

In 1692 the government had access to a variety of non-parliamentary sources of income. Some had arisen from earlier permanent legislative provision and some from older Crown common law entitlements and rights. The old hereditary revenue, in existence prior to the 1660s, consisted of tonnage and poundage, Crown and composition rents, ale and aqua-vitae licences, prizage, lighthouse duties, aulnage duties and other casual revenues. The new hereditary revenues were those granted by statute to Charles II and his successors and comprised quit rents, customs, import and inland excise, hearth tax, ale, wine and strong-water licences, and aulnage duties. From the 1660s onwards the customs and excise duties provided the main sources of ordinary or non-parliamentary revenue for the government. However, unlike in England, the Irish Crown and quit rents still represented a significant levy on land ownership well into the eighteenth century as one of the main branches of the ordinary revenues and, alongside the hearth tax, were one of the reasons why an equivalent ongoing land tax along the lines of that in England was not introduced in Ireland in the 1690s or thereafter.[23]

Customs duties were, in origin, an ancient tax of tonnage and poundage on goods imported and exported. They were regularized, expanded, consolidated and granted to the Crown in perpetuity in the 1662 Customs Act, which imposed a basic rate of 12*d.* in 20*s.* on all imported and exported goods alongside various other gradations and increases for specified reasons. Excise was a much newer levy, having first being introduced to Ireland in 1643 following its imposition in England. As with customs, excise was regularized and consolidated in perpetuity in the 1662 Excise Act in which an import excise duty ranging from 6*d.* to 2*s.* 6*d.* on foreign goods was levied on retailers and an inland excise duty ranging from 6*d.* to 2*s.* 6*d.* on every thirty-two gallons of beer or ale and 4*d.* per gallon of aqua-vitae and strong-waters was levied on brewers and distillers.[24] Both customs and excise were uncertain in that the financial return was dependent upon extraneous and internal economic, political and social conditions, though some indication of their capacity is demonstrated by the average annual yield over a five-year period from 1684 to 1688 which for customs was £81,402 and for excise was £118,542. By comparison, the other two main branches of the revenue, rents and hearth tax, produced an average yearly return in that period of £67,743 and £32,142 respectively.[25]

But while rents and hearth tax were certain revenues, in that their annual yield was more assured and less susceptible to the vagaries of national and international political and economic swings and roundabouts, they were also incapable of any significant growth. Hence in the eighteenth century in relative terms customs and excise became even more dominant as the main sources of the increasing government income needed to fuel the expanded military establishment. The vehicle for such growth was parliament.

Parliamentary Taxation

A pre-existing taxation system that was flexible, functioning and capable of expansion was an essential ingredient in the financial revolution that occurred in England in the late seventeenth century, which in turn enabled the expansion of empire in the eighteenth century. At the heart of that flexible English tax system was the excise. Initially outshone by the annual land tax during the reigns of William III and Anne, the excise dominated eighteenth-century English tax yields. More than any other levy or duty, excise could readily and discretely be increased with great regularity.[26]

In Ireland the Restoration financial settlement of the 1660s, and in particular the 1662 Customs and Excise Acts, provided a similar flexible and functioning tax system capable of expanding when necessary. The primary means by which that expansion was achieved was by use of the parliamentary 'additional duty', which involved the imposition of an increased levy upon an existing duty for a regulated period of time so as to provide an estimated amount of money.[27] The first use of this fiscal device in the British Isles occurred in England in 1666, when a small additional customs duty was imposed on imported liquors. In 1668 more substantial additional duties were imposed on imported wine and brandy for two years; in 1670 an eight-year additional customs duty was imposed on wine; and in 1671 a six-year additional excise was imposed on domestic and imported beer. With later renewals of some of these duties, a pattern and practice was established which was further developed following the Glorious Revolution.[28]

The idea was also adopted and further developed in Ireland in the 1690s and thereafter, though it had been first mooted as far back as the 1670s when consecutive Irish governments made initial preparations for parliaments that were never summoned. In 1674 Lord Lieutenant Essex put forward proposals for a five-year additional excise duty on beer and ale as well as additional customs and excise duties on imports of beer, ale, wine, tobacco and sugar. Essex justified his proposition on the grounds that an Irish parliament would never again agree to the voting of taxes in perpetuity as had been done in the 1660s. Lord Lieutenant Ormond also favoured presenting government bills for short-term duties, in 1678 proposing additional customs and excise duties on tobacco, beer, ale, wine and other alcoholic beverages. Despite nothing coming of any of these considerations, the recognition by the Irish government that parliament would not agree to any enlargement of the hereditary revenue paved the way for the use of short-term parliamentary additional duties in the future.[29]

The first additional duties imposed by the Irish parliament were in the 1692 Additional Excise Act. The duration of the act was for one year, with an additional 50–60 per cent increase in the level of duty charged on domestic beer and ale and a 75 per cent increase on spirits distilled in Ireland, which together were intended to bring in £20,000. As detailed in Table 7.2, on the next occasion parliament met, in 1695, the same one-year additional excise was enacted alongside two more measures, one of which simply extended the existing one-year inland excise duties for a further two years and two months and the other which imposed additional customs and import excise duties on tobacco, linen, muslin, calicoes, drapery and wine for four years. The most significant money-generating aspect of the latter act was a 60 per cent increase in the level of duty charged on tobacco. The final supply act of the 1695 session was a once-off poll tax, which demonstrated that, as in England, there was still scope for direct taxation in Ireland. The poll set a basic rate of 1s. per person rising to as much as £50 for archbishops and dukes, though poundage rates for public officials, absentee clergy, pensioners, sinecures and salaried servants meant some people ending up paying £300 or more. The expected yield from all of these measures combined was £163,000.[30]

The two remaining sessions of the Irish parliament during William III's reign, in 1697 and 1698–9, continued these developments in short-term additional supply, as demonstrated in Table 7.2. In 1697 the three additional duty acts from 1695 were amalgamated into one measure which extended the duties on beer, ale and liquors for four years and those on tobacco, linen, muslin, calicoes and wine for three years, the different durations simply serving to provide the same terminal date for all taxes. The additional duty on drapery was allowed to lapse, while the only raised rate was on tobacco, which increased from 60 per cent to 100 per cent of the hereditary duty. A second act imposed another poll tax, which doubled the basic rate of the first but allowed for collection over two years in quarterly instalments rather than as a once-off levy. These two measures were aimed at raising at least £150,000. In 1698–9 the only additional duty imposed was a further increase on tobacco to 140 per cent of the hereditary duty to run consecutively with the existing four-year levy enacted in 1697 and with an extension thereafter for a further six months. A second act imposed a land tax, to be collected in half-yearly instalments over two years. Together these two measures were aimed at raising £139,000, of which £120,000 was to be raised on land. A third act imposed additional duties on Irish woollen manufacture exports, but rather than being a revenue-raising measure was instead an unsuccessful attempt to prevent the Westminster parliament legislating to prohibit such exports.[31]

Table 7.2: Supply legislation in the Irish parliament, 1692–9.

Session	Commodities	Duration
1692	1: Beer, ale, liquors	1 year
1695	1: Beer, ale, liquors	1 year
	2: Beer, ale, liquors	2 years, 2 months
	3: Tobacco, linen, calicoes, muslin, drapery, wine	4 years
	4: Poll tax	1 year
1697	1: Beer, ale, liquors	4 years
	2: Tobacco (rate increased 1697–1702), linen, muslin, calicoes, wine	3 years
	3: Poll tax	2 years
1698–9	1: Tobacco (rate increased 1698–1702)	6 months
	2: Land tax	2 years
	3: Woollen manufactures	3 years

The money raised from the taxes voted in the 1690s were central to the post-1691 recovery in Irish finances and the facilitating of an expanded military establishment. The government's pay arrears were reduced to manageable proportions by the later 1690s, the initial injection of capital into the barrack-building project was made possible and public finances more generally were put back on an even keel.[32] In total between 1696 and 1703, and excluding all income raised from the parliamentary additional inland excise duties (the figures for which were subsumed into the general inland excise account), at least £600,500 was raised from the parliamentary taxation voted between 1695 and 1699. Averaged over eight years, the annual yield, excluding the additional inland excise duties, was £75,063. This represented about 21 per cent of the overall annual net yield from all revenue sources in those years, suggesting that with the additional inland excise duties, which are known to have produced £18,414 in 1696 and £26,659 in 1698, at least a quarter of the government's financial requirements arose from parliamentary taxation at that time.[33] As long as the standing army remained in Ireland, the government would therefore always be reliant upon parliament to make up that extra 25 per cent of income required to cover expenditure. As had been seen in the first half of the 1690s, when that extra money was not available the pay arrears escalated out of all proportion and created a financial crisis in government. Providing an army for Ireland and the empire made the Irish parliament an essential and central institution of the state and gave Irish MPs a bigger role in the running of the country and in establishing its place in the wider imperial nexus.

As itemized in Table 7.3, the consolidation of additional duties as the bedrock of Irish parliamentary supply in the eighteenth century occurred in the seven sessions of parliament held during Queen Anne's reign, as direct taxation became even more peripheral. The existing additional inland excise duties on beer, ale and liquors and the import excise on tobacco and muslin were renewed in each session for durations of between one and two years apart from 1713 when they were all extended for only three months. The additional duties on linen were also continued each session until 1710 when they were extended for seven years along with those on calicoes, which had been increased in 1703 and renewed thereafter. However, the additional duties on wine from the 1690s were dropped in 1703 though at the same time new additional import duties were introduced on molasses for seven years alongside a new two-year tax of 4*s.* in 20*s.* on specific pensions and grants made out of Irish revenue, while in 1705 new additional import duties were imposed upon silk, which were continued each session thereafter. The molasses duties were renewed in 1711.[34] By 1714 the average annual yield from all of the additional duties was about £85,000.[35]

Table 7.3: Supply legislation in the Irish parliament, 1703–13.

Session	Commodities	Duration
1703–4	1: Beer, ale, liquors	1 year
	2: Beer, ale, liquors	1 year
	Tobacco, linen, muslin, calicoes (increased)	2 years
	Molasses	7 years
	Pensions, grants	2 years
1705	1: Beer, ale, liquors	2 years
	Tobacco, linen, muslin, calicoes, silk	1 year, 10 months
1707	1: Beer etc., tobacco, linen, muslin, calicoes, silk	1 year, 9 months
1709	1: All duties	session
	2: Beer etc., tobacco etc.	1 year
1710	1: Beer etc., tobacco, muslin, silk	session
	2: Beer etc., tobacco, muslin, silk	1 year, 6 months
	3: linen, calicoes	7 years
1711	1: Beer etc., tobacco, muslin, silk	2 years
	Molasses	7 years
1713–14	1: Beer etc., tobacco, muslin, silk	3 months

The short-term additional duty system was well-established by the beginning of the reign of George I. The duration for all of the main revenue-raising duties and other taxes was clarified and confirmed in the 1715–16 parliament at two years, thereby ensuring biennial sessions of parliament for the following seven decades.[36] The main point of note thereafter, as shown in Table 7.4, was the occasions when the rate of taxation was increased on commodities already included on the schedule of goods liable to additional duties or when new commodities were added to that schedule. In 1715–16 the additional inland excise duties on beer, ale and liquors and import excise duties on tobacco, muslin and silk were reimposed, while that on wine which had lapsed in 1703 was reintroduced alongside a wholly new additional import excise duty on strong-waters and spirits. A new direct tax on government salaries, profits of employments, fees and pensions paid to any person not resident in Ireland was also introduced. All of these taxes were continued in every session thereafter apart from the direct tax, which was allowed to lapse between 1753 and 1767. In 1717 a new additional import excise duty was imposed upon brandy and 'spirits above proof' while the rates of the inland excise duties on beer, ale and liquors were increased by one-third. In 1719 new import excise duties were imposed on molasses, treacle, tea, coffee, chocolate and cocoa-nuts. In 1725–6 further duties were levied on brandy and spirits above proof while those on brandy were increased again in 1727–8 and 1729–30, when increases were also levied on all other imported spirits, wine and silk goods. In 1731–2 the most recent increased duties on brandy and other imported spirits were allowed to lapse, though those on wine were increased yet again, while new additional import excise duties were levied on hops, china, earthen, japanned or lacquered ware and vinegar. In 1737–8 new import excise duties were imposed on romals, cotton goods, cotton/linen goods and cambrics, while in 1743–4 additional customs duties were imposed on exported hides. In 1745–6 the import excise on cambrics and lawns and the import excise on wine, velvet and silk goods were increased again, while in 1751–2 and 1757–8 the import excise on cambrics and lawns was increased even further. In the meantime, the 1731–2 increased duty on wine and those on hops, china, earthen, japanned or lacquered ware and vinegar were allowed to lapse between 1753 and 1759. In 1759–60 additional import excise duties were imposed on paper.[37]

The beginning of George III's reign saw the start of a further extension of the schedule of commodities liable for increased taxation alongside ongoing increases for the additional duty staples. As Table 7.5 details, in 1761–2 increased rates were imposed on domestic liquors and imported brandy and other spirits above the quality of single spirits as well as wine and vinegar, while new additional duties were imposed on imported coffee and domestic cider, with retailers of the latter being required to pay a licence fee. A new additional customs duty was imposed on exported soap-boilers' waste alongside a tax on private coaches, chariots, berlins, calashes and chaises with four wheels. The latter tax had been levied since 1729–30 but had always been appropriated solely for the improvement of tillage, employment of the poor, the draining of bogs and for river navigation and canal-building projects. The new tax was therefore levied on top of the existing rates for the appropriated income. In 1763–4 new additional customs duties were introduced on exported linen rags while the duties on velvet, silk and soap-boilers' waste were increased further, as was the case once again for the latter item in 1765–6.[39]

Table 7.4: New and increased additional duties and other taxes, 1715–60.[38]

Session	Acts	Sources of taxation revenue
1715–16	2 GI 1 & 7	*inland excise:* beer, ale, aqua-vitae, strong-waters, spirits
		import excise: tobacco, muslin, silk
	2 GI 3	*import excise:* wine, strong-waters, spirits
		income tax: government salaries, profits of employments, fees, pensions
1717–18	4 GI 2	*import excise:* brandy, spirits above proof
		inland excise: beer, ale, aqua-vitae, strong-waters, spirits
1719	6 GI 4	*import excise:* molasses, treacle, tea, coffee, chocolate, cocoa-nuts
1725–6	12 GI 1	*import excise:* brandy, spirits above proof
1727–8	1 GII 4	*import excise:* brandy
1729–30	3 GII 2	*import excise:* wine, brandy, spirits, silk goods
1731–2	5 GII 2	*import excise:* wine, hops, china, earthen, japanned or lacquered ware, vinegar
1737–8	11 GII 1	*import excise:* romals, cotton goods, cotton/linen goods, cambrics
1743–4	17 GII 1	*customs outwards:* hides
1745–6	19 GII 2	*import excise:* cambrics, lawns
	19 GII 3	*import excise:* wine, velvet and silk goods
1751–2	25 GII 1	*import excise:* cambrics, lawns
1757–8	31 GII 1	*import excise:* cambrics, lawns
1759–60	33 GII 1	*import excise:* paper
	33 GII 2	*import excise:* wine, hops, china, earthen, japanned or lacquered ware, vinegar

Table 7.5: New and increased additional duties and other taxes, 1760–70.

Session	Acts	Sources of taxation revenue
1761–2	1 GIII 1	*import excise:* brandy, spirits above the quality of single spirits
	1 GIII 5	*inland excise:* aqua-vitae, strong-waters, spirits, cider
		import excise: wine, vinegar, coffee
		customs outwards: soap-boilers' waste
		licences: cider
		transport tax: private coaches, chariots, berlins, calashes, chaises with four wheels
1763–4	3 GIII 2	*import excise:* velvet and silk goods
		customs outwards: soap-boilers' waste, linen rags
1765–6	5 GIII 2	*customs outwards:* soap-boilers' waste
1767–8	7 GIII 2	*income tax:* government salaries, profits of employments, fees, pensions

The legislative provision every two years in parliament of additional duties and other taxes, with new commodities and increased rates as required, ensured that the government's income deriving from those sources remained steady before slowly increasing over the decades from the 1710s to the 1770s. The ten-yearly annual average for gross income from the additional duties between March 1719 and March 1729 was £135,292. In the following three decades to March 1759 it stood at £128,653, £133,370 and £168,239 respectively. Throughout that time these additional duties accounted for between 26–34 per cent of the annual net income arising from all of the sources of revenue available to the Irish government, excluding government borrowing.[40] By the second half of the 1770s the annual yield from the additional duties was averaging about £240,000 per annum, which accounted for about 35 per cent of total net income, excluding loans, at that time.[41]

As had been the case since the second half of the 1690s, the income arising from the additional duties and other parliamentary taxes provided the Irish government with the essential one-quarter to one-third top-up of the annual yield from the hereditary or permanent revenues and thereby facilitated the maintenance of a standing army on the Irish establishment during the first seven decades of the eighteenth century. As had been seen in the early 1690s, without that top-up, the government's finances quickly descended into crisis as pay arrears escalated within two to three years to a level beyond that of the establishment itself. Hence the vast majority of Irish MPs, once the system had been established and understood, were happy to vote these additional duties and other taxes every two years while also being cognizant of, and vigilant about, not providing the government with more money than it needed. That mistake had been made in the late 1690s, which had allowed for a gap of over four years between parliaments, but was not to be made again as parliamentary supply was managed thereafter so as to always keep the government a little money-hungry and thereby to ensure biennial parliaments.[42]

MPs were also cognizant of what commodities could handle additional duties. At times, recently increased rates were once again reduced when they served to be counterproductive in terms of diminished returns or increased smuggling, as happened with brandy in the early 1730s.[43] Debates also took place that ensured the exclusion of commodities such as potatoes and salt because they were staples of the population's diet.[44] The addition of new rates of duties and, especially, of new commodities was always an issue of particular attention. It was harder to justify such additions in peacetime, though ultimately increasing financial demand upon the government saw advances made in this respect when necessary even if begrudgingly conceded by MPs.[45] Such debates were particularly pertinent when the subject of a national debt arose, which in itself was caused by increasing government expenditure on the army and yet was also the cause of significant additions to the schedule of commodities liable to additional duties. The national debt represented the second main parliamentary-sanctioned source of money provided to the government for the purpose primarily of financing Ireland's military contribution to the empire in the period 1716–70. The question of how that debt was created, maintained and justified therefore needs to be addressed.

8 THE NATIONAL DEBT

As already demonstrated, the public commitment of Irish money towards the maintenance of the army and the barracks by means of parliamentary taxation constituted a key contribution to the British Empire in the period 1692–1770. However, at times of particular political or economic crisis or emergency, additional funds were required at short notice. In England, the provision of such funds via the creation and maintenance of a national debt constitutes a key aspect of the late seventeenth-century financial revolution. The emergence of an English national debt was directly related to the expansion of the empire, as the debt was created in order to finance the maintenance of a naval and military establishment capable of winning wars and defending newly acquired territories.[1]

Parliament-sanctioned government borrowing and the build-up of a permanent national debt in order to finance war commenced in earnest in England in the early 1690s. The Nine Years' War saw existing practices in short-term borrowing extended and the new innovation of long-term borrowing introduced, the Bank of England established in 1694 and other fiscal experiments embarked upon. At the centre of these developments was the Westminster parliament, which, as the ultimate beneficiary of the constitutional revolution of 1688–9, facilitated the move from insecure, volatile and unsustainable royal debt to secure, safe and sustainable national debt. By enshrining in statute the repayment of public debts, be it at the outset of a new loan, the creation of a new financial institution, or through the conversion of short-term unfunded liabilities into long-term funded debts, the Westminster parliament revolutionized England's public finances and the country's ability to wage war, conquer new territories and, ultimately, to build an overseas empire.[2]

Parliament-sanctioned government borrowing and the creation of a permanent national debt built upon a legislative foundation commenced in Ireland in 1716.[3] As had been the case in England in the 1690s, the introduction of a permanent national debt to Ireland was a highly significant occurrence directly related to security concerns of both a national and an international character, on this occasion concerning Ireland, England, Scotland and France. This chapter examines the reasons for the establishing of an Irish national debt, the methods adopted thereafter for its maintenance and the degree to which it constituted a contribution to the British Empire during the period 1716–70.

The Irish national debt was from the outset an integral part of the evolving constitutional framework centred on short-term additional supply and biennial sessions, which was epitomized by the gradual increase in the power and influence of the Irish Commons in particular.[4] In keeping with similar developments in England in the 1690s, the commencement of parliament-sanctioned government borrowing in Ireland in 1716 conceded further power and influence to the legislature, as not only the imprimatur for public borrowing now lay with that assembly, but at a more practical level the essential assurance that the debt would be serviced and repaid was derived from, and dependent upon, parliamentary legislation. Such assurance was crucial both for the government, as it ensured that public creditors came forward to lend money, and for the public creditors, as it ensured that the return on their investment was secured on funds voted by parliament. But there was another reciprocity in these arrangements that to some extent served to counterbalance the increased power of parliament. The main public creditors were leading members of the Irish Protestant community who, by lending their money to the government, were investing in the continued survival of their community in Ireland on the basis of the post-Glorious Revolution settlement in church and state.[5] The maintenance of an army capable of defending their interest in Ireland and, in a wider context, actively contributing to the expansion of the British Empire was the fundamental reason why parliament and the wider Protestant community lent money to the government and ensured that the debt was serviced.

The first official record of a national debt actually occurred in 1715. In 1711 the Irish parliament had chosen not to make any provision for 'about £17,000 [of pay arrears] which must go on as a national debt till next session'. In 1715 that sum remained unpaid and the more exact figure of £16,107 was accounted by the treasury as a floating national debt.[6] However, it was not until January 1716 that a more substantial, and permanent, national debt began to be incurred with the advent of parliament-sanctioned government borrowing.[7]

The immediate financial necessity for creating a national debt in 1716 was the Jacobite rebellion in Scotland. With the army in Ireland depleted following the departure for Britain of twelve regiments, the Commons resolved on 16 January that 'whatever forces his majesty shall think fit to raise, or whatever expense [he] ... shall think necessary for the defence of this kingdom, this house shall enable [him] ... to make good the same', and presented an address to that effect to the lords justices two days later. It was this need to raise new regiments that prompted the sanctioning of a loan to government. On 28 January the lords justices notified parliament 'that there is reason to believe that this kingdom will be very suddenly invaded' and that the King desired that they 'take such measures thereupon as may best conduce to the defence and security of your country', including the raising of new forces. Given that it was accepted that responsibility for raising supply lay with the Commons, the lords justices then appealed directly to the lower house for money for the purpose. The Commons reacted by passing a vote of credit, in which it was stated that

> whatever sum or sums of money shall be advanced and paid into the treasury by any person or persons, at the instance of ... the lords justices ... for the defence of this kingdom, shall be made good by this house, with legal interest for the same, out of such aids as shall be granted ... the next session of parliament.[8]

The significance of these events was not lost on the Irish executive. Chief Secretary Delafaye expressed the view on 30 January that 'never [a] parliament did greater things, especially the vote of credit the like to which was never known here before'.[9] On the same day, the lords justices informed Stanhope that the

> vote of credit is a resolution without precedent here, and as it shows their unlimited affection for his majesty, so we are persuaded it will very much contribute to his service which could not possibly have been carried on any other way at this time, in a country where we have no bank nor East India Company to supply the emergencies of the government.[10]

Almost six months later they reiterated that sentiment in their closing speech to parliament: 'We must ... thankfully acknowledge the several marks of confidence you have placed in us, more particularly your seasonable and unprecedented vote of credit'.[11]

The absence of both a national bank and a joint-stock company demonstrated that the institutions and organizations associated with the financial revolution had not been replicated in Ireland. This was in part owing to the lack in the 1690s of an overriding need or the requisite economic and financial climate, insufficient ready specie and the absence both of public creditors and a robust capital market.[12] Yet in 1716 a buoyant economy following a boom in the wake of the peace of 1713, stability in Irish financial practice owing to twenty years of regular short-term additional parliamentary supply and a real, immediate and justifiable need for public borrowing ensured that in the absence of such institutions and organizations alternative public creditors emerged.[13]

The uniqueness of what had occurred was highlighted by the fact that during February the executive felt it necessary to make inquiries as to the best way to raise the loan.[14] Yet with interest to be set at the legal rate in Ireland, which was 8 per cent per annum, payment of which, along with repayment of the principal sum, was to be secured by parliamentary legislation, investment in the loan scheme represented an attractive proposition to a person with capital. It was little surprise therefore that there was 'more money ready' in Ireland than was needed to fill the required subscription to the treasury.[15] The government was therefore readily able to borrow £50,000 which it spent on raising thirteen new regiments.[16]

The actual loan legislation was included in the third and final supply bill passed by the 1715–16 parliament. In accordance with procedures on supply developed since the 1690s, the token government supply bill had been enacted in November. At the same time the Commons commenced assessment of the government's further financial needs and the heads of a second supply bill was ready for transmission to London on 22 December, being returned and passed into law by the end of January 1716. The heads of a third and final supply bill had also been ordered in December but had been proceeded upon more slowly because its commencement date was further in the future, an occurrence which allowed for it to become the vehicle for the loan legislation. The drafting committee finally presented the heads on 27 January and the Commons took them into consideration on 1 February.[17] Two days later a new clause was introduced and agreed 'for making effectual the vote of credit of this house' and the finalized heads were sent to the lords justices for transmission to London.[18] Thus the first 'loan bill' was actually three clauses in an additional duties bill that had been under consideration before the need for a loan had become apparent. The bill was returned from London without amendment and received the royal assent on 19 May.[19]

Although the bill was not opposed at any stage in its passage, a degree of opposition had arisen more generally. On 3 May it was moved in the Commons that the lords justices 'be addressed for an account of what had been done in pursuance of the former vote of credit', which was considered to be 'pretty odd' and intended 'to have it appear in the votes that this account was demanded on purpose to insinuate with the people a jealousy of the government'. However, the 'great cry' of the opposition, computed at about twenty-eight MPs, was more specifically 'against pensions and loading the establishment', as was traditionally the case.[20] At the end of May debate centred on unnecessary pensions and a more general concern over the increased debt, with one speaker promising to confine his remarks to the 'great burden that was growing upon us' and 'the immense debt we were running into', which he computed would be £140,000 by the time parliament met again in 1717. However, the debate was concluded on a division in the government's favour by 124 votes to 60, the opposition comprising thirty Tories and thirty 'discontented Whigs'.[21] What these debates most readily demonstrated was that the national debt had almost immediately been subsumed within opposition politics into the grand cornucopia of discontent that derived from long-standing extravagances of government – both perceived and real – in certain areas of the establishment.

As to the loan act itself, the preamble confirmed that parliament had agreed to sanction the advent of a national debt because of the restless and treasonable practices and attempts of the enemies of your majesty, and of our happy constitution, to deprive us of our religion, laws, and liberties ... and being highly sensible, that the security, peace, and prosperity of this ... kingdom under God does alone depend upon the support of your majesty's government, and your lawful and undoubted right and title to the Crown of these realms.

Clause III specified that the loan was raised owing to the fact that 'the exigence of the public affairs ... may require an expense and greater supplies, than the funds already granted ... this session', and directed that the principal sum and the interest should be repaid 'out of the next aids to be granted by parliament'. In so doing, parliament promised to service the debt and act as security for the loan. As the representative body for the nation, parliament had therefore initiated public borrowing that was ultimately secured upon the credit of that nation and was therefore a truly 'national' debt.[22]

Clarification of the loan repayment provision was included in Clause V of the act. Interest payments were to be made every six months from the date of the initial loan out of the general body of supplies granted in 1715–16 and out of all supplies to be granted in the future until such time as full payment of both the interest and principal was achieved. The act therefore secured the interest payments upon the 1715–16 parliamentary additional supplies in general, without appropriation of a specific fund, and offered a general undertaking to repay the principal. In strictly legal terms, the only certain provision for servicing the debt related to the interest and would terminate in eighteen months when the main 1715–16 supply acts expired.[23] The absence of a specific appropriated fund also reduced the degree of assurance attached to the servicing of the debt, an assurance that was crucial for public creditor confidence and which accounted for the first attempt at clarifying such matters in 1717.

The second supply act of the 1717 session acknowledged that the debt of £50,000 'may not be fully ... paid out of the aids granted this present session' and so the public creditors were to continue to receive interest payments every six months 'until they are respectively paid ... [their] principal sums'. However, the fact that the act allowed for the debt to be serviced out of the public revenue in general, inclusive of the hereditary revenue (which represented an even more generalized provision than that of May 1716), meant that the issue of a specific appropriated fund remained unaddressed, while in legal terms it was still theoretically possible that interest might only be paid during the two-year duration of the two 1717 supply acts. On the other hand, the general undertaking regarding the continued payment of interest and eventual repayment of the principal constituted an acceptance by parliament of its obligation to ensure that at some unspecified point in the future the public creditors would be repaid their money and that in the interim parliament would, at each biennial session, ensure that provision was made for the continuation of interest payments, as was seen to be done in the supply acts passed in the following five sessions to 1727–8.[24]

As with the main supply acts passed by the Irish parliament since the 1690s, the secondary supply legislation for servicing the national debt during the years 1716 to 1727–8 was comprehended within the parameters of the Commons' understanding of the politics of supply, whereby all of the main supply legislation was restricted to a two-year duration which ensured the continuation of biennial parliamentary sessions and kept the government financially dependent upon parliament. During these years only the interest was paid on the debt, and payments were always in arrears of anywhere between about £850 and £1,400.[25] In 1724 the interest rate was reduced to 7 per cent following the introduction by parliament in 1722 of the same rate reduction for legal interest throughout Ireland, which had been occasioned by the 'very great abatement in the value of divers merchandises, wares, and commodities of this kingdom both at home' and abroad. This fall in prices had been construed as damaging to the economy because the gentry, merchants, traders and others who had borrowed money for business were unable to repay their debts.[26]

The reduction in interest rates was symptomatic of a greater malaise arising out of a general economic downturn and loss of confidence in Irish trade and manufactures which was exacerbated by various other related factors, the first of which was the proposal in 1720 for a national bank such as had been established in England in 1694 as part of the financial revolution. Unsuccessful proposals for an Irish bank had been made in the late seventeenth century, but it was not until after the creation of the national debt that the idea was pursued with real vigour and intent.[27] In early 1720 a notice was published calling for subscriptions for the establishment of a bank and paper credit in Ireland as a means of addressing the various economic and financial problems that were emerging at that time, including a trade imbalance and the drain of Irish money to Britain and elsewhere through salaries, pensions, rents and the prevailing mania for purchasing stocks in both the Mississippi and South Sea Companies in the hopes of 'extravagant gain'.[28] The subscription was quickly filled, directors elected, and a petition presented to George I desiring a royal charter for the bank.[29] A counter-proposal emerged from another group and a minor bidding war ensued which included a proposal to discharge £50,000 of the national debt within five years, an offer the lords justices felt would contravene 'the usual and known methods' of parliament which was wholly and solely responsible for providing 'any money which shall be necessary to be applied to the use of the kingdom'.[30]

The idea that a national bank might obviate the need for the government to continue to have regular recourse to parliament for financial supplies was highly relevant, as the bank proposals coincided with the English government briefly considering in the aftermath of the 1720 Declaratory Act whether it might be possible to govern Ireland without parliament. However, such an idea was quickly dismissed as too much of a political risk.[31] In May 1721 the English treasury commissioners recommended that a charter for a bank be granted but that 'an act of the Irish parliament would be necessary in order to make effective certain important provisions'.[32] The drafting of the bill commenced in late September but quickly ran into trouble with the first clause being thrown out on a division of 103 to 95 and further consideration being put off for two months on a vote of 98 to 91.[33] When the Commons eventually returned to the bill in December it was rejected, as were the proposal and charter on a division of 150 to 80 on the question that the house 'cannot find any safe foundation for establishing a public bank, so as to render it beneficial to Ireland'.[34]

The bank proposal failed for a variety of reasons, including the significant financial losses people had suffered in the interim from the collapse of the South Sea Company in late 1720 and the ensuing detrimental effect upon the Irish economy and public confidence in general. Trade restrictions due to quarantines to prevent the plague spreading from the Continent increased the hardship, as did the impact of bad weather, which caused famine conditions in the winter of 1720–1. These factors, combined with a general fear that the bank might facilitate non-parliamentary government, the innate conservatism of the landed country gentlemen in parliament and ongoing conflicts within Irish politics, made the task of the bank's critics a great deal easier.[35]

The increasing shortage of ready specie also led to the British government issuing a patent in 1722 for coining copper halfpence and farthings for Ireland which resulted in the protracted Wood's halfpence affair of 1722–5.[36] However, while all of these economic and political difficulties could be construed as reasons for the government's failure to keep up to date with interest payments on the national debt, a more obvious cause lay in the fact that most MPs were opposed to the regular imposition of new additional duties, in part out of fear that the government might in time be able to survive financially without parliament. Even though new duties were introduced during the period 1716–1728, they were never sufficient to match government expenditure nor were any such duties appropriated specifically for servicing the national debt.

The difficulties arising from the failure to implement a proper system for servicing the national debt resulted in another fiscal experiment in 1726. In keeping with a Commons' request, £10,000 from supplies granted in the 1725–6 session was used to pay 7 per cent interest to those who advanced money to clear army pay warrants that were in arrears, which also served the secondary purpose of giving the resulting debentures 'a currency among the people'.[37] In accordance with the scheme, £59,967 was advanced to clear warrants and during the next two years £8,395 7s. 8d. was paid in interest. The success was such that at the end of 1727 the Commons again requested that £10,000 from the duties voted in the 1727–8 session be applied to the same use. The government readily complied.[38]

The 1726 scheme was significant in two ways. First, the Commons had created a method for transforming a percentage of the army pay arrears into part of the national debt. As with the first parliament-sanctioned loan in 1716, this new debt was ultimately secured on the credit of the nation, a fact that had prompted a degree of unsuccessful opposition in parliament in 1726.[39] In the future, the practice of transforming establishment pay arrears into national debt was to become common practice and was an Irish variation on the English theme of consolidating and transforming short-term floating liabilities into long-term funded debts. Second, the formalization of a process for private investors to advance money on the security of army pay warrants removed the less edifying aspects of the older system of compounding. Now, the investor's financial return came from an official interest-bearing debenture rather than a top slice from the soldier's pay. At the same time, the debenture gained a currency in its own right.

As applied in 1726 and 1727, however, the scheme was only an interim measure. It did not address the bigger question of making more comprehensive and substantive provision for servicing the national debt, which was the only way to ensure the sustainability of that debt over a longer period of time. The first step in that direction occurred in 1729, with the introduction of new measures that included official adoption of some of the key aspects of the interim scheme of 1726 and 1727.

The establishment pay arrears at the end of 1729 stood at £317,169 16s. 2d. Towards clearing that sum the 1729–30 Commons legislated for a new loan to government of £150,000, which served to transform part of the army pay arrears into a national debt, the principal of which thereby increased to £200,000 with a new interest rate of 6 per cent. Apart from increasing the principal debt fourfold, the 1729 secondary supply act was most significant in that it finally introduced a schedule of additional duties appropriated solely for paying the debt interest and, if any surplus arose thereafter from those duties, for reducing or 'sinking' the principal, thereby transforming the whole thing into a funded national debt. In taking subscriptions to the loan, priority was to be given to debentures and warrants for army pay arrears, which were to be treated as 'ready money', were to be preferred over ready specie and were to include those debentures upon which interest had been paid since 1726.[40]

The process had not been wholly straightforward, however. The government was initially rebuffed over a proposal that all of the taxes to be voted should be included in one supply act, the Commons choosing to keep the appropriated duties separate from those voted for the government's revenue-at-large so as to retain greater control over the two different financial provisions. A second government proposal to have the duration of the appropriated duties open-ended was rejected out of fear that those taxes might in time assume a permanency and thereby be beyond the control of parliament and endanger that institution's regular assembly. Instead the usual two-year duration was imposed. The final threat came from amendments carried out in London that were intended to restore the pre-existing general undertaking to continue interest payments to public creditors until such unspecified time as their principal was repaid and to clarify that any surplus arising from the appropriated duties would be applied towards clearing the principal and no other use whatsoever in accordance with future acts of the Irish parliament. Both amendments were clearly aimed at clarifying and confirming the evident wishes of the Irish parliament, yet they allowed the opposition to attack the returned bill in relation to Poynings' Law, the Crown's prerogative and the long-standing principle that supply bills were not to be altered in Britain, in part out of fear that such alterations might lead to non-par-liamentary government. The opposition was persistent though unsuccessful. A series of divisions went the government's way: 124 votes to 62 for consideration of the bill; 99 to 27 for engrossing; 75 to 14 for the third reading; and finally 95 to 21 on passing into law. In the end, the fear of increased pay arrears and the financial injury to the existing public creditors among other concerns resulted in MPs siding with the government.[41]

As in 1716, there was no shortage of people willing to lend their money to the government in 1729–30 and the loan was fully subscribed within a few months.[42] The following years were to demonstrate how a more comprehensive and substantive provision for servicing the national debt had been achieved in 1729, a provision which ensured the sustainability of that debt over a longer period of time.

A new loan was legislated for in the next session in 1731–2 which served to transform another £100,000 of army pay arrears into part of the funded national debt, the principal of which increased thereby to £300,000. In accordance with the British government's amendment of 1729, the sinking fund was established on a more practical basis with provision being made for the names of public credi-tors to be drawn by lottery for the repayment of principal sums whenever a surplus of more than £5,000 arose from the appropriated duties. The interest rate for the whole debt was reduced to 5 per cent while that for all other financial transac-tions in Ireland was set at 6 per cent on the grounds that parliament-secured debt offered the best security for invested capital and therefore would still attract suffi-cient public creditors at a lower interest rate than the national legal limit.[43] There was little difficulty in securing this new loan or in finding subscribers for the full amount, to the extent that many MPs had their subscriptions refused. The only point of debate arose over the government's unsuccessful request that the dura-tion of the appropriated duties be set at twenty-one years rather than the usual two years.[44] The 1731 act also demonstrated how, as had been the case since 1716, the Commons made certain that the national debt was tied into the politics of supply, which ensured the continuation of biennial sessions. As Robert Clayton,

Bishop of Killala, noted in January 1732, 'as they now have experience that they can raise money on parliamentary security from two years to two years, I believe they will hardly be prevailed upon to grant it for a longer time'.[45]

At the same time, however, there was some general unease expressed with the growing debt. Prior to the 1731–2 session, a pamphlet had been published which argued against any new loans on the grounds that 'the nation is [already] run so much into debt' because a number of people were determined 'to serve a certain party':

> Pray what is all this, but laying the nation under the severest bonds, to do whatever the prime minister directs? The joke too is, that the money lent on the public faith, is all supplied by members of parliament, by which means they must be pensioners to the court, and obliged ... to comply with all future desires, on pain of forfeiting what is already advanced.[46]

It was true that many of the public creditors were MPs, but that only served to show how the creation and maintenance of the national debt had strengthened the mutual dependence and obligation between government and parliament. The pamphlet's author also advocated a reduction of interest 'on all money lent' to 6 per cent, in which respect, at least, he reflected events as they actually transpired.[47] Another pamphlet opposed the reduction of the national debt interest below the 'common interest for money lent on other securities', because money so 'secured on the public faith, and the interest of it well paid, would make debentures, or any share in that stock, very valuable, and yield a high premium on every transfer'. All such premiums could then be paid into the treasury to be applied to the discharge of the debt. However, no method was offered for enforcing such a process.[48]

It was also the case that although parliament had readily agreed to increasing the size of the national debt, some disquiet arose over the procedures for doing so. In December 1731 the Commons had made it a standing order for the future that they should not proceed upon any petition, motion, address, bill or vote of credit for giving any money other than in a committee of the whole house on supply or ways and means.[49] While ultimately about proper procedures, the standing order demonstrated that MPs were conscious of the need to ensure that sufficient checks and balances were in place to sustain continued parliamentary control of the parameters of the national debt.

The provisions put in place for servicing the national debt in 1729 and 1731 were renewed in individual acts in each of the following four sessions to 1739–40.[50] The government's adherence to these provisions, and the extent to which they were both practical and successful, was demonstrated from 1733 onwards when a sufficient surplus had built up in the sinking fund. An initial £20,000 was cleared at the end of 1733 and, with further repayments thereafter, by 1741 the principal debt was down to £227,000. Such repayments also indicated that the interest was also being cleared, with annual amounts of anywhere between £7,000 and £14,000 being remitted to public creditors during that decade. As a counterbalance however, the establishment pay arrears, which had been reduced to £182,695 by 1733, grew slowly to £210,180 in 1741 because of the continuing practice in the Commons of reducing the amount of the government's reported pay arrears to a lower figure upon which the ensuing vote of supplies would be based.[51]

The renewed security crisis following the outbreak of war with Spain in 1739 provided the Commons with the motivation for dealing with the pay arrears because a significant part of government expenditure was diverted to more immediate military needs. Having passed a vote of credit in early 1740 on the basis of which the government borrowed £25,000 for buying arms for the militia, the Commons at the end of 1741 legislated for a new loan of £125,000, including the £25,000 borrowed in 1740, so that £100,000 of army pay arrears was transformed into part of the funded national debt. The loan was quickly subscribed, raising the principal of the debt in early 1742 to £352,000, of which £250,000 paid a new 4 per cent interest rate while the remaining £102,000, which was to be cleared first, remained at 5 per cent.[52]

The appropriated duties continued to produce a surplus during the following years, so that the principal reduced in size to £340,700 by the end of 1743.[53] However, the outbreak of hostilities with France and the Jacobite rebellion in Scotland resulted in another loan in 1745 for up to £70,000 at 4 per cent interest for the purchase of 30,000 firelocks and bayonets and 10,000 broadswords for the use of the militia and for an artillery battery at Cork. The government borrowed £58,500 on the security of the act.[54]

The fact that the government did not need to avail itself of the whole amount of borrowing sanctioned by parliament in 1745 was symptomatic of changed financial circumstances in Ireland in general. As with all previous loans, the official justification for borrowing in the 1745 act was a desire not to overburden the people with additional taxes at an economically difficult time.[55] Yet the stated purpose of the loan in purchasing arms and building fortifications was, with the exception of 1740, different from all that had gone before. For only the second time since 1716, and despite occurring in the middle of a war, the loan was not directly related to raising or paying soldiers. While still focused on a primarily military concern, a subtle shift had occurred in the justification for increasing the national debt.

An improving economy and increasing public income in the mid-1740s, combined with savings made on the establishment owing to the large number of regiments sent overseas, had resulted in significant surpluses starting to accrue in the Irish treasury. By the end of 1745 the establishment pay arrears had reduced to a very manageable £118,879, while the principal of the funded national debt had been lowered as well to £335,300. Indeed, the government's accounts were in such a healthy state that the Commons in that year reported an overall 'credit to the nation' of £71,947, which was a wholly new concept in eighteenth-century Irish public finances and implied that the existing sources of public revenue were sufficient for the government's needs and that there was therefore no necessity for transforming any of the army pay arrears into part of the funded national debt.[56] The government's continued healthier finances in the later 1740s, especially following further economic improvement in the wake of the peace of 1748, did not preclude the biennial renewal of the main parliamentary duties or the continued provision of appropriated duties for servicing the national debt in 1747, 1749 and 1751, but it did preclude the imposition of any new duties, appropriated or otherwise, and represented the start of a sustained period of funded debt repayment.[57]

The build-up of a substantial surplus in the Irish treasury prompted the Commons in 1749 to take the unprecedented step of passing legislation for the appropriation of £128,500 of existing general public income for repayment of the funded national debt. The 1749 Debt Repayment Act was the first step along the road to conflict between the executive and legislature over control of expenditure. The statutory sinking fund was officially comprised of the surplus arising from the appropriated additional duties only, but the 1749 act, while continuing to impose those duties, also appropriated a substantial amount of existing treasury funds of less certain origin, which from the government's perspective impinged upon the Crown's prerogative with regard to expenditure arising from the hereditary revenues and non-appropriated parliamentary taxation.[58]

The 1749 Debt Repayment Act resulted in the clearing of £128,500 of the principal of the national debt, which thereby reduced from £378,500 to £250,000. All creditors holding bonds which still paid 5 per cent interest were cleared first, with those on 4 per cent being drawn by way of a lottery, in keeping with previous practice. Interest payments were also maintained with almost £30,000 being paid out between March 1749 and March 1751.[59] The ongoing build-up of a surplus in the treasury led to the passage in December 1751 of a second Debt Repayment Act which resulted in £120,000 more being cleared from the principal debt, which in the interim had increased by £2,500 borrowed on the basis of the 1745 act but yet had also had £15,000 cleared from the sinking fund, so that it stood at £237,500 before being reduced by the 1751 act to £117,500.[60] The creditors for repayment were again decided by lottery, while interest of £15,559 was paid to the remainder over two years to March 1753.[61]

The conflict simmering since the first appropriation of the general treasury surplus in 1749 came to a boil in late 1753. Although the dispute took place against the background of a power struggle among the leading Irish political undertakers, the focus of the conflict between the executive and legislature was upon the control of expenditure.[62] In keeping with the previous two sessions in 1749 and 1751, in late 1753 the Commons drafted a bill for appropriating £77,500 from the general surplus for repayment of the principal of the funded national debt. However, unlike its predecessors, the 1753 bill did not include any clauses for continuing the appropriated additional duties for servicing the debt so that they would lapse at the end of 1753 regardless, the reason being that the surplus sum to be appropriated was intended to clear the outstanding principal debt completely.[63]

The Commons' heads of a bill was sent to England without any reference to either the King's recommendation or consent to the appropriation of the surplus, which had been incorporated by amendment in London in the 1751 version and passed with resistance in Dublin.[64] When the 1753 bill was returned from London, the preamble had again been amended so as to express explicitly the granting by George II of his consent and recommendation. As a result, on 17 December the bill was defeated in the Commons by 123 votes to 118.[65] While the power struggle among Ireland's leading politicians and the contest over control of expenditure accounted for the bill's rejection, the willingness of MPs to vote against it may also have been owing to the fact that the bill did not contain any provisions for imposing additional duties. In 1751 MPs recognized the financial damage they would cause to the remaining public creditors if the Commons rejected a bill which provided appropriated duties for the continued servicing of the funded national debt. In 1753, that latter consideration was no longer relevant. While rejection in theory threatened the repayment of the remainder of the national debt, in reality the government chose to continue repayments by king's letter during the 1750s, with the principal eventually being reduced by 1759 to £5,200 and outstanding interest to £206, the lowest figures attained since the debt's inception in 1716.[66]

The conflict over the appropriation of surplus public income served to clarify certain developments in Irish politics and public finance since the 1690s. The dispute ultimately centred on who had the right to direct public expenditure. While government argued that the surplus was at the disposal of the Crown because it arose from the hereditary revenue and the non-appropriated parliamentary additional duties (an argument based on the view that the hereditary revenues in particular were the property of the Crown), the majority of MPs believed that all public income, from wherever it derived, was part of the 'public wealth', and therefore at the disposal of the nation, as represented by parliament.[67] Having laid the foundations in the 1660s, from the 1690s through to the 1710s the focal point of parliament had been upon gaining control of public income. Having achieved that aim, attention began to shift to control of expenditure, an endeavour that was made more realistic by the creation and maintenance of a national debt. The appropriation of specific additional duties and then of general surpluses delineated significant initial stages along that path. The journey was far from complete in 1754, but the return to parliament-sanctioned government borrowing in 1759 was to help advance the process further in the 1760s and 1770s.

In retrospect, the treasury surpluses of the late 1740s and early 1750s were an anomaly. The return to war in 1756 combined with a serious economic downturn resulted in the renewal of parliament-sanctioned borrowing in December 1759, when that assembly once again legislated for a new loan to the government of £150,000 for the 'security and defence' of Ireland and the King. The immediate cause of the loan was the widespread fear of a Franco-Jacobite invasion, and in particular the activities of Thurot, the French privateer. Within two months of the loan legislation, the Commons felt obliged to pass a vote of credit for £300,000 (the government availing of £200,000), which was occasioned by Thurot's landing at Carrickfergus. By that time the principal had risen to £350,000.[68] The continuing concerns over defence in the early 1760s saw the national debt rapidly increase. In the new parliament convened in late 1761 following the accession of George III, an act was passed to secure repayment of the £200,000 borrowed upon the 1760 vote of credit and to allow further borrowing 'not exceeding in the whole the sum of' £400,000 'to supply such deficiency as might arise in the aids, granted that session ... for the support of the civil and military establishments, and other necessary expenses of government for the defence of this kingdom'. With the same official justification, the Commons passed a vote of credit in February 1762 to allow for further borrowings of up to £200,000.[69] At the end of 1763, with the principal of the debt already risen to £650,000, a new loan of £100,000 was legislated for to make up any deficiencies in the taxes voted that session. By the end of 1765 the principal was down to £600,000, though another loan of £100,000 was sanctioned at that time, while in 1767, with the principal at £675,000, a further loan of £100,000 was allowed by parliament.[70]

Such loan legislation did not pass without opposition, particularly from among Patriot MPs who either looked to divert the money towards public works or to defeat the bills completely. However, they were never able to muster sufficient support to truly challenge or derail the process, though the three acts passed between 1763 and 1767 did include public works as part of the purpose of the loans.[71] As before, on all occasions the legislation made continuing provision for a sinking fund out of surpluses arising from the appropriated additional duties after payment of the interest, which decreased from 5 per cent to 4 per cent during the decade. In keeping with the increasing debt, the schedule of commodities for appropriated additional duties expanded throughout the 1760s as well.[72]

The government exercised a degree of caution in its borrowings and did not always avail itself of the full amounts sanctioned. Coupled with a functioning sinking fund, the debt did not escalate on a par with the amount of borrowing actually allowed. Even still, by the end of 1769 the principal stood at £655,000, at which time a new era was entered into with the legislated augmentation of the army. The financial foundation for payment of the additional 3,235 soldiers was a new loan of £100,000, which gave parliament another direct role in the control of expenditure.[73] Every two years thereafter the continued support of those soldiers was dependent upon parliamentary legislation, which was provided in 1771 by means of a further loan of £200,000 and thereafter out of the main supply act for the government's revenue-at-large.[74] Further loans were made during the 1770s to address military concerns and general deficiencies in the revenue with a corresponding increase in the overall debt.[75] By 1783 the combined national debt and pay arrears, as computed by parliament as the 'debt of the nation', stood at £1,919,386. It continued to escalate thereafter.[76]

The importance of the national debt for the provision of that essential extra income required for Irish governance in general and support of the military establishment in particular is evident. Of the fifty-one main supply acts passed in the period 1715–70, twenty-six related to the national debt, a fact which reveals the extent to which that debt quickly became an integral part of the considerations and procedures of the eighteenth-century Irish parliament. Of those twenty-six acts, nineteen appropriated specific additional duties for servicing the debt while twelve sanctioned the borrowing of money by government.[77] The question remains however as to where the loans came from in the first place. Who were the people who lent money to the government, and to what extent did a community of lenders or public creditors exist whose actions represented an expression of confidence in the state and a commitment to the role Ireland played within the British Empire? The answer to those questions is explored in Chapter 9.

9 THE PUBLIC CREDITORS

In order to create and maintain a national debt, there had to be a community of people willing to lend money to government. Such a community required certain assurances, most notably a credible commitment on the part of the government to repay loans, provision against deferment of repayment or default, and a secure tax base for financing interest payments and principal repayments. Such assurances could be provided in a number of ways. In eighteenth-century Britain and Ireland, the essential feature was a representative political institution in the form of a bicameral legislature which assembled on a regular basis, controlled taxation, and functioned primarily on the basis of majority coalition groupings that necessitated compromise and concession. Allied with recognizable and accepted procedures and institutions of executive government, ranging from the long-established Privy Council to the recently professionalized revenue collection service, the apparatus of state provided the credible commitment needed in eighteenth-century Britain and Ireland for a community of public creditors to exist.[1]

There was a reciprocity in the relationship between government and the public creditors. The people who lent money expressed confidence in the apparatus of the state because they attested, in a public manner, to the existence of sufficient assurance, or security, for the safe return of their investment. Ultimately, a national debt tied the community of lenders and the state more closely together in a relationship of mutual dependence that became self-perpetuating.[2] In both Britain and Ireland that relationship extended beyond national boundaries, because the creation and maintenance of a national debt was directly related to the expansion of the British Empire.[3]

Examination of the community of lenders in Ireland provides further insight into the extent to which Ireland played a role in the British Empire in the period 1692–1770. The emerging confidence within the Irish Protestant community in the apparatus of the state as represented by the Irish executive and legislature was most readily demonstrated by the willingness of a section of that community to lend its money to government from 1716 onwards. Admittedly, unlike in England, Protestants were a minority of the population in Ireland, but as the community from which the ruling elite was drawn, and as the main focus of both economic

and political power, they were no less significant for that fact. The Irish government's public creditors were Protestant peers, judges, MPs, clergymen, merchants
and the like, who, as part of the Irish Protestant community, already depended
for their survival upon the maintenance of the Revolution settlement in church
and state. Therein, although the creation of a national debt increased the government's reliance upon the Irish parliament, it also ensured that parliament, and the
wider Protestant community, developed an even greater vested interest in supplying the necessary funds for servicing the national debt and, in the wider context,
for maintaining an army capable of defending Ireland and actively contributing to
the expansion of the British Empire in the eighteenth century.

The Emergence of an Irish Public Credit System, 1716–29

The first Irish public creditors predated an Irish national debt. Three Irish people
were recorded as subscribers to the first long-term loans to the English government in 1693–4, a figure which had risen to 109 by the early 1720s, though
admittedly 100 of this latter number (eighty-three of whom lived in Dublin)
were South Sea stockholders whose investments amounted in total to £81,988.
The other nine held between them Bank of England stock worth £6,809.
Compared to Scottish investment, which remained negligible even in the mid-
eighteenth century, Irish involvement was worthy of note from the earliest days
of the development of a public credit system in England.[4]

However, the first parliament-sanctioned loan in Ireland was not raised
until 1716.[5] The government did not encounter any difficulty in accessing the
required £50,000, the availability of money being in part a reflection of a buoyant economic climate but even more so of the Protestant community's vested
interest in the defence of the Hanoverian succession and their sense of confidence built up over the previous two decades in the apparatus of the state.[6]
The profiles of the subscribers to the loan reflected this confidence. The largest
subscription, of £5,000, came from Speaker Conolly. At the same time, seventeen more MPs, four past or future MPs, six peers, four women, three bishops,
three judges (one of whom was also a peer), three clergymen, two aldermen
and twenty unidentified private people were included on the list of sixty-three
individual subscribers. Among the names were Conolly's two main political
rivals, Lord Chancellor Brodrick (£1,000) and his son, St John (£1,000). Others
included James Hamilton, Earl of Abercorn (£500); Robert Fitzgerald, Earl of
Kildare (£500); Chaworth Brabazon, Earl of Meath (£1,000); William Stewart,
Viscount Mountjoy (£500); Richard Boyle, Viscount Shannon (£1,000); Henry
Petty, Baron Shelburne (£1,000); St George Ashe, Bishop of Clogher (£500);
John Stearne, Bishop of Dromore (£300); Nicholas Forster, Bishop of Killaloe
(£300); William Whitshed, Lord Chief Justice of the King's Bench (£2,000);

John Forster, Lord Chief Justice of the Common Pleas (£1,000); Revenue Commissioner Thomas Medlycott (£1,000); Attorney-General George Gore (£500); Solicitor-General John Rogerson (£500); the private bankers Benjamin Burton (£2,000) and Francis Harrison (£2,000); Luke Gardiner, the future deputy vice-treasurer (£200); Charles Delafaye (£500) and his fellow chief secretary, Martin Bladen (£1,000); Undersecretary Eustace Budgell (£500); Postmaster-General Isaac Manley (£500); and the infamous Colonel Henry Luttrell (£200). Of the four women, the largest subscription came from Mrs Mary Bury (£2,000), followed by Mrs Jane Pigott (£800).[7]

In terms of the amount of the national debt, the variety of methods used by government and parliament for raising loans and providing for repayment, and the actual number of public creditors, Britain in 1716 clearly offered a far more complex and developed example of a public credit system at work. The estimated number of British public creditors stood at about 5,000 by the mid-1690s, at 10,000 by 1709, and at 40,000 by 1719–20. In 1697–8 the national debt stood at £16.7 million, by 1714 at £40.3 million, and by 1719 at over £50 million.[8] In such circumstances, comparisons with Ireland are meaningless. Little more can be deduced other than that Ireland, as a smaller country with a less developed economy and commercial trading sector, a much smaller population and political, social and religious divisions that were for the most part alien to England, could never be expected to replicate in comparatively equal terms the financial innovations of eighteenth-century England and Britain. However, in 1716, Ireland had commenced upon building a public credit system suited to its own economic, political and social abilities, its particular peculiar circumstances and its unique place in the emerging empire.

In the years after 1716 the Irish national debt was serviced through legislation passed in each biennial session of parliament. As the next parliament-sanctioned loan to the Irish government did not occur until 1729, there is little available evidence to assess the emerging community of lenders in the years between 1716 and 1729. The one area in which such a possibility does arise, however, is with regard to the proposed national bank in 1720–1.[9] Although the proposal ultimately met with failure, the initial process for establishing the bank made substantial progress and included the completion of three lists of people willing to subscribe money to fund the project. In 1720 two alternative proposals both included lists of potential subscribers, numbering 219 and 255 individuals respectively, though with a significant replication of names on each. A third list of 210 names, again with significant replication, was compiled in late 1721 as the proposal entered its final death throes in parliament. Taking account of name replication on the three lists, a total of 488 individuals were prepared in theory to subscribe to a national bank, though in reality a much smaller number would actually have been able to do so given that each individual list contained the projected maximum number of subscribers required to provide the necessary capital fund. If the bank had been a success, it would have been greatly over-subscribed, and there would have been many disappointed potential creditors. Within the composite figure of 488, there were sixteen peers, four bishops, a judge, 117 MPs, thirty past or future MPs, eighteen women, eleven Protestant clergymen, fifty-one merchants, five bankers, one goldsmith, twenty-three military officers, four aldermen, a lord mayor, and a further 206 unidentified people. Not all of the amounts to be subscribed were included on the lists, though when figures were given they varied in round numbers from £500 to £5,000 per person. Both of the proposals in 1720 were aimed at raising £500,000 and both had their subscriptions filled in quick time.[10]

The rejection of the national bank project by parliament ensured that none of these people actually had to hand over any cash in the end, and thus the majority of them remained, for the time being at least, only potential public creditors. It was also the case that many who had subscribed in mid-1720 had changed their minds by late 1721 owing to the drastically altered economic and political circumstances both in Ireland and abroad. This change in fortunes for the bank was most clearly reflected by the voting pattern of the 117 MPs who were on the subscription lists. There were three divisions in parliament which all went against the proposal by 103 to 95, 98 to 91 and 150 to 80 respectively. As Table 9.1 demonstrates, a significant minority of the 117 MPs chose to vote against the bank in the two divisions for which lists are extant. Of these 117, forty-six voted for the bank on both occasions, while twenty-five voted against; ten who voted for and one who voted against in October did not vote in December; five who voted for and eight who voted against in December had not voted in October; four who voted for in October voted against in December; and one who voted against in October voted for in December. Of the remaining eighteen unaccounted for MPs, one died before the 1721 session commenced, another was elevated to the Lords and the remainder were either absent or abstained from voting. The total number who voted for the bank at some point was sixty-six, while the total who voted against was thirty-nine.[11] Thus, despite the changed economic and political climate in late 1721, the majority of the subscriber MPs remained in favour of the project.

Table 9.1: Voting pattern of MPs on the national bank lists, for and against the bank proposal, October and December 1721.

October		December	
For	Against	For	Against
60 [95]	27 [103]	52 [80]	37 [150]

(Totals for the two divisions are given in square brackets)

It is more difficult to assess the attitude of the wider Protestant community. Only ninety-three of the original subscribers to the two lists in 1720 appeared among the 210 names listed in late 1721. This absence at least 278 of the original subscribers suggests that much of the early enthusiasm outside parliament had been dispelled by late 1721. However, it cannot be assumed that all 278 had lost interest in the project, but rather that some may have been excluded because the subscription was full. Likewise, the presence of 117 wholly new subscribers in 1721 offered some counterbalance to the apparently significant swing in opinion. The new subscribers included fifteen MPs, among whom was the pro-bank pamphleteer, Henry Maxwell. They were joined by twenty-eight MPs from the original 1720 lists, signifying that seventy-four MPs had fallen by the wayside in the interim, though once again the reasons are unclear. Of the MPs on the 1721 list, forty voted for the bank, including Maxwell and twelve other new subscribers who presumably had felt the need to show a public financial commitment, at least on paper, to the beleaguered project. Less easily explained is the presence of three MPs who voted against the bank, two of whom were making their first appearance as subscribers. Presumably they had a late change of mind, as they only voted against the proposal in the third division.[12]

Ultimately, the history of the bank project suggests that many more potential public creditors existed within the Irish Protestant community in the early 1720s. More definitive proof began to emerge when a second parliament-sanctioned loan to government of £150,000 was legislated for in 1729 and the first steps towards a more comprehensive provision for servicing the debt occurred with the appropriation of specific additional duties and the creation of a sinking fund, both of which innovations provided potential public creditors with further credible commitments for the payment of interest and the repayment of the principal.[13]

As in 1716, there was no shortage of willing public creditors in 1729. Given that the loan was aimed at clearing part of the army pay arrears, priority was to be given to subscriptions in the form of debentures or warrants for such arrears. Held for the most part by army officers, regimental agents and private individuals and bankers who had advanced cash to the army,[14] these debentures and warrants were to be treated as 'ready money' in the loan subscription, receiving interest and principal repayments in the same fashion as cash amounts.[15] By March 1730, £52,000 had been subscribed in this form by eighty-four people, of whom forty-four were army officers. It is unclear whether these officers were subscribing debentures for their own arrears or that of the soldiers under their command. Over half of the army officers had Huguenot or non-English surnames. The non-military subscribers of debentures included amounts between £50 and £300 from seven women who were probably relatives of army officers, given that most of their surnames also appeared to be of Huguenot origin. Three clergymen (£50, £300, and £550 respectively) and Josiah Hort, Bishop of

Kilmore (£1,000), also subscribed debentures, as did the private bankers Daniel Falkiner (£100) and David La Touche (£50), and Lord Chancellor Thomas Wyndham (£2,000). The single largest debenture subscription, of £5,300, came from Undersecretary Thomas Tickell. In total £59,758 was subscribed in debentures, all of which appeared to be the same as those upon which interest had been allowed to their owners since 1726. The refusal to accept any debentures grown due after that time was owing to the need to allow for the subscription of sufficient amounts of ready specie to meet immediate cash requirements, in particular the exporting of £40,000 to England for the pay of soldiers in Gibraltar.[16]

To that end, a further £90,242 was subscribed in ready money by eighty-six individuals. These cash subscribers included the new undertakers Sir Ralph Gore (£2,000) and Marmaduke Coghill (£1,500); the future undertaker Henry Boyle (£1,500); the leading opponent of the altered loan bill Richard Bettesworth (£350); Solicitor-General Robert Jocelyn (£1,000); Chief Secretary Thomas Clutterbuck (£3,600); Richard Coote, Earl of Bellomont (£500); Richard Lambart, Earl of Cavan (£1,000); Robert Howard, Bishop of Elphin (£500); Revenue Commissioner Thomas Medlycott (£1,000); and Baron of the Exchequer St John St Leger (£2,200). Eight women subscribed ready specie in varying amounts from £100 to £1,000. Six army officers, five of whom had not subscribed debentures, lent sums varying from £400 to £2,000. The single largest cash subscription, of £6,000, came from a privy councillor, Sir Gustavus Hume. Seven people, including Tickell (£5,300 and £1,400), were creditors for both debentures and ready specie, so that the total number of individual subscribers was 163, comprising two peers, two bishops, two judges, fifty MPs, three past or future MPs, fifteen women, four Protestant clergymen, one banker, forty-nine military officers and thirty-five unidentified others.[17]

The list of subscribers to the loan demonstrated, as in 1716, not only the business aptitude of people, but also the confidence of many individuals in the central apparatus of the state and of their understanding of a public credit system. Indeed, the competition among potential subscribers led to several MPs objecting in March 1730 that the act had been contravened because ready specie was being prioritized over debentures in order to pay the soldiers in Gibraltar. Partly for that reason the Lord Lieutenant had chosen to take cash subscriptions 'from about fifty parliament men, and several others whom he had a mind to gratify'. Yet it was also the case that many of the arrears 'due to the officers were in such small sums ... that it was impossible to make out debentures to answer them all with their interest, without great difficulty and infinite number of such debentures'.[18]

Such a competitive atmosphere would suggest that even more potential public creditors existed. Comparison of the two loan lists from 1716 and 1729 shows that money was lent on both occasions by the following seven people: Hume (£1,000 and £6,000), Manley (£500 and £1,500), Medlycott (£1,000 and £1,000), Henry Sandford (£500 and £500), Anthony Sheppard (£1,000 and £2,000), Major-General Owen Wynne (£1,000 and £1,500), and John Curtis (£1,000 and £1,950). All but Curtis were also MPs. Therefore a total of 219 individual people were successful in subscribing to a loan between 1716 and 1729. As overviewed in Table 9.2, a projection of how many more willing lenders might have existed can be facilitated by comparison with the 488 names on the bank lists, of whom forty-six subscribed to one loan and a bank, with a possible two more, while seven others, plus possible one more, subscribed to both loans and a bank. That still left 432 individuals who had been prepared to subscribe to a bank but were not on either loan list.[19]

Table 9.2: Public creditors and potential creditors, 1716–29.

Subscribers	1716	1720–1	1729
Peers	6	16	2
Bishops	3	4	2
Judges	3	1	2
MPs	18	117	50
Past or future MPs	4	30	3
Women	4	18	15
Clergy	3	11	4
Merchants	—	51	—
Bankers	—	2	1
Merchant/bankers	—	3	—
Goldsmiths	—	1	—
Military officers	—	23	49
Aldermen	2	4	—
Lord Mayor	—	1	—
Other	20	206	35
Totals	63	488	163

It was not surprising that the seven subscribers to both loans had also subscribed to a bank. Of the six MPs, Hume initially voted against and then for the bank, while Manley, Medlycott, Sandford, Sheppard and Wynne voted for it. Twelve people can also be identified who subscribed to the 1716 loan and a bank, of whom six were MPs. Benjamin Burton, Francis Harrison and Jacob Peppard voted against and Benjamin Parry and Oliver St George voted for the bank, while St John Brodrick initially voted for and then against. Burton and Harrison were also partners in one of the most important and reputedly safe private banks in Ireland, which had survived the South Sea crisis and had close links to the government. Thus their decision to vote against the proposal may well have convinced other MPs to do likewise.[20] Brodrick's decision to vote against, despite being one of the original petitioners for a bank charter, may also have influenced MPs.[21] Of these six, only Parry and St George were alive in 1729–30, but there is no evidence as to why they were not included in the 1729 loan subscription.[22]

Of the remaining six subscribers to the 1716 loan and a bank, it is impossible to assess the attitude of four of them in 1729 as they remain little more than unidentified names.[23] The fifth was Lord Abercorn, who had been a leading promoter of the bank in 1720. The absence of his name in 1729 is less easily explained given that he was still a willing investor, as his financial backing of the colony of Georgia in 1733 attested. The sixth was Gardiner, whose appointment as deputy vice-treasurer in 1725 may account for his absence in 1729 given that he was responsible for taking subscriptions and therefore may have been excluded on ethical grounds.[24] It was certainly the case that his predecessor, John Pratt, although a subscriber to a bank, had not lent money in 1716. The right of the deputy vice-treasurer to make use of public revenue in his hands for his own private use most also have served as grounds for exclusion.[25]

Thirty-four people subscribed to a bank and the 1729 loan. Fifteen were MPs, of whom James Barry, Thomas Carter, Hugh Henry,[26] Accountant-General Mathew Pennefather, Richard Tighe, Frederick Trench and Richard Warburton ultimately voted against the bank, Thomas Bligh, Francis Burton,[27] David Chaigneau, Chancellor of the Exchequer Sir Ralph Gore, Francis Lucas, Henry Singleton and Sir Thomas Taylor voted for it, and Arthur Hill[28] initially voted for and then against. The remainder included Falkiner,[29] Thomas Staunton and Major-General Robert Napper, all of whom were first elected to parliament in 1727, and La Touche, Baron of the Exchequer St Leger, Bishop Hort and Captain Theophilus Desbrisay.[30] Little is known of the remaining twelve.[31]

It was not surprising that the seven individuals who lent money in both 1716 and 1729 had ultimately been in favour of the bank proposal and that seven of the bank-subscriber MPs who voted for it in 1721 also subscribed to the 1729 loan. That a further seven bank-subscriber MPs who had in the end voted against the project but were still prepared to lend money in 1729 adds weight to the argument that a significant number of MPs opposed the bank owing to concern about specific economic difficulties rather than suspicion of the concept of a national bank or a public credit system. Either way, by 1729 a significant community of public creditors clearly existed in Ireland.

Administering the Debt, 1745–59

As already seen, further loans to the government were sanctioned in 1731, 1740, 1741 and 1745.[32] As in 1716 and 1729, there proved little difficulty in finding people to lend money to the government on each occasion. The names of these public creditors and the administrative and financial details of the management of the national debt from 1745 to 1759 were recorded in a series of ledgers kept by the teller of the exchequer, Nathaniel Clements.[33] For the year 1745–6 there were a total of 404 names listed in the relevant ledger, the first two of whom received £100 each as repayment of the principal they had lent, the standard value of one loan debenture being £100. The remaining 402 people received interest payments on their principal sums. From June 1745 to March 1746, the total interest paid out was £14,545 5s. The largest single interest payment was £615 to the private bank, Henry Mitchell and John Macarrell, one of five banks included in the ledger. Mitchell and Macarrell also received £563 in another payment, bringing their total receipts to £1,178. The four other banks were those of La Touche, Lunell, Fade and Swift. As Table 9.3 shows, many other individuals also received substantial payments, which demonstrated the significant income that a public creditor could receive from investing in the Irish government. There were numerous multiple entries for the same individuals, with the largest number of eleven separate payments amounting to £162 being made to John Chaigneau. In total there were about 118 multiple entries, while the actual number of individual public creditors paid interest during the period was 236, though the inclusion of at least five private banks would suggest that there was a larger unknown number of people whose money was also being lent to government.[34]

Table 9.3: Interest payments in excess of £100, 1745–6.

Subscriber	Amount	Subscriber	Amount
Mitchell & co.	£1,178	Johnston, Capt.	£199
Dayly, Mr	£626	Desbrisay, Capt.	£178
Swift & co.	£619	Caldwell, Mr	£176
Bayly, Mr	£493	La Touche & co.	£167
Pelletreau, Mr	£452	Chaigneau, John	£162
Gervais, Mr	£377	Pallisier, Mr	£162
Bernard, Mr	£333	Elphin, Bishop of	£144
Lennox, Mr	£327	Cockburn, Mr	£140
Morgan, Mr	£314	Sandys, Mr	£140
Gibson, Dr	£276	Bragg, General	£132
Clements, Mr	£274	Putland, Mr	£128
Brickenden, Mr	£244	Parker, Capt.	£125
Cooke, Mr	£243	Fairbrother, Mr	£120
Colvill, Mr	£240	Finlay, Mr	£120
Bowes, Baron	£231	Card, Mr	£118
Tighe, Robert	£226	Clarke, Mr	£114
Cooper, Mr	£220	Killaloe, Bishop of	£104
Barrington, Mr	£217	Stopford, Mr	£100

The majority of the subscribers to the 1745 loan were listed in the ledger for 1746–7. The debentures were in units of £100 each and the total subscribed between March 1746 and February 1747 was £50,000 recorded in seventy-seven separate entries. However, as usual, several persons subscribed more than once, while others contributed as part of a group. As detailed in Table 9.4, the single largest subscription was £10,000 by Gleadowe and company. The number of

people for whom the bank was acting, either with the depositors' knowledge or
not, was not recorded. Discounting the identifiable multiple subscriptions, there
remained sixty separate individual subscriptions, although some of these may
still have been replications of the same person with variant names or individuals
acting for larger private groupings or for specific organizations such as the ministers and dean of St Anne's (£100), the trustees of Steevens' hospital (£1,800)
and the governors of the Erasmus Smith's charities (£2,800).[35]

Table 9.4: Subscriptions of more than £1,000, 1746–7.

Subscriber	Amount
Gleadowe & co.	£10,000
Erasmus Smith charities, governors of	£2,800
Chrismas, Thomas	£2,000
Cooper, William	£2,000
Malone, Anthony	£2,000
Steevens' hospital, trustees of	£1,800
Dublin, Archbishop of, Dr Charles Cobbe	£1,800
Tilson, Mrs Elizabeth	£1,800
Dawson, Arthur & Prior, Thomas	£1,500
Newburgh, Mr	£1,500
Crosbie, Sir Warren (by sundry persons)	£1,300
Gardiner, Mr	£1,100
Barry, Edward, esq.	£1,000
Monck, Charles, esq.	£1,000

The list of subscribers in 1746–7 demonstrated once again that a substantial
pool of public creditors existed in Ireland. At the same time, the normal routine
of interest payments went on. In 1746–7 the total amount paid out was £14,185
15s. in 362 entries of which about 105 were multiple, so that the actual number
of individual creditors was 230. While many names were the same as those listed
in 1745–6, there were a number of notable new arrivals such as Gleadowe and
company, whose £10,000 subscription in 1746–7 had made them one of the
highest earners of interest payments at £537. However, Mitchell and Macarrell
were still in front on £1,105. Others were noticeable by their absence, in particular Swift and company. As before, at the lower levels people received as little as
£2 or £4 in interest. In 1747–8 the total amount paid out in interest was £14,715
5s. on 366 entries of which about 103 were multiple, so that the total for individuals was 228, though the inclusion of banks as ever made for a higher, unknown
number of public creditors. Overall, the ledger lists for 1746–8 demonstrated
once again the substantial and regular incomes public creditors received from
investing in government.[36]

     There were no extant records for 1748–9, though in 1749–50 a new require-
ment appeared in Clements's ledgers for repayment of the debt principal on the
basis of the 1749 Debt Repayment Act.[37] It was not specified in the ledger for

1749–50 what amount of the debt repayment was made by way of the act, though the amount repaid was substantial, totalling £79,450. Many of the repayments were recorded by debenture number only (nineteen cases did not even have that), thereby hiding the identity of the majority of subscribers. Thus, although there were 102 separate entries, only thirty-five included a name, with three multiple payments reducing the number of individuals to thirty-two, to whom £22,800 was paid. As detailed in Table 9.5, the entry for 'N. C.' may have referred to Nathaniel Clements, as may the entry for Mr Clements. The number of individual debentures entered for the other repayments cannot be used as a means of identifying the unnamed subscribers, given that some owned multiple debentures, others owned one, and some debentures were owned by groups, so that the total number of public creditors repaid principal sums in 1749–50 is not quantifiable.[38]

Table 9.5: Principal repayments made to public creditors, 1749–50.

Subscriber	Amount	Subscriber	Amount
N. C.	£5,700	Barry, Carleton	£100
Clements, Mr, for C.C.	£4,700	Becheser, Col.	£100
Dayly, Mr	£2,600	Belcher, Mr	£100
Lennox, Mr	£2,200	Bibby, Mr	£100
La Touche, Mr	£1,800	Cook, Mr	£100
Malone, Councillor	£1,100	Cuppaidge, Mr	£100
Leeson, Mr	£600	Enraight, Mr	£100
Hart, Alderman	£500	Houlding, Mr	£100
Gervais, Mr	£400	Meares, Mr	£100
Malone, Edmond	£400	Morell, Maj.	£100
Mercer, Mr	£300	Nicholson, Mr	£100
Bragg, General	£200	Prior, Mr	£100
Ewing, Mr	£200	Rousiliere, Capt.	£100
Rousiliere, Mr	£200	Stopford, Mr	£100
Usher, Mr	£200	Studholme, Mr	£100
Nesbitt, Mr	£150	Gleadowe, Mr	£50

In October 1751 it was recorded in the Commons that £147,400 of the principal debt had been repaid between March 1749 and March 1751.[39] Given that the 1749 act had provided for £128,500 to be repaid out of the general revenue surplus, it was evident that a further £18,900 had been cleared from the appropriated duties sinking fund at the same time. As only £79,450 of this amount was accounted for in Clements's extant ledgers, the details for almost half of the repayments remain unknown.

As before, interest continued to be paid with £16,835 6s. 8d. being issued in 1749–50 on 458 separate entries of which about 113 were multiple, thereby leaving a total of 263 separate individuals. Mitchell and Macarrell were no longer the recipients of the largest payments, which would suggest that the bank's debenture holdings had been reduced. A Mr Prior received the single largest payment of £770, though if 'N. C.' and 'Mr Clements' were both references to Nathaniel Clements himself, then he would have topped the list on £1,275. As before, there were five banks,[40] which with a new entry for 'several persons' (£56), signified a further unknown number of public creditors.[41]

The 1751 Debt Repayment Act appropriated £120,000 to repay principal debt to those debenture-holders drawn in a lottery.[42] A list of 1,200 debenture numbers of £100 value each drawn in January 1752 was advertised in print on 4 February, starting with debenture number 2 and rising by random selection up to 3107. All were to be repaid on 25 March. A further 100 debentures were advertised for repayment on 12 May, the last of which was debenture number 3110, which also happened to be the highest debenture number recorded anywhere in the ledgers.[43] While the first 1,200 debentures were those cleared by the 1751 act, the remainder were presumably repaid from the appropriated duties sinking fund. Some of these repayments were recorded in Clements's ledger for 1752–3 under the heading of 'loan principal great drawing'. The total amount paid to named individuals was £77,500, though the overall total recorded was £120,000 owing to a number of general entries for repayments and an amount from another non-extant account. The repayments were dated from April 1752 to March 1753. The debenture numbers were recorded as well, including sixty without names or payments which were 'standing out' on 25 March 1752 presumably because the owners had not as yet redeemed them. Eighteen appear to have been cleared subsequently. There were 196 separate entries of people of which about thirty-four were multiple, so that the number of individuals was 137, the top twenty-two of whom are detailed in Table 9.6.[44]

Table 9.6: Principal repayments in excess of £1,000, 1752–3.

Subscriber	Amount	Subscriber	Amount
Gleadowe, Mr	£7,600	Machony, Dr	£1,400
Curtis, Mr	£3,800	Cary, Archdeacon	£1,300
Stopford, Dr	£3,700	Gleadowe & co.	£1,300
J. C.	£3,000	Hutchinson, Mrs	£1,200
Mitchell & co.	£2,300	Killaloe, Bp of	£1,200
Elphin, Bishop of	£2,100	Gervais, Mr	£1,100
Morris, Mr	£1,900	Hume, Mr	£1,100
Fairbrother, Mr	£1,800	Macartney, Mr	£1,100
Meredyth, Mr	£1,700	Patrick, Mr	£1,100
Lennox, Mr	£1,500	Card, Mr	£1,000
Lawson, Dr	£1,400	Chaigneau, John	£1,000

Repayment of such substantial amounts of principal debt reduced the number of people who continued to receive interest in the 1750s. Payments in March 1752 totalled only £2,766 15*s*. with 202 separate entries of which about thirty-one were multiple, leaving 147 separate individuals. Only four payments exceeded

£100, to Gleadowe and company (£253), Dr Stopford (£182), Mr Fairbrother (£167) and Mr Curtis (£114). A similar pattern emerged in June with £4,284 paid out on 243 separate entries of which about fifty-seven were multiple, leaving 169 separate individuals. The payments in excess of £100 were made to John Chaigneau (£240), Dr Stopford (£206), Mr Meredyth (£203), Mr Fairbrother (£169), Gleadowe and company (£166), Mitchell and Macarrell (£160), and Captain Johnston (£104).[45]

The failure of the 1753 debt repayment bill did not ultimately undermine the continued clearing of the principal debt out of the general revenue surplus in the 1750s. In March 1754 a king's letter directing that the national debt be reduced was issued, an action which it was felt would help to maintain credit.[46] Indeed, with the belated release of this cash from the treasury, difficulties arising from an economic downturn in the early 1750s and the concomitant decline in credit for normal commercial activity were alleviated to a degree.[47] In late 1754 it was rumoured that the legality of 'the order for the payment of the surplus' by king's letter was to be raised at Westminster,[48] but this was dismissed in Ireland, from whence it was reported 'that no men ... ha[ve] ever doubted the legality of the act[ion] and there is not a single creditor who has not received his money'.[49]

The repayment of both interest and principal by way of king's letter, or licence, in 1754–5 amounted to £65,517 13s. 3d. on 172 separate entries of which about twenty-four were multiple, so that the actual number of individuals was 137. There were no payments under £100, and most were between £100 and £1,000. As Table 9.7 shows, however, there were some who still received much more substantial amounts, such as Mitchell and Macarrell and John Chaigneau.[50]

Table 9.7: Principal repayments in excess of £1,000 made by king's letter, 1754–5.

Subscriber	Amount	Subscriber	Amount
Mitchell & co.	£5,602	Ford, Mr	£1,113
Chaigneau, John	£4,584	Bayly, Mr	£1,019
Eyre, Mr	£1,935	Dawson, Alderman	£1,019
Stopford, Mr	£1,730	Fairbrother, Mr	£1,019
Meredyth, Mr	£1,630	Faulkner, Mr	£1,019
Daly, Mr	£1,528	Yorke, LCJ	£1,019
Elphin, Bishop of	£1,324	Cavendish, Mr	£1,018
La Touche & co.	£1,118		

At the same time, the remaining principal debt continued to be repaid out of the appropriated duties sinking fund. Between April 1754 and March 1755 a total of £6,300 was repaid by this means on twenty-three entries of which three were multiple, leaving a total of seventeen individuals. The only payments over £1,000 were to Mitchell and Macarrell (£1,600) and a Mr Lennox (£1,300). Interest payments also continued with £1,534 being paid during the same period on 117 separate entries of which about nineteen were multiple, leaving eighty-eight separate individuals. The only payments over £100 were to the Archbishop of Dublin (£210) and Mitchell and Macarrell (£153). In the following years to 1759, sinking fund payments continued to be recorded in the ledgers, though in decreasing numbers. The number of interest payments totalled only twenty of which four were multiple, leaving a total of thirteen separate individuals with only one in excess of £100, paid to Mitchell and Macarrell (£300). Principal repayments amounted to £4,000 on twelve entries of which only three were identified, being a Mr Putland (£1,900), Mr Bowen (£200) and Captain Desbrisay (£100).[51]

The final account relating to the national debt in Clements's ledgers was for £14,668 4s. loan principal repaid by king's letters between 1755 and 1759. Of thirty-one separate entries, twenty-nine included names. Of the two unnamed, one actually accounted for forty separate debentures to the value of £4,074 10s. Seven were multiple payments, and there was a total of nineteen separate individuals. The only payments in excess of £1,000 were made to Mitchell and Macarrell (£3,973) and Mr Besnard (£1,222).[52] As is evident, by 1759, on the eve of the recommencement of parliament-sanctioned government borrowing, the principal debt and the number of public creditors had been greatly reduced. But both would readily and rapidly escalate once again in the 1760s beyond the highest levels achieved in both respects in the period 1716–59.[53]

Numbers and Names

The question remains as to the number of public creditors in existence in the 1740s and 1750s, and the overall total for the period 1716–59. The total number of individual subscribers in Clements's ledgers was 700, inclusive of each group entry such as the banks, Trinity College Dublin, the Erasmus Smith charities, Steevens's and the Royal hospital, and the various 'several persons' and 'sundry persons' being counted as a single individual. When amalgamated with the loan lists from 1716 and 1729, the number of possible public creditors increases to 919.

In Clements's ledgers, many names were entered with surname and title only, so that it is difficult to ascertain if they are the same person as equivalent surnames on the 1716 and 1729 loan lists. Some overlaps can be clarified, however. The unqualified entry for the Protestant Bishop of Clogher who lent £500 in 1716 was St George Ashe, while the incumbent who received interest payments in 1749–50 and 1754–5 and a principal repayment of £101, 3s. 4d. in 1754–5 was Robert Clayton.[54] What is less certain is whether the original loan was a personal investment by Ashe, whether further loans were made by John Stearne when bishop between 1717 and 1745, or if the loan or loans were part of the bishopric's endowments. These financial dealings may best be explained by the fact that Clogher was considered to be a wealthy bishopric. Stearne, who as Bishop of

Dromore in 1716 had also subscribed £300, became renowned for his generosity and it was he and a later Clogher incumbent, John Garnett, bishop from 1758 to 1782, who were able to afford the rebuilding of the episcopal palace and cathedral.[55] The unqualified entry for the Bishop of Elphin who subscribed £500 in 1729 was probably Robert Howard as he had just succeeded Theophilus Bolton on his translation to Cashel, while the incumbent who received various payments between 1745 and 1755 was Edward Synge.[56] Having collected at least £382 in interest by 1752, Synge had also received principal repayments of £3,424 4s. 3d. by 1755.[57] Little wonder then that at his death in 1762 he was said to be worth £100,000, while his daughter was worth £50,000 at the time of her marriage.[58] The Bishop of Killaloe in 1716, Nicholas Forster, lent £300, while a later incumbent, Nicholas Synge, brother of Edward, received interest of £259 between 1746 and 1752 and principal repayments of £1,913 9d. in 1752–5.[59] Following his translation to Waterford in January 1746 the previous incumbent at Killaloe, Richard Chenevix, received £37 in interest and also lent £700 in 1746–7.[60] Other bishops included Hort of Kilmore who lent £1,000 in debentures and £550 in cash in 1729 and then as Archbishop of Tuam received interest of £144 in 1745–7; Robert Downes, who as Bishop of Ferns received £50 interest in 1749–50 and as Bishop of Raphoe received £38 interest and £203 15s. 2d. principal in 1752–5; John Hoadly, Archbishop of Armagh, who received £93 interest in 1745; and Charles Cobbe, Archbishop of Dublin, who lent £1,800 in 1746–7 and received interest of at least £488 between 1746 and 1755.[61]

Of all these bishops, however, only Hort can readily be identified as being on both a loan list and in Clements's Ledgers. There are eleven other such instances: Richard Wolseley, who lent £2,400 in 1729 is probably the MP who, having been made a baronet in 1745, received £160 interest in 1749–50; Francis Bindon, subscriber of £100 in 1729 and £500 in 1746; John Bowes, subscriber of £650 in 1729 and, as Lord Chief Baron of the Exchequer, recipient of £459 interest between 1745 and 1748; David Chaigneau MP, a Dublin merchant of Huguenot descent who lent £500 in 1729 and received interest of £12 in 1746–7; Dean Cross, subscriber of £1,850 in 1729 and recipient of £892 interest between 1746 and 1750; Theophilus Desbrisay, subscriber of £100 in 1729 and, when serving as one of the regimental agents, recipient of £715 interest and £601 17s. 3d. principal between 1745 and 1759; Deputy Vice-Treasurer Gardiner, subscriber before his appointment of £200 in 1716, recipient of £24 interest in 1746–7 and a governor of Steevens's hospital and the Erasmus Smith charities, both of which were grouped public creditors; Robert Jocelyn MP, subscriber of £1,000 in 1729 and, as Baron Newport, of £800 in 1746–7, recipient of £174 interest in 1745–7 and £305 11s. 9d. in 1754–5, and a governor of both Steevens's and the Royal hospital; David La Touche, son of the founder of the bank, who subscribed £50 in 1729, while La Touche and company received £715 interest and

£2,017 12*s.* 6*d.* principal between 1745 and 1755; Francis Lucas MP, a governor of the Erasmus Smith charities who lent £1,000 in 1729 and received £61 interest in 1746; and Robert Tighe, who subscribed £600 in 1729 and either he or his son received £328 interest and £304 principal between 1746 and 1755.[62]

These twelve replications reduce the figure for public creditors between 1716 and 1759 to 907. This total can be further reduced to 844 by discounting one equivalent surname from Clements's ledgers where surnames are the same or similar to those on the 1716 or 1729 lists. Such a process implies that on top of the twelve creditors already identified, a further sixty-three people from 1716–29 were still public creditors in 1745–59 and an extra 625 people had invested their money in government since 1729, which represents a significant growth in that community.

As before, comparison with Britain places the Irish situation in context. In the 1750s the British national debt was more than £70 million, with between 53,000 and 60,000 estimated public creditors. About 14–15 per cent of the debt was owned by non-English creditors. However, Irish holdings and the number of individual creditors had decreased since the 1720s. Thirty-one Irish investors held between them £27,031 worth of stock in the Bank of England, the East India Company and South Sea Annuities.[63] In terms of Irish investors in other money-raising ventures for the British government, the most significant was Clements himself, whose short-term investment schemes for making money with Irish treasury funds for his own benefit included the purchase in late 1749 of £51,000 worth of stock from the 1748 loan to the British government.[64]

The problems identified in comparing the 1716 and 1729 loan lists with those from 1745–59 are replicated when Clements's ledgers are compared with the bank lists. While many surnames are the same or similar, the use of military and other titles such as 'Mr', 'Mrs', 'Dr', 'Miss' and 'Rev.' rather than first names in Clements's ledgers prevents any significant assessment of replications. As already ascertained, David Chaigneau was on a bank list and lent money in 1729 and received interest in 1746–7. Others who can be cross-referenced with a degree of certainty include the merchant James Swift, who was described as a banker on the bank lists and was most probably associated with the bank of Swift and company, Captain Theophilus Desbrisay, Deputy Vice-Treasurer Gardiner, Francis Lucas MP and Sir Robert Maude MP. The William Tighe listed in 1720–1 may have been father of the William Tighe who was a public creditor in the 1740s-50s, as was the case for Richard Wolseley MP in 1720–1, who was probably the father of the Richard Wolseley who lent money in 1729 and, as a baronet, received interest in 1749–50.[65]

It is difficult to identify more names in Clements's ledgers. On the basis of title, 283 out of the maximum calculation of 700 public creditors for 1745–59 can be grouped in some form. As detailed in Table 9.8, the largest number, though the most general individual grouping, is ninety-eight women. Of these, few can be readily identified. Mrs Judith Cramer, who lent £200 in 1746–7, was probably the only daughter of Brinsley Butler, Viscount Lanesborough. Mrs Conolly, who received interest payments of at least £444 between 1745 and 1750, was possibly Katherine, widow of Speaker Conolly. Mrs Anne Henry, who lent £500 in 1746–7, may have been the widow of the banker Hugh Henry. Lady Kildare, who received interest of £30 in 1747–8, may well have been Emilia Mary Lennox, wife of James Fitzgerald, Earl of Kildare, or indeed his mother, Mary, given that her late husband, the nineteenth earl, had subscribed to the 1716 loan. Likewise, Lady Catherine Meade, who lent £500 in 1746–7, may have been the wife of Sir Richard Meade MP, who died in 1744. Mrs Jane Pearson, who lent £500 in 1746–7, may have been a niece of Speaker Conolly and the widow of Thomas Pearson MP. Mrs Eleanor Westenra, who lent £200 in 1746–7, may have been the wife of Henry Westenra and daughter of Sir Joshua Allen.[66]

Table 9.8: Public creditors, 1745–59.

Identifier	Number of subscribers
Women	98
Military Officers	78
Protestant Clergy	39
Doctors (Dr)	31
Aldermen/councillors	19
Banks	8
Judges	4
Hospitals	2
Trinity College Dublin	2
Peers	1
Charities	1
Total	283

While some of the women may have been the beneficiaries of investments made by husbands, fathers or other male relatives, many others, as in 1716 and 1729, were investors in their own right. In 1746–7, eleven women were recorded among the sixty individuals who subscribed to the 1745 loan. These were Cramer (£200), Henry (£500), Meade (£500), Pearson (£500), Mrs Mary Coghill (£100), Mrs Alice Dowdall (£100), Mrs Ann Durand (£300), Mrs Jane Maziere (£500), Mrs Elizabeth Tilson (£1,800), Eleanor Westenra (£200) and Mrs Penelope Westenra (£100). As before, women with disposable income in the 1740s were prepared to invest their money in government.[67]

Among the seventy-eight military officers noted in Table 9.8, there was a particularly large number of names that appear to be of Huguenot origin. While the already identified Captain Desbrisay's involvement as a public creditor was presumably connected with his emerging role as one of the regimental agents, others may simply have had private income or have been business-minded. It was certainly the case that in 1729 a large number of officers subscribed to the loan in the form of debentures for army pay arrears, possibly because they had financed their men's pay out of their own pocket. The only names recorded for people who, as allowed in the legislation, cashed in their loan debentures in between formal repayment periods were also army officers. In May 1738, Captain Sheyne (£329 6s. 6d.), Captain Banastre (£100), and Major Stewart (£109 18s. 3d.) were paid by the treasury for the return of five debentures in total. A further thirteen debentures were returned between 17 May and 12 July 1738, though the owners were not recorded. Almost as quickly as the debentures came in, however, new creditors purchased them, with fifteen of the eighteen resubscribed by 12 July. Although the new creditors were not named, in all but two cases they were purchased for the usual sum of £100 each. For the remaining two, the new subscribers seem to have been obliged, or willing, to also pay an equivalent of interest on their purchases.[68] These transactions demonstrate how readily new subscribers could be found and how easily the number of public creditors could increase and their profiles change over the years.

Apart from the bishops already identified, there is little evidence as to who the remainder of the thirty-nine Protestant clergy were owing to the use of titles such as 'Dean' or 'Rev.' rather than first names. Even less can be said about the thirty-one entries with the title 'Dr'. There is no certainty as to whether these people were medical doctors or clergymen, apart from Dr Mosse who received £21 in interest in 1747–8 and was probably Dr Bartholomew Mosse, founder of the women's lying-in hospital in Dublin.[69] Likewise, little can be said about the nineteen aldermen and councillors. The eight private banks or companies speak for themselves, while the investments made by the trustees and governors of the two hospitals, the Erasmus Smith charities and the bursar and fellows of Trinity College Dublin seem to represent good business practice, either for the benefit of the named institutions or, less edifyingly, for the trustees, governors and fellows themselves.

The presence in Clements's ledgers of only one peer, Charles, Baron Moore of Tullamore, the muster-master-general, was in keeping with a rapidly diminishing financial interest on the part of the Irish peerage in the country's national debt and public credit system.[70] In 1716, Lords Abercorn, Kildare, Meath, Shelburne, Shannon and Mountjoy had subscribed to the loan, while in 1729 only Lords Bellomont and Cavan did so. By the 1740s not only had all of these individuals themselves ceased to be public creditors, but in the cases where the original lender had died their heirs had also disappeared from the lists.[71] Only the House of Kildare can with any certainty be identified, through Lady Kildare, as still being among the public creditors. Whether owing to absenteeism, other financial commitments, private financial crises or other factors, by the mid-eighteenth century the Irish peerage, for all intents and purposes, had ceased to be a factor in relation to public credit and debt. However, such a situation was not exceptional, as a similar lack of involvement was evident on the part of the British peerage in relation to Britain's national debt.[72]

The four judges in Clements's ledgers were all originally from England. Lord Chancellor Jocelyn was actually raised to the Irish peerage in 1743 as Baron Newport, though he had been a public creditor long before that time. As an ambitious young lawyer making a career in Ireland, he had been elected to parliament in 1727 and first lent money in 1729.[73] The other judges were Lord Chief Baron Bowes who made his career in Ireland in the 1730s as an MP and as solicitor- and attorney-general, Richard Mountney who first came to Ireland in 1741 as an exchequer baron and William Yorke, Lord Chief Justice of the Common Pleas.[74]

Of course there are those who are not included in the computation of 283 but who have already been identified, such as MPs and government officials like Clements, Gardiner, Lucas, Wolseley, Maude and Chaigneau. Others who can be identified include John Chaigneau, first clerk to Clements; Sir Compton Domvile MP, clerk of the Crown and hanaper and grandson of Sir William Domvile; Anthony Malone, prime serjeant and one of the most influential and active MPs in mid-eighteenth-century Irish politics who, despite being a public creditor, led the opposition to the amended debt repayment bill in 1753 and voted against it, for which he was removed from his position of prime serjeant; and Edmond Malone MP, brother of Anthony, who also voted against the 1753 bill.[75] But it is not possible to identify many more from these groups so that any useful computation of MPs or government officials is not viable.

*　　*　　*

The overall impression portrayed by the foregoing assessment of the various lists of public creditors is of a complex and diverse community of people lending money to the government for a variety of reasons. While financial profit might appear to be the most obvious justification, the readiness to seek such profit through investment in government was synonymous with a more nuanced reasoning. Self-interest extended beyond financial gain to the more fundamental question of the security of their personal and private estates and, ultimately, of their lives. For the vast majority of Irish public creditors the survival of the Irish government, the British government and the expanding empire was essential for their own survival in a country in which they were a social, political, cultural and religious minority who held sway over a disempowered majority. The mainstay of their power in Ireland was the continued presence and ongoing maintenance of a permanent British military establishment capable of defending their Irish interests in the event of internal unrest or external threat. Thus, from the 1690s onwards Irish Protestants were willing to provide the necessary finance to maintain a standing army of

12,000 men, which with increasing demands from 1716 onwards required the creation and maintenance of a national debt and public credit system. By making such financial commitments, Ireland became actively committed to the ongoing expansion of the British Empire. For the public creditors, it was therefore both a personal and a public commitment.

However, in order for the public creditors to make that commitment in the first place, certain preconditions had to exist, most notably a realistic assurance that the government would repay the loans without deferring or defaulting on payments and the existence of a secure tax base that was capable of raising the money needed to cover interest and principal payments. By 1716 such preconditions had been met in Ireland following over twenty years of regular parliamentary supply, greater financial accountability on the part of government and a more settled administration of the country in general.[76] Thus, the creation and maintenance of a national debt and public credit system in the decades after 1716 demonstrated the extent to which the Protestant community had developed a significant degree of confidence and trust in the apparatus of the state that had emerged in Ireland after the Glorious Revolution of 1688–9, a state which was inextricably connected with, and dependent upon, Britain and its empire.

Many questions regarding the Irish public creditors remain to be answered, not least the extent to which the Catholic moneyed interest invested in government during the first half of the eighteenth century. However, what can be ascertained is that the decades after 1716 witnessed the emergence of a newfound confidence and sense of identity within the Protestant community which was expressed in part through the willingness of individuals and groups within that community to act as public creditors.

In the early 1750s it appeared, for a time, that an unprecedented period of economic prosperity in the late 1740s and the related increase in the government's annual income from traditional sources of revenue had created a circumstance in which the public creditors would no longer be needed. However, a renewed decline in the economy in the 1750s and the outbreak of the Seven Years' War ensured that by 1759 the government needed to return to parliament-sanctioned public borrowing.[77] Extant records for the new generation of people who chose to lend money in ever-increasing amounts to the Irish government from 1759 onwards have not yet come to light. Until such time as they do, we must rely on the evidence available from the existing accounts for the years 1716 to 1759 in order to assess the numbers, identities, motivations and attitudes of Ireland's first public creditors, and the extent to which their actions made it possible for Ireland to play a role in the emergence and consolidation of the British Empire.

CONCLUSION

In 1770 Ireland was on the cusp of a new era with regard to politics, religion and society. Internal and external pressures brought about the commencement of the repeal of the penal laws against Catholics in the 1770s and Patriot politics finally secured significant constitutional alterations in the relationship with Britain in 1782. The American and French Revolutions also encouraged existing and created new and varying degrees of radicalization within certain sectors of Irish society in political terms. One result of these various changes was the outbreak of rebellion in 1798, more than 100 years since countrywide violence had last engulfed Ireland. Another was the passage of the Act of Union in 1800, which put an end to the Irish parliament and the associated constitutional anomalies of the preceding centuries.[1] These two events were synonymous with a seismic shift in Irish–British relations, as the subordination of Ireland as a dominion or province of the empire was finally clarified, confirmed and concluded. Thereafter, Ireland's role in the empire began to change, as did the variety of ideas about Irish identity, separateness and, eventually, nationality, with dramatic and at times violent results at political, constitutional, religious, social and economic levels.[2]

The 1798 Rebellion and the Act of Union therefore also marked the end of a very particular phase in Ireland's role within the empire. In 1770 the army in Ireland had finally been augmented beyond the 12,000 limit set in 1699. Thereafter Ireland was able to make an even more telling contribution of men and money to the empire in the final thirty years of the eighteenth century. The American War of Independence required more soldiers from Ireland, which, as has already been seen, resulted in among other things Catholic recruitment increasing dramatically. It also required a significant escalation in Ireland's financial commitment to the empire, which was compounded by the French Revolutionary wars.[3] Total expenditure increased fairly steadily from £1,142,269 in 1784 to £6,615,959 in 1800. A new requirement entered Irish governmental expenditure in 1783, with £49,478 being spent on the navy. Such payments did not reoccur again until 1791 but from 1796 onwards were made on an annual basis. Even though in theory as part of the provisions of the 1662 Customs Act Ireland was meant to make a contribution to 'the better guarding and defending of the seas', in reality Irish public income had last contributed to naval costs in the 1670s.[4]

By 1782 the cost of the civil list on the Irish establishment had reached £236,758, rising eventually to a wholly unprecedented £1,025,510 in 1800. During the same timeframe, the military list rose from £609,131 to £4,596,762.[5] In order to cover such escalating costs, total net income, excluding loans, had reached £1,106,504 by 1783 and continued to increase during the following years to £3,017,758 in 1800, with concomitant dramatic expansions of the schedules of parliamentary duties and taxes being levied. The difference between net income and expenditure continued to be made up through larger loans and the legislative provision of more innovative fiscal devices such as lotteries, annuities, treasury bills and the creation of a national bank, so that by 1800 the national debt had escalated to £5,502,462.[6]

The financial, military and other commitments by Ireland to empire in the last thirty years of the eighteenth century had been made possible by what had gone before in the period 1692–1770. The maintenance of a standing army from 1692 onwards, the provision of a permanent countrywide network of barracks from 1697–8 onwards, the provision of soldiers for overseas service from 1702 onwards, the development of regular parliamentary additional supply from the 1690s onwards and the creation and maintenance of a parliament-sanctioned national debt from 1716 onwards had all been part of Ireland's demonstrable commitment to the growth of the British Empire in the period 1692–1770 as a subordinate, yet separate, sister kingdom to England. Ultimately, however, in 1800 that subordinate sister kingdom was subsumed completely within the empire and became part of the United Kingdom of Great Britain and Ireland. Seen by many as a final solution to Ireland's problems and the best way 'to consolidate the strength, power and resources of the British Empire', in fact the Act of Union of 1800 might more readily be seen as the catalyst for the start of the end of that empire.[7]

NOTES

1 Contexts

1. *An Account of the Revenue and National Debt of Ireland. With Some Observations on the Late Bill for Paying off the National Debt* (London, 1754), pp. 19–20. The pamphlet was one of many written at the time as part of the controversy surrounding a dispute in parliament in late 1753 regarding legislation for repayment of the national debt. See D. O'Donovan, 'The Money Bill Dispute of 1753', in T. Bartlett and D. W. Hayton (eds), *Penal Era and Golden Age: Essays in Irish History, 1690–1800* (Belfast: Ulster Historical Foundation, 1979), pp. 55–87; J. Hill, '"Allegories, Fictions, and Feigned Representations": Decoding the Money Bill Dispute', *Eighteenth Century Ireland*, 21 (2006), pp. 66–88.
2. Chapters 2–3, 7–9. See also C. I. McGrath, *The Making of the Eighteenth-Century Irish Constitution: Government, Parliament and the Revenue, 1692–1714* (Dublin: Four Courts Press, 2000), passim; idem, 'Parliamentary Additional Supply: The Development and Use of Regular Short-Term Taxation in the Irish Parliament, 1692–1716', *Parliamentary History*, 20 (2001), pp. 27–54; idem, 'Central Aspects of the Eighteenth-Century Constitutional Framework in Ireland: The Government Supply Bill and Biennial Parliamentary Sessions, 1715–82', *Eighteenth Century Ireland*, 16 (2001), pp. 9–34; D. W. Hayton, *Ruling Ireland, 1685–1742: Politics, Politicians and Parties* (Woodbridge: Boydell & Brewer, 2004), passim.
3. *An Account of the Revenue*, p. 19.
4. Chapters 4–9.
5. J. Brewer, *The Sinews of Power: War, Money and the English State* (London: Unwin Hyman, 1989), p. xvii. See also J. Brewer, 'The Eighteenth-Century British State: Context and issues', in L. Stone (ed.), *An Imperial State at War: Britain from 1689 to 1815* (London: Routledge, 1994), pp. 52–71; Stone, 'Introduction', in ibid., pp. 1–32, on pp. 9–17.
6. Brewer, *The Sinews of Power*, passim.
7. P. J. Marshall, *The Making and Unmaking of Empires: Britain, India and America c.1750–1783* (Oxford: Oxford University Press, 2005), p. 58.
8. H. Roseveare, *The Financial Revolution 1660–1760* (London: Longman, 1991), passim; P. G. M. Dickson, *The Financial Revolution in England: A Study in the Development of Public Credit 1688–1756* (London: Macmillan, 1967), passim.
9. Brewer, *The Sinews of Power*, pp. 29–32, and passim.
10. Marshall, *Empires*, p. 63.
11. On consent to taxation see J. P. Greene, *Peripheries and Center: Constitutional Development in the Extended Polities of the British Empire and the United States, 1607–1788* (Athens, GA: University of Georgia Press, 1986), pp. 79–90; E. Mancke, 'The Languages

of Liberty in British North America, 1607–1776', in J. P. Greene (ed.), *Exclusionary Empire: English Liberty Overseas, 1600–1900* (Cambridge: Cambridge University Press, 2010), pp. 25–49, on pp. 26, 28, 34, 41, 43–4. See also Chapter 2. On standing armies see Chapter 4.

12. See Chapter 3.
13. See Chapters 2, 5.
14. For considerations on the complexities of Irish identity see S. J. Connolly, *Contested Island: Ireland 1460–1630* (Oxford: Oxford University Press, 2009), pp. 10–58, 333–403; idem, *Religion, Law and Power: The Making of Protestant Ireland 1660–1760* (Oxford: Clarendon Press, 1992), pp. 103–42; T. Bartlett, *Ireland: A History* (Cambridge: Cambridge University Press, 2010), pp. 34–78, 84–99, 155–8.
15. See Chapters 5–6.
16. Connolly, *Contested Island*, pp. 1–2.
17. Ibid., p. 2.
18. See Chapter 3.
19. A. Pagden, *Peoples and Empires: Europeans and the Rest of the World, from Antiquity to the Present* (London: Phoenix Press, 2002), p. 98.
20. S. Howe, *Ireland and Empire: Colonial Legacies in Irish History and Culture* (Oxford: Oxford University Press, 2000), p. 11.
21. S. Duffy, *Ireland in the Middle Ages* (Dublin: Gill & Macmillan, 1997), pp. 10–22, 29–36; M. Richter, *Medieval Ireland: The Enduring Tradition* (Dublin: Gill & Macmillan, 1988), pp. 8–9, 13–25, 29–40, 43–117; R. Dudley Edwards, *An Atlas of Irish History*, 3rd edn (London: Routledge, 2005), pp. 71–5; A. Cosgrove (ed.), *A New History of Ireland, II: Medieval Ireland 1169–1534* (Oxford: Oxford University Press, 1987), pp. 1–42, 205–39, 314–51, 397–438 (hereafter *NHI*, vol. 2).
22. Duffy, *Middle Ages*, pp. 57–181; Richter, *Medieval Ireland*, pp. 129–88; Dudley Edwards, *An Atlas*, pp. 76–82; *NHI*, vol. 2, pp. 43–201, 240–302, 352–96, 525–636.
23. Richter, *Medieval Ireland*, pp. 166–7.
24. *NHI*, vol. 2, pp. 638–87; B. Bradshaw, *The Irish Constitutional Revolution of the Sixteenth Century* (Cambridge: Cambridge University Press, 1979), passim; C. Lennon, *Sixteenth-Century Ireland: The Incomplete Conquest* (Dublin: Gill & Macmillan, 1994), pp. 65–175.
25. Lennon, *Sixteenth-Century Ireland*, pp. 303–24; A. Clarke, *The Old English in Ireland, 1625–42* (Dublin: Four Courts Press, 2000), pp. 15–27.
26. T. W. Moody, F. X. Martin and F. J. Byrne (eds), *A New History of Ireland, III: Early Modern Ireland 1534–1691* (Oxford: Oxford University Press, 1976), pp. 77–8, 104–15, 195–206, 219–23, 357–73 (hereafter *NHI*, vol. 3); T. W. Moody, and W. E. Vaughan (eds), *A New History of Ireland, IV: Eighteenth-Century Ireland, 1691–1800* (Oxford: Oxford University Press, 1986), pp. 10–13 (hereafter *NHI*, vol. 4); Lennon, *Sixteenth-Century Ireland*, pp. 180–1, 216–302; N. Canny, *Making Ireland British 1580–1650* (Oxford: Oxford University Press, 2001), pp. 121–300, 402–550; R. Gillespie, *Seventeenth-Century Ireland: Making Ireland Modern* (Dublin: Gill & Macmillan, 2006), pp. 42–55, 97–103, 142–211; Dudley Edwards, *An Atlas*, pp. 156–63; J. G. Simms, *The Williamite Confiscation in Ireland 1690–1703* (London: Faber & Faber, 1956), passim.
27. See Chapter 2.
28. See Chapter 3.
29. For the 1541 Act for Kingly Title see Bradshaw, *Constitutional Revolution*, pp. 231–44; C. Brady, *The Chief Governors: The Rise and Fall of Reform Government in Tudor Ireland,*

1536–1588 (Cambridge: Cambridge University Press, 1994), pp. 25–7, 30, 50; Connolly, *Contested Island*, pp. 111–13.

30. On the lord lieutenancy see P. Gray and O. Purdue (eds), *The Irish Lord Lieutenancy c. 1541–1922* (Dublin: UCD Press, forthcoming 2012), passim; *NHI*, vol. 4, pp. 57–64.

31. K. Costello, *The Court of Admiralty of Ireland 1575–1893* (Dublin: Four Courts Press, 2011), passim; J. G. Crawford, *A Star Chamber Court in Ireland: The Court of Castle Chamber, 1571–1641* (Dublin: Four Courts Press, 2005), passim; *NHI*, vol. 4, pp. 66–7.

32. J. McCavitt, *Sir Arthur Chichester: Lord Deputy of Ireland 1605–16* (Belfast: Institute of Irish Studies, 1998), pp. 91–110; Crawford, *Castle Chamber*, pp. 14, 41–58; Connolly, *Religion, Law and Power*, pp. 198–9; Canny, *Making Ireland British*, pp. 301–2; *NHI*, vol. 4, pp. 67–70, 78–81.

33. C. I. McGrath, 'The Irish Revenue System: Government and Administration, 1689–1702' (PhD, University of London, 1997), pp. 141–218, 359–72; P. Walsh, *The Making of the Irish Protestant Ascendancy: The Life of William Conolly, 1662–1729* (Woodbridge: Boydell & Brewer, 2010), pp. 125–52.

34. See Chapter 4.

35. Connolly, *Religion, Law and Power*, pp. 200–17; McGrath, 'The Irish Revenue System', pp. 211–13; Canny, *Making Ireland British*, pp. 302–6; *NHI*, vol. 4, pp. 81–2.

36. Connolly, *Religion, Law and Power*, pp. 171–90, 198; Canny, *Making Ireland British*, pp. 306–8.

37. See Chapter 3.

38. C. I. McGrath, 'The Parliament of Ireland to 1800', in C. Jones (ed.), *A Short History of Parliament: England, Great Britain, the United Kingdom, Ireland and Scotland* (Woodbridge: Boydell & Brewer, 2009), pp. 321–38. See also Chapter 4.

39. J. P .Greene, 'Introduction: Empire and Liberty', in idem (ed.), *Exclusionary Empire*, pp. 1–24, on pp. 7–10.

40. See Chapters 2–3.

41. N. Canny, 'The Origins of Empire: An Introduction', in idem (ed.), *The Oxford History of the British Empire, vol. I: The Origins of Empire* (Oxford: Oxford University Press, 1998), pp. 1–33, on pp. 1–4; A. Pagden, 'The Struggle for Legitimacy and the Image of Empire in the Atlantic to c.1700', in ibid., pp. 34–54; J. C. Appleby, 'War, Politics, and Colonisation, 1558–1625', in ibid., pp. 55–78; J. Horn, 'Tobacco Colonies: The Shaping of English Society in the Seventeenth-Century Chesapeake', in ibid., pp. 170–92; P. E. H. Phair and R. Law, 'The English in Western Africa to 1700', in ibid., pp. 241–63, on pp. 243–9; P. J. Marshall, 'The English in Asia to 1700', in ibid., pp. 264–85, on pp. 264–7; P. Lawson, *The East India Company: A History* (London: Longman, 1987), pp. 1–63.

42. Canny, 'The Origins of Empire', pp. 6–18; J. Ohlmeyer, 'A Laboratory for Empire? Early Modern Ireland and English Imperialism', in K. Kenny (ed.), *Ireland and the British Empire* (Oxford: Oxford University Press, 2004), pp. 26–60; T. Barnard, 'New Opportunities for British Settlement: Ireland, 1650–1700', in Canny (ed.), *The Origins of Empire*, pp. 309–27.

43. See Chapters 2–3.

44. See for example T. Bartlett, 'Ireland, Empire, and Union, 1690–1801', in Kenny (ed.), *Ireland and the British Empire*, pp. 61–89, on pp. 61–3; F. G. James, *Ireland in the Empire 1688–1770* (Cambridge, MA: Harvard University Press, 1973), pp. 1–4.

45. Howe, *Ireland and Empire*, pp. 22–9.

46. D. H. Akenson, *The Irish Diaspora: A Primer* (Belfast: Institute of Irish Studies, 1993), pp. 142–51.

47. J. Horn, 'British Diaspora: Emigration from Britain, 1680–1815', in P. J. Marshall (ed.), *The Oxford History of the British Empire, vol. II: The Eighteenth Century* (Oxford: Oxford University Press, 1998), pp. 28–52, on pp. 31–2; K. Kenny, 'The Irish in the Empire', in idem (ed.), *Ireland and the British Empire*, pp. 95–122; idem, *The American Irish: A History* (London: Longman, 2000), pp. 7–23; L. M. Cullen, 'The Irish Diaspora of the Seventeenth and Eighteenth Centuries', in N. Canny (ed.), *Europeans on the Move: Studies on European Migration, 1500–1800* (Oxford: Clarendon Press, 1994), pp. 113–49, on pp. 126–7; G. Kirkham, 'The Origins of Mass Emigration from Ireland', in R. Kearney (ed.), *Migrations: The Irish at Home and Abroad* (Dublin: Wolfhound, 1990), pp. 81–90; C. J. Houston and W. J. Smyth, *Irish Emigration and Canadian Settlement: Patterns, Links and Letters* (Belfast: Ulster Historical Foundation, 1990), pp. 8–9, 13–20; K. A. Miller, *Emigrants and Exiles: Ireland and the Irish Exodus to North America* (Oxford: Oxford University Press, 1985), pp. 137–68; D. Fitzpatrick, *Irish Emigration 1801–1921* (Dublin: Economic and Social History Society of Ireland, 1984), pp. 1–13.
48. Cullen, 'Diaspora', pp. 114, 117–18.
49. Kenny, 'The Irish in the Empire', p. 93. See also K. Jeffery, 'Introduction', in idem (ed.), *'An Irish Empire'? Aspects of Ireland and the British Empire* (Manchester: Manchester University Press, 1996), pp. 1–24, on p. 1.
50. See for example R. Davis, *The Rise of the Atlantic Economies* (New York: Cornell University Press, 1973), passim; J. H. Parry, *Trade and Dominion: The European Overseas Empires in the Eighteenth Century* (London: Phoenix Press, 2000), passim.
51. See Chapter 3.
52. T. M. Truxes, *Irish-American Trade, 1660–1783* (Cambridge: Cambridge University Press, 1988), passim; D. Dickson, *Old World Colony: Cork and South Munster 1630–1830* (Cork: Cork University Press, 2005), pp. 113–69; L. M. Cullen, *An Economic History of Ireland since 1660*, 2nd edn (London: B. T. Batsford Ltd, 1993), pp. 7–76; I. McBride, *Eighteenth-Century Ireland: The Isle of Slaves* (Dublin: Gill & Macmillan, 2009), pp. 10–13, 110–12, 126–9; James, *Ireland in the Empire*, pp. 190–217; R. Gillespie, *The Transformation of the Irish Economy 1550–1700* (Dublin: Economic & Social History Society of Ireland, 1991), pp. 3–60.
53. For an earlier endeavour at addressing some of these questions see James, *Ireland in the Empire*, passim.

2 Religion

1. I. McBride, '"The Common Name of Irishman": Protestantism and Patriotism in Eighteenth-Century Ireland', in T. Claydon and I. McBride (eds), *Protestantism and National Identity: Britain and Ireland, c.1650–c.1850* (Cambridge: Cambridge University Press, 1998), pp. 236–61, on pp. 236, 238; L. Colley, *Britons: Forging the Nation 1707–1837*, 3rd edn (London: Pimlico, 2003), p. 54.
2. McBride, 'Common Name', p. 238.
3. For Ireland see B. Bradshaw, 'Sword, Word and Strategy in the Reformation in Ireland', *Historical Journal*, 21 (1978), pp. 475–502; Canny, *Making Ireland British*, pp. 53–5, 64, 107, 170–1, 266–7, 402–18, 422–32, 435–6; R. Dudley Edwards, *Church and State in Tudor Ireland: A History of Penal Laws against Irish Catholics 1534–1603* (London: Longman, 1935), pp. 192–303; A. Ford, *The Protestant Reformation in Ireland, 1590–1641* (Dublin: Four Courts Press, 1997), passim; Lennon, *Sixteenth-Century Ireland*, pp. 113–43, 303–25; S. A. Meigs, *The Reformations in Ireland: Tradition and Confes-*

sionalism, 1400–1690 (Dublin: Gill & Macmillan, 1997), pp. 57–107; S. J. Connolly, *Divided Kingdom: Ireland 1630–1800* (Oxford: Oxford University Press, 2010), pp. 4–8; *NHI*, vol. 3, pp. 39–141, 187–232. For England see E. Duffy, *The Stripping of the Altars: Traditional Religion in England c.1400–c.1580* (New Haven, CT: Yale University Press, 1992), pp. 377–593; A. Ryrie, *The Age of Reformation: The Tudor and Stuart Realms 1485–1603* (London: Longman, 2009), passim.

4.   See for example G. Bossenga, 'Society', in W. Doyle (ed.), *Old Regime France, 1648–1788* (Oxford: Oxford University Press, 2001), pp. 42–77, on p. 56; D. A. Bell, 'Culture and Religion', in ibid, pp. 78–104, on pp. 79–80, 85–6; J. Swann, 'Politics: Louis XIV', in ibid, pp. 195–222, on pp. 179–81; George Rudé, *Europe in the Eighteenth Century: Aristocracy and the Bourgeois Challenge* (London: Phoenix Press, 2002), pp. 131–2; E. Norman, *Roman Catholicism in England* (Oxford: Oxford University Press, 1986), pp. 8–10; J. Kelly, 'Sustaining a Confessional State: The Irish Parliament and Catholicism', in D. W. Hayton, J. Kelly and J. Bergin (eds), *The Eighteenth-Century Composite State: Representative Institutions in Ireland and Europe, 1689–1800* (Basingstoke: Palgrave, 2010), pp. 44–77, on pp. 44–7.

5.   D. M. Downey, 'Accommodations with the Protestant State and Church: A Comparative Study of Respective Dutch and Irish Catholic Experiences', in J. Bergin, E. Magennis, L. Ní Mhunghaile and P. Walsh (eds), *New Perspectives on the Penal Laws: Eighteenth-Century Ireland Special Issue No. 1* (Dublin: Eighteenth-Century Ireland Society, 2011), pp. 75–92, on p. 76.

6.   Dudley Edwards, *Church and State*, pp. 14, 181–3; Lennon, *Sixteenth-Century Ireland*, pp. 133–4, 306–9.

7.   Connolly, *Religion, Law and Power*, pp. 103–43.

8.   Canny, *Making Ireland British*, p. 540; Tadhg Ó hAnnracháin, *Catholic Reformation in Ireland: The Mission of Rinuccini, 1645–1649* (Oxford: Oxford University Press, 2002), pp. 33, 194.

9.   Canny, *Making Ireland British*, pp. 412–13.

10.   See D. W. Hayton and J. Kelly, 'The Irish Parliament in European Context: A Representative Institution in a Composite State', in Hayton, Kelly and Bergin (eds), *Composite State*, pp. 3–16.

11.   See for example Canny, *Making Ireland British*, pp. 402–13, 456–9, 540; Connolly, *Religion, Law and Power*, p. 19; *NHI*, vol. 3, pp. 189–90; A. Creighton, 'The Remonstrance of December 1661 and Catholic Politics in Restoration Ireland', *Irish Historical Studies*, 34 (2004–5), pp. 16–41, on p. 27.

12.   Clarke, *The Old English*, pp. 32–3, 37, 48, 52, 121, 242–3.

13.   Orders made and established by the General Assembly for the kingdom of Ireland, Kilkenny, 24 October 1642 (BL, Add. MS 4781, f. 4).

14.   Acts agreed upon, ordained and concluded at Kilkenny, 10, 11, 13 May 1642 (BL, Stowe MS 82, f. 271); M. Ó Siochrú, *Confederate Ireland 1642–1649: A Constitutional and Political Analysis* (Dublin: Four Courts Press, 1999), p. 40.

15.   Orders made ... at Kilkenny, 24 October 1642 (BL, Add. MS 4781, f. 4); Ó Siochrú, *Confederate Ireland*, pp. 43–8.

16.   Confederate oaths, *c.* 1643–6 (BL, Add. MS 4781, ff. 12–14).

17.   Canny, *Making Ireland British*, p. 540.

18.   Ó hAnnracháin, *Catholic Reformation*, pp. 20, 81, 133, 128, 159, 185, 194, 228–30.

19.   P. Walsh, *The History and Vindication of the Loyal Formulary, or Irish Remonstrance ...* (London, 1674), pp. 7–9; *Calendar of State Papers, Ireland, 1669–70 and Addenda* (Lon-

don: Stationery Office, 1910), pp. 560–3; Creighton, 'The Remonstrance', pp. 17–20, 26–30; Connolly, *Religion, Law and Power*, p. 19; idem, *Divided Kingdom*, p. 147.

20. Ryrie, *Reformation*, p. 248; G. R. Elton, *The Tudor Constitution: Documents and Commentary*, 2nd edn (Cambridge: Cambridge University Press, 1982), pp. 423–8.

21. Creighton, 'The Remonstrance', pp. 28–41; Connolly, *Religion, Law and Power*, pp. 19–21; idem, *Divided Kingdom*, pp. 147–8.

22. *NHI*, vol. 3, pp. 429–30.

23. Creighton, 'The Remonstrance', pp. 33, 39.

24. J. Hoppit, *A Land of Liberty? England 1689–1727* (Oxford: Oxford University Press, 2000), pp. 34–6, 216–17; G. M. Trevelyan, *The English Revolution 1688–1689* (Oxford: Oxford University Press, 1965), pp. 78–9.

25. For the war see J. G. Simms, *Jacobite Ireland 1685–91* (London: Routledge, 1969); R. Doherty, *The Williamite War in Ireland 1688–1691* (Dublin: Four Courts Press, 1998).

26. J. G. Simms, *The Treaty of Limerick* (Dundalk: Dundalgan Press, 1965), p. 22; J. I. McGuire, 'The Treaty of Limerick', in B. Whelan (ed.), *The Last of the Great Wars: Essays on the War of the Three Kings in Ireland 1688–91* (Limerick: University of Limerick Press, 1995), pp. 127–38, on p. 128.

27. P. Fagan, *Divided Loyalties: The Question of an Oath for Irish Catholics in the Eighteenth Century* (Dublin: Four Courts Press, 1997), p. 9; E. Kinsella, 'In Pursuit of a Positive Construction: Irish Catholics and the Williamite Articles of Surrender, 1690–1701', *Eighteenth Century Ireland*, 24 (2009), pp. 11–35, on pp. 20–1.

28. Kelly, 'Confessional State', pp. 47–8.

29. Canny, *Making Ireland British*, passim; Lennon, *Sixteenth-Century Ireland*, pp. 144–302; Gillespie, *Seventeenth-Century Ireland*, passim; *NHI*, vol. 3, pp. 69–141, 187–386, 420–53. On the figures for percentages of land and the difficulties associated with them see Connolly, *Religion, Law and Power*, pp. 147–8, 309; idem, *Divided Kingdom*, pp. 5, 137; L. M. Cullen, 'Catholics under the Penal Laws', *Eighteenth Century Ireland*, 1 (1986), pp. 23–36, on pp. 27–8; T. Bartlett, *The Fall and Rise of the Irish Nation: The Catholic Question, 1690–1830* (Dublin: Gill & Macmillan, 1992), pp. 22, 47–8; Gillespie, *Seventeenth-Century Ireland*, p. 3; E. Lyons, 'Morristown Lattin: A Case Study of the Lattin and Mansfield Families in County Kildare, c. 1660–1860' (PhD, UCD, 2011), pp. 37–9.

30. McGrath, 'The Parliament of Ireland', pp. 331–3; Gillespie, *Seventeenth-Century Ireland*, p. 3.

31. BL, Add. MS 18022, ff. 62–3; *Calendar of State Papers, Domestic Series* (hereafter, *CSPD) 1690–1*, pp. 385–6; *CSPD 1695 and addenda*, pp. 176, 178–9; HMC, *Finch MSS*, vol. 3, p. 302; *NHI*, vol. 4, pp. 630; P. Wauchope, *Patrick Sarsfield and the Williamite War* (Dublin: Irish Academic Press, 1992), pp. 277–83.

32. Bossenga, 'Society', p. 56; Bell, 'Culture and Religion', pp. 79–80, 85–6; Swann, 'Louis XIV', pp. 179–81; Rudé, *Europe*, pp. 131–2; Kelly, 'Confessional State', pp. 44–7; J. Morrill, 'The Causes of the Penal Laws: Paradoxes and Inevitabilities', in Bergin, Magennis, Ní Mhunghaile and Walsh (eds), *New Perspectives*, pp. 55–73.

33. Morrill, 'Paradoxes and Inevitabilities', pp. 55–73.

34. Dudley Edwards, *Church and State*, pp. 14, 181–3; Lennon, *Sixteenth-Century Ireland*, pp. 133–4, 306–9; J. McCafferty, *The Reconstruction of the Church of Ireland: Bishop Bramhall and the Laudian Reforms, 1633–1641* (Cambridge: Cambridge University Press, 2007), pp. 4, 10–11; Meigs, *Reformations in Ireland*, pp. 69–70; A. Ford, 'The Church of Ireland, 1558–1624: A Puritan Church?', in A. Ford, J. I. McGuire and K.

Milne (eds), *As by Law Established: The Church of Ireland since the Reformation* (Dublin: Lilliput Press, 1995), pp. 52–68, on pp. 56–7.

35. Dudley Edwards, *Church and State*, pp. 187–307; Clarke, *The Old English*, pp. 116–24; *NHI*, vol. 3, pp. 208–9, 224–5, 244–5; Connolly, *Divided Kingdom*, pp. 6–7.

36. M. A. Mullett, *Catholics in Britain and Ireland, 1558–1829* (Basingstoke: Macmillan, 1998), pp. 1–2, 10, 13–14; Elton, *The Tudor Constitution*, pp. 419–42; Morrill, 'Paradoxes and Inevitabilities', pp. 55–60, 64; J. Miller, *Popery and Politics in England, 1660–1688* (Cambridge: Cambridge University Press, 1973), pp. 52–6, 67–93, 100; Norman, *Catholicism*, pp. 12–15, 33–4.

37. Miller, *Popery*, pp. 90, 93, 121, 125, 163; J. Miller, *Charles II* (London: Weidenfield & Nicolson, 1991), pp. 175, 178, 191, 199, 203; Norman, *Catholicism*, p. 38.

38. Dudley Edwards, *Church and State*, pp. 199–200; McCavitt, *Chichester*, pp. 178–98.

39. *Proclamation. By the King, James Rex, Dublin, 1605* (TNA, SP 63/217/127–8).

40. Canny, *Making Ireland British*, p. 174; McCavitt, *Chichester*, pp. 111–28; *NHI*, vol. 3, pp. 190–2.

41. McCavitt, *Chichester*, pp. 178, 188–207; *NHI*, vol. 3, pp. 224–6.

42. Clarke, *The Old English*, pp. 61–2, 116–24; McCafferty, *Church of Ireland*, pp. 42–3, 152, 158, 170–7, 219–20; Ó hAnnracháin, *Catholic Reformation*, pp. 41–68.

43. *NHI*, vol. 3, pp. 288–386; Connolly, *Religion, Law and Power*, pp. 17–24; Miller, *Popery*, pp. 56, 67–93, 106, 121, 125, 163.

44. Disarming Proclamation, 8 November 1673 (NLI, MS 1793); *Proclamations by the Lord Lieutenant and Council. Ormonde,* 16 October 1678, 12 December 1678 (Dublin, 1678); HMC, *Ormond MSS*, vol. 2, pp. 352–9; C. I. McGrath, 'Securing the Protestant Interest: The Origins and Purpose of the Penal Laws of 1695', *Irish Historical Studies*, 30 (1996–7), pp. 25–46, on pp. 27–8.

45. *Proclamations by the Lord Lieutenant and Council. Ormonde,* 26 March 1679, 26 April 1680 (Dublin, 1679; 1680); *CSPD 1693*, pp. 8–9.

46. Extract of letters, orders and proclamations, 1678 (BL, Add. MS 27382, ff. 20–1).

47. Ibid.

48. J. E. Aydelotte, 'The Duke of Ormond and the English Government of Ireland, 1677–85' (PhD, Iowa University, 1975), p. 78.

49. Disarming Proclamation, 25 February 1689 (NLI, MS 1793); McGrath, 'The Origins and Purpose of the Penal Laws', p. 34.

50. McGrath, 'The Origins and Purpose of the Penal Laws', pp. 25–6, 28–34; Connolly, *Religion, Law and Power*, p. 267. For the advent of regular parliaments see Chapter 3.

51. Connolly, *Religion, Law and Power*, pp. 263–4; J. Kelly, 'The Historiography of the Penal Laws', in Bergin, Magennis, Ní Mhunghaile and Walsh (eds), *New Perspectives*, pp. 27–54, on pp. 29–35.

52. HMC, *Ormond MSS*, vol. 2, p. 449; HMC, *Buccleuch and Queensberry MSS*, vol. 2, pp. 163–5, 169–70, 183–4, 187, 205; HMC, *Downshire MSS*, vol. 1, pp. 509, 529, 534–5; *CSPD 1693*, pp. 196, 238, 251, 277, 364, 413, 418; *CSPD 1694–5*, pp. 41–2, 57, 59, 76–7, 94, 117–18, 154, 227, 353–4, 434; *CSPD 1695 and addenda*, pp. 37, 45, 182, 185, 188, 193–4, 204, 251, 265, 280, 319–20; McGrath, 'The Origins and Purpose of the Penal Laws', pp. 25–6, 28–42; J. F. Bosher, 'The Franco-Catholic danger, 1660–1715', *History*, 79 (1994), pp. 5–30; Morrill, 'Paradoxes and Inevitabilities', pp. 72–3; Hoppit, *A Land of Liberty?*, pp. 138, 221–2; Mullett, *Catholics*, p. 86; Norman, *Catholicism*, pp. 40–1.

53. *The Journals of the House of Commons of the Kingdom of Ireland* (1st and) 3rd edn , 21 vols (Dublin, 1796-1800) (hereafter, *CJI*) (1st edn), vol. 2, pp. 599–600, 621–7; *CSPD*

1695 and addenda, pp. 192, 199; J. I. McGuire, 'The Irish Parliament of 1692', in Bartlett and Hayton (eds), *Penal Era and Golden Age*, pp. 1–31, on pp. 17–18, 21–2; McGrath, *Constitution*, pp. 82–7; idem, 'The Origins and Purpose of the Penal Laws', p. 35.

54. HMC, *Buccleuch and Queensberry MSS*, vol. 2, p. 99; McGrath, *Constitution*, pp. 94–102; idem, 'The Origins and Purpose of the Penal Laws', pp. 33–46.

55. BL, Add. MS 40771, f. 33; McGrath, 'The Origins and Purpose of the Penal Laws', pp. 25–46.

56. *CSPD 1694–5*, p. 500.

57. Gillespie, *Seventeenth-Century Ireland*, pp. 226–8; D. Dickson, *New Foundations: Ireland 1660–1800* (Dublin: Helicon, 1987), p. 13; M. Wall, *The Penal Laws, 1691–1760* (Dundalk: Dundalgan Press, 1976), pp. 19–20.

58. Alan Brodrick to St John Brodrick, 21 September 1695 (SHC, Midleton papers, 1248/1, ff. 274–5).

59. Warburton to Ellis, 19 September 1695 (BL, Add. MS 28879, ff. 138–9).

60. *The Statutes at Large Passed in the Parliaments Held in Ireland*, 21 vols (Dublin, 1765-1804) (hereafter, *Stat. Ire.*), vol. 3, pp. 260–7.

61. TCD, MS 1178, ff. 56, 62; PRONI, De Ros MSS, D638/18/3; McGrath, 'The Origins and Purpose of the Penal Laws', pp. 39–41.

62. *Stat. Ire.*, vol. 3, pp. 260–7.

63. Capell and Privy Council to English lords justices, 17 June 1695 (BL, Add. MS 40771, f. 33).

64. *Stat. Ire.*, vol. 3, pp. 254–60.

65. Ibid., pp. 254–67.

66. C. I. McGrath, 'The Provisions for Conversion in the Penal Laws, 1695–1750', in M. Brown, C. I. McGrath and T. P. Power (eds), *Converts and Conversion in Ireland, 1650–1850* (Dublin: Four Courts Press, 2005), pp. 35–59, on pp. 36–8.

67. *A Journal of the Life of Thomas Story: Containing, an Account of his Remarkable Convincement of, and Embracing the Principles of Truth, as held by the People called Quakers ...* (Newcastle-upon-Tyne, 1747), pp. 131–2.

68. *Stat. Ire.*, vol. 3, pp. 339–43; J. G. Simms, 'The Bishops' Banishment Act of 1697 (9 Will. III, c. I)', *Irish Historical Studies*, 17 (1970–1), pp. 185–99, on pp. 187–92.

69. *CSPD 1693*, pp. 3, 8–10, 15–18, 51, 141, 162, 179.

70. Elton, *The Tudor Constitution*, pp. 422, 433–7.

71. Simms, 'Banishment Act', pp. 196–7; C. I. McGrath, 'Securing the Protestant Interest: Parliament, Policy and Politics in Ireland in the Aftermath of the Glorious Revolution 1690–1695' (MA, UCD, 1991), pp. 72–7.

72. *Stat. Ire.*, vol. 3, pp. 339–40.

73. *CSPD 1693*, pp. 8–9.

74. *Stat. Ire.*, vol. 3, pp. 340–3.

75. W. P. Burke, *The Irish Priests in the Penal Times (1660–1760)* (Shannon: Irish University Press, 1969), p. 120.

76. BL, Add. MS 18022, f. 69; Burke, *Priests*, pp. 120–8, 144. Simms gives the secular figure as 872 (Simms, 'Banishment Act', p. 197).

77. Burke, *Priests*, pp. 128–9.

78. Wall, *Penal Laws*, p. 12; Burke, *Priests*, p. 132. Simms gives a total figure of 424 (Simms, 'Banishment Act', p. 198).

79. Burke, *Irish Priests*, p. 132; Simms, 'Banishment Act', p. 198.

80. Fagan, *Divided Loyalties*, p. 2, fn. 3.

81. *Stat. Ire.*, vol. 3, pp. 349–53; vol. 5, pp. 148–50; vol. 6, pp. 765–6; vol. 7, pp. 42–4; Burke, *Priests*, pp. 186–8.

82. *Stat. Ire.*, vol. 3, pp. 512–14; McGrath, 'Conversion', p. 40.

83. *Stat. Ire.*, vol. 4, pp. 121–5; McGrath, 'Conversion', pp. 44–5; Fagan, *Divided Loyalties*, pp. 25–6.

84. J. G. Simms, 'The Making of a Penal Law (2 Anne, c. 6), 1703–4', *Irish Historical Studies*, 12 (1960–1), pp. 105–18, on p. 116; idem, 'Irish Catholics and the Parliamentary Franchise, 1692–1728', *Irish Historical Studies*, 12 (1960–1), pp. 28–37, on pp. 31–2.

85. Fagan, *Divided Loyalties*, pp. 26–7; H. Maynard, 'Butler, Sir Theobald (Toby)', in *Dictionary of Irish Biography* (Cambridge: Cambridge University Press, 2009) (hereafter *DIB*), at <http://dib.cambridge.org/viewReadPage.do?articleId=a1307>.

86. *Stat. Ire.*, vol. 5, pp. 287–9; McGrath, 'Conversion', pp. 51–2; Fagan, *Divided Loyalties*, p. 26.

87. *Letters Written by His Excellency Hugh Boulter, D.D. Lord Primate of All Ireland, &c. to Several Ministers of State in England, and Some Others*, 2 vols (Oxford, 1769), vol. 1, p. 226, 229–31; C. Kenny, 'The Exclusion of Catholics from the Legal Profession in Ireland, 1537–1829', *Irish Historical Studies*, 25 (1986–7), pp. 337–57, on pp. 353–4.

88. *Stat. Ire.*, vol. 6, pp. 13–20; McGrath, 'Conversion', pp. 52–3; Fagan, *Divided Loyalties*, p. 26.

89. *Stat. Ire.*, vol. 4, pp. 342–9; vol. 6, pp. 20–1; McGrath, 'Conversion', p. 54.

90. *Stat. Ire.*, vol. 5, pp. 222–6; McGrath, 'Conversion', pp. 48, 50–1; Simms, 'Franchise', pp. 28–37.

91. *Stat. Ire.*, vol. 4, pp. 5–6; Burke, *Priests*, pp. 167–8, 183.

92. *Stat. Ire.*, vol. 4, pp. 31–3, 71–2, 199; McGrath, 'Conversion', p. 44; Connolly, *Religion, Law and Power*, pp. 274–6; Burke, *Priests*, pp. 181–2.

93. *Stat. Ire.*, vol. 4, pp. 12–14; McGrath, 'Conversion', pp. 40–1.

94. *Stat. Ire.*, vol. 4, pp. 12–31; W. N. Osborough, 'Catholics, Land and the Popery Acts of Anne', in T. P. Power and K. Whelan (eds), *Endurance and Emergence: Catholics in Ireland in the Eighteenth Century* (Dublin: Irish Academic Press, 1990), pp. 21–56, on pp. 23–5; McGrath, 'Conversion', pp. 41–4.

95. *Stat. Ire.*, vol. 4, pp. 21–4; McGrath, 'Conversion', pp. 42–4; Fagan, *Divided Loyalties*, pp. 24–5.

96. Simms, 'Making of a Penal Law', pp. 112–16; Connolly, *Religion, Law and Power*, pp. 162–3; P. Kilroy, *Protestant Dissent and Controversy in Ireland 1660–1714* (Cork: Cork University Press, 1994), pp. 188–93.

97. Kilroy, *Protestant Dissent*, pp. 1–7; McCafferty, *Church of Ireland*, pp. 178–90; Gillespie, *Seventeenth-Century Ireland*, p. 159.

98. Connolly, *Religion, Law and Power*, p. 162.

99. Kilroy, *Protestant Dissent*, pp. 41, 174, 180–1, 188–93, 228–9, 238–41, 243–4; Connolly, *Religion, Law and Power*, pp. 79–80, 159–71; T. Barnard, 'The Government and Irish Dissent, 1704–1780', in K. Herlihy (ed.), *The Politics of Irish Dissent 1650–1800* (Dublin: Four Courts Press, 1997), pp. 9–27; D. W. Hayton, 'Exclusion, Conformity, and Parliamentary Representation: The Impact of the Sacramental Test on Irish Dissenting Politics', in ibid, pp. 52–73.

100. *Stat. Ire.*, vol. 4, pp. 508–16; Connolly, *Religion, Law and Power*, pp. 165–6; J. Kelly, '1780 Revisited: The Politics of the Repeal of the Sacramental Test', in Herlihy (ed.), *Politics of Irish Dissent*, pp. 74–92; McGrath, 'Conversion', p. 49.

101. Eileen O'Byrne (ed.), *The Convert Rolls: The Calendar of the Convert Rolls, 1703–1838, with Fr Wallace Clare's Annotated List of Converts, 1703–18, Edited by Anne Chamney* (Dublin: Irish Manuscripts Commission, 2005), pp. xi–xiii; T. P. Power, 'Converts', in Power and Whelan (eds), *Endurance and Emergence*, pp. 101–27; M. Brown, C. I. McGrath and T. P. Power, 'Introduction: Converts and Conversion in Ireland', in Brown, McGrath and Power (eds), *Converts*, pp. 11–34, on pp. 13–18.

102. Connolly, *Religion, Law and Power*, p. 151, fn. 24.

103. O'Byrne (ed.), *Convert Rolls*, pp. xiii–xviii; Connolly, *Religion, Law and Power*, pp. 294–307; T. P. Power, '"A Weighty, Serious Business": The Conversion of Catholic Clergy to Anglicanism', in Brown, McGrath and Power (eds), *Converts*, pp. 183–213; idem, 'Conversions among the Legal Profession in Ireland in the Eighteenth Century', in D. Hogan and W. N. Osborough (eds), *Brehons, Serjeants and Attorneys* (Dublin: Irish Academic Press, 1990), pp. 153–74; Brown, McGrath and Power, 'Converts and Conversion', pp. 17–18.

104. T. P. Power, 'The Theology and Liturgy for Conversion from Catholicism to Anglicanism', in Brown, McGrath and Power (eds), *Converts*, pp. 60–78; J. Kelly, 'The Conversion Experience: The Case of Fr James O'Farrell, OP, 1785–7', in ibid, pp. 214–36; Connolly, *Religion, Law and Power*, p. 298.

105. Morrill, 'Paradoxes and Inevitabilities', pp. 69–70. See also pp. 55–6, 65. Osborough states that the aspects of the 1704 act relating to land purchase and forms of lease were based upon an English statute from William III's reign (Osborough, 'Popery Acts', p. 26).

106. *Stat. Ire.*, vol. 4, pp. 190–216; Osborough, 'Popery Acts', pp. 25–6; McGrath, 'Conversion', pp. 45–7.

107. Osborough, 'Popery Acts', pp. 26–43; Lyons, 'Morristown Lattin', pp. 209–47.

108. Lyons, 'Morristown Lattin', pp. 209–47; K. Harvey, *The Bellews of Mount Bellew: A Catholic Gentry Family in Eighteenth-Century Ireland* (Dublin: Four Courts Press, 1998), passim; T. P. O'Neill, 'Discoverers and Discoveries: The Penal Laws and Dublin Property', *Dublin Historical Record*, 37 (1983–4), pp. 2–13; idem, 'Discoverers and Discoveries – a Preliminary Note' (NLI, unpublished paper); Osborough, 'Popery Acts', pp. 26–51; Connolly, *Religion, Law and Power*, pp. 308–10.

109. Connolly, *Religion, Law and Power*, pp. 147–8, 309–10; idem, *Divided Kingdom*, pp. 5, 137; Cullen, 'Penal Laws', pp. 27–8; Bartlett, *The Fall and Rise*, pp. 22, 47–8; Gillespie, *Seventeenth-Century Ireland*, p. 3; Lyons, 'Morristown Lattin', pp. 37–9.

110. Osborough, 'Popery Acts', pp. 22–3.

111. Connolly, *Religion, Law and Power*, pp. 276–7.

112. Burke, *Priests*, pp. 182–4.

113. Connolly, *Religion, Law and Power*, p. 276.

114. *Boulter Letters*, vol. 1, p. 223.

115. Connolly, *Religion, Law and Power*, pp. 150–1.

116. McBride, *Seventeenth-Century Ireland*, pp. 215–70; G. O'Brien (ed.), *Catholic Ireland in the Eighteenth Century: Collected Essays of Maureen Wall* (Dublin: Geography Publications, 1989), pp. 73–114.

117. Burke, *Priests*, p. 185; Fagan, *Divided Loyalties*, p. 26.

118. Fagan, *Divided Loyalties*, pp. 67–8.

119. I. McBride, 'Catholic Politics in the Penal Era: Father Sylvester Lloyd and the Delvin Address of 1727', in Bergin, Magennis, Ní Mhunghaile and Walsh (eds), *New Perspectives*, pp. 115–48; Fagan, *Divided Loyalties*, pp. 62–80.

120. See Chapters 5–6.

121. Fagan, *Divided Loyalties*, pp. 81–192.

3 Politics

1. In general see N. Canny, *Kingdom and Colony: Ireland in the Atlantic World* (Baltimore, MD: Johns Hopkins University Press, 1988), passim; Connolly, *Religion, Law and Power*, pp. 103–43; Howe, *Ireland and Empire*, pp. 7–36; McBride, *Eighteenth-Century Ireland*, pp. 100–69; Bartlett, *Ireland*, pp. 155–8.

2. S. Conway, *War, State, and Society in Mid-Eighteenth-Century Britain and Ireland* (Oxford: Oxford University Press, 2006), p. 37.

3. *Calendar of Treasury Books, 1660–1718*, 32 vols (London: Stationery Office, 1904–59) (hereafter *CTB*) *1698–9*, p. 107.

4. A. Cosgrove, 'Parliament and the Anglo-Irish Community: The Declaration of 1460', in A. Cosgrove and J. I. McGuire (eds), *Parliament and Community* (Belfast: Ulster Historical Foundation, 1983), pp. 25–42, on p. 31.

5. W. Molyneux, *The Case of Ireland's Being Bound by Acts of Parliament in England, Stated* (Dublin, 1698); J. G. Simms, *Colonial Nationalism 1698–1776: Molyneux's The Case of Ireland ... stated* (Cork: Mercier Press, 1976), pp. 28–9.

6. A. Clarke, 'Colonial Constitutional Attitudes in Ireland, 1640–60', *Proceedings of the Royal Irish Academy*, 90, section C (1990), pp. 357–75; F. G. James, 'Historiography and the Irish Constitutional Revolution of 1782', *Éire-Ireland*, 18 (1983), pp. 6–16, on p. 7.

7. W. J. Johnston, 'The First Adventure of the Common Law', *Law Quarterly Review*, 36 (1920), pp. 9–30; P. Brand, 'The Birth and Early Development of a Colonial Judiciary: The Judges of the Lordship of Ireland', in W. N. Osborough (ed.), *Explorations in Law and History* (Dublin: Four Courts Press, 1995), pp. 1–48; Cosgrove, 'Parliament', pp. 25–38; J. Kelly, '"Era of Liberty": The Politics of Civil and Political Rights in Eighteenth-Century Ireland', in Greene (ed.), *Exclusionary Empire*, pp. 77–111, on pp. 78–9.

8. Connolly, *Contested Island*, pp. 26–51; Bradshaw, *Constitutional Revolution*, pp. 3–31; Dudley Edwards, *An Atlas*, pp. 32–41, 76–84; Cosgrove, 'Parliament', pp. 25–38.

9. Bradshaw, *Constitutional Revolution*, pp. 231–44; Brady, *The Chief Governors*, pp. 25–7, 30, 50; Clarke, 'Constitutional Attitudes', p. 364; Connolly, *Contested Island*, pp. 111–13.

10. Cosgrove, 'Parliament', pp. 29–30.

11. Bradshaw, *Constitutional Revolution*, p. 29; Connolly, *Contested Island*, p. 39; Cosgrove, 'Parliament', pp. 25–41.

12. Cosgrove, 'Parliament', p. 31.

13. Ibid., pp. 28–9.

14. E. W. Ives, 'Fortescue, Sir John (c.1397–1479)', in *ODNB*, at <http://www.oxforddnb.com/view/article/9944>; Greene, 'Introduction', pp. 1–2.

15. Cosgrove, 'Parliament', p. 29.

16. E. Curtis, 'The Acts of the Drogheda Parliament, 1494–5, or "Poynings' Laws"', in A. Conway, *Henry VII's Relations with Scotland and Ireland 1485–1498. With a Chapter on the Acts of the Poynings Parliament 1494–5 by Edmund Curtis* (Cambridge: Cambridge University Press, 1932), pp. 129, 137–8.

17. *CJI*, vol. 1, pp. 174–5; J. G. Simms, *William Molyneux of Dublin 1656–1698* (Dublin: Irish Academic Press, 1982), p. 102.

18. P. Darcy, *An Argument Delivered by Patrick Darcy Esquire, by the Express Order of the House of Commons in the Parliament of Ireland, 9 Iunii, 1641* (Waterford, 1643), pp. 41, 67, 81–2; A. Clarke, 'Patrick Darcy and the Constitutional Relationship between Ireland and Britain', in J. Ohlmeyer (ed.), *Political Thought in Seventeenth-Century Ireland* (Cambridge: Cambridge University Press, 2000), pp. 35–55, on pp. 35–46.

19. Ó Siochrú, *Confederate Ireland*, pp. 62–3; M. Ó Siochrú, 'Catholic Confederates and the Constitutional Relationship between Ireland and England, 1641–1649', in C. Brady and J. Ohlmeyer (eds), *British Interventions in Early Modern Ireland* (Cambridge: Cambridge University Press, 2005), pp. 207–29, on pp. 215–29; Simms, *Colonial Nationalism*, pp. 14–15; Clarke, 'Constitutional Attitudes', pp. 358–9; P. Little, 'The English Parliament and the Irish Constitution, 1641–9', in M. Ó Siochrú (ed.), *Kingdoms in Crisis: Ireland in the 1640s* (Dublin: Four Courts Press, 2001), pp. 106–21.

20. Simms, *Colonial Nationalism*, pp. 14–16; Ó Siochrú, *Confederate Ireland*, pp. 60–4, 79, 239; Clarke, 'Constitutional Attitudes', pp. 357–9, 364–5; idem, 'Darcy', pp. 47, 49–50; N. L. York, *Neither Kingdom nor Nation: The Irish Quest for Constitutional Rights, 1698–1800* (Washington, DC: Catholic University of America Press, 1994), pp. 15–16.

21. Sir R. Bolton, 'A Declaration Setting forth, How, and by What Means, the Laws and Statutes of England, from Time to Time, Came to Be of Force in Ireland', in W. Harris, *Hibernica. Part II. Or, Two Treatises Relating to Ireland* (Dublin, 1770), pp. 9–45. Authorship was for a time ascribed to Darcy (Clarke, 'Constitutional Attitudes', pp. 357–8; Simms, *Colonial Nationalism*, pp. 14–15), though it has recently been ascribed beyond doubt to Bolton (P. Kelly, 'Sir Richard Bolton and the Authorship of "A Declaration Setting Forth, How, and by What Means, the Laws and Statutes of England, from Time to Time, Came to Be of Force in Ireland", 1644', *Irish Historical Studies*, 35 (2006), pp. 1–16).

22. Bolton, 'A Declaration', pp. 11, 14–17, 20–1.

23. Sir S. Mayart, 'Serjeant Mayart's Answer to a Book Intitled, A Declaration ...', in Harris, *Hibernica*, pp. 47–231.

24. Kelly, 'Bolton', pp. 12–13; R. Armstrong, 'Ormond, the Confederate Peace Talks and Protestant Royalism', in Ó Siochrú (ed.), *Kingdoms in Crisis*, pp. 122–40, on p. 133.

25. Clarke, 'Constitutional Attitudes', pp. 360–2; Kelly, 'Bolton', pp. 13–14.

26. Clarke, 'Constitutional Attitudes', p. 363.

27. A. Clarke, *Prelude to Restoration in Ireland: The End of the Commonwealth, 1659–1660* (Cambridge: Cambridge University Press, 1999), p. 158.

28. Ibid., pp. 249, 318–19; Clarke, 'Darcy', pp. 51–2; Simms, *Colonial Nationalism*, p. 16.

29. Sir W. Domville, 'A Disquisition Touching that Great Question Whether an Act of Parliament Made in England Shall Bind the Kingdom and People of Ireland without Their Allowance and Acceptance of Such Act in the Kingdom of Ireland', ed. P. Kelly, *Analecta Hibernica*, 40 (2007), pp. 17–70, on pp. 21–7, 35–70; Clarke, *Restoration*, p. 319; idem, 'Constitutional Attitudes', p. 363; idem, 'Darcy', pp. 52–3; York, *Kingdom nor Nation*, pp. 19–22; Kelly, 'Era of Liberty', p. 82.

30. Domville, 'A Disquisition', pp. 55–7, 68.

31. *The Statutes at Large*, 8 vols (London, 1770), vol. 3, pp. 182–5, 267–71, 299–300, 317–18, 374–6, 401–2; Cullen, *An Economic History*, pp. 12–13, 15–18, 37–9; C. A. Edie, 'The Irish Cattle Bills: A Study in Restoration Politics', *Transactions of the American Philosophical Society*, new series, 60 (1970), pp. 1–66; Truxes, *Irish-American Trade*, pp. 7–13.

32. Simms, *Jacobite Ireland*, pp. 19–77; idem, *The Jacobite Parliament of 1689* (Dundalk: Dundalgan Press, 1974), pp. 4–7; McGrath, 'The Parliament of Ireland', p. 332; Clarke, *The Old English*, pp. 255–61.

33. For versions of the act see *A List of Such of the Names of the Nobility, Gentry and Commonalty of England and Ireland ... Attainted of High Treason* (London, 1690), pp. 5–8; *The Acts of That Short Session of Parliament Held in Dublin, May 7, 1689. Under the Late King James II* (Dublin, 1756), pp. 1–7; T. Davis, *The Patriot Parliament of 1689*, ed. C.

G. Duffy (London: T. Fisher Unwin, 1893), pp. 43–8; Simms, *The Jacobite Parliament*, p. 27.

34. I. Victory, 'The Making of the 1720 Declaratory Act', in G. O'Brien (ed.), *Parliament, Politics and People: Essays in Eighteenth-Century Irish History* (Dublin: Irish Academic Press, 1989), pp. 9–29, on p. 9. See also *CJI*, vol. 1, pp. 174–5.

35. *A List*, pp. 5–8; *The Acts*, pp. 1–7; Davis, *Patriot Parliament*, pp. 43–8. See also Simms, *Jacobite Ireland*, pp. 80–1; idem, *The Jacobite Parliament*, pp. 8–9.

36. *A List*, pp. 49–52; *The Acts*, pp. 27–35; Davis, *Patriot Parliament*, pp. 55–62; Simms, *Jacobite Ireland*, p. 92; idem, *The Jacobite Parliament*, p. 17.

37. Simms, *Jacobite Ireland*, pp. 42–57, 77–8, 81–5, 93–4; idem, T*he Jacobite Parliament*, pp. 3–4, 9–14, 18–19; idem, *Molyneux*, p. 103; McGrath, 'Parliament of Ireland', p. 331.

38. Molyneux, *The Case*, pp. 111–12; Simms, *Colonial Nationalism*, pp. 46–7.

39. McGuire, 'Parliament', pp. 6–7; Connolly, *Divided Kingdom*, p. 194; McGrath, *Constitution*, p. 87.

40. M. Powell, *Britain and Ireland in the Eighteenth-Century Crisis of Empire* (Basingstoke: Palgrave, 2003), pp. 104, 188–91, 200, 205, 211; V. Morley, *Irish Opinion and the American Revolution, 1760–1783* (Cambridge: Cambridge University Press, 2002), pp. 90, 247–8, 260, 263–5, 267–8, 274, 288, 290, 297; Connolly, *Divided Kingdom*, pp. 406–8, 410.

41. K. P. Ferguson, 'The Army in Ireland from the Restoration to the Act of Union' (PhD, TCD, 1981), p. 54.

42. BL, Add. MS 31237, ff. 72–3.

43. O'Donovan, 'The Money Bill Dispute', pp. 55–87; T. Bartlett, 'The Augmentation of the Army in Ireland 1767–1769', *English Historical Review*, 96 (1981), pp. 540–59. See also Chapter 5.

44. McGrath, *Constitution*, pp. 73–152.

45. *CTB 1693–6*, pp. 278–9; *CTB 1698–9*, pp. 89–90; *CTB 1700–1*, pp. 326, 338–9; McGrath, 'The Irish Revenue System', pp. 89, 98–102.

46. C. I. McGrath, 'Late Seventeenth- and Early Eighteenth-Century Governance and the Viceroyalty', in Gray and Purdue (eds), *Lord Lieutenancy*; Ferguson, 'The Army', pp. 64–5; A. J. Guy, *Oeconomy and Discipline: Officership and Administration in the British Army 1714–63* (Manchester: Manchester University Press, 1985), p. 34.

47. See Chapters 5–6.

48. Guy, *Oeconomy and Discipline*, p. 5.

49. PRONI, De Ros MSS, D638/13/69, 74; *CSPD 1695 and addenda*, p. 177.

50. BL, Add. MS 31237, ff. 72–3.

51. *Modus tenendi Parliamenta et consilia in Hibernia* (Dublin, 1692); Domville, 'A Disquisition', pp. 46–7; Connolly, *Divided Kingdom*, p. 195.

52. J. I. McGuire, 'Dopping, Anthony', in *DIB*, at <http://dib.cambridge.org/viewReadPage.do?articleId=a2714>; idem, 'Parliament', pp. 11–12, fn. 38.

53. Molyneux, *The Case*, pp. 29–36; P. Kelly, 'Recasting a Tradition: William Molyneux and the Sources of *The Case of Ireland … Stated* (1698)', in Ohlmeyer (ed.), *Political Thought*, pp. 83–106, on pp. 94–5.

54. Kelly, 'Tradition', pp. 84–9; H. F. Kearney, 'The Political Background to English Mercantilism, 1695–1700', *Economic History Review*, 2nd series, 9 (1958–9), pp. 484–96; P. Kelly, 'The Irish Woollen Export Prohibition Act of 1699: Kearney Re-visited', *Irish Economic and Social History*, 7 (1980), pp. 22–44; McGrath, *Constitution*, pp. 135–52; Simms, *Colonial Nationalism*, pp. 24–6.

55. F. G. James, *Lords of the Ascendancy: The Irish House of Lords and Its Members, 1600–1800* (Dublin: Irish Academic Press, 1995), pp. 68–72; Simms, *Colonial Nationalism*, pp. 26–7; M. S. Flaherty, 'The Empire Strikes Back: *Annesley V. Sherlock* and the Triumph of Imperial Parliamentary Supremacy', *Columbia Law Review*, 87 (1987), pp. 593–622, on pp. 603–12; D. W. Hayton, 'The Stanhope/Sunderland Ministry and the Repudiation of Irish Parliamentary Independence', *English Historical Review*, 113 (1998), pp. 610–36, on p. 611; Victory, 'Declaratory Act', pp. 10–12.

56. Kelly, 'Tradition', pp. 83–4, 91–100; C. Robbins, *The Eighteenth-Century Commonwealthman* (New York: Atheneum, 1968), pp. 135–8.

57. Molyneux, *The Case*, pp. 29, 40, 55, 163–4.

58. Ibid., pp. 148–9.

59. Ibid., pp. 56, 118–19, 150–2, 158–9, 168–70.

60. Ibid., pp. 124, 170–1; Kelly, 'Tradition', p. 98; Simms, *Colonial Nationalism*, pp. 35–6.

61. P. Kelly, 'Conquest *versus* Consent as the Basis of the English Title to Ireland in William Molyneux's *Case of Ireland … Stated* (1698)', in Brady and Ohlmeyer (ed.), *British Interventions*, pp. 334–56.

62. Molyneux, *The Case*, pp. 69, pp. 95–8.

63. See for example W. Atwood, *The History and Reasons, of the Dependency of Ireland upon the Imperial Crown of the Kingdom of England. Rectifying Mr Molyneux's State of the Case …* (London, 1698); J. Cary, *A Vindication of the Parliament of England, In Answer to a Book, Written By William Molyneux …* (London, 1698); idem, *An Answer to Mr Molyneux His Case of Ireland …* (London, 1698); J. G. Simms (ed.), *The Case of Ireland Stated by William Molyneux* (Dublin: Cadenus Press, 1977), pp. 143–4; idem, *Molyneux*, pp. 113–15.

64. Kelly, 'Tradition', pp. 104–5; Simms, *Colonial Nationalism*, pp. 38–47; idem, *Molyneux*, pp. 112–13; McGrath, *Constitution*, pp. 136–7.

65. P. Kelly, 'William Molyneux and the Spirit of Liberty in Eighteenth-Century Ireland', *Eighteenth Century Ireland*, 3 (1988), pp. 133–48, on pp. 134–6; Simms, *Molyneux*, pp. 104, 122.

66. Kearney, 'Mercantilism', pp. 491–6; Kelly, 'Kearney Re-visited', pp. 39–44; Hayton, *Ruling Ireland*, pp. 66–71; F. G. James, 'The Irish Lobby in the Early Eighteenth Century', *English Historical Review*, 81 (1966), pp. 543–57, on p. 546.

67. Simms, *The Williamite Confiscation*, pp. 96–157; Walsh, *Protestant Ascendancy*, pp. 48–60; Hayton, *Ruling Ireland*, pp. 71–84.

68. Simms, *Colonial Nationalism*, p. 9. For a cautionary note see Morley, *Irish Opinion*, p. 16.

69. Kelly, 'Tradition', p. 83; idem, 'Spirit of Liberty', pp. 136–48; Simms (ed.), *The Case*, pp. 141–2; idem, *Colonial Nationalism*, pp. 48–77; M. J. Bric, *Ireland, Philadelphia and the Re-invention of America, 1760–1800* (Dublin: Four Courts Press, 2008), pp. 201–2. See also Greene, *Peripheries*, p. 140.

70. Simms, *Colonial Nationalism*, p. 49; idem, *Molyneux*, p. 116.

71. Flaherty, 'Empire', pp. 603–12; Victory, 'Declaratory Act', pp. 12–14; James, *Lords*, pp. 69–70; Hayton, 'Stanhope/Sunderland', p. 611.

72. Victory, 'Declaratory Act', pp. 14–29; Flaherty, 'Empire', pp. 614–19; Hayton, 'Stanhope/Sunderland', pp. 612–36; James, *Lords*, pp. 70–2.

73. E. Curtis and R. B. McDowell (eds), *Irish Historical Documents 1172–1922* (London: Methuen, 1943), p. 186.

74. J. Toland, *Reasons Most Humbly Offered to the Honourable House of Commons, Why the Bill Sent Down to Them from the Most Honourable House of Lords …* (London, 1720). See also *A Letter from a Member of the House of Commons of Ireland to a Gentleman of the*

Long Robe in Great-Britain (Dublin, 1720); *A Second Letter to a Gentleman of the Long Robe in Great-Britain* (Dublin, 1720).

75. Hayton, 'Stanhope/Sunderland', pp. 615, 620–1, 625–31; Victory, 'Declaratory Act', pp. 22–6. See also TNA, SP 63/379/61–70.
76. M. A. Lyons, 'FitzGerald, Gerald (Gearóid Mór) 8th Earl of Kildare', in *DIB*, at <http://dib.cambridge.org/viewReadPage.do?articleId=a3148>; Connolly, *Contested Island*, pp. 5, 62.
77. *Stat. Ire.*, vol. 1, p. 44; D. B. Quinn, 'The Early Interpretation of Poynings' Law, 1494–1534', *Irish Historical Studies*, 2 (1940–1), pp. 241–54, on pp. 241–2; Curtis, 'Drogheda Parliament', pp. 120–1, 130–43; C. I. McGrath, 'Government, Parliament and the Constitution: The Reinterpretation of Poynings' Law, 1692–1714', *Irish Historical Studies*, 35 (2006–7), pp. 160–72, on p. 161.
78. *Stat. Ire.*, vol. 1, pp. 89–90, 157–9, 320–22; Quinn, 'Poynings' Law', pp. 243–54; R. Dudley Edwards and T. W. Moody, 'The Early Interpretation of Poynings' Law: Part 1, 1494–1615', *Irish Historical Studies*, 2 (1940–1), pp. 415–24, on pp. 418–21; Bradshaw, *Constitutional Revolution*, pp. 147–54.
79. *Stat. Ire.*, vol. 1, pp. 246–8; McGrath, 'Reinterpretation', p. 162; Dudley Edwards and Moody, 'Interpretation', pp. 419–20.
80. Dudley Edwards and Moody, 'Interpretation', pp. 419–20.
81. Ibid., p. 421; McCavitt, *Chichester*, pp. 177–8.
82. *CJI*, vol. 1, pp. 27, 42, 44, 46, 53–6; Dudley Edwards and Moody, 'Interpretation', p. 422; McGrath, 'Reinterpretation', p. 162.
83. Dudley Edwards and Moody, 'Interpretation', p. 422.
84. TNA, SP 63/247/128, 141, 143; A. Clarke, 'The History of Poynings' Law, 1615–41', *Irish Historical Studies*, 18 (1972–3), pp. 207–22, on pp. 207–10; idem, *The Old English*, pp. 28–59.
85. Clarke, 'The History of Poynings' Law', pp. 210–14.
86. *CJI*, vol. 1, pp. 69–71, 80, 90, 141–2, 145–8, 155, 157, 161–7, 169–71, 174–7, 183, 186, 196; Clarke, 'The History of Poynings' Law', pp. 214–21.
87. Ó Siochrú, 'Confederates', pp. 212–14.
88. BL, Stowe MS 82, ff. 271–4; Add. MS 4781, ff. 4–11; TCD, MS 840, ff. 59–60.
89. Ó Siochrú, 'Confederates', pp. 215–25; Armstrong, 'Royalism', pp. 132–4.
90. Ó Siochrú, 'Confederates', pp. 214, 217–18.
91. Ibid., pp. 226–9.
92. *CJI*, vol. 1, p. 161.
93. *CJI*, vol. 1, pp. 394, 396–401, 419, 440–1, 459–60, 463–9, 479–80; F. O'Donoghue, 'The Irish Parliament under Charles II' (MA, UCD, 1970), pp. 57–8; J. Kelly, 'The Making of Law in Eighteenth-Century Ireland: The Significance and Import of Poynings' Law', in N. M. Dawson (ed.), *Reflections on Law and History* (Dublin: Four Courts Press, 2006), pp. 259–77, on pp. 262–3.
94. *CJI*, vol. 1, pp. 440–1.
95. *CJI*, vol. 1, pp. 503–5, 513–14, 526–9; Kelly, 'The Making of Law', pp. 262–6; J. Kelly, *Poynings' Law and the Making of Law in Ireland 1660–1800* (Dublin: Four Courts Press, 2007), pp. 18–46; O'Donoghue, 'Parliament', pp. 99–100; James, *Ireland in the Empire*, pp. 12–13.
96. McGrath, 'Reinterpretation', p. 164.
97. Simms, *Jacobite Ireland*, pp. 78–80; idem, *The Jacobite Parliament*, pp. 7–9; Kelly, *Poynings' Law*, p. 48.
98. HMC, *Le Fleming MSS*, p. 279; HMC, *Various Collections*, vol. 8, *Clements MSS*, p. 216.

99. McGrath, *Constitution*, pp. 49–55; Connolly, *Divided Kingdom*, pp. 192–3.
100. *CSPD 1690*, pp. 201–6; *CSPD 1690–1*, p. 512; HMC, *Buccleuch MSS*, vol. 2, pp. 111–12, 145; HMC, *Portland MSS*, vol. 3, p. 480; J. Kelly, 'Public and Political Opinion in Ireland and the Idea of an Anglo-Irish Union, 1650–1800', in D. G. Boyce, R. Eccleshall and V. Geoghegan (eds), *Political Discourse in Seventeenth- and Eighteenth-Century Ireland* (Basingstoke: Palgrave, 2001), pp. 110–41, on pp. 113–14; D. W. Hayton, 'Ideas of Union in Anglo-Irish Political Discourse, 1692–1720: Meaning and Use', in ibid., pp. 142–68, on pp. 144–7.
101. McGuire, 'Parliament', pp. 2–5; Hayton, *Ruling Ireland*, pp. 23–4, 36–41; D. W. Hayton, 'Constitutional Experiments and Political Expediency, 1689–1725', in S. G. Ellis and S. Barber (eds), *Conquest and Union: Fashioning a British State 1485–1725* (London: Longman, 1995), pp. 276–305, on pp. 280–4; McGrath, *Constitution*, pp. 74–5; C. I. McGrath, 'English Ministers, Irish Politicians, and the Making of a Parliamentary Settlement in Ireland, 1692–5', *English Historical Review*, 119 (2004), pp. 585–613, on pp. 587–8; Connolly, *Divided Kingdom*, p. 192.
102. McGuire, 'Parliament', p. 4; McGrath, *Constitution*, pp. 75–6; Kelly, 'The Making of Law', pp. 266–7; idem, *Poynings' Law*, pp. 48–60.
103. Aydelotte, 'Ormond', pp. 30–4, 48–53, 56–61, 64, 78; McGrath, 'Parliamentary Additional Supply', pp. 30–1; idem, *Constitution*, pp. 36–7.
104. *CSPD 1695 and addenda*, pp. 204–5; McGrath, *Constitution*, pp. 77–8.
105. McGrath, 'Parliamentary Additional Supply', pp. 27–54.
106. BL, Add. MS 27382, ff. 3–6; McGrath, 'English Ministers', pp. 588–9; idem, *Constitution*, pp. 74–5, 77, 154–5; S. J. Connolly, 'The Glorious Revolution in Irish Protestant Thinking', in idem (ed.), *Political Ideas in Eighteenth-Century Ireland* (Dublin: Four Courts Press, 2000), pp. 27–63; idem, 'Precedent and Principle: The Patriots and Their Critics', in ibid., pp. 130–58; idem, *Divided Kingdom*, pp. 195–6; D. W. Hayton, 'Introduction: The Long Apprenticeship', *Parliamentary History*, 20 (2001), pp. 1–26, on p. 8.
107. McGuire, 'Parliament', pp. 11–12; idem, 'Dopping'; Connolly, *Divided Kingdom*, p. 195.
108. *CJI*, vol. 2, pp. 10–11; McGrath, 'Reinterpretation', pp. 165–6; Kelly, *Poynings' Law*, p. 60.
109. *CSPD 1695 and addenda*, p. 213; McGuire, 'Parliament', p. 15.
110. McGuire, 'Parliament', pp. 11–19; McGrath, *Constitution*, pp. 78–100; idem, 'English Ministers', pp. 589–613.
111. *CJI*, vol. 2, p. 28; McGrath, *Constitution*, pp. 84–5; McGuire, 'Parliament', pp. 19–20; Kelly, *Poynings' Law*, pp. 61–2; Connolly, *Divided Kingdom*, p. 194.
112. J. P. Kenyon (ed.), *The Stuart Constitution 1603–1688: Documents and Commentary* (Cambridge: Cambridge University Press, 1966), p. 419.
113. McGrath, *Constitution*, pp. 85–6; idem, 'English Ministers', p. 590; idem, 'Reinterpretation', pp. 166–7; McGuire, 'Parliament', pp. 20–1.
114. McGuire, 'Parliament', pp. 16–20; McGrath, *Constitution*, pp. 78–87; idem, 'Reinterpretation', pp. 165–6.
115. *CJI*, vol. 2, pp. 35–6; McGuire, 'Parliament', pp. 21–2; McGrath, *Constitution*, pp. 86–8; Kelly, *Poynings' Law*, pp. 62–3.
116. McGrath, 'English Ministers', pp. 591–611; idem, *Constitution*, pp. 90–100; idem, 'Reinterpretation', p. 167; Hayton, *Ruling Ireland*, pp. 52–6; Kelly, *Poynings' Law*, pp. 63–8.
117. *CJI*, vol. 2, pp. 44–5.

118. McGrath, *Constitution*, pp. 100–17; idem, 'The Origins and Purpose of the Penal Laws', pp. 25–46; idem, 'Reinterpretation', p. 167; Hayton, *Ruling Ireland*, pp. 56–62, 96–105; Kelly, *Poynings' Law*, pp. 69–79; Connolly, *Divided Kingdom*, p. 196.
119. McGrath, 'Parliamentary Additional Supply', pp. 27–54; idem, 'Central Aspects', pp. 9–34.
120. Hayton, 'Apprenticeship', pp. 11–13.
121. McGrath, *Constitution*, pp. 118–52; idem, 'Reinterpretation', pp. 168–9; Kelly, *Poynings' Law*, 79–112.
122. TNA, PC 2/79, pp. 413–14, 430–1; *CSPD 1703–4*, pp. 56–7; McGrath, *Constitution*, pp. 156–60, 212, 234, 250; idem, 'Reinterpretation', pp. 169–70; idem, 'Parliamentary Additional Supply', pp. 40–54; Kelly, *Poynings' Law*, pp. 160–3.
123. Kelly, *Poynings' Law*, pp. 152–63; Hayton, 'Apprenticeship', p. 11.
124. McGrath, 'Parliamentary Additional Supply', pp. 32–54; Hayton, 'Apprenticeship', pp. 8, 23–5; Connolly, *Divided Kingdom*, p. 197.
125. McGrath, *Constitution*, pp. 193–246; idem, 'Parliamentary Additional Supply', pp. 40–54.
126. Hayton, *Ruling Ireland*, pp. 106–30; T. Bartlett, 'The Townshend Viceroyalty, 1767–72', in Bartlett and Hayton (eds), *Penal Era and Golden Age*, pp. 88–112; M. J. Powell, 'The Reform of the Undertaker System: Anglo-Irish Politics, 1750–67', *Irish Historical Studies*, 31 (1998–9), pp. 19–36.
127. TNA, SP 63/369/154, 158, 160; PC 2/85, pp. 279–80, 282–4, 293–4; *CJI*, vol. 3, pp. 9, 14, 16, 20, 22, 29, 38, 40, 43, 50, 64–5, 73, 77–8.
128. Kelly, *Poynings' Law*, pp. 242–4; Hayton, 'Apprenticeship', p. 11.
129. *CJI*, vol. 3, pp. 463, 468, 470, 475, 479–85; vol. 7, pp. 12, 16, 20–1, 24, 30, 54, 63–5, 67–89, 70–1, 73, 76–7, 90–2; vol. 9, p. 296; TNA, PC 2/90, pp. 51–3, 66–8, 78–80; PC 2/108, pp. 191–2, 208–10, 213–15.
130. TNA, SP 63/430/162–6; *Calendar of Home Office Papers, 1760–69*, 2 vols (London: Stationery Office, 1878–9) (hereafter, *CHOP*) *1766–9*, pp. 520–22; *CJI*, vol. 8, pp. 288, 323, 328.
131. Kelly, *Poynings' Law*, pp. 242–4, 310–12 (for the remainder of the eighteenth century see pp. 355–7); Hayton, 'Apprenticeship', p. 11.
132. Kelly, *Poynings' Law*, pp. 47–112, 133–58, 210–41, 273–309.
133. McGrath, *Constitution*, pp. 218–20, 237–40, 267–8; idem, 'Parliamentary Additional Supply', pp. 50.
134. McGrath, 'Central Aspects', pp. 13–17.
135. *CJI*, vol. 3, pp. 91, 483.
136. McGrath, 'Central Aspects', pp. 21–2, 24, 30.
137. Kelly, 'Era of Liberty', p. 86; idem, 'Anglo-Irish Union', pp. 113–14; Hayton, 'Ideas of Union', pp. 144–7; J. Kelly, 'The Origins of the Act of Union: An Examination of Unionist Opinion in Britain and Ireland, 1650–1800', *Irish Historical Studies*, 25 (1986–7), pp. 236–63; J. Smyth, '"Like Amphibious Animals": Irish Protestants, Ancient Britons, 1691–1707', *Historical Journal*, 36 (1993), pp. 785–97; idem, 'Anglo-Irish Unionist Discourse, c.1656–1707: From Harrington to Fletcher', *Bullán*, 2 (1995), pp. 17–34; idem, '"No Remedy More Proper": Anglo-Irish Unionism before 1707', in B. Bradshaw and P. Roberts (eds), *British Consciousness and Identity: The Making of Britain, 1533–1707* (Cambridge: Cambridge University Press, 1998), pp. 301–20; idem, *The Making of the United Kingdom, 1660–1800* (London: Longman, 2001), pp. 99–102; J. Hill, 'Ireland without Union: Molyneux and His Legacy', in John Robertson (ed.), *A Union for*

Empire: Political Thought and the British Union of 1707 (Cambridge: Cambridge University Press, 1995), pp. 271–96.

138. Molyneux, *The Case*, pp. 95–8.

139. *CJI*, vol. 2, pp. 341–2; C. I. McGrath, 'The "Union" Representation of 1703 in the Irish House of Commons: A Case of Mistaken Identity?', *Eighteenth Century Ireland*, 23 (2008), pp. 11–35; Hayton, 'Ideas of Union', pp. 144, 159–60.

140. *CJI*, vol. 2, pp. 320, 322; McGrath, 'Representation', pp. 22–3.

141. [H. Maxwell], *An Essay upon an Union of Ireland with England: Most humbly Offered to the Consideration of the Queen's Most Excellent Majesty and Both Houses of Parliament* (Dublin, 1704).

142. D. W. Hayton, 'Henry Maxwell, M.P., Author of *An Essay upon an Union of Ireland with England* (1703)', *Eighteenth Century Ireland*, 22 (2007), pp. 28–63.

143. G. Davies, 'Swift's *The Story of the Injured Lady*', *Huntington Library Quarterly*, 6 (1943), pp. 473–89.

144. J. Swift, *The Story of the Injured Lady. Being a True Picture of Scotch Perfidy, Irish Poverty, and English Partiality* (London, 1746); Hayton, 'Ideas of Union', pp. 154–5.

145. Kelly, 'Anglo-Irish Union', pp. 119–25; E. Magennis, *The Irish Political System, 1740– 1765: The Golden Age of the Undertakers* (Dublin: Four Courts Press, 2000), pp. 137–40.

146. See P. McNally, *Parties, Patriots and Undertakers: Parliamentary Politics in Early Hanoverian Ireland* (Dublin: Four Courts Press, 1997), pp. 174–95; J. Leerssen, *Mere Irish and Fíor-Ghael: Studies in the Idea of Irish Nationality, Its Development and Literary Expression Prior to the Nineteenth Century*, 2nd edn (Cork: Cork University Press, 1996), pp. 294–376; idem, 'Anglo-Irish Patriotism and its European Context: Notes Towards a Reassessment', *Eighteenth Century Ireland*, 3 (1988), pp. 7–24; Bartlett, *Ireland*, pp. 153–63; McBride, 'Common Name', pp. 236–61.

147. Simms, *Colonial Nationalism*, p. 50; idem, *Molyneux*, p. 116; R. Mahony, *Jonathan Swift: The Irish Identity* (New Haven, CT: Yale University Press, 1995), p. 1.

148. A. Goodwin, 'Wood's Halfpence', *English Historical Review*, 51 (1936), pp. 647–55; S. Baltes, *The Pamphlet Controversy about Wood's Halfpence (1722–25) and the Tradition of Irish Constitutional Nationalism* (Frankfurt: Peter Lang, 2003), pp. 105–9.

149. P. McNally, 'Wood's Halfpence, Carteret, and the Government of Ireland, 1723–6', *Irish Historical Studies*, 30 (1996–7), pp. 354–76, on p. 355.

150. TNA, SP 63/380/110; McNally, 'Carteret', pp. 355–6.

151. Goodwin, 'Halfpence', pp. 647–63; McNally, *Parties*, pp. 127–30; Baltes, *Pamphlet Controversy*, pp. 109–17, 159, 171–3.

152. *CJI*, vol. 3, p. 325; TNA, SP 63/381/3–4, 122–4, 145–6, 147, 149, 165–6, 168, 172, 178–9, 180–3, 184–5; SP 63/383/208–9, 227–8; SP 63/384/18, 66, 136–8, 189–91.

153. [J. Swift], *A Letter to the Shopkeepers, Tradesmen, Farmers and Common-People of Ireland, Concerning the Brass Half-Pence Coined by Mr Woods, with a Design to Have Them Pass in This Kingdom* (Dublin, 1724); H. Williams (ed.), *The Correspondence of Jonathan Swift*, 5 vols (Oxford: Clarendon Press, 1963–5), vol. 3, pp. 11–13.

154. [J. Swift], *A Letter to the Whole People of Ireland. By M.B. Drapier* (Dublin, 1724); [idem], *Seasonable Advice* ([Dublin,] 1724).

155. TNA, SP 63/384/226–8; McNally, 'Carteret', pp. 362–8.

156. McNally, *Parties*, pp. 174–85; Magennis, *Political System*, pp. 22, 34–6; B. Harris, *Politics and the Nation: Britain in the Mid-Eighteenth Century* (Oxford: Oxford University Press, 2002), pp. 199–207; Connolly, *Divided Kingdom*, pp. 240–1; idem, *Religion, Law and Power*, pp. 92–3, 123–4.

157. McGrath, *Constitution*, pp. 74–283; C. I. McGrath, "'The Public Wealth Is the Sinew, the Life, of Every Public Measure": The Creation and Maintenance of a National Debt in Ireland, 1716–45', in D. Carey and C. J. Finlay (eds), *The Empire of Credit: The Financial Revolution in the British Atlantic World, 1688–1815* (Dublin: Irish Academic Press, 2011), pp. 171–208, on pp. 181–4; Kelly, *Poynings' Law*, pp. 152–62, 237–44, 302–12; idem, 'Era of Liberty', pp. 93–6; Connolly, *Divided Kingdom*, pp. 240–1.

158. Simms, *Colonial Nationalism*, p. 51; idem, *Molyneux*, pp. 116–17; Kelly, 'Spirit of Liberty', pp. 138–9; Connolly, *Divided Kingdom*, pp. 241–4.

159. Harrington to Bedford, 17 November 1749 (TNA, SP 63/411/214–16).

160. TNA, PC 2/101, pp. 370–71.

161. Dorset and Irish Privy Council to [Holdernesse], 14 November 1751 (TNA, SP 63/412/206–207). See also TNA, PC 2/102, pp. 378–9; *Stat. Ire.*, vol. 7, pp. 104–11.

162. *Stat. Ire.*, vol. 7, pp. 104–11; TNA, PC 2/102, pp. 378–9.

163. Magennis, *Political System*, pp. 66–8; C. I. McGrath, 'Money, Politics and Power: The Financial Legislation of the Irish Parliament', in D. W. Hayton, J. Kelly and J. Bergin (eds), *Composite State*, pp. 21–43, on p. 35.

164. TNA, SP 63/413/73; PC 2/102/363–4, 378–9, 383–5; PC 2/103/515–16, 518–19, 525, 546; *CJI*, vol. 5, pp. 187–8, 190; O'Donovan, 'The Money Bill Dispute', pp. 55–87; McGrath, 'Money, Politics and Power', pp. 35–6.

165. Magennis, *Political System*, p. 82; O'Donovan, 'The Money Bill Dispute', p. 64.

166. TNA, SP 63/452/302–7, 326–9; Lord J. Russell (ed.), *Correspondence of John, Fourth Duke of Bedford*, 3 vols (London: Longman, 1842–6), vol. 2, pp. 421–3, 427–9; vol. 3, pp. 1–2; HMC, *Various Collections*, vol. 6, pp. 75, 78–80; *The Representation of the L[ord]s J[ustice]s of Ireland, Touching the Transmission of a Privy Council Money Bill Previous to the Calling of a New Parliament in Two Letters. Addressed to His Grace the Duke of Bedford* (Dublin, 1770), pp. 1–11, 16–26; *CHOP 1760–5*, pp. 6, 69–71; McGrath, 'Central Aspects', pp. 20–1; J. Kelly, 'Monitoring the Constitution: The Operation of Poynings' Law in the 1760s', *Parliamentary History*, 20 (2001), pp. 87–106, on pp. 89, 95–9; Magennis, *Political System*, pp. 146–51, 158–60; R. E. Burns, *Irish Parliamentary Politics in the Eighteenth Century*, 2 vols (Washington, DC: Catholic University of America Press, 1989–90), vol. 2, pp. 300–12.

167. *CJI*, vol. 3, pp. 91, 483.

168. *CHOP 1760–5*, pp. 73, 76, 78–80; *CJI*, vol. 7, pp. 11–14, 18–19, 22, 24, 28, 57, 60–2, 64, 67, 68, 69–71, 73; *Stat. Ire.*, vol. 7, pp. 801–7; McGrath, 'Central Aspects', pp. 21–2; Magennis, *Political System*, pp. 159–61; D. Lammey, 'The Growth of the "Patriot Opposition", in Ireland during the 1770s', *Parliamentary History*, 7 (1988), pp. 257–81, on pp. 261–2.

169. *Stat. Ire.*, vol. 9, p. 504; Bartlett, 'The Augmentation', pp. 554–6; T. Bartlett, 'Opposition in Late Eighteenth-Century Ireland: The Case of the Townshend Viceroyalty', *Irish Historical Studies*, 22 (1980–1), pp. 313–30, on pp. 313–16; James, *Ireland in the Empire*, pp. 264–70; J. Kelly, *Prelude to Union: Anglo-Irish Politics in the 1780s* (Cork: Cork University Press, 1992), pp. 19–22; Lammey, 'Opposition', pp. 261–2; Powell, 'Undertaker system', pp. 28–36.

170. *CJI*, vol. 8, pp. 295–7, 316, 322–3; TNA, SP 63/430/162–3, 211–13; *CHOP 1766–9*, pp. 520–2; McGrath, 'Central Aspects', pp. 24–5; J. Kelly, *Henry Flood: Patriots and Politics in Eighteenth-Century Ireland* (Dublin: Four Courts Press, 1998), pp. 135–6; T. Bartlett, 'The Irish House of Commons' Rejection of the "Privy Council" Money Bill in 1769: A Re-Assessment', *Studia Hibernica*, 19 (1979), pp. 63–77.

171. TNA, SP 63/430/163, 185–6; Bartlett, 'Money Bill', p. 65.

172. *CJI*, vol. 8, pp. 332–40, 345–6, 353–4; TNA, SP 63/430/185–6, 205–6, 209, 211–16, 230, 232, 236–8, 240, 242, 244–6, 259, 261, 263–4, 273; *Stat. Ire.*, vol. 10, pp. 1–22.
173. TNA, SP 63/430/248–54; Curtis and McDowell (eds), *Documents*, pp. 220–1; McGrath, 'Central Aspects', pp. 25–6.
174. Simms, *Colonial Nationalism*, pp. 53–63; Greene, *Peripheries*, p. 103.
175. Greene, 'Introduction', p. 12.
176. W. E. Harcourt (ed.), *Harcourt Papers*, 15 vols (privately printed, 1876–1903), vol. 10, pp. 95–6, 98–9, 136–7, 166–7; TNA, SP 63/452/299–300, 302–7, 324, 326–9, 332; SP 63/453/65, 93–4, 147, 149–53, 222–3; *CJI*, vol. 9, pp. 286, 289–90, 295–6, 299–302; McGrath, 'Central Aspects', pp. 28–31.
177. Curtis and McDowell (eds), *Documents*, pp. 186–8, 203–4; Kelly, *Poynings' Law*, pp. 315–54; idem, *Prelude to Union*, pp. 59–61, 66, 235–6; Connolly, *Divided Kingdom*, pp. 402–16.
178. Connolly, *Divided Kingdom*, pp. 416–98; G. C. Bolton, *The Passing of the Irish Act of Union* (Oxford: Oxford University Press, 1966); P. M. Geoghegan, *The Irish Act of Union* (Dublin: Gill & Macmillan, 1999); T. D. Ingram, *A History of the Legislative Union of Great Britain and Ireland* (London: Macmillan, 1887).
179. Cosgrove, 'Parliament', pp. 28–9.
180. Greene, *Peripheries*, pp. 79–90; Morley, *Irish Opinion*, pp. 97–106, 119, 125–9; Simms, *Colonial Nationalism*, pp. 53–61; Mancke, 'Languages of Liberty', pp. 26, 28, 34, 41, 43–4; Bric, *Philadelphia*, pp. 201–2.

4 Barracks for a Standing Army

1.   J. H. Andrews, *Shapes of Ireland: Maps and Their Makers 1564–1839* (Dublin: Geography Publications, 1997), p. 157.
2.   G. Parker, *The Army of Flanders and the Spanish Road 1567–1659* (Cambridge, 1972), p. 166; idem, *The Military Revolution: Military Innovation and the Rise of the West, 1500–1800* (Cambridge, 1988), p. 78; J. Douet, *British Barracks 1600–1914: Their Architecture and Role in Society* (London: Stationary Office, 1998), p. 3.
3.   Douet, *Barracks*, pp. 3–4, 17; Parker, *The Army of Flanders*, pp. 166–7; J. Black, *European Warfare 1660–1815* (London: University College London Press, 1994), p. 225.
4.   P. Wilson, 'Warfare in the Old Regime 1648–1789', in J. Black (ed.), *European Warfare 1453–1815* (Basingstoke: Palgrave, 1999), pp. 69–95, on p. 75.
5.   S. J. Connolly, 'The Defence of Protestant Ireland, 1660–1760', in T. Bartlett and K. Jeffery (eds), *A Military History of Ireland* (Cambridge: Cambridge University Press, 1996), pp. 231–45, on p. 244; Ferguson, 'The Army', pp. 79–80. See also P. M. Kerrigan, *Castles and Fortifications in Ireland 1485–1945* (Cork: Collins Press, 1995), p. 133.
6.   S. Brumwell, 'Wade, George (1673–1748)', *ODNB*, at <http://www.oxforddnb.com/view/article/28377>.
7.   C. M. Clode, *The Military Forces of the Crown: Their Administration and Government*, 2 vols (London: John Murray, 1869), vol. 1, p. 223. See also H. C. B. Rogers, *The British Army of the Eighteenth Century* (London: Allen & Unwin, 1977), p. 38; Brewer, *The Sinews of Power*, p. 48.
8.   L. G. Schwoerer, *'No Standing Armies!': The Anti-Army Ideology in Seventeenth-Century England* (Baltimore, MD: Johns Hopkins University Press, 1974), passim; J. Childs,

Armies and Warfare in Europe 1648–1789 (New York: Holmes and Meier, 1982), pp. 185–6.

9. Clode, *The Military Forces*, vol. 1, pp. 17, 19–20, 61; B. Coward, *The Stuart Age: England 1603–1714*, 3rd edn (London: Longman, 2003), pp. 162–3, 312, 518.

10. Clode, *The Military Forces*, vol. 1, p. 20; Coward, *The Stuart Age*, pp. 162–3, 518; Schwoerer, *No Standing Armies*, pp. 19–32; P. Christianson, 'Arguments on Billeting and Martial Law in the Parliament of 1628', *Historical Journal*, 37 (1994), pp. 539–67; L. Boynton, 'Billeting: The Example of the Isle of Wight', *English Historical Review*, 74 (1959), pp. 23–40; idem, 'Martial Law and the Petition of Right', *English Historical Review*, 79 (1964), pp. 255–84.

11. Schwoerer, *No Standing Armies*, p. 56.

12. See Schwoerer, *No Standing Armies*, pp. 99–101; Coward, *The Stuart Age*, pp. 312, 532.

13. Clode, *The Military Forces*, vol. 1, pp. 65–6; J. Childs, *The Army, James II, and the Glorious Revolution* (Manchester: Manchester University Press, 1980), pp. 85–6.

14. Childs, *The Army*, pp. 1–4, 85–91; Clode, *The Military Forces*, vol. 1, pp. 80–2; Schwoerer, *No Standing Armies*, p. 143.

15. Clode, *The Military Forces*, vol. 1, pp. 229–30; Rogers, *The British Army*, p. 38.

16. Schwoerer, *No Standing Armies*, p. 137; Childs, *The Army, James II*, p. 87; Brewer, *The Sinews of Power*, pp. 48–9.

17. R. E. Scouller, *The Armies of Queen Anne* (Oxford: Clarendon Press, 1966), p. 164; Rogers, *The British Army*, p. 38; Brewer, *The Sinews of Power*, p. 48.

18. Clode, *The Military Forces*, vol. 1, pp. 230–7, 569–77; Brewer, *The Sinews of Power*, p. 49.

19. W. Hogarth, *The March to Finchley*, 1749–1750 (Oil on canvas); idem, *The Invasion, Plate 2: England*, 8 March 1756 (Etching and engraving on paper); Scouller, *The Armies of Queen Anne*, pp. 164–5.

20. Scouller, *The Armies of Queen Anne*, p. 164.

21. Childs, *The Army, James II*, pp. 86–8.

22. See Schwoerer, *No Standing Armies*, pp. 21–2; P. Edwards, 'Logistics and Supply', in J. Kenyon and J. Ohlmeyer (eds), *The Civil Wars: A Military History of England, Scotland, and Ireland 1638–1660* (Oxford: Oxford University Press, 1998), pp. 234–71, on p. 257.

23. *By the Lords Justices of Ireland, A Proclamation [Regarding Winter Quarters]* (Dublin, 1691); *By the Lords Justices of Ireland, A Proclamation. Requiring all Officers and Soldiers to Observe Strict Discipline, and for Payment of Quarters* (Dublin, 1692). See also I. Gentles, *The English Revolution and the Wars of the Three Kingdoms 1638–1652* (London: Longman, 2007), pp. 445–6; Schwoerer, *No Standing Armies*, pp. 143, 150; Ferguson, 'The Army', p. 43–4.

24. Clode, *The Military Forces*, vol. 1, pp. 222–3.

25. Simms, *Jacobite Ireland*, p. 130; Wauchope, *Sarsfield*, p. 89; Doherty, *The Williamite War*, pp. 98–100; Ferguson, 'The Army', pp. 30–4.

26. For the controversy over the standing army see Schwoerer, *No Standing Armies*, pp. 155–87; Hoppit, *A Land of Liberty?*, pp. 156–7.

27. J. Trenchard, *An Argument Shewing, That a Standing Army Is Inconsistent with A Free Government, and Absolutely Destructive to the Constitution of the English Monarchy* (London, 1697), pp. 28–9.

28. W. Moyle, *The Second Part of An Argument, Shewing, That a Standing Army Is Inconsistent with A Free Government, and Absolutely Destructive to the Constitution of the English Monarchy* (London, 1697), p. 6.

29. J. Trenchard, *A Short History of Standing Armies in England* (London, 1731), p. 12. It has been suggested that Moyle was in fact Trenchard's amanuensis, and that the two men collaborated on the writing of Moyle's *Second Part of An Argument*, which would account for the similarity of argument and wording in Trenchard's *Short History*. See Schwoerer, *No Standing Armies*, pp. 175–6 and n. 90.

30. Trenchard, *Short History*, p. 18. See also Hoppit, *A Land of Liberty?*, pp. 158–9.

31. D. Defoe, *An Argument Shewing, That a Standing Army, with consent of Parliament, Is Not Inconsistent with a Free Government* (London, 1698), p. 21.

32. M. Prior, *A New Answer to an Argument against a Standing Army* ([London], 1697).

33. Rogers, *The British Army*, p. 38; Brewer, *The Sinews of Power*, p. 48.

34. *The History and Proceedings of the House of Commons 1660–1743*, 14 vols (London, 1742–4), vol. 12, pp. 148–9, 178. See also Clode, *The Military Forces*, vol. 1, p. 234.

35. *Letters on the Impolicy of a Standing Army, in Time of Peace. And, on the Unconstitutional and Illegal Measure of Barracks ...* (London, 1793); *A Political and Military Rhapsody, on the Invasion and Defence of Great Britain and Ireland ...*, 3rd edn (London, 1794).

36. *The State of the Nation, with Respect to Its Public Funded Debt, Revenue, and Disbursement; Comprised in the Reports of the Select Committee on Finance (with the Appendices to Each Report) Appointed by The House of Commons ...*, 3 vols (London, 1799), vol. 3, pp. 1–29; Douet, *Barracks*, pp. 60, 67–94.

37. S. S. Webb, *The Governors-General: The English Army and the definition of the Empire, 1569–1681* (Williamsburg, VA: Chapel Hill, 1979), p. 280.

38. Scouller, *The Armies of Queen Anne*, p. 169.

39. Clode, *The Military Forces*, vol. 1, p. 228.

40. *An Abridgement of the Laws of Jamaica*, 2 vols (Jamaica, 1793), vol. 1, pp. 20–1. See also Greene, 'Introduction', pp. 8–9.

41. Webb, *The Governors-General*, p. 474.

42. W. S. Fields and D. T. Hardy, 'The Third Amendment and the Issue of the Maintenance of Standing Armies: A Legal History', *The American Journal of Legal History*, 35 (1991), pp. 393–431, on p. 414; V. D. Anderson, 'New England in the Seventeenth Century', in Canny (ed.), *The Origins of Empire*, pp. 193–217, on pp. 214–15.

43. Webb, *The Governors-General*, pp. 384–5.

44. Fields and Hardy, 'The Third Amendment', p. 414.

45. Ibid., pp. 411–14.

46. C. E. Carter, 'The Significance of the Military Office in America, 1763–1775', *American Historical Review*, 28 (1923), pp. 475–88, on p. 476; Marshall, *Empires*, p. 63.

47. Carter, 'Military Office', p. 485; F. Anderson, *Crucible of War: The Seven Years War and the Fate of Empire in British North America 1754–1766* (London: Faber & Faber, 2000), pp. 719–24.

48. Fields and Hardy, 'The Third Amendment', p. 417, fn. 113; Carter, 'Military Office', p. 475.

49. Fields and Hardy, 'The Third Amendment', p. 418.

50. Ibid., pp. 393, 420–31.

51. Scouller, *The Armies of Queen Anne*, pp. 81, 83–6; Clode, *The Military Forces*, vol. 1, pp. 52–4.

52. Scouller, *The Armies of Queen Anne*, pp. 86–7.

53. Clode, *The Military Forces*, vol. 1, p. 222; Rogers, *The British Army*, p. 39; Scouller, *The Armies of Queen Anne*, p. 166; Ferguson, 'The Army', p. 79.

54. Scouller, *The Armies of Queen Anne*, p. 85.

55. Clode, *The Military Forces*, vol. 1, p. 221; Scouller, *The Armies of Queen Anne*, pp. 163–4.
56. Quoted in Scouller, *The Armies of Queen Anne*, p. 166.
57. Mr Waite's paper about the present state of Ireland, [1749] (BL, Add. MS 35919, f. 268); E. Magennis, 'Select Document: "The Present State of Ireland", 1749', *Irish Historical Studies*, 36 (2009), pp. 581–97, on p. 592.
58. C. I. McGrath, 'Waging War: The Irish Military Establishment and the British Empire, 1688–1763', in W. Mulligan and B. Simms (eds), *The Primacy of Foreign Policy in British History, 1660–2000* (Basingstoke: Palgrave, 2010), pp. 102–18, on p. 105.
59. Orrery to Lord Lieutenant, 22 November 1678 (NAI, Wyche papers, 1/1/25).
60. Thomas Brodrick to Sir St John Brodrick, 16 December 1690 (SHC, Midleton papers, 1248/1, ff. 251–2).
61. Alan Brodrick to St John Brodrick, 11 November 1691 (SHC, Midleton papers, 1248/1, ff. 255–6).
62. *CSPD 1693*, p. 445. See also pp. 109, 124–5, 147, 165–6, 176–7, 192.
63. *CSPD 1695 and addenda*, p. 198.
64. Ibid., p. 175.
65. See BL, Add. MS 21136, f. 12; BL, Harleian MS 6274, f. 116; McGrath, 'Parliament, Policy and Politics', pp. 108–11.
66. Information given to the English House of Commons on the state of Ireland, 24 February 1693 (BL, Harleian MS 4892, ff. 127–90); SHC, Midleton papers, 1248/1, ff. 261–2.
67. *CJI* (1st), vol. 2, p. 726.
68. W. N. Osborough, 'The Failure to Enact an Irish Bill of Rights: A Gap in Irish Constitutional History', *Irish Jurist*, 33 (1998), pp. 392–416.
69. Alan Brodrick to St John Brodrick, 17 December 1695 (SHC, Midleton papers, 1248/1, ff. 278–9).
70. Douet, *Barracks*, p. 29.
71. *CSPD 1693*, p. 115. The year is given incorrectly as 1692 in McGrath, 'Waging War', p. 106.
72. *CSPD 1693*, pp. 227–8, 247.
73. *CSPD 1695 and addenda*, p. 146.
74. Ibid., p. 59.
75. D. Fleming, *Politics and Provincial People: Sligo and Limerick, 1691–1761* (Manchester: Manchester University Press, 2010), p. 198.
76. See McGrath, 'Revenue', pp. 52–4.
77. See L. G. Schwoerer, 'The Role of King William III of England in the Standing Army Controversy – 1697–1699', *Journal of British Studies*, 5 (1966), pp. 74–94.
78. C. Rose, *England in the 1690s: Revolution, Religion and War* (Oxford: Blackwell, 1999), p. 142.
79. *CJI* (1st), vol. 2, pp. 833–4; *CSPD 1690–1*, pp. 216–17 (this copy of the opening speech has been calendared under the wrong year).
80. Budgell to Addison, 9 February 1715 (BL, Add. MS 61636, ff. 163–4).
81. PRONI, De Ros MSS, D638/166/21; *CSPD 1697*, pp. 492–3; T. G. Doyle, 'The Politics of Protestant Ascendancy: Politics, Religion and Society in Protestant Ireland, 1700–1710' (PhD, UCD, 1996), p. 339.
82. *CSPD 1697*, p. 299; McGrath, *Constitution*, pp. 124–9.
83. *Stat. Ire.*, vol. 3, pp. 353–8; McGrath, *Constitution*, pp. 40, 131.
84. *Stat. Ire.*, vol. 3, pp. 353.

85. Ibid.
86. Ibid., p. 356.
87. *Calendar of Treasury Papers* (hereafter, *CTP*) *1697–1702*, p. 138; *CTB 1697–8*, p. 279; *CSPD 1698*, p. 149.
88. Henry Horwitz, *Parliament, Policy and Politics in the Reign of William III* (Manchester: Manchester University Press, 1977), pp. 222–70; Schwoerer, 'King William', pp. 74–94.
89. See Chapter 5.
90. *CJI* (1st), vol. 2, p. 994.
91. McGrath, *Constitution*, pp. 142–3.
92. Lords justices to Blathwayt, 26 November, 3 December 1698 (NAI, MS M2456, [unfol.]); same to Vernon, 3 December 1698 (NAI, MS 2447, p. 34).
93. Schwoerer, 'King William', pp. 87–8.
94. *CSPD 1699–1700*, pp. 2–4, 11, 17.
95. *CJI* (1st), vol. 2, pp. 1098, 1103, 1107, 1109, 1115; *Stat. Ire.*, vol. 3, pp. 471; T. G. Doyle, 'Parliament and Politics in Williamite Ireland 1690–1703' (MA, UCD, 1992), p. 308.
96. *CTP 1697–1702*, p. 296; *CTB 1698–9*, p. 88; *CTB 1699–1700*, pp. 196–7; *CSPD 1699–1700*, p. 281.
97. *CTB 1699–1700*, p. 307; *CSPD 1699–1700*, p. 409.
98. *CTB 1700–1*, p. 280.
99. *CTB 1700–1*, pp. 326, 340; *CSPD 1700–2*, p. 405.
100. *Rules, Orders, Powers, and Directions, For the Good Government and Preservation of the Barracks and Redoubts, for Quartering the Army in Ireland* (Dublin, 1701), p. 15; *CSPD 1700–2*, p. 183.
101. *CTB 1699–1700*, pp. 365–7; *CTB 1700–1*, p. 339; *CSPD 1700–2*, p. 157; *CSPD 1702–3*, p. 157; *CSPD 1704–5*, pp. 48, 143; [H. Brooke], *The Secret History and Memoirs of the Barracks of Ireland* (London, 1747), pp. 20–1.
102. *Rules, Orders, Powers, and Directions*, pp. 3–7.
103. *CTB 1699–1700*, p. 260; *CSPD 1702–3*, p. 157.
104. E. McParland, *Public Architecture in Ireland 1680–1760* (New Haven, CT: Yale University Press, 2001), p. 129.
105. *CSPD 1700–2*, p. 183; *Rules, Orders, Powers, and Directions*, pp. 8–14.
106. *Rules, Orders, Powers, and Directions*, pp. 10–11.
107. E. McParland, 'The Office of the Surveyor-General in Ireland in the Eighteenth Century', *Architectural History*, 38 (1995), pp. 91–101, on p. 93.
108. *Rules, Orders, Powers, and Directions*, p. 13.
109. *CSPD 1700–2*, p. 183; *Rules, Orders, Powers, and Directions*, pp. 16–18.
110. *Rules, Orders, Powers, and Directions*, p. 14.
111. *The Statutes at Large*, 6 vols (London, 1758), vol. 3, p. 383. For the Williamite forfeitures see Simms, *The Williamite Confiscation*, passim.
112. E. M. Johnston-Liik, *History of the Irish Parliament 1692–1800: Commons, Constituencies and Statutes*, 6 vols (Belfast: Ulster Historical Foundation, 2002), vol. 6, pp. 168–9; J. Gibney, 'Robinson, Sir William', *DIB*, at <http://dib.cambridge.org/viewReadPage.do?articleId=a7736>.
113. *Rules, Orders, Powers, and Directions*, pp. 21–39.
114. Ibid., p. 29.
115. Ibid., p. 40.
116. Ibid., pp. 28, 42; Ferguson, 'The Army', p. 93.
117. *CSPD 1702–3*, p. 78.
118. *State of the Nation*, p. 1; Douet, *Barracks*, pp. 67–9.

119. *A Warrant for the Regulation of Barracks* (London, 1795), p. 2.
120. Budgell to Addison, 9 February 1715 (BL, Add. MS 61636, ff. 163–4). For Galway see M. Léoutre, 'Life of a Huguenot Exile: Henri de Ruvigny, Earl of Galway, 1648–1720' (PhD, UCD, 2012), passim.
121. *CSPD 1700–2*, pp. 54, 57, 69, 98, 104–5, 107, 171, 173.
122. *Rules, Orders, Powers, and Directions, for the Good Government and Preservation of the Barracks and Redoubts for Quartering the Army in Ireland* (Dublin, 1726), pp. 15–18.
123. *Rules, Orders, Powers, and Directions* … (1726), pp. 19–22.
124. TNA, PRO 30/26/60, ff. 13–17; Ferguson, 'The Army', p. 81.
125. *Rules, Orders, Powers, and Directions* … (1726), pp. 23–9.
126. Ibid., p. 27.
127. Ibid., p. 29.
128. Ibid., pp. 30–3.
129. Ibid., pp. 35–51.
130. McParland, *Architecture*, p. 125; J. A. Houlding, *Fit for Service : The Training of the British Army, 1715–1795* (Oxford: Clarendon Press, 1981), p. 52.
131. *CSPD 1703–4*, p. 101.
132. *CSPD 1704–5*, p. 156.
133. For the 1703–4 session see McGrath, *Constitution*, pp. 156–81; C. I. McGrath, 'Alan Brodrick and the Speakership of the House of Commons, 1703–4', in J. Kelly, J. McCafferty and C. I. McGrath (eds), *People, Politics and Power: Essays on Irish History 1660–1850 in Honour of James I. McGuire* (Dublin: UCD Press, 2009), pp. 70–93; idem, 'Representation', pp. 11–35.
134. *CJI* (1st), vol. 3, pp. 11–12; *CSPD 1703–4*, p. 122.
135. Memorandum on the state of the Irish revenue, 30 September 1703 (BL, Add. MS 28947, ff. 83–6); *CSPD 1703–4*, pp. 138–9; *CJI* (1st), vol. 3, p. 27.
136. On the basis of the figures provided in the various warrants and establishments, the total expenditure between 1699 and December 1703 would have been £139,147 4s. 5d., or an excess of £80,513, 14s. 5d. See *CTB 1699–1700*, pp. 307, 365–7; *CTB 1700–1*, pp. 326, 339–40; *CSPD 1699–1700*, p. 409; *CSPD 1700–2*, pp. 157, 405; *CSPD 1702–3*, p. 157; *CSPD 1704–5*, pp. 48, 143; [Brooke], *Secret History*, pp. 20–1.
137. *CSPD 1703–4*, pp. 145–6, 149–50; Minute book of the committee of public accounts, 1–2 October 1703 (NAI, Frazer MSS 10, [unfol.]); *CJI* (1st), vol. 3, pp. 25, 32, 72–3.
138. Chetwood to Ellis, 12 October 1703 (BL, Add. MS 28891, ff. 129–30).
139. *CJI* (1st), vol. 3, pp. 72–3.
140. Ibid.
141. McGrath, *Constitution*, pp. 168–70.
142. Lloyd to Ellis, 22 October 1703 (BL, Add. MS 28891, f. 152); *CSPD 1703–4*, pp. 169–70; *Stat. Ire.*, vol. 4, pp. 7–10.
143. An account of some matters in the session of 1703 and particularly with regard to the Speaker's behaviour, [1704] (BL, Add. MS 9715, f. 65); McGrath, *Constitution*, p. 175; idem, 'Brodrick', pp. 70–93; idem, 'Parliamentary Additional Supply', p. 43.
144. *CSPD 1703–4*, p. 282; Ferguson, 'The Army', p. 79.
145. McParland, *Architecture*, p. 123.
146. BL, Add. MS 9715, ff. 112–13; McGrath, *Constitution*, pp. 183–7.
147. *CJI* (1st), vol. 3, pp. 220, 297–8; TNA, SP 63/365/120, 122–3, 143.
148. SHC, Midleton papers, 1248/2/183–4.
149. State of the case as to the address presented to the Lord Lieutenant, 21 March 1705 (BL, Add. MS 9715, f. 113); McGrath, *Constitution*, pp. 187–8.

150. Cox to Southwell, 11 March 1707 (BL, Add. MS 38154, f. 172).
151. *Stat. Ire.*, vol. 4, p. 156; Ferguson, 'The Army', p. 79.
152. McParland, *Architecture*, p. 123.
153. Scouller, *The Armies of Queen Anne*, p. 165.
154. *Stat. Ire.*, vol. 4, p. 156; Clode, *The Military Forces*, vol. 1, pp. 396–7. For later examples of how government in both London and Dublin were fully cognizant of, and abided by, the laws in Ireland regarding quartering in barracks except when on the march, see TNA, SP 63/403/39–40; SP 63/406/32–3.
155. TNA, SP 63/365/97–9; Minute book of the committee of public accounts, 14 July 1707, 15 May 1709, 25 May 1710, 20 July 1711 (NAI, Frazer MSS 10, [unfol.]); *CJI* (1st), vol. 3, pp. 566–7, 823.
156. TCD, MS 2022, f. 283.
157. TNA, WO 78/419/19.
158. Information provided by Dr Linda Doran (ed.), *Irish Historic Towns Atlas: New Ross* (Dublin: Royal Irish Academy, forthcoming). For the 1750s see Fleming, *Provincial People*, p. 193.
159. H. Murtagh, *Irish Historic Towns Atlas: Athlone* (Dublin: Royal Irish Academy, 1994), pp. 10–11.
160. K. M. Davies, *Irish Historic Towns Atlas: Bray* (Dublin: Royal Irish Academy, 1998), p. 11.
161. J. Bradley, *Irish Historic Towns Atlas: Kilkenny* (Dublin: Royal Irish Academy, 2000), p. 15.
162. S. Gearty, M. Morris and F. O'Ferrall, *Irish Historic Towns Atlas: Longford* (Dublin: Royal Irish Academy, 2009), p. 11.
163. Kerrigan, *Castles and Fortifications*, p. 131.
164. C. Lennon, *Irish Historic Towns Atlas: Dublin Part II, 1610 to 1756* (Dublin: Royal Irish Academy, 2010), p. 26.
165. R. Lewis, *The Dublin Guide: or a Description of the City of Dublin, and the Most Remarkable Places within Fifteen Miles …* (Dublin, 1787), p. 99.
166. TNA, WO 78/419/19.
167. McParland, *Architecture*, p. 126; Fleming, *Provincial People*, p. 199.
168. E. O'Flaherty, *Irish Historic Towns Atlas: Limerick* (Dublin: Royal Irish Academy, 2010), p. 1. See also Simms, *Jacobite Ireland*, pp. 158–73, 240–9; H. Murtagh, 'The War in Ireland, 1689–91', in W. A. Maguire (ed.), *Kings in Conflict: The Revolutionary War in Ireland and its Aftermath 1689–1750* (Belfast: Ulster Historical Foundation, 1990), pp. 61–91, on pp. 79–80, 89–91; J. Burke, 'Limerick in the Golden Age of Siege Warfare', in Whelan (ed.), *Last of the Great Wars*, pp. 83–107.
169. *CSPD 1693*, pp. 227–8, 247; *CSPD and addenda*, pp. 59, 146.
170. O'Flaherty, *Limerick*, p. 27.
171. Simms, *Jacobite Ireland*, pp. 174–86; Murtagh, 'War in Ireland', pp. 80–1.
172. D. J. Butler, 'Defence from the Dispossessed: The State-Sponsored Garrisoning of the South Tipperary Landscape, c. 1650– c. 1730', *Irish Sword*, 24 (2004), pp. 45–56, on pp. 53–5; Douet, *Barracks*, p. 33. On the redoubts in general see Kerrigan, *Castles and Fortifications*, pp. 131–3; Ferguson, 'The Army', pp. 79–80.
173. TNA, WO 78/419/19.
174. Butler, 'Defence', p. 53; Kerrigan, *Castles and Fortifications*, pp. 131–3.
175. TNA, WO 78/419/19.
176. P. Robinson, *Irish Historic Towns Atlas: Carrickfergus* (Dublin: Royal Irish Academy, 1986), p. 11.

177. A. Thomas, *Irish Historic Towns Atlas: Derry – Londonderry* (Dublin: Royal Irish Academy, 2005), p. 20.
178. A. Simms, H. Clarke, and R. Gillespie, *Irish Historic Towns Atlas: Armagh* (Dublin: Royal Irish Academy, 2007), p. 14.
179. R. Gillespie and S. Royle, *Irish Historic Towns Atlas: Belfast, part 1 to 1840* (Dublin: Royal Irish Academy, 2003), p. 22.
180. R. H. Buchanan, *Irish Historic Towns Atlas: Downpatrick* (Dublin: Royal Irish Academy, 1997), p. 10.
181. McParland, *Architecture*, p. 131.
182. TNA, WO 78/419/19.
183. *CTB 1699–1700*, pp. 365–7.
184. *CSPD 1702–3*, p. 157.
185. *CSPD 1704–5*, p. 143; R. W. Jackson, 'Queen Anne's Irish Army Establishment in 1704', *Irish Sword*, 1 (1949–53), pp. 133–5. on pp. 134–5.
186. TNA, WO 78/419/19.
187. *CTB 1699–1700*, pp. 365–7; *CSPD 1704–5*, p. 143; Jackson, 'Army Establishment', pp. 134–5; TNA, WO 78/419/19.
188. For later maps and lists see the following: UCD Special Collections, W1.U.2/1–2; W1.U.4/1–4; TNA, PRO 30/26/60, ff. 13–17, 80–1; MPF 1/315; *The Quarters of the Army in Ireland in 1744 (1745, 1748–52). To Which Is Added, the Succession of Colonels to All His Majesty's Land Forces and Marines ...* (Dublin, 1744–52); *A List of the General and Field Officers ... to Which Are Added, the Quarters of the Army in Ireland, in the Year 1755 ...* (Dublin, 1755); Andrews, *Shapes of Ireland*, p. 189; Fleming, *Provincial People*, pp. 192–3; Houlding, *Fit for Service*, p. 53; Ferguson, 'The Army', pp. 76–7, 134.
189. J. C. T. MacDonagh, 'An Eighteenth-Century Redoubt in County Donegal', *Irish Sword*, 1 (1949–53), pp. 338–40; Ferguson, 'The Army', p. 80.
190. Walsh, *Protestant Ascendancy*, pp. 153–8.
191. Conolly to [Sunderland], 18 January 1715 (BL, Add. MS 61636, ff. 208–9).
192. McParland, *Architecture*, p. 126; Fleming, *Provincial People*, pp. 199–200.
193. Budgell to Addison, 9 February 1715 (BL, Add. MS 61636, ff. 163–4).
194. Fleming, *Provincial People*, p. 199.
195. BL, Add. MS 61636, f. 167.
196. BL, Add. MS 61636, f. 226.
197. TNA, PRO 30/26/60, ff. 13–17, 80–1; McParland, *Architecture*, p. 125.
198. [Brooke], *Secret History*, pp. 11, 33–4; McParland, *Architecture*, pp. 126, 131; Fleming, *Provincial People*, pp. 199–200.
199. Johnston-Liik, *Parliament*, vol. 6, pp. 126–7.
200. Cox to Southwell, 30 November 1706 (BL, Add. MS 38154, f. 110).
201. Fleming, *Provincial People*, p. 199.
202. Ibid., pp. 204–5.
203. TNA, PRO 30/26/60, ff. 80–1; *Hiberniae Notitia: Or, A List of the Present Officers in Church and State, and of All Payments to Be Made for Civil and Military Affairs for the Kingdom of Ireland, upon the Establishment Which Commenced on the 24th Day of August 1717 ...* (London, 1723), pp. 39–42. The figures given above for the total number of barracks in 1717 are a correction to those given in McGrath, 'Waging War', p. 107.
204. *Quarters of the Army*, passim; *Field Officers*, passim; Andrews, *Shapes of Ireland*, p. 189; Fleming, *Provincial People*, pp. 192–3; Houlding, *Fit for Service*, p. 53.

205. BL, Add. MS 35919, f. 269; TNA, MPF 1/315; Magennis, 'State of Ireland', p. 593; Andrews, *Shapes of Ireland*, p. 189; Fleming, *Provincial People*, pp. 200, 202.

206. Fleming, *Provincial People*, p. 204.

207. H. P. E. Pereira, 'Barracks in Ireland, 1729, 1769', *Irish Sword*, 1 (1949–53), pp. 142–4.

208. H. P. E. Pereira, 'Quarters of the Army in Ireland, 1769', *Irish Sword*, 2 (1954–6), pp. 230–1.

209. TNA, T 1/393/44.

210. TNA, SP 63/430/5–11; *CHOP 1766–9*, pp. 488–93.

211. J. A. Claffey, *Irish Historic Towns Atlas: Tuam* (Dublin: Royal Irish Academy, 2009), p. 13.

212. P. O'Flanagan, *Irish Historic Towns Atlas: Bandon* (Dublin: Royal Irish Academy, 1988), p. 11.

213. Andrews, *Shapes of Ireland*, pp. 157–8, 182, fn. 13. See also Ferguson, 'The Army', pp. 77–8.

214. Andrews, *Shapes of Ireland*, p. 158.

215. TNA, WO 78/419/19; MPF 1/315; UCD Special Collections, W1.U.2/1–2; W1.U.4/1–4; Andrews, *Shapes of Ireland*, pp. 160–4, 182.

216. TNA, PC 2/86, pp. 54–60, 63–5; *CJI*, vol. 3, pp. 173.

217. *CJI*, vol. 3, p. 137; app. pp. cxvi–cxxvii; Minute book of the committee of public accounts, 12–14, 17–18, 20, 23, 25 September 1717 (NAI, Frazer MSS 10, [unfol.]). On the 'debt of the nation' see McGrath, 'The Public Wealth', pp. 171–208.

218. TNA, SP 63/384/198; *Rules, Orders, Powers, and Directions ...* (1726); McParland, *Architecture*, p. 129.

219. *CJI*, vol. 3, pp. 400–1, 424.

220. Ibid., vol. 4, pp. 13, 40; app. p. iii.

221. Coghill to Southwell, 20 November 1733 (BL, Add. MS 21123, f. 66); *CJI*, vol. 4, pp. 74, 83; app. pp. xxii, xliii–xliv.

222. *CJI*, vol. 4, pp. 168, 175, 244; app. pp. lx–lxi, lxxxiii; BL, Add. MS 21138, f. 80.

223. *CJI*, vol. 4, pp. 302, 369, 408; app. pp. cxviii, cliii, clxxiii.

224. Potter to Wilmot, 14 December 1745 (PRONI, Wilmot papers, T3019/709); *CJI*, vol. 4, p. 458; app. p. cclxi.

225. *CJI*, vol. 4, pp. 481–3; app. pp. cclxi–cclxx.

226. Ibid., p. 486.

227. Chesterfield to lords justices, 10 June 1746 (PRONI, Wilmot papers, T3019/758).

228. Chesterfield to Newcastle, 11 March 1746 (TNA, SP 63/409/84, 92); McParland, 'Surveyor-General', pp. 92, 100, fn. 7; idem, *Architecture*, p. 129.

229. *CJI*, vol. 4, app. p. ccxc.

230. S. P. Donlan, 'Brooke, Henry', *DIB*, at <http://dib.cambridge.org/viewReadPage.do?articleId=a0990>; J. Leerssen, 'Brooke, Henry', *ODNB*, at <http://www.oxforddnb.com/view/printable/3545>.

231. [Brooke], *Secret History*. See also Ferguson, 'The Army', p. 81.

232. Henry Brooke, *The Farmer's Letter to the Protestants of Ireland. Number I* (Dublin, 1745).

233. [Brooke], *Secret History*, p. 14.

234. Ibid., pp. 21–2; McParland, *Architecture*, p. 129.

235. [Brooke], *Secret History*, pp. 33, 46–7.

236. Ibid., pp. 11–12, 23–4, 27–34, 46–7.

237. Ibid., pp. 64–5. This passage is reproduced verbatim in Waite's 1749 paper on Ireland in BL, Add. MS 35919, ff. 268–9; Magennis, 'State of Ireland', p. 593.

238. [Brooke], *Secret History*, p. 70. See also P. D. O'Donnell, 'Dublin Military Barracks', *Dublin Historical Record*, 25 (1972), pp. 141–2.

239. [Brooke], *Secret History*, pp. 73–4.

240. Harrington to Newcastle, 12 December 1747 (TNA, SP 63/410/142–3); *CJI*, vol. 4, p. 524.

241. Weston to Andrew Stone, 7 November 1747 (BL, Add. MS 32713, f. 408).

242. *CJI*, vol. 4, p. 525; app. p. cclxxxix.

243. Ibid., app. p. ccxc; McParland, *Architecture*, p. 129.

244. Harrington to Newcastle, 12 December 1747 (TNA, SP 63/410/143); *CJI*, vol. 4, p. 541; McParland, *Architecture*, p. 130.

245. Harrington to Newcastle, 12 December 1747 (TNA, SP 63/410/142–4).

246. *CJI*, vol. 4, pp. 548–53, 559–61, 563, 567; TNA, PC 2/100, pp. 541–2, 557–8, 600–3; SP 63/410/157–8, 162–4.

247. *The Cabinet: Containing, A Collection of Curious Papers, Relative to the Present Political Contests in Ireland; Some of Which Are Now First Published* (London, 1754), pp. 6–7; McParland, *Architecture*, p. 130.

248. McParland, 'Surveyor-General', pp. 91–3.

249. Johnston-Liik, *Parliament*, vol. 4, pp. 510–11; *Dictionary of Irish Architects 1720–1940* (electronic database, Dublin, 2011), at <http://www.dia.ie/architects/view/4012/NEVILL-ARTHURJONES>.

250. *CJI*, vol. 5, p. 18; app. pp. xix–xxiv, xviii.

251. Magennis, *Political System*, pp. 62–7.

252. *CJI*, vol. 5, pp. 91–2.

253. Waite to Wilmot, 7 January 1752 (PRONI, Wilmot papers, T3019/1836; J. Walton (ed.), *The King's Business: Letters on the Administration of Ireland, 1740–1761, from the Papers of Sir Robert Wilmot* (New York: AMS Press, 1996), p. 46); *CJI*, vol. 5, pp. 98, 104, 112, 114, 116–17; app. pp. xlv, lxx–lxxi.

254. Walton (ed.), *The King's Business*, pp. 46–7, 50; *CJI*, vol. 5, pp. 128–32; app. pp. lxv–lxvi, lxviii–lxix.

255. Walton (ed.), *The King's Business*, p. 47.

256. Ibid., p. 48; Magennis, *Political System*, p. 68.

257. *The Cabinet*, p. 2; Magennis, *Political System*, p. 69. An alternative view is provided by Archbishop Stone in BL, Egerton MS 3435, ff. 18–20.

258. Walton (ed.), *The King's Business*, p. 48.

259. Ibid., p. 51.

260. *CJI*, vol. 5, pp. 143–6; app. pp. lxv–ccxxviii; McParland, *Architecture*, pp. 135–6.

261. BL, Add. MS 32726, ff. 246–8; C. L. Falkiner (ed.), 'Correspondence of Archbishop Stone and the Duke of Newcastle', *English Historical Review*, 20 (1905), pp. 508–42, 735–63, on p. 511; Magennis, *Political System*, p. 67.

262. Walton (ed.), *The King's Business*, pp. 51–2.

263. Archbishop Stone to Andrew Stone, 10 March 1752 (BL, Add. MS 32726, ff. 246–8); Magennis, *Political System*, p. 70.

264. Falkiner (ed.), 'Correspondence', p. 511; P. A. Walsh and A. O'Brien, 'Nevill, Arthur Jones', *DIB*, at <http://dib.cambridge.org/viewReadPage.do?articleId=a6164>.

265. Dorset to Holdernesse, 10 March 1652 (TNA, SP 63/412/266).

266. *CJI*, vol. 5, app. pp. lxvii, cvii.

267. Holdernesse to Newport, 29 June 1753 (BL, Add. MS 35592, ff. 85–6; PRONI, Wilmot papers, T3019/2144–5); BL, Egerton MS 3435, ff. 16–17; PRONI, Shannon papers, D2707/A1/4/26; Magennis, *Political System*, pp. 76–7; idem, 'Fitzgerald, James, 20th

Earl of Kildare, 1st Duke of Leinster', *DIB*, at <http://dib.cambridge.org/viewRead-Page.do?articleId=a3157>.

268. *The Cabinet*, pp. 1–6.

269. Walton (ed.), *The King's Business*, p. 59.

270. Magennis, *Political System*, pp. 76–7.

271. Archbishop Stone to Holdernesse, 11 July 1753 (BL, Egerton MS 3435, ff. 18–20).

272. Magennis, *Political System*, p. 79.

273. Walton (ed.), *The King's Business*, pp. 70–1; Magennis, *Political System*, p. 79.

274. Walton (ed.), *The King's Business*, pp. 70–1.

275. Harris, *Politics and the Nation*, p. 210; Hill, 'Allegories', pp. 66–88.

276. *A Fragment of the History of Patrick* ([Dublin], 1753), p. 13; Hill, 'Allegories', pp. 72–4.

277. *The Groans of Ireland. Humbly Address'd to the L-r-d-s and C-mm-s of This Kingdom. With Some Interesting Arguments in Behalf of the Right Honourable the Earl of K—d—e* ([Dublin], 1753), pp. 1–14.

278. *Court and No Country. A Seri-Tragi-Comi-Farcical Entertainment, (Not Acted but Once, These Twenty Years.) Wherein Are Occasionally Exhibitted, the Groans of the Barracks. Or, The History of Sir Arthur Vantrype* ... ([Dublin], 1753), pp. 1–53; Hill, 'Allegories', pp. 76, 81.

279. BL, Add. MS 35592, ff. 173–4; Walton (ed.), *The King's Business*, p. 63.

280. Walton (ed.), *The King's Business*, p. 63.

281. Sackville to Holdernesse, 28 October 1753 (BL, Egerton MS 3435, ff. 30–1).

282. Walton (ed.), *The King's Business*, pp. 63–4; *CJI*, vol. 5, pp. 180, 189, 191, 194–6.

283. *CJI*, vol. 5, p. 183; app. p. cclxiv.

284. Seven handbills printed between 25 October and 6 December were published together as *The Patriot; Or, The Irish Packet Open'd* (London, [1753?]). For number 4, see pp. 19–26.

285. Walton (ed.), *The King's Business*, p. 66.

286. Ibid., pp. 66–7; Falkiner (ed.), 'Correspondence', pp. 524–5; *CJI*, vol. 5, p. 192.

287. BL, Add. MS 35592, f. 229; Walton (ed.), *The King's Business*, pp. 67–8; Falkiner (ed.), 'Correspondence', p. 525; *CJI*, vol. 5, pp. 193–5; Magennis, *Political System*, p. 80. The reasons for the divisions are unknown.

288. Walton (ed.), *The King's Business*, p. 68.

289. Falkiner (ed.), 'Correspondence', p. 525.

290. *CJI*, vol. 5, p. 196; PRONI, Wilmot papers, T3019/2194; *A List of the Members of the Honourable House of Commons of I—d, Who Voted on the Question Previous to the Expulsion of Arthur Jones Nevill, Esq; Late Engineer and Surveyor-General of That Kingdom* (Dublin, 1753), [p. 2].

291. *CJI*, vol. 5, pp. 197–8, 201, 204, 208–10; Walton (ed.), *The King's Business*, p. 70; Kelly, *Poynings' Law*, pp. 206–7; Magennis, *Political System*, pp. 83–4; O'Donovan, 'The Money Bill Dispute', pp. 61–4.

292. Walton (ed.), *The King's Business*, pp. 70–1; Magennis, *Political System*, pp. 81–3; O'Donovan, 'The Money Bill Dispute', pp. 64–9; McParland, *Architecture*, pp. 134, 136.

293. Falkiner (ed.), 'Correspondence', p. 527; Magennis, *Political System*, p. 80.

294. *A Letter to the Right Honourable the Lord ********, Occasion'd by a Pamphlet, Just Publish'd, Entitled, Thoughts on the Affairs of Ireland, with an Account of the Expulsion of A—r J—s N—ll, Esq; Late Surveyor and Engineer-General, from the Hon. the H—se of C—mm—ns in That Kingdom. By M. B. Drapier* (London, 1754), p. 25. The second edition in 1754 was dedicated to Archbishop Stone.

295. Walsh and O'Brien, 'Nevill'.
296. PRONI, Wilmot papers, T3019/2119; McParland, *Architecture*, p. 137.
297. Walton (ed.), *The King's Business*, pp. 71–2.
298. *Letter*, p. 19.
299. McParland, *Architecture*, p. 135.
300. *Letter*, p. 19.
301. McParland, *Architecture*, p. 123.
302. PRONI, Wilmot papers, T3019/2555; Chatsworth papers, T3158/639; *CJI*, vol. 5, pp. 221–2, 236, 362–3, 371–2, 374; app. p. cclxxxv; Walton (ed.), *The King's Business*, pp. 129–30; Magennis, *Political System*, pp. 95, 99–100.
303. *Reasons for Building of Barracks; Disencumbering the Inn-Keepers and Publicans; Restoring Discipline to the Army; and A Right Understanding between the Soldiers and the People* ... (London, 1756), pp. 1–42; Conway, *War, State, and Society*, pp. 22–5; Douet, *Barracks*, p. 43.
304. *CJI*, vol. 6, pp. 14, 16, 18–19, 25, 30, 60–1, 72–3, 76, 84–5, 92, 1016; app. pp. xxxvii–xxxviii, xxxviii–li, lxiii; Walton (ed.), *The King's Business*, pp. 157–8; TNA, PC 2/106, pp. 65, 104; Magennis, *Political System*, p. 127. The warranted overrun for 1757 was £17,059 13s. 5d.
305. *Bedford Correspondence*, vol. 2, pp. 350–1.
306. Magennis, *Political System*, p. 132.
307. McParland, *Architecture*, p. 137.
308. McParland, 'Surveyor-General', p. 92.
309. Walton (ed.), *The King's Business*, pp. 216–17; *CJI*, vol. 6, p. 194.
310. *CJI*, vol. 7, pp. 12–14, 57; app. p. lxxx. The warranted overspend for 1761 was £17,219 15s. 2d.
311. Magennis, *Political System*, p. 129.
312. McParland, 'Surveyor-General', pp. 93, 96; idem, *Architecture*, pp. 137–8.
313. *CJI*, vol. 7, pp. 189, 227–8, 244, 259, 263–7, 269–71, 273–4, 276, 281, 284; app. pp. ccxlvi, ccliii–cclvii, cclxvi–cclxviii. The warranted overrun in 1763 was £42,070 1s. 1d.
314. Northumberland to Halifax, 8 February 1764 (TNA, SP 63/423/28–9); PRONI, Wilmot papers, T3019/4798.
315. *CJI*, vol. 7, pp. 286–7, 309; TNA, SP 63/423/36–7.
316. McParland, *Architecture*, p. 125.
317. Thomas Eyre, *A Reply to the Report of the Commissioners and Others, upon the Condition of the Dublin Barracks* (Dublin, 1760), p. 7.
318. Ibid., pp. 4, 6–16.
319. McParland, *Architecture*, p. 125.
320. *The History and Antiquities of the City of Dublin, from the Earliest Accounts* ... (Dublin, 1766), p. 473; Ferguson, 'The Army', p. 79.
321. Lewis, *Dublin Guide*, p. 41; O'Donnell, 'Barracks', p. 142.
322. Eyre, *Reply*, p. 10.
323. McParland, *Architecture*, p. 139.
324. *CJI*, vol. 6, pp. 64–5, 71, 76, 80; app. pp. xcv–xcvi.
325. McParland, 'Surveyor-General', p. 91.
326. Devonshire to Newcastle, 30 September 1737 (BL, Add. MS 32690, f. 376).
327. Mr Waite's paper about the present state of Ireland, [May 1749] (BL, Add. MS 35919, ff. 269–70); Magennis, 'State of Ireland', p. 593; O'Donnell, 'Barracks', pp. 141–2.

5 A Standing Army for Ireland

1. Brewer, *The Sinews of Power*, p. 32.
2. Marshall, *Empires*, p. 340.
3. On this system see Houlding, *Fit for Service*, pp. 47–51.
4. S. H. F. Johnston, 'The Scots Army in the Reign of Anne', *Transactions of the Royal Historical Society*, fifth series, 3 (1953), pp. 1–21, on pp. 12–16.
5. S. H. F. Johnston, 'The Irish Establishment', *Irish Sword*, 1 (1949–53), pp. 33–6, on pp. 34–5; Houlding, *Fit for Service*, pp. 47–51; Brewer, *The Sinews of Power*, p. 32.
6. J. L. Bullion, 'Security and Economy: The Bute Administration's Plans for the American Army and Revenue, 1762–3', *William and Mary Quarterly*, 45 (1988), pp. 499–509, on pp. 501–3, 505–6. Bullion does not seem aware that the system already existed in Ireland.
7. J. L. Bullion, 'The Ten Thousand in America: More Light on the Decision on the American Army, 1762–3', *William and Mary Quarterly*, 43 (1986), pp. 646–57.
8. T. Bartlett, 'Army and Society in Eighteenth-Century Ireland', in Maguire (ed.), *Kings in Conflict*, pp. 173–82; idem, 'The Augmentation', pp. 541–2; Guy, *Oeconomy and Discipline*, pp. 9–10, 34–7; A. J. Guy, 'A Whole Army Absolutely Ruined in Ireland: Aspects of the Irish Establishment', *Annual Report of the National Army Museum* (1978/9), pp. 30–43; idem, 'The Irish Military Establishment, 1660–1776', in Bartlett and Jeffery (eds), *A Military History*, pp. 220–8. A more careful approach is taken in N. Garnham, 'Military Desertion and Deserters in Eighteenth-Century Ireland', *Eighteenth Century Ireland*, 20 (2005), pp. 91–103, on pp. 91–2.
9. On this point see F. G. James, 'Illustrious or Notorious? The Historical Reputation of Ireland's Pre-Union Parliament', *Parliamentary History*, 6 (1987), pp. 312–25; Hayton, 'Long Apprenticeship', pp. 2–3.
10. Howe, *Ireland and Empire*, p. 43. Howe also notes the stereotyping of Irish people as drunken, feckless, unintelligent and with a criminal or motiveless propensity towards violence (ibid, pp. 52–3), demonstrating that uniformed and biased opinion can work both ways.
11. Scouller, *The Armies of Queen Anne*, pp. 253–309; Rogers, *The British Army*, pp. 53–65; Brewer, *The Sinews of Power*, pp. 46–63.
12. TCD, Southwell MSS 1180, f. 87; NLI, MS 1793; *CSPD 1690–1*, pp. 154–5, 161, 168; *CSPD 1695 and addenda*, pp. 155, 157, 159–61; HMC, *Finch MSS*, vol. 2, pp. 418, 450; HMC, *Ormond MSS*, vol. 2, pp. 410–39; *By the King: A Declaration. For the Better Government of the Army. James R.* (Dublin, 1689); *By the Lords-Justices and Council, A Proclamation* (Dublin, 1690); *By the Lords-Justices of Ireland. A Proclamation* (Dublin, 1691); *By the Lords Justices of Ireland, A Proclamation. Requiring All Officers and Soldiers to Observe Strict Discipline, and for Payment of Quarters* (Dublin, 1692); Sir J. Dalrymple, *Memoirs of Great Britain and Ireland*, 3 vols (London, 1790), vol. 3, p. 49; Ferguson, 'The Army', pp. 43–4.
13. Hogarth, *The March to Finchley*; idem, *The Invasion*; Scouller, *The Armies of Queen Anne*, pp. 164–5. See also Colley, *Britons*, pp. 44–6.
14. Bartlett, 'Army and Society', p. 178.
15. Garnham, 'Desertion', p. 92; Scouller, *The Armies of Queen Anne*, pp. 292–309.
16. BL, Add. MS 35919, f. 267; Magennis, 'State of Ireland', p. 592; Ferguson, 'The Army', pp. 64–5.
17. Ferguson, 'The Army', pp. 65–7.

18. D. W. Hayton, 'Ireland and the English Ministers 1707–16. A Study in the Formulation and Working of Government Policy in the Early 18th Century' (D.Phil, Oxford, 1975), pp. 49, 197; Houlding, *Fit for Service*, pp. 45–7; Magennis, *Political System*, pp. 49–51; Guy, *Oeconomy and Discipline*, pp. 34–7; idem, 'Military Establishment', pp. 223–4; Ferguson, 'The Army', pp. 64–5.

19. Porter to Coningsby, 8 June 1693 (PRONI, De Ros MSS, D638/18/8).

20. Mr Waite's paper about the present state of Ireland, [May 1749] (BL, Add. MS 35919, f. 267); Magennis, 'State of Ireland', p. 592.

21. Bartlett, 'Army and Society', pp. 174–5; Ferguson, 'The Army', p. 53.

22. Mr Waite's paper ... [May 1749] (BL, Add. MS 35919, f. 268); Magennis, 'State of Ireland', p. 592.

23. *CSPD 1695 and addenda*, p. 176.

24. Johnston-Liik, *Parliament*, vol. 2, p. 404; vol. 4, pp. 179–80.

25. TCD, MS 2022, f. 283.

26. Walton (ed.), *The King's Business*, p. 159.

27. TCD, Southwell MSS 1180, f. 87; *CSPD 1690–1*, pp. 154–5, 161, 168; *CSPD 1695 and addenda*, pp. 155, 157, 159–61; HMC, *Finch MSS*, vol. 2, pp. 418, 450; Dalrymple, *Memoirs*, vol. 3, p. 49.

28. Ferguson, 'The Army', pp. 43–4; E. Berwick (ed.), *Rawdon Papers* (London, 1819), p. 326.

29. Porter to Coningsby, 20 June 1693 (PRONI, De Ros MSS, D638/18/10).

30. *CSPD 1693*, p. 391.

31. *CJI* (1st), vol. 2, pp. 646, 677; Johnston-Liik, *Parliament*, vol. 3, pp. 556–7; vol. 4, pp. 294–5.

32. TCD, MS 2022, ff. 283, 285; J. Kelly, *'That Damn'd Thing Called Honour': Duelling in Ireland 1570–1860* (Cork: Cork University Press, 1995), pp. 43–53.

33. Parker, *The Army of Flanders*, pp. 87–101; idem, *Military Revolution*, pp. 75–81.

34. Fleming, *Provincial People*, p. 195.

35. James, *Ireland in the Empire*, p. 180.

36. Bartlett, 'Army and Society', p. 178.

37. James, *Ireland in the Empire*, p. 180.

38. Walton (ed.), *The King's Business*, pp. 42–3.

39. James, *Ireland in the Empire*, p. 180.

40. Bartlett, 'Army and Society', p. 176; Guy, 'Military Establishment', pp. 222–3.

41. Fleming, *Provincial People*, p. 194.

42. James, *Ireland in the Empire*, p. 180.

43. Magennis, *Political System*, p. 55; Guy, 'Military Establishment', pp. 225–6; Ferguson, 'The Army', pp. 100–1.

44. PRONI, De Ros MSS, D638/18/73.

45. Lords justices to Blathwayt, 31 May 1698 (NAI, MS M2455, [unfol.]); *CTB 1697–8*, p. 327.

46. BL, Add. MSS 28890, f. 271; 28892, f. 201; 38154, f. 170.

47. TNA, SP 63/374/42–3, 63–5; *CJI*, vol. 3, p. 46; É. Ó Ciardha, *Ireland and the Jacobite Cause, 1685–1766: A Fatal Attachment* (Dublin: Four Courts Press, 2002), pp. 135–6; Ferguson, 'The Army', p. 101.

48. Chesterfield to Newcastle, 1 April 1746 (TNA, SP 63/409/124–5).

49. BL, Egerton MS 3435, ff. 85–6.

50. Lords justices to Bedford, 31 August 1759 (TNA, SP 63/416/65–6). See also TNA, SP 63/416/139–40; Ferguson, 'The Army', p. 101.

51. TNA, SP 63/417/185–6; SP 63/418/234–6, 238, 250–1; Ferguson, 'The Army', p. 101.
52. Fleming, *Provincial People*, p. 194.
53. For the British Isles in general see Houlding, *Fit for Service*, pp. 57–90. For Ireland specifically see Ferguson, 'The Army', pp. 82–4; Connolly, *Religion, Law and Power*, pp. 200–17; Guy, 'Military Establishment', p. 220; idem, *Oeconomy and Discipline*, pp. 34–5; Magennis, *Political System*, pp. 136–7; McGrath, 'Revenue', pp. 211–13.
54. Connolly, 'The Defence', pp. 231–45; Bartlett, 'Army and Society', pp. 173–4.
55. TNA, SP 63/421/245–7, 249–50, 255–8; Connolly, *Divided Kingdom*, pp. 300–5; Magennis, *Political System*, pp. 54, 56, 165–8, 176; Guy, *Oeconomy and Discipline*, pp. 34–5; Ferguson, 'The Army', pp. 83–4.
56. Fleming, *Provincial People*, p. 195.
57. BL, Add. MS 18022, ff. 62–3; *CSPD 1690–1*, pp. 385–6; *CSPD 1695 and addenda,* pp. 176, 178–9; HMC, *Finch MSS*, vol. 3, p. 302; *NHI*, vol. 4, p. 630; Wauchope, *Sarsfield*, pp. 277–83.
58. HMC, *Finch MSS*, vol. 3, p. 302; Wauchope, *Sarsfield*, pp. 280–1.
59. *CSPD 1690–1,* pp. 385–6. See also Chapter 6.
60. *CSPD 1693*, pp. 33, 106.
61. *CSPD 1695 and addenda*, p. 176.
62. *CJI* (1st), vol. 2, pp. 599–600.
63. Information on the state of Ireland, 24 February 1693 (BL, Harleian MS 4892, f. 164).
64. *CSPD 1695 and addenda*, pp. 55–6.
65. *CSPD 1693*, p. 205.
66. Ibid., pp. 160–1.
67. Ibid., p. 206.
68. Southwell to Blathwayt, 27 November 1703 (BL, Add. MS 34774, ff. 10–11).
69. *CSPD 1693*, pp. 380–2, 389.
70. *CSPD 1694–5*, p. 71.
71. *CSPD 1695 and addenda*, p. 59.
72. *CSPD 1697*, p. 219. An infantry battalion was 'an army unit made up of several companies and forming part of a regiment' (*OED*), though often in the eighteenth century the term appeared to be used interchangeably with that of regiment, which was defined as 'a permanent unit of an army, usually divided into companies, troops, or battalions' (*OED*). However, bigger elite regiments such as the Guards tended to contain two or more battalions.
73. T. Denman, "*Hibernia officina militum*': Irish Recruitment to the British Regular Army, 1660–1815', *Irish Sword*, 20 (1996–7), pp. 148–66, on p. 151.
74. *CSPD 1697*, p. 223.
75. *Stat. Ire.*, vol. 3, pp. 260–7; McGrath, 'The Origins and Purpose of the Penal Laws', pp. 33–42; idem, 'Conversion', pp. 36–8.
76. Denman, 'Recruitment', p. 151; Guy, 'Military Establishment', p. 217; Ferguson, 'The Army', p. 56.
77. Ferguson, 'The Army', pp. 57, 69.
78. Lloyd to Ellis, 14 June 1703 (BL, Add. MS 28890, f. 271).
79. BL, Add. MS 34774, ff. 14–15.
80. Lloyd to Ellis, 12 August 1704 (BL, Add. MS 28892, f. 201).
81. TCD, MS 2022, f. 283; *CJI*, vol. 3, p. 74.
82. Bladen to Stanhope, 22 May 1716 (TNA, SP 63/374/233–4).

83. James, *Ireland in the Empire*, p. 179; Bartlett, 'Army and Society', p. 165; Guy, 'Military Establishment', pp. 217, 219; Ferguson, 'The Army', pp. 56, 68–73.

84. [—] to Molesworth, 27 March 1716 (TNA, SP 63/374/185–6).

85. TNA, SP 67/8, f. 21.

86. TNA, SP 67/8, f. 115.

87. TNA, SP 41/6, ff. 30–1, 34–5, 48–9.

88. Ferguson, 'The Army', p. 71; Denman, 'Recruitment', p. 153.

89. Grafton to Carteret, 24 February [1724] (TNA, SP 63/383/64).

90. Ferguson, 'The Army', pp. 70–1; Denman, 'Recruitment', p. 153.

91. Boulter to Newcastle, 11 March 1727 (TNA, SP 63/388/196); *Boulter Letters*, vol. 1, p. 148.

92. Ferguson, 'The Army', pp. 71–2; Denman, 'Recruitment', p. 153.

93. Devonshire to Newcastle, 30 September 1737 (BL, Add. MS 32690, f. 376).

94. TNA, SP 63/406/32–3; PRONI, Wilmot papers, T3019/640, 647, 675, 687; Denman, 'Recruitment', p. 155.

95. TNA, SP 63/408/70, 96, 98–9, 100–1, 106–8, 110–12, 200; Ferguson, 'The Army', p. 73.

96. TNA, SP 63/410/23, 68–9; PRONI, Wilmot papers, T3019/858; Denman, 'Recruitment', p. 155.

97. Denman, 'Recruitment', p. 155; Magennis, *Political System*, p. 53.

98. *CJI*, vol. 5, pp. 407–9.

99. Bartlett, 'Army and Society', p. 175; T. Bartlett, 'Defence, Counter-Insurgency and Rebellion: Ireland, 1793–1803', in Bartlett and Jeffery (eds), *A Military History*, pp. 247–93, on pp. 248–9.

100. T. Bartlett, *'The Academy of Warre': Military Affairs in Ireland, 1600 to 1800* (Dublin: National University of Ireland, 2002), pp. 22–3; idem, 'Counter-Insurgency', pp. 248–9.

101. TNA, SP 63/417/49–55.

102. Magennis, *Political System*, p. 50; Guy, *Oeconomy and Discipline*, pp. 35–6.

103. Ferguson, 'The Army', pp. 67–8.

104. Pitt to Bedford, 13 January 1760 (TNA, SP 63/418/9).

105. Walton (ed.), *The King's Business*, pp. 137–8, 140; PRONI, Wilmot papers, T3019/3046.

106. PRONI, Wilmot papers, T3019/3085.

107. *Bedford Correspondence*, vol. 2, p. 364.

108. Waite to Wilmot, 4 January 1757 (PRONI, Wilmot papers, T3019/3085).

109. PRONI, Wilmot papers, T3019/3089, 3094.

110. PRONI, Wilmot papers, T3019/3158.

111. Rigby to the secretary-at-war, 13 November 1757 (TNA, SP 63/418/17). See also Conway, *War, State, and Society*, pp. 74–5.

112. TNA, SP 63/418/19–25.

113. TNA, SP 63/415/166, 194.

114. Bedford to Pitt, 3 January 1758 (TNA, SP 63/415/170–2). See also TNA, SP 63/415/174.

115. *Bedford Correspondence*, vol. 2, pp. 386–7; TNA, SP 63/416/119–25. See also Conway, *War, State, and Society*, p. 75.

116. TNA, SP 63/416/105–7.

117. TNA, SP 63/416/146–7, 148–50, 152, 154, 191, 193–4, 201–9, 211, 222, 224, 241–5, 251, 253, 255, 265; SP 63/417/116–20, 128, 130, 132, 134–6, 138, 140; Guy, 'Military Establishment', p. 220.

118. TNA, SP 63/416/156–60, 195, 199, 213, 237–8, 263, 269; SP 63/417/153–4; A. P. W. Malcomson, *Nathanial Clements: Government and the Governing Elite in Ireland, 1725–75* (Dublin: Four Courts Press, 2005), pp. 393–4.

119. TNA, SP 63/419/100, 102, 104, 106, 130, 132, 136, 138–9, 145, 147; SP 63/421/15, 23.

120. Denman, 'Recruitment', p. 158.

121. Ibid., pp. 158–66; Bartlett, *Military Affairs*, pp. 22–3; idem, 'Counter-Insurgency', pp. 247–93; Guy, 'Military Establishment', pp. 228–30.

122. Guy, 'Military Establishment', pp. 211–12.

123. Essex to William Harbord, 30 November 1674 (NAI, Wyche papers, 1/4/1). See NAI, Wyche papers, 1/1/30; H. Murtagh, 'Irish Soldiers Abroad, 1600–1800', in Bartlett and Jeffery (eds), *A Military History*, pp. 294–314, on p. 305; Ferguson, 'The Army', p. 16.

124. Guy, 'Military Establishment', p. 213.

125. Doherty, *The Williamite War*, p. 23.

126. Aydelotte, 'Ormond', passim; Hayton, 'English Ministers', p. 42.

127. TNA, SP 63/351/317–18; Ferguson, 'The Army', pp. 18–23; Doherty, *The Williamite War*, p. 24.

128. *CSPD 1689–90*, p. 265; J. Childs, 'The Williamite War, 1689–1691', in Bartlett and Jeffery (eds), *A Military History*, pp. 188–210, on pp. 190, 193–6, 201.

129. HMC, *Portland MSS*, vol. 3, p. 478.

130. PRONI, De Ros MSS, D638/13/76, 69, 74.

131. *CSPD 1695 and addenda*, p. 177.

132. BL, Add. MS 4761, f. 205; *CTB 1689–92*, p. 1595; NAI, Wyche papers, 2/6.

133. *An Exact List of All Their Majesties Forces in Flanders, England, Scotland, and Ireland, for the Year 1692. And the Charges of Each Regiment* (London, 1692).

134. *CTB 1689–92*, p. 1710; TCD, MS 1178, f. 69; PRONI, De Ros MSS, D638/18/6.

135. Porter to Coningsby, 20 December 1692 (PRONI, De Ros MSS, D638/18/6).

136. *CSPD 1693*, p. 3.

137. NAI, Wyche papers, 2/7; *CSPD 1693*, pp. 33, 106.

138. *CTB 1696–7*, p. 304.

139. *CJI*, vol. 2, app. pp. xv–xviii; BL, Add. MS 4761, f. 41; *CTB 1697–8*, pp. 118–19.

140. Guy, 'Military Establishment', p. 216.

141. *The Argument against a Standing Army, Discussed. By a True Lover of His Country* (London, 1698), p. 18.

142. Trenchard, *Argument*, p. 19.

143. Trenchard, *Short History*, pp. 15–16, 20.

144. Ferguson, 'The Army', p. 54.

145. *CTB 1702*, pp. ccx–ccxi.

146. Johnston, 'Scots Army', pp. 12, 14.

147. Houlding, *Fit for Service*, pp. 28, 35–6.

148. McGrath, *Constitution*, pp. 134–5.

149. *CJI* (1st), vol. 2, p. 994.

150. G. P. R. James (ed.), *Letters Illustrative of the Reign of William III, from 1696 to 1708, addressed to the Duke of Shrewsbury, by James Vernon, Esq. Secretary of State*, 3 vols (London, 1841), vol. 2, pp. 206–7; BL, Add. MS 28883, ff. 209, 213, 221, 224; SHC, Midleton papers, 1248/1, f. 316; *CSPD 1698*, pp. 403, 409; W. Coxe (ed.), *Private and Original Correspondence of Charles Talbot, Duke of Shrewsbury, with King William, the Leaders of the Whig Party, and Other Distinguished Statesmen* (London, 1821), pp. 557–8; *CJI* (1st), vol. 2, pp. 1003–5, 1008–9, 1012; Doyle, 'Parliament and Politics', p. 290.

151. *CSPD 1699–1700,* pp. 2–4; *CJI* (1st), vol. 2, pp. 1082–3.

152. *CSPD 1699–1700,* pp. 11, 17; McGrath, *Constitution,* pp. 147–8.

153. Alan Brodrick to Thomas Brodrick, 28 December 1699 (SHC, Midleton papers, 1248/1, f. 316).

154. *CTB 1700–1,* p. 169; Ferguson, 'The Army', pp. 55–6.

155. Delafaye to [Pringle], 19 April 1716 (TNA, SP 63/374/215–16).

156. HMC, *Portland MSS,* vol. 3, p. 603; *CSPD 1700–2,* pp. 60–1.

157. BL, Add. MS 21136, f. 80; *CTP 1697–1702,* pp. 134, 296, 315–16; *CTB 1697–8,* pp. 62, 73, 97, 290, 293–4, 363; *CTB 1698–9,* pp. 68, 70, 75, 296, 308, 319, 323, 348; *CTB 1699–1700,* p. 213; *CTB 1700–1,* pp. 152, 169; Ferguson, 'The Army', pp. 55–6.

158. *CTB 1699,* p. 149; Ferguson, 'The Army', p. 55.

159. *CTB 1700,* pp. 364, 367; *CTB 1701,* pp. 338–9.

160. Singleton to Ellis, 13 July 1702 (BL, Add. MS 28889, f. 50).

161. Rochester to Keightley, 18 July, 1 August 1702 (NLI, Keightley papers, folder 2600).

162. Alan Brodrick to St John Brodrick, 29 [December] 1702 (SHC, Midleton papers, 1248/2, ff. 74–5); McGrath, *Constitution,* pp. 157–8.

163. BL, Add. MS 28888, f. 75; Minute book of the committee of public accounts, 1 October 1703 (NAI, Frazer MSS, 10 [unfol.]).

164. John Isham to Sir Justinian Isham, 12 March 1703 (Northamptonshire Record Office, Isham MSS, I.C. 2205).

165. BL, Add. MS 28890, f. 271; Ferguson, 'The Army', p. 57.

166. *CSPD 1703–4,* p. 148.

167. BL, Add. MS 34774, f. 8; Ferguson, 'The Army', p. 57.

168. The Irish Establishment, 1709 (NLI, MS 2097, [unfol.]).

169. [Southwell] to [Dartmouth], 28 July 1711 (TNA, SP 63/367/11–12, 327).

170. TNA, SP 63/367/25–6.

171. TCD, MS 2022, ff. 9, 44–6, 234, 238, 245–50, 257, 260–1; D. Murphy, *The Irish Brigades, 1685–2006: A Gazetteer of Irish Military Service, Past and Present* (Dublin: Four Courts Press, 2007), pp. 139–40, 145.

172. TCD, MS 2022, ff. 60–1, 63–6, 107–8, 111, 113–36.

173. McNally, *Parties, Patriots and Undertakers,* p. 73.

174. PRONI, De Ros MSS, D638/145.

175. BL, Add. MS 61636, ff. 214–15.

176. Alan Brodrick to Sunderland, 25 January 1715 (BL, Add. MS 61636, f. 131).

177. Delafaye to [Pringle], 6 December 1715 (TNA, SP 63/373/296); *CJI,* vol. 3, p. 39.

178. Lords justices to [Stanhope], 5 January 1716 (TNA, SP 63/374/11–11a). See also NAI, Wyche papers, 2/51; BL, Add. MSS 4761, f. 41; 35919, f. 267; TNA, PRO 30/26/60, ff. 9, 65; SP 63/375/37–8.

179. TNA, SP 63/373/256–7; *CJI,* vol. 3, pp. 46, 54.

180. TNA, SP 63/374/11–11a.

181. Lords justices to [Sunderland], 30 July 1715 (BL, Add. MS 61635, f. 125).

182. Ó Ciardha, *Jacobite Cause,* pp. 113–14, 134–6.

183. *CJI,* vol. 3, pp. 9–10.

184. Lords justices to Stanhope, 13, 20 January 1716 (TNA, SP 63/374/26–7, 42–3).

185. TNA, SP 63/374/235–6.

186. Lords justices to Stanhope, 18 January 1716 (TNA, SP 63/374/38); *CJI,* vol. 3, pp. 60, 62.

187. Lords justices to Stanhope, 20 January 1716 (TNA, SP 63/374/42–3); *CJI,* vol. 3, p. 46.

188. *CJI,* vol. 3, pp. 73–5.

189. TNA, SP 63/374/59–60, 63–5, 80–1, 84–5; Ferguson, 'The Army', pp. 57–8.
190. TNA, SP 63/374/103–4, 169–70, 175–6, 201–3, 205–6, 233–4.
191. *CJI*, vol. 3, pp. 100–1.
192. Grafton to Paul Methuen, 10 November 1716 (TNA, SP 63/374/274–5).
193. Grafton to Stanhope, 6 February 1716 (TNA, SP 63/374/82–3); TCD, MS 2022, ff. 145–50; TNA, SP 63/374/211–12, 215–16; A. E. Murray, *A History of the Commercial and Financial Relations between England and Ireland from the Period of the Restoration* (London: P. S. King & Son, 1903), pp. 185–6.
194. TNA, SP 63/374/82–3, 211–12.
195. Delafaye to [Pringle], 19 April 1716 (TNA, SP 63/374/215–16).
196. TNA, SP 63/374/211–12.
197. TNA, SP 63/375/9–10, 59, 66–7.
198. *CJI*, vol. 3, pp. 119–21, 137; app. pp. cxx–cxxi.
199. Conolly to [Delafaye], 21 September 1717 (TNA, SP 63/375/188–9).
200. TNA, SP 63/374/42–3; SP 63/375/204–5, 206–7; *CJI*, vol. 3, pp. 127–8, 137, 139, 146–7; app. pp. cxiv–cxv, cxvii, cxvix, cxxxv–cxxxvi.
201. Houlding, *Fit for Service*, p. 47.
202. See Chapter 6.
203. *CJI*, vol. 3, pp. 202–3; app. pp. clxvi, clxviii–clxxi.
204. Houlding, *Fit for Service*, p. 48.
205. *CJI*, vol. 3, pp. 264, 330, 424, 489, 594; app. pp. ccxiii–ccxiv, ccxliv–ccxlv, ccciv–cccv, cccxxxvi–cccxxxvii, ccclxxvii, ccclxxxi; vol. 4, pp. 18, 83; app. pp. xi–xiii.
206. TNA, SP 67/8, ff. 21, 115. See also Table 5.1.
207. *CJI*, vol. 4, pp. 168, 235, 244, 302; app. pp. lx–lxi, lxxix–lxxxii, xliv, cviii, cxvi.
208. Ibid., pp. 342–3, 363; app. pp. cxxviii, ccxxxvi, cxlvi, cxliii–cxliv.
209. TNA, SP 63/403/63; *CJI*, vol. 4, pp. 364, 369; app. pp. cxlvi–cxlvii, clii; PRONI, Wilmot papers, T3019/413.
210. TNA, SP 63/408/100–1.
211. TNA, SP 63/409/56; Walton (ed.), *The King's Business*, p. 21.
212. PRONI, Wilmot papers, T3019/711; BL, Add. MS 47002 A, f. 15.
213. TNA, SP 63/410/7–8.
214. Harrington to Newcastle, 5 October 1747 (TNA, SP 63/410/67–9).
215. TNA, SP 63/410/71; *CJI*, vol. 4, pp. 406–8, 454, 458, 521, 525; app. pp. clxi–clxiv, clxvi, clxx, ccliv–cclvi, cclx, cclxxix–cclxxxi, cclxxxiii–cclxxxv, cclxxxviii.
216. PRONI, Wilmot papers, T3019/1088–9, 1107, 1130; Walton (ed.), *The King's Business*, pp. 14–25; Magennis, *Political System*, p. 169.
217. PRONI, Wilmot papers, T3019/1163–4, 1177, 1180, 1183, 1185, 1189; Walton (ed.), *The King's Business*, pp. 25–6.
218. *CJI*, vol. 5, pp. 15, 18; app. pp. xiii–xiv, xvii; Murphy, *Irish Brigades*, p. 110.
219. BL, Add. MS 35919, f. 270; Magennis, 'State of Ireland', pp. 593–4.
220. *CJI*, vol. 5, pp. 95, 98, 172, 183; app. pp. xli–xlii, xliv–v, cclviii–cclix, cclxi–cclxii.
221. For more detailed consideration of these annual costs see Chapter 7.
222. TNA, SP 63/413/231–2; *CJI*, vol. 5, pp. 225, 227, 236; app. pp. cclxxiv–cclxxvi, cclxxviii–cclxxxiv; PRONI, Wilmot papers, T3019/2573.
223. TNA, SP 63/417/49–55.
224. BL, Egerton MS 3435, ff. 85–6.
225. *CJI*, vol. 5, pp. 225, 227, 236; app. pp. cclxxiv–cclxxvi, cclxxviii–cclxxxiv; Walton (ed.), *The King's Business*, pp. 99–100.

226. *CJI*, vol. 5, pp. 221–2; Walton (ed.), *The King's Business*, p. 132.

227. Conway to Wilmot, 1 January 1756 (PRONI, Wilmot papers, T3019/2736); Walton (ed.), *The King's Business*, pp. 137–8.

228. BL, Egerton MS 3435, ff. 88, 90.

229. *CJI*, vol. 5, p. 359; Walton (ed.), *The King's Business*, pp. 140–1. See also PRONI, Wilmot papers, T3019/2752.

230. *CJI*, vol. 5, pp. 392, 393–4; app. p. ccxcviii. See also Chapter 6.

231. BL, Add. MSS 32862, f. 303; 32863, ff. 77–8, 117, 341; Egerton MS 3435, ff. 94, 96; Walton (ed.), *The King's Business*, pp. 144–5.

232. *Journals of the House of Commons*, 51 vols (London, 1803), vol. 27, pp. 539–40; *Journals of the House of Lords*, 61 vols (London, 1767–1830), vol. 28, p. 538. See also TNA, SP 63/420/26–8; BL, Add. MS 35892, ff. 31–2.

233. *CJI*, vol. 5, p. 394; TNA, SP 63/414/134–40.

234. TNA, SP 63/414/146, 160; PRONI, Wilmot papers, T3019/2790, 2792–3, 2796; Walton (ed.), *The King's Business*, pp. 149–50.

235. PRONI, Wilmot papers, T3019/2847; *Bedford Correspondence*, vol. 2, pp. 215–16.

236. *CJI*, vol. 6, pp. 13–14, 16, 19, 21; app. pp. x–xiii, xv–xix, xxvii–xxviii, xxxiii–xxxv, lix. See also Chapter 6.

237. Ibid., pp. 176, 179; app. pp. cclxxxviii–cclxxxix.

238. Bedford to Pitt, 3 January 1758 (TNA, SP 63/415/170–2). See also TNA, SP 63/415/333.

239. *Bedford Correspondence*, vol. 2, pp. 363–4.

240. *Bedford Correspondence*, vol. 2, p. 374; Magennis, *Political System*, p. 133.

241. TNA, SP 63/416/101, 103.

242. *CJI*, vol. 6, pp. 128, 150–1; TNA, SP 63/416/119–25, 127; 63/417/110–11; *Bedford Correspondence*, vol. 2, pp. 386–91; Walton (ed.), *The King's Business*, pp. 195–6, 196–8, 200–1; Magennis, *Political System*, pp. 133–4.

243. TNA, SP 63/416/105–7, 146–7, 148–50, 152, 154, 156–60, 191, 193–5, 199, 201–9, 211, 213, 222, 224, 237–8, 241–5, 251, 253, 255, 263, 265, 269; SP 63/417/116–20, 128, 130, 132, 134–6, 138, 140, 153–4.

244. Walton (ed.), *The King's Business*, pp. 210–11.

245. TNA, SP 63/416/156–60, 195, 199, 213, 237–8, 263, 269; SP 63/417/153–4; Malcomson, *Clements*, pp. 393–4.

246. TNA, SP 63/417/159–60; *CJI*, vol. 6, p. 187; Walton (ed.), *The King's Business*, pp. 213–16.

247. *CJI*, vol. 6, pp. 172–3, 180, 187, 190–1, 194; app. pp. cccxci–cccxcv; BL, Add. MS 35596, f. 95; TNA, SP 63/416/75–7, 101, 103; Walton (ed.), *The King's Business*, pp. 202–3, 210–11, 216–17; Magennis, *Political System*, p. 141; Powell, *Crisis of Empire*, p. 54; M. Beresford, 'Francois Thurot and the French Attack at Carrickfergus, 1759–60', *Irish Sword*, 10 (1971–2), pp. 255–74, on pp. 264–5.

248. TNA, SP 63/419/68, 98, 100, 102, 104, 106, 128–30, 132, 136, 138, 143–5, 147; SP 63/421/15, 23; PRONI, Wilmot papers, T3019/3832, 4246, 4253, 4255, 4267; *CHOP 1760–5*, pp. 81–2.

249. Halifax to Egremont, 29 November 1761 (TNA, SP 63/419/114–15; *CHOP 1760–5*, p. 82); Magennis, *Political System*, p. 161.

250. TNA, SP 63/419/110–11, 128–9, 161–2; SP 63/421/21, 29, 31, 33; PC 2/109, p. 4; PRONI, Wilmot papers, T3019/4250; Magennis, *Political System*, p. 161.

251. TNA, SP 63/419/149–50; 63/421/49–51.

252. *CJI*, vol. 7, pp. 108–10; PRONI, Wilmot papers, T3019/4275.

253. Halifax to Egremont, 12 February 1762 (TNA, SP 63/421/91); *CJI*, vol. 7, p. 118; Magennis, *Political System*, pp. 161–2.

254. NAI, 999/308/3/13.

255. *CJI*, vol. 7, pp. 57, 127, 129, 145–6, 227–8: app. pp. lxxix, clxxix–clxxxii, clxxxiv–clxxxviii, cxcvi–cxcix, ccxliv.

256. J. W. Shy, *Toward Lexington: The Role of the British Army in the Coming of the American Revolution* (Princeton, NJ: Princeton University Press, 1965), pp. 73–8; Magennis, *Political System*, pp. 169–70.

257. PRONI, Wilmot papers, T3019/4378, 4383, 4414, 4426.

258. Report to his majesty, 27 December 1762 (TNA, SP 63/420/26–8; BL, Add. MS 35892, f. 31–2).

259. BL, Add. MS 35892, f. 29; TNA, SP 63/420/29, 31; Bullion, 'Security and Economy', p. 503; idem, 'More Light', pp. 650–3; Shy, *Toward Lexington*, pp. 74–8; Magennis, *Political System*, pp. 170–1.

260. Bullion, 'More Light', pp. 651–2.

261. TNA, SP 63/421/308–9.

262. *CJI*, vol. 7, pp. 227–8; app. p. ccxliv.

263. Northumberland to Halifax, 10 November 1763 (TNA, SP 63/422/99–103).

264. *CJI*, vol. 7, pp. 198, 239, 255–6; TNA, SP 63/422/109–10, 111–12, 119–21, 143–8, 167; PRONI, Wilmot papers, T3019/4752.

265. *CJI*, vol. 7, pp. 255–6.

266. *The Public Register: Or, Freeman's Journal*, 4:86, 27–30 June 1767; 5:40, 16–19 January 1768; Morley, *Irish Opinion*, pp. 60–1.

267. *CJI*, vol. 7, pp. 255–6.

268. For more detailed consideration of these annual costs see Chapter 7.

269. PRONI, Wilmot papers, T3019/5187; Bartlett, 'The Augmentation', p. 543.

270. TNA, SP 63/420/138–9; [R. Jephson], *Considerations upon the Augmentation of the Army. Addressed to the Public* (Dublin, 1768), p. 6; *Reasons for an Augmentation of the Army on the Irish Establishment, Offered to the Consideration of the Public* (Dublin, 1768), pp. 5–13; Bartlett, 'The Townshend Viceroyalty', pp. 88, 90, 93–4; Guy, 'Military Establishment', p. 228; Ferguson, 'The Army', pp. 61–2.

271. Bartlett, 'The Augmentation', pp. 550–1; Morley, *Irish Opinion*, pp. 40–62.

272. *Freeman's Journal*, 5:40, 16–19 January 1768.

273. Bartlett, 'The Augmentation', pp. 540–59; Morley, *Irish Opinion*, pp. 52–63.

274. [Sir C. Bingham], *An Essay on the Use and Necessity of Establishing a Militia in Ireland, and Some Hints towards a Plan for That Purpose* (Dublin, 1767), pp. 9–14; Charles Lucas, *To the Right Honourable the Lord Mayor, the Worshipful the Board of Aldermen, The Sheriffs, Commons, Citizens, and Freeholders of Dublin, ... upon the Proposed Augmentation of the Military Establishment* (Dublin, 1768), pp. 3–35; *Considerations on the Present State of the Military Establishment of This Kingdom, Addressed to the Knights, Citizens, and Burgesses of Ireland, in Parliament Assembled* (Dublin, 1768), pp. 3–52; Morley, *Irish Opinion*, pp. 60–1.

275. *Some Impartial Observations on the Proposed Augmentation. By a Country Gentleman* (Dublin, 1768), pp. 3, 5–8; [Jephson], *Considerations*, pp. 4–7, 9–21; *Reasons*, pp. 14–24.

276. Waite to Wilmot, 19 April, 3 May 1768 (PRONI, T3019/5732, 5742–3); Bartlett, 'The Augmentation', p. 558; Morley, *Irish Opinion*, p. 62.

277. *Reasons*, p. 25.

278. Bartlett, 'The Augmentation', p. 556.

279. Weymouth to Townshend, 9 June 1769 (TNA, SP 63/429/241; *CHOP 1766–9*, p. 476).

280. TNA, SP 63/429/282–7; SP 63/430/5–12, 27–9; *CHOP 1766–9*, pp. 478–80, 488–93, 496–7.

281. *CJI*, vol. 8, pp. 288–9, 313–14; TNA, SP 63/430/76–7, 154.

282. Townshend to Weymouth, [15] November 1769 (TNA, SP 63/430/152–3; *CHOP 1766–9*, pp. 518–20).

283. *CJI*, vol. 8, pp. 300, 313–14; TNA, SP 63/430/152–3; *CHOP 1766–9*, pp. 518–20.

284. *CJI*, vol. 8, pp. 329–31.

285. TNA, SP 63/430/181, 189–90.

286. *Freeman's Journal*, 7:28, 16–18 November 1769; 7:38, 9–12 December 1769.

287. Townshend to Weymouth, 17 October 1769 (TNA, SP 63/430/76–7).

288. Bartlett, 'The Augmentation', p. 559.

289. *CJI*, vol. 8, pp. 339–40, 345–6, 353–4; TNA, SP 63/430/97–9, 101, 103, 105, 107–10, 113–18, 152–3; *CHOP 1766–9*, pp. 518–20; *Stat. Ire.*, vol. 10, pp. 6–22, 71–87, 333–41, 681–9; vol. 11, pp. 3–12, 303–11, 374–86; vol. 12, pp. 1–18.

290. TNA, SP 63/430/199–201, 207–8.

291. TNA, SP 63/420/165, 167–94; *Stat. Ire.*, vol. 10, pp. 71–87, 333–41, 681–9; vol. 11, pp. 3–12, 303–11, 374–86; vol. 12, pp. 1–18.

292. TNA, SP 63/430/207–8.

293. Ferguson, 'The Army', p. 62.

294. N. Garnham, 'Defending the Kingdom and Preserving the Constitution: Irish Militia Legislation 1692–1793', in Hayton, Kelly and Bergin (eds), *Composite State*, pp. 107–35; idem, 'Ireland's Protestant Militia, 1715–76: A Military Assessment', *Irish Sword*, 20 (1996–7), pp. 131–6; Bartlett, 'Counter-Insurgency', pp. 247–93; Ferguson, 'The Army', pp. 138–200; E. A. Coyle, 'Talbot's Fencibles and the Drogheda Mutiny', *Journal of the County Louth Archaeological and Historical Society*, 24 (1997), pp. 39–50.

295. E. M. Spiers, 'Army Organisation and Society in the Nineteenth Century', in Bartlett and Jeffery (eds), *A Military History*, pp. 335–57, on p. 335; Ferguson, 'The Army', pp. 199–200.

6 An Army for Empire

1. B. P. Lenman, 'Colonial Wars and Imperial Instability, 1688–1793', in Marshall (ed.), *Eighteenth Century*, pp. 151–68, on p. 151.

2. Marshall, *Empires*, p. 58.

3. The numbers in the navy were always less, rising from 40,262 during the Nine Years' War to 82,022 in the American War. See Brewer, *The Sinews of Power*, p. 30.

4. Marshall, *Empires*, p. 59; Brewer, *The Sinews of Power*, p. 32.

5. Ferguson, 'The Army', p. 16.

6. Murray, *Financial Relations*, p. 161.

7. *CSPD 1687–9*, p. 154.

8. Trenchard, *Argument*, p. 19. A year later he had changed his mind and argued against a standing army in Ireland. See Trenchard, *Short History*, pp. 15–16, 20; Ferguson, 'The Army', p. 54.

9. Guy, 'Military Establishment', p. 212.

10. This work is concerned throughout with the regular units of the British army. For recruitment to the army of the East India Company see T. Bartlett, 'The Irish Soldier in India, 1740–1947', in M. Holmes and D. Holmes (eds.), *Ireland and India: Connections, Comparisons, Contrasts* (Dublin: Folens, 1997), pp. 12–28; Conway, *War, State, and Society*, pp. 56, 65–6.

11. Denman, 'Recruitment', pp. 151, 153–4. Johnston, 'Irish Establishment', p. 35; Garnham, 'Desertion', p. 94; Bartlett, 'Army and Society', p. 179. See also Chapter 5.

12. Murtagh, 'Soldiers Abroad', pp. 305–7.

13. HMC, *Finch MSS*, vol. 3, pp. 114–15, 290, 295, 304.

14. TNA, SP 63/353/206; PC 2/75, f. 145; BL, Add. MS 18022, ff. 62–3; *CSPD 1691–2*, p. 91; *CSPD 1695 and addenda*, pp. 177–9, 180–4, 188; *NHI*, vol. 4, p. 630; Denman, 'Recruitment', p. 150.

15. TCD, MS 1178, f. 69; PRONI, De Ros MSS, D638/18/6.

16. *CSPD 1693*, p. 3.

17. Licence to Colonel Henry Luttrell, 22 April 1693 (NAI, Wyche papers, 1/2/25). See also NAI, Wyche papers, 1/3/28; *CSPD 1693*, p. 105; Wauchope, *Sarsfield*, pp. 229–36, 272–4, 301–2.

18. *NHI*, vol. 4, p. 630; *CTB 1693–6*, p. 707; Wauchope, *Sarsfield*, p. 302.

19. Rochester to Keightley, 20 June 1702 (NLI, Keightley Papers, folder 2599).

20. See Chapter 5.

21. *CSPD 1703–4*, p. 99.

22. *CSPD 1703–4*, p. 116.

23. Narcissus Luttrell, *A Brief Historical Relation of State Affairs from September 1678 to April 1714*, 6 vols (Oxford: Oxford University Press, 1857), vol. 5, p. 355.

24. BL, Add. MS 38153, f. 88.

25. Denman, 'Recruitment', p. 152.

26. Cox to Southwell, 21 February 1706 (BL, Add. MS 38153, f. 162).

27. Cox to Southwell, 31 December 1706 (BL, Add. MS 38154, f. 124).

28. Cox to Southwell, 19 January 1707 (BL, Add. MS 38154, f. 132).

29. Nylan to [Fingal], 10 February 1707[8] (NLI, Fingall papers, MS 8020(3)).

30. *Supplement* [London], 11 February 1708; BL, Add. MS 61634, ff. 47–8.

31. Murtagh, 'Soldiers Abroad', pp. 296–300, 307–12; Ó Ciardha, *Jacobite Cause*, pp. 32–5; Cullen, 'The Irish Diaspora', pp. 123–5; Murphy, *Irish Brigades*, pp. 1–64; J. C. O'Callaghan, *History of the Irish Brigades in the Service of France* (Glasgow: Cameron and Ferguson, 1870), passim.

32. Garnham, 'Desertion', pp. 91–103.

33. Denman, 'Recruitment', p. 152.

34. Denman, 'Recruitment', pp. 152–5. See also Chapter 5.

35. Bartlett, 'Army and Society', p. 179; Denman, 'Recruitment', p. 155; Garnham, 'Desertion', p. 94.

36. Denman, 'Recruitment', pp. 154–5; Conway, *War, State, and Society*, pp. 177–8.

37. Harrington to Bedford, 23 February 1748 (TNA, SP 63/410/170–2); PRONI, Wilmot papers, T3019/980; TNA, SP 63/410/182–3; Denman, 'Recruitment', p. 155.

38. Denman, 'Recruitment', p. 156.

39. TNA, SP 63/421/117–18, 151–2, 221–2.

40. T. Bartlett, '"A Weapon of War Yet Untried": Irish Catholics and the Armed Forces of the Crown, 1760–1830', in T. G. Fraser and K. Jeffery (eds), *Men, Women and War* (Dublin: Lilliput Press, 1993), pp. 66–85, on p. 69; Denman, 'Recruitment', pp. 156–7.

41. Bedford to Pitt, 3 January 1758 (TNA, SP 63/415/170–2). See also TNA, SP 63/415/174.
42. *Bedford Correspondence*, vol. 2, pp. 371–2; TNA, SP 63/416/263; SP 63/418/11–13.
43. TNA, SP 63/417/159–61, 164–5; SP 63/418/61–4, 106–7; Ferguson, 'The Army', pp. 70, 73.
44. Fagan, *Divided Loyalties*, p. 125; Conway, *War, State, and Society*, pp. 182–4.
45. McBride, 'Delvin Address', pp. 115–48; Fagan, *Divided Loyalties*, pp. 62–6, 126–7.
46. Halifax to Egremont, [*c*.12] February 1762 (TNA, SP 63/421/75–9, 81–2).
47. Circular letter, February 1762 (TNA, SP 63/421/83).
48. TNA, SP 63/421/115–17, 151–2, 193.
49. TNA, SP 63/421/195–6, 235, 237–41, 261–2; *London Chronicle*, 30 March 1762.
50. Halifax to Egremont, 8, 13 April 1762 (TNA, SP 63/421/227, 249–50).
51. *CJI*, vol. 7, pp. 154, 161.
52. TNA, SP 63/421/253; M. Wall, 'The Quest for Catholic Equality, 1745–1778', in O'Brien (ed.), *Catholic Ireland*, pp. 115–34, on p. 119; Bartlett, 'A Weapon of War', pp. 69–70; Fagan, *Divided Loyalties*, p. 129.
53. Denman, 'Recruitment', p. 157.
54. Halifax to Egremont, 13 April 1762 (TNA, SP 63/421/249–50).
55. R. K. Donovan, 'The Military Origins of the Roman Catholic Relief Programme of 1778', *Historical Journal*, 28 (1985), pp. 79–102.
56. Marshall, *Empires*, p. 62. See also Denman, 'Recruitment', pp. 156–66.
57. Ferguson, 'The Army', pp. 73–5; Bartlett, 'A Weapon of War', pp. 70–6; Denman, 'Recruitment', pp. 158–66.
58. Guy, 'Military Establishment', pp. 229–30; Marshall, *Empires*, p. 341.
59. Ferguson, 'The Army', p. 74; Bartlett, 'A Weapon of War', pp. 76–7.
60. PRONI, De Ros MSS, D638/13/67, 69, 74.
61. PRONI, De Ros MSS, D638/13/90, 137; D638/14/46; Murphy, *Irish Brigades*, pp. 110, 116, 128.
62. *CSPD 1695 and addenda*, p. 185.
63. *CSPD 1693*, p. 66.
64. *CSPD 1691–2*, pp. 408–9; *CTB 1693–6*, pp. 278–9.
65. *CTB 1693–6*, pp. 502, 517.
66. *CSPD 1694–5*, pp. 41–2.
67. Abstract of subsistence, [undated] (NLI, MS 174, [unfol.]); BL, Add. MS 4761, f. 246; NAI, MS M2465/20; *CTB 1696–7*, p. 304; Murphy, *Irish Brigades*, p. 139.
68. *CTP 1557–1696*, p. 434.
69. *CTB 1689–92*, p. 1710; *CTB 1697–8*, pp. 118–19.
70. McGrath, *Constitution*, pp. 49–64.
71. See Chapter 5.
72. *CSPD 1700–2*, p. 260; Murphy, *Irish Brigades*, p. 110.
73. *CTB 1700–1*, pp. 74, 280, 312, 350–1, 370, 410, 430–1; *CTB 1702*, p. 141; *CSPD 1700–2*, pp. 416–17, 425; Rochester to Keightley, 28 June 1701 (NLI, Keightley papers, folder 2598); Ferguson, 'The Army', pp. 57, 69.
74. *CSPD 1700–2*, pp. 406–7; *CTB 1700–1*, pp. 314, 318, 320.
75. *CSPD 1700–2*, pp. 406–7, 410, 412.
76. Scouller, *The Armies of Queen Anne*, p. 275; Ferguson, 'The Army', p. 58. See also Rochester to Keightley, 11 April 1702 (NLI, Keightley papers, folder 2599).

77. *CTB 1702*, pp. 165, 167, 180; Ferguson, 'The Army', p. 58; Murphy, *Irish Brigades*, p. 139.
78. NLI, Keightley papers, folder 2601, no. 7.
79. BL, Add. MS 28946, f. 356; Ferguson, 'The Army', p. 57.
80. Keightley to Rochester, 5 September, 22 October 1702 (NLI, Keightley papers, folders 2600–1); Ferguson, 'The Army', p. 61; Murray, *Financial Relations*, p. 161.
81. Rochester to Keightley, 20 June 1702 (NLI, Keightley papers, folder 2599).
82. E. Murphy, 'O'Brien, William, 2nd earl of Inchiquin', *DIB*, at <http://dib.cambridge.org/viewReadPage.do?articleId=a6502>.
83. Ferguson, 'The Army', p. 57.
84. Alan Brodrick to St John Brodrick, 29 [December] 1702, 4 June 1703 (SHC, Midleton papers, 1248/2, ff. 74–5, 98–9).
85. *CJI* (1st), vol. 3, pp. 11–12.
86. *CSPD 1703–4*, pp. 149–50; McGrath, 'Brodrick', p. 78.
87. BL, Add. MS 28947, ff. 91–2.
88. *CSPD 1703–4*, pp. 185–7; McGrath, *Constitution*, pp. 173–4.
89. BL, Add. MS 34774, ff. 26–7, 55.
90. [Southwell] to [Hedges], 1 March 1705 (TNA, SP 63/365/97–9); McGrath, *Constitution*, pp. 184–6.
91. BL, Add. MS 28890, f. 220.
92. BL, Add. MSS 28890, f. 271; 34774, ff. 1, 8, 10–11; 28891, f. 9; 28947, ff. 91–2; *CJI* (1st), vol. 3, pp. 46–8.
93. BL, Add. MS 38153, ff. 64, 66, 70, 72, 76, 78, 80; PRONI, De Ros MSS, D638/48/1–4; Ferguson, 'The Army', pp. 58–9.
94. BL, Add. MSS 38153, ff. 74, 82, 84, 88; 28892, f. 399; Ferguson, 'The Army', p. 58.
95. Southwell to Ellis, 24 January 1704[5] (BL, Add. MS 28893, f. 27); Murphy, *Irish Brigades*, p. 144.
96. Cox to Southwell, 15 December 1705 (BL, Add. MS 38153, f. 126).
97. NAI, MS 2447, pp. 93–4.
98. BL, Add. MSS 38153, ff. 90, 106, 108, 126, 138, 140; 38154, f. 1; TNA, SP 63/365/252, 254, 257–9, 301–2.
99. BL, Add. MS 34774, ff. 10–11, 14–15; *CJI* (1st), vol. 3, pp. 60–4; NAI, MS M2461, ff. 137–40.
100. BL, Add. MSS 38154, ff. 82, 100, 104; 61638, f. 26.
101. BL, Add. MS 38154, f. 170.
102. Cox to Southwell, 16 March 1707 (BL, Add. MS 38154, f. 176).
103. BL, Add. MSS 38154, ff. 149, 156, 170, 176, 178; 61638, f. 26.
104. Conway, *War, State, and Society*, p. 15.
105. BL, Add. MS 61633, ff. 74–6, 124, 220.
106. PRONI, De Ros MSS, D638/25/2.
107. Additional instructions, 30 March 1709 (BL, Add. MS 61634, ff. 15–16); *CJI* (1st), vol. 3, pp. 566–7.
108. Ó Ciardha, *Jacobite Cause*, pp. 113, 122–5, 127–8; T. M. Devine, *The Scottish Nation, 1700–2000* (London: Penguin, 2000), p. 36.
109. BL, Add. MS 61634, ff. 85, 92–3; TNA, SP 63/367/11–12, 25–6, 29–30.
110. BL, Add. MS 37674, ff. 5–10, 13, 15–16; TNA, SP 63/367/25–6; McGrath, *Constitution*, pp. 252–3; G. Holmes, *British Politics in the Age of Anne*, revised edn (London: Hambledon Press, 1987), pp. 78, 454.

111. BL, Add. MS 37674, f. 47.
112. Opening speech to parliament, November 1713 (TCD, MS 2022, f. 11).
113. TCD, MS 2022, f. 234; Ferguson, 'The Army', p. 61; Brewer, *The Sinews of Power*, pp. 35, 172; L. Colley, *Captives: Britain, Empire and the World, 1600–1850* (London: Pimlico, 2003), pp. 35, 69–71.
114. TCD, MS 2023, ff. 59, 76–7, 81; BL, Add. MS 61635, ff. 33, 41.
115. Alan Brodrick to Sunderland, 25 January 1715 (BL, Add. MS 61636, f. 131).
116. BL, Add. MS 61635, f. 125; TNA, PC 2/85, pp. 250–7, 260–6.
117. Lords justices to [Sunderland], 28 July 1715 (BL, Add. MS 61635, f. 123); BL, Add. MSS 61635, f. 128; 61636, ff. 191–2; TNA, SP 63/373/7–8, 21, 30–3, 37–42, 58–9, 72–3, 88.
118. See TNA, PC 2/85, pp. 288–90; Ó Ciardha, *Jacobite Cause*, pp. 113–14, 134–6; Devine, *Scottish Nation*, pp. 37–8; Murphy, *Irish Brigades*, p. 121.
119. TNA, SP 63/373/112, 144, 150, 193.
120. *CJI*, vol. 3, app. p. lxxvi; Rogers, *The British Army*, p. 20.
121. TNA, SP 63/373/242–3.
122. [W. King], 'Some Observations on the Taxes Paid by Ireland to Support the Government' ([undated, *c.* 1726], NLI, MS 694, p. 68); P. Kelly, 'The Politics of Political Economy in Mid-Eighteenth-Century Ireland', in Connolly (ed.), *Political Ideas*, pp. 105–29, on p. 121 fn. 82.
123. TNA, SP 63/375/49.
124. Conway, *War, State, and Society*, p. 1; Hoppit, *A Land of Liberty?*, pp. 504, 508.
125. *CJI*, vol. 3, pp. 202–3; app. pp. clxvi, clxviii–clxxi; TNA, SP 63/377/28–9, 59–60, 171–2; SP 63/378/35–6; Ferguson, 'The Army', p. 99.
126. Ferguson, 'The Army', p. 61; Murphy, *Irish Brigades*, pp. 110, 129.
127. TNA, SP 63/377/28–9, 59–60, 171–2; SP 63/378/35–6; 67/8, ff. 114–15; Ferguson, 'The Army', p. 99.
128. TNA, SP 63/387/197–8; SP 63/389/117, 119, 121; *CJI*, vol. 3, app. p. ccclxxvii.
129. TNA, SP 63/390/234.
130. Bolton to Craggs, 8 July 1719 (TNA, SP 63/377/171–2). See also TNA, SP 63/377/28–9, 59–60; SP 63/378/35–6.
131. *CJI*, vol. 3, pp. 579–80.
132. Boulter to [Newcastle], 23 October 1729 (TNA, SP 63/391/184–5).
133. Carteret to Southwell, 9 December 1729 (BL, Add. MS 38016, ff. 11–12); TNA, SP 63/391/254.
134. TNA, SP 63/392/3; BL, Add. MS 21123, ff. 2–3.
135. *CJI*, vol. 4, pp. 9–10; app. pp. xi–xiii.
136. PRONI, Shannon papers, D2707/A1/7, pp. 48–50.
137. *CJI*, vol. 4, app. p. xliii.
138. PRONI, Shannon papers, D2707/A1/7, pp. 10–11, 51–3.
139. See TNA, SP 63/397/88, 90–1, 97–9, 111, 115–16, 129, 143; Swann, 'Louis XV', pp. 201–2.
140. Cary to [Delafaye], 19 April 1734 (TNA, SP 63/397/117–18).
141. Lords justices to Dorset, 19 July 1735 (PRONI, Shannon papers, D2707/A1/7, pp. 48–53). See also BL, Add. MS 21123, ff. 104–5.
142. *CJI*, vol. 4, app. pp. lx–lxi, lxxxi.
143. TNA, SP 63/399/7, 9, 42, 46, 58.
144. PRONI, Chatsworth papers, T3158/48.

145. *CJI*, vol. 4, app. pp. cxxviii, cxlvi, cxliii–cxliv.

146. TNA, SP 63/408/72–3, 98, 107–8, 117–18, 130, 142; SP 63/409/16; *CJI*, vol. 4, p. 521; Murphy, *Irish Brigades*, p. 129.

147. Chesterfield to Newcastle, 8 February 1746 (TNA, SP 63/409/58–9). See also TNA, SP 63/409/60–3; Conway, *War, State, and Society*, pp. 203–4.

148. *CJI*, vol. 4, app. pp. cclxxix–cclxxxi.

149. Observations on the Irish economy by Henry Boyle, [1747] (PRONI, Shannon papers, D2707/A1/12/3).

150. TNA, SP 63/404/70, 82, 98, 128–31, 184; SP 63/406/1; SP 63/410/21; PRONI, Wilmot papers, T3019/503, 506, 532; Ferguson, 'The Army', p. 99.

151. TNA, SP 63/406/30–1, 37–8, 79, 118–19, 139.

152. TNA, SP 63/407/146–8, 152, 154; SP 63/410/45–7, 67–9, 95; Ferguson, 'The Army', p. 99.

153. TNA, SP 63/409/189, 193; SP 63/410/7–8; PRONI, Wilmot papers, T3019/819, 957.

154. *CJI*, vol. 5, pp. 15, 18; app. pp. xiii–xiv, xvii; Walton (ed.), *The King's Business*, p. 25.

155. Walton (ed.), *The King's Business*, pp. 16, 19, 25.

156. Ibid., p. 35.

157. Ferguson, 'The Army', p. 61.

158. Bedford to Harrington, 29 March 1750 (TNA, SP 63/412/112–13).

159. TNA, SP 63/412/124, 129; Walton (ed.), *The King's Business*, p. 41. See also PRONI, Wilmot papers, T3019/1605.

160. See Table 6.2 below.

161. *CJI*, vol. 5, app. pp. xxxvi–xxxix.

162. A reduced horse regiment in Ireland cost between £11,000 and £12,000 in 1699 and 1717, while a foot regiment cost about £9,000 and dragoons were anywhere between £8,000 and £12,000. The Royal Regiment of Foot, which was more than twice the size of normal infantry regiments, cost around £17,000 (*CTB 1699–1700*, pp. 150–1; *Hiberniae Notitia*, pp. 23–9). During wartime in 1760 the estimated cost of a newly raised full strength dragoon regiment was £18,000 while foot regiments varied between £10,500 and £18,000 (TNA, SP 63/418/65–6). In 1762 a standard full strength foot regiment of 1,034 soldiers on the British establishment cost £18,400 (Guy, *Oeconomy and Discipline*, p. 55).

163. *CJI*, vol. 5, app. pp. ccliv–cclvi, cclxxiv–cclxxvi.

164. Conway, *War, State, and Society*, pp. 22–4.

165. TNA, SP 63/413/105–6, 109–10, 117; Ferguson, 'The Army', p. 61.

166. PRONI, Wilmot papers, T3019/2422, 2429, 2437.

167. BL, Egerton MS 3435, ff. 59–60; Walton (ed.), *The King's Business*, p. 132.

168. TNA, SP 63/413/231–2; PRONI, Wilmot papers, T3019/2524; *CJI*, vol. 5, app. pp. cclxxviii–cclxxx; vol. 6, app. p. xxviii; Rogers, *The British Army*, p. 63.

169. BL, Egerton MS 3435, ff. 85–6, 96; Walton (ed.), *The King's Business*, p. 137; PRONI, Wilmot papers, T3019/2736.

170. BL, Add. MSS 32862, f. 303; 32863, f. 77; TNA, SP 63/414/27, 55, 59, 61, 76, 78, 82, 84, 90, 92, 107, 109; *CJI*, vol. 6, app. pp. xvi–xviii, xxviii; Ferguson, 'The Army', p. 100; Murphy, *Irish Brigades*, p. 129.

171. Walton (ed.), *The King's Business*, p. 140.

172. *CJI*, vol. 5, p. 359; app. p. ccxcviii. Also see Chapter 5.

173. PRONI, Wilmot papers, T3019/2736; BL, Egerton MS 3435, f. 96; Walton (ed.), *The King's Business*, p. 137.

174. See PRONI, Wilmot papers, T3019/2865, 2971, 3014.

175. See Chapter 5.

176. Walton (ed.), *The King's Business*, p. 145.

177. PRONI, Wilmot papers, T3019/2926; TNA, SP 63/414/274; *CJI*, vol. 6, app. pp. xvi–xviii, xxviii; Johnston, 'Irish Establishment', p. 35.

178. TNA, SP 63/415/174; *Bedford Correspondence*, vol. 2, pp. 225, 228; *CJI*, vol. 6, app. p. xxviii; Ferguson, 'The Army', p. 100.

179. TNA, SP 63/415/41, 174.

180. *CJI*, vol. 6, app. p. xxviii.

181. BL, Add. MS 51385, ff. 176–7; TNA, SP 63/415/196; Walton (ed.), *The King's Business*, p. 182.

182. Johnston, 'Irish Establishment', p. 34.

183. Bedford to Pitt, 3 January 1758 (TNA, SP 63/415/170).

184. TNA, SP 63/415/331, 333.

185. PRONI, Wilmot papers, T3019/3619; TNA, SP 63/417/108.

186. TNA, SP 63/416/59–60, 61–2, 79, 81.

187. *CJI*, vol. 6, p. 165; app. pp. cclxxv, cclxxxviii–cclxxxix.

188. TNA, SP 63/417/159, 163–5; SP 63/418/8–10, 45, 61–4, 80–1, 104–7; PRONI, Wilmot papers, T3019/3532, 3685, 3791.

189. TNA, SP 63/421/49–51, 117–18, 151–2, 221–2.

190. Marshall, *Empires*, p. 63.

191. See Tables 5.4 and 6.2.

192. Houlding, *Fit for Service*, pp. 20–1, 50–1.

193. Payments to Regiments Serving Abroad, June 1750 to December 1778 (NAI, 999/308/3/12).

194. Halifax to Northumberland, 28 February 1764 (TNA, SP 63/423/59–60).

195. Halifax to Northumberland, 15 March 1764 (TNA, SP 63/423/89–90); Ferguson, 'The Army', p. 61; Conway, *War, State, and Society*, pp. 53–4.

196. TNA, SP 63/423/57, 61, 63, 83, 91, 93, 95, 107, 109, 128; PRONI, Wilmot papers, T3019/4808.

197. Hamilton to Weston, 24 March 1764 (TNA, SP 63/423/111).

198. Halifax to Northumberland, 3 April 1764 (TNA, SP 63/423/126).

199. Wilmot to Waite, 1 September 1764 (PRONI, Wilmot papers, T3019/4906).

200. TNA, SP 63/423/200–2; PRONI, Wilmot papers, T3019/4989, 5034; Ferguson, 'The Army', p. 61.

201. Anderson, *Crucible of War*, pp. 35, 250–8, 387–415.

202. PRONI, Wilmot papers, T3019/5477; Ferguson, 'The Army', p. 61; Murphy, *Irish Brigades*, pp. 110, 129.

203. See Chapter 5.

204. TNA, SP 63/430/207–8.

205. TNA, SP 63/420/165, 167–94.

206. Ferguson, 'The Army', p. 99.

7 Income, Expenditure and Taxation

1. McCavitt, *Chichester*, pp. 37–41.

2. T. J. Kiernan, *A History of the Financial Administration of Ireland to 1817* (London: P. S. King & Son, 1930), pp. 62, 79.

3. S. Egan, 'Finance and the Government of Ireland, 1660–85', 2 vols (PhD, TCD, 1983), vol. 1, p. 25; vol. 2, pp. 196–224; Kiernan, *Administration*, pp. 79–80.

4. BL, Add. MSS 18022, f. 52; 36651, f. 23; 4761, ff. 174–5; NLI, MS 50, f. 4; Egan, 'Finance', vol. 2, pp. 196–224; McGrath, *Constitution*, p. 291.

5. Dickson, *New Foundations*, pp. 21–2; Murray, *Financial Relations*, pp. 160–1; Ferguson, 'The Army', p. 16; Kiernan, *Administration*, p. 86; Egan, 'Finance', vol. 2, pp. 5–7, 222–4.

6. The average net yield is calculated from figures in Egan, 'Finance', vol. 2, p. 223.

7. *CSPD 1687–9*, p. 154.

8. BL, Add. MSS 18022, ff. 57–8; 36651, f. 25; 4761, ff. 174–5, 159–60, 167, 181, 203, 208; NLI, MSS 50, ff. 6, 12; 1437, ff. 6–8; TCD, MS 1179, ff. 146–7; McGrath, *Constitution*, pp. 50–72, 293; idem, 'Revenue', pp. 317, 329–30.

9. BL, Add. MSS 18022, ff. 52–9; 36651, ff. 23, 25; 4761, ff. 174–5, 159–60, 167, 181, 203, 208; Egerton MS 790, ff. 4–10; NLI, MSS 50, ff. 4–6, 12; 1437, ff. 6–8; TCD, MS 1179, ff. 145–7; *CJI*, vol. 2, app. pp. v, xxxii, cviii–cix; McGrath, *Constitution*, pp. 50, 291–3.

10. BL, Add. MS 4761, ff. 41, 205, 244, 266; TCD, MS 2022, ff. 110–11; *CTB 1689–92*, pp. 1180–1, 1595–6; *CTB 1698*, pp. 139–43; *CTB 1699–1700*, pp. 141–57, 364–7; *CTB 1700–1*, pp. 338–9, 433–46.

11. *CSPD 1697*, pp. 462, 528, 593; *CSPD 1698*, pp. v–vi, 23, 29, 33–4, 57–8, 427–8, 430–1, 437–40; *CSPD 1699–1700*, pp. viii–x, 5, 11, 43–4, 65, 68; *CSPD 1703–4*, pp. 172–3; *CTB 1681–5*, pp. 738, 1002–12; *CTB 1685–9*, pp. 1742–7; *CTB 1698*, pp. 139–43; *CTB 1699–1700*, pp. 141–57, 364–7; *CTB 1700–1*, pp. 338–9, 433–46; *CTB 1703*, pp. 123–5; *CTB 1709*, pp. 114–23; McGrath, *Constitution*, pp. 66–7, 293–5.

12. BL, Add. MS 4761, ff. 39, 41, 154, 246; NAI, MS M2465/20–4; Wyche papers, 2/50, 53; *CSPD 1698*, pp. 437–40; *CTB 1689–92*, pp. 1180–1, 1595–6; *CTB 1698*, pp. 139–43; *CTB 1699–1700*, pp. 141–57, 364–7; *CTB 1700–1*, pp. 338–9, 433–46; *CJI*, vol. 2, app. pp. ii–iii, xi–xvi, xxxiii, xlviii, cv–cvii; *Accounts of Net Public Income and Expenditure of Great Britain and Ireland, 1688–1800*, pp. 227–53, H.C. 1868–9 (366), xxxv, 1, 483; McGrath, *Constitution*, pp. 54, 291–5.

13. *Net Public Income*, pp. 227–53; McGrath, *Constitution*, pp. 294–5; idem, 'Revenue', p. 326.

14. *CJI*, vol. 3, app. pp. cxcix, ccxl, ccxcii–ccxciii, ccxcvi, cccxxxi, cccxxxiv, ccclxii; vol. 4, app. pp. vi–viii, xix, xxviii, xxix, lvi–lvii, lxxiii, lxxiii, lxxv, cv–cvi, cxxxix–cxl, clvii–clviii, ccxlviii–ccxlix, cclxxiv–cclxxv; vol. 5, app. pp. vi–vii, xxxii, ccl–ccli, cclxx–cclxxi; vol. 6, app. pp. vi–vii, clxxii–clxxiii.

15. P. K. O'Brien, 'The Political Economy of British Taxation, 1660–1815', *Economic History Review*, 2nd series, 41 (1988), pp. 1-32, on pp. 1–2; Brewer, *The Sinews of Power*, pp. 40–1.

16. *Net Public Income*, pp. 434–9.

17. Eoin Magennis, 'Coal, Corn and Canals: The Dispersal of Public Moneys, 1695–1772', *Parliamentary History*, 20 (2001), pp. 71–86; Chapters 8–9.

18. *CJI*, vol. 3, app. pp. vi–vii, cvi, clvi, cxciv, ccxxxvi, ccxc, cccxxx, ccclxii; vol. 4, app. pp. iii, xxii, li–lii, lxxiii, cv–cvi, cxxxix–cxl, clvii–clviii, ccxlviii–ccxlix, cclxxiv–cclxxv; vol. 5, app. pp. vi–vii, xxxii, ccl–ccli, cclxx–cclxxi; vol. 6, app. pp. vi–vii, clxxii–clxxiii; vol. 7, app. pp. xii–xiii.

19. *Net Public Income*, pp. 255–321.

20. Ibid., pp. 434–9.

21. See Chapters 8–9.

22. *Net Public Income*, pp. 434–9. The annual amount is given for 25 December each year until 1725. Thereafter the end date is 25 March in the following year, so that the figure for 1726 is actually for one and one-quarter years.

23. McGrath, 'Revenue', pp. 60–2, 317–20; idem, *Constitution*, pp. 24–5; Egan, 'Finance', vol. 2, pp. 196–224.

24. *Stat. Ire.*, vol. 2, pp. 365–418, 419–93; McGrath, *Constitution*, pp. 26–32.

25. BL, Add. MSS 18022, f. 52; 36651, f. 23; 4761, ff. 174–5; NLI, MS 50, f. 4; McGrath, *Constitution*, pp. 26–32; idem, 'Revenue', pp. 317–19.

26. Brewer, *The Sinews of Power*, pp. 88–101; J. V. Beckett, 'Land Tax or Excise: The Levying of Taxation in Seventeenth- and Eighteenth-Century England', *English Historical Review*, 100 (1985), pp. 285–308; O'Brien, 'British Taxation', pp. 1–32; P. K. O'Brien and P. A. Hunt, 'The Rise of a Fiscal State in England, 1485–1815', *Bulletin of the Institute of Historical Research*, 46 (1993), pp. 129–76.

27. R. Eaton, *A Book of Rates, Inwards and Outwards* (Dublin, 1767), pp. iv–v.

28. C. D. Chandaman, *The English Public Revenue 1660–1688* (Oxford: Oxford University Press, 1975), pp. 11–17, 37–48; W. Kennedy, *English Taxation 1640–1799* (London: G. Bell & Sons, 1913), pp. 24–5, 56; M. Braddick, *The Nerves of State: Taxation and the Financing of the English State, 1558–1714* (Manchester: Manchester University Press, 1996), p. 99; Dickson, *The Financial Revolution*, pp. 48–9; Beckett, 'Land Tax', pp. 298–307.

29. Aydelotte, 'Ormond', pp. 30–4, 48–53, 56–61, 64, 78, 80, 108; McGrath, 'Parliamentary Additional Supply', pp. 30–1; idem, *Constitution*, pp. 36–7.

30. *Stat. Ire.*, vol. 3, pp. 245–6, 289–95, 312–13, 328; PRONI, De Ros MSS, D638/18/40; McGrath, *Constitution*, pp. 37–9, 42; idem, 'Parliamentary Additional Supply', pp. 32–6.

31. *Stat. Ire.*, vol. 3, pp. 353–8, 374–96, 451–73; McGrath, *Constitution*, pp. 39–43; idem, 'Parliamentary Additional Supply', pp. 37–40, 54.

32. McGrath, *Constitution*, pp. 62–8, 90–152.

33. BL, Add. MSS 4761, ff. 146, 159, 163, 181, 196, 200, 203; 18022, ff. 54–5; NLI, MS 1437, f. 7; TCD, MS 1179, ff. 145–8; *CJI*, vol. 3, app. p. cviii; McGrath, *Constitution*, pp. 62–5; idem, 'Revenue', pp. 315, 329–30.

34. *Stat. Ire.*, vol. 4, pp. 1–2, 7–10, 69–70, 109–12, 187–90, 251–7, 291–3; McGrath, *Constitution*, pp. 44–8; idem, 'Parliamentary Additional Supply', pp. 40–51, 54.

35. TCD, MS 2022, ff. 110–12.

36. McGrath, 'Central Aspects', pp. 13–34.

37. *Stat. Ire.*, vol. 4, pp. 315–20, 325–7, 431–8, 504–8; vol. 5, pp. 1–5, 75–81, 137–42, 193–8, 201–15, 333–63, 483–92; vol. 6, pp. 1–9, 171–80, 389–98, 479–89, 601–12, 639–50, 698–710, 805–17; vol. 7, pp. 1–15, 99–111, 255–60, 271–6, 491–7, 613–22.

38. The table only records new additions to the schedule of commodities and increased rates on existing ones, and the sessions in which those changes occurred. The ongoing renewals of unaltered existing rates, which accounted for the majority of year-to-year taxes, are not recorded.

39. *Stat. Ire.*, vol. 7, pp. 801–7, 809–20; vol. 9, pp. 1–17, 261–85, 479–503; vol. 10, pp. 1–22.

40. *CJI*, vol. 3, app. pp. cccxxviii–cccxxix, ccclxi, ccclxxvii; vol. 4, app. pp. vi–vii, xx–xxi, xxviii, l, liii–lvi, lxxi–lxxv, ciii–civ, cvi–cvii, cxxxvii–cxli, clv–clvi, clviii–clix, ccxlvi–cci, cclxxi–cclxxvi, vol. 5, app. pp. iii–v, vii–viii, xxix–xxxiv, ccxlvii–ccliii, cclxvii–cclxxii; vol. 6, app. pp. iii–viii, clxx–clxxi, clxxiv. For the national debt see Chapters 8–9.

41. *CJI*, vol. 10, app. pp. xii–xiii, xix; *Net Public Income*, pp. 434–9.

42. McGrath, 'Money, Politics, and Power', pp. 26–7; idem, 'Central Aspects', pp. 9–34; idem, *Constitution*, passim.

43. TNA, SP 63/394/93–4, 121–2.

44. NAI, MS 2447, pp. 23, 27–30; *CSPD 1695 and addenda*, pp. 207–8; McGrath, *Constitution*, pp. 77, 144–5.
45. BL, Add. MS 61636, ff. 131–2, 214–15; TNA, SP 63/373/296, 336–7; McGrath, *Constitution*, passim.

8 The National Debt

1. Dickson, *The Financial Revolution*, p. 12; N. Ferguson, *Empire: How Britain Made Modern Europe* (London: Penguin, 2004), pp. 23, 34–5, 46.
2. Roseveare, *The Financial Revolution*, pp. 3–4, 8–9, 16–25, 34–40, 52–3; Brewer, *The Sinews of Power*, pp. 114–26.
3. Kiernan, *Administration*, pp. 145–6.
4. McGrath, *Constitution*, passim; idem, 'Central Aspects', pp. 9–34.
5. See Chapter 9.
6. Southwell to Dartmouth, 28 July 1711 (TNA, SP 63/367/11–12); R. V. Clarendon, *A Sketch of the Revenue and Finances of Ireland and of the Appropriated Funds, Loans and Debt of the Nation from Their Commencement* (Dublin, 1791), pp. xvi, 70, 93; McGrath, *Constitution*, pp. 255, 284–6. On floating debts see Roseveare, *The Financial Revolution*, p. 108.
7. Kiernan, *Administration*, pp. 145–6.
8. *CJI*, vol. 3, pp. 60, 62, 73–5; TNA, SP 63/374/59–60.
9. Delafaye to [Pringle], 30 January 1716 (TNA, SP 63/374/59–60).
10. Lords justices to Stanhope, 30 January 1716 (TNA, SP 63/374/63–5).
11. *CJI*, vol. 3, p. 112.
12. Dickson, *The Financial Revolution*; Brewer, *The Sinews of Power*; Roseveare, *The Financial Revolution*; McGrath, 'Revenue', pp. 1–7.
13. *Net Public Income*, pp. 227–53; Cullen, *An Economic History*, pp. 43–4; McGrath, *Constitution*, pp. 50, 54–5, 64, 70–2.
14. TNA, SP 63/374/70–1, 101–2.
15. King to [—], 15 February 1716 (TNA, SP 63/374/101–2).
16. *CJI*, vol. 3, p. 86; app. p. xxxviii; TNA, SP 63/374/63–5.
17. *CJI*, vol. 3, pp. 14, 16, 20, 22, 53–5, 59, 66, 68, 70–3, 78; *Stat. Ire.*, vol. 4, pp. 315–20; TNA, SP 63/373/308–9, 322–4, 336–7; SP 63/374/18, 57–8; PC 2/85, pp. 329, 331–5; McGrath, 'Central Aspects', pp. 14–15.
18. *CJI*, vol. 3, p. 80.
19. TNA, SP 63/374/163, 169–71, 175–6, 201–3, 205–6, 221–2, 225–6, 240–1; PC 2/85, pp. 359–67; *CJI*, vol. 3, pp. 86, 88–90, 92.
20. Delafaye to [Pringle], 4 May 1716 (TNA, SP 63/374/219–20).
21. Delafaye to [Pringle], 31 May 1716 (TNA, SP 63/374/246–7).
22. *Stat. Ire.*, vol. 4, pp. 325–7; *CJI*, vol. 3, pp. 60, 73–6, 80, 86, 92–3, 98, 112; vol. 3, app. p. xxxviii; Kiernan, *Administration*, pp. 145–6; McGrath, *Constitution*, pp. 286–7.
23. *Stat. Ire.*, vol. 4, pp. 325–7; *CJI*, vol. 3, p. 92; McGrath, 'Central Aspects', pp. 15–16.
24. *Stat. Ire.*, vol. 4, pp. 433–8, 504–8; vol. 5, pp. 1–5, 75–81, 137–42, 201–6; McGrath, 'Central Aspects', pp. 16–17.
25. *CJI*, vol. 3, app. pp. cvi, clvi, cxciv, ccxxxvi, ccxc, cccxxx, ccclxii; McGrath, 'Central Aspects', pp. 9–34.
26. *Stat. Ire.*, vol. 5, pp. 63–5.
27. R. Lawrence, *The Interest of Ireland in Its Trade and Wealth Stated. In Two Parts* (Dublin, 1682), vol. 2, pp. 3–5, 10; Hugh Chamberlen, *A Proposal and Considerations Relating to*

an *Office of Credit upon Land Security: Proposed to Their Excellencies the Lords Justices: And to the Lords of the Privy Council; and the Parliament of Ireland* (London, 1697); F. G. Hall, *The Bank of Ireland, 1783–1946* (Dublin: Hodges Figgis, 1949), p. 15.

28. *To the Nobility, Gentry and Commonalty of this Kingdom of Ireland* [Dublin, 1720]; NLI, MS 2256, ff. 59–61; M. Ryder, 'The Bank of Ireland, 1721: Land, Credit and Dependency', *Historical Journal*, 25 (1982), pp. 557–82, on p. 560.

29. NLI, MS 2256, ff. 8–9, 17–18; Ryder, 'The Bank', pp. 559–61.

30. *CJI*, vol. 3, app. p. cci; NLI, MS 2256, ff. 11, 21–2; Ryder, 'The Bank', p. 560.

31. See Chapter 3.

32. Privy Council minutes, Whitehall, 28 May 1721 (TNA, PC 2/87/212); Ryder, 'The Bank', pp. 563–4.

33. *CJI*, vol. 3, pp. 267–8; J. Griffin, 'Parliamentary Politics in Ireland during the Reign of George I' (MA, UCD, 1977), pp. 102, 190–3; Ryder, 'The Bank', p. 565.

34. *CJI*, vol. 3, p. 289.

35. Roseveare, *The Financial Revolution*, pp. 54–8; Ryder, 'The Bank', pp. 557–82; Griffin, 'Parliamentary Politics', pp. 100–12; J. Johnston, 'Berkeley and the Abortive Bank Project of 1720–21', in idem (ed.), *Bishop Berkeley's Querist in Historical Perspective* (Dundalk, 1970), pp. 44–51; Hall, *The Bank of Ireland*, pp. 15–29; J. Kelly, 'Harvests and Hardship: Famine and Scarcity in Ireland in the Late 1720s', *Studia Hibernica*, 26 (1992), pp. 65–105, on pp. 66–9; Cullen, *An Economic History*, pp. 44–6.

36. C. I. McGrath, 'The Irish Experience of "Financial Revolution", 1660–1760', in C. I. McGrath and C. Fauske (eds), *Money, Power and Print: Interdisciplinary Studies on the Financial Revolution in the British Isles* (Newark, NJ: University of Delaware Press, 2008), pp. 157–88, on pp. 173–5.

37. Manley to [—], 25 February 1726 (TNA, SP 63/387/73). See also TNA, SP 63/386/214–15, 221–5, 292–4, 308, 312–13; SP 63/387/13–14, 17–19, 21, 50–1, 55–6, 59–60, 75, 77, 79–82, 114, 130; BL, Add. MS 21122, ff. 24–6, 29; *CJI*, vol. 3, pp. 442–5; McGrath, 'The Public Wealth', pp. 178–9.

38. TNA, SP 63/389/123–4, 133; SP 63/390/1; *CJI*, vol. 3, pp. 490–1, 495; McGrath, 'The Public Wealth', pp. 178–9.

39. TNA, SP 63/387/73.

40. *CJI*, vol. 3, pp. 579–80, 594–5, 599, 600–1; app. pp. ccclxii, ccclxxvii; TNA, SP 63/391/184, 210–11, 234, 236–9; *Stat. Ire.*, vol. 5, pp. 337–40.

41. TNA, SP 63/391/184, 204, 238, 254, 260–1, 264, 268, 272, 280, 286–7; PC 2/91, pp. 92–3; BL, Add. MSS 21122, ff. 91–2, 95, 97–9, 103; 38016, f. 11; *CJI*, vol. 3, pp. 596–8, 621–4; McGrath, 'The Public Wealth', pp. 179–85.

42. TNA, SP 63/391/254; BL, Add. MS 21123, ff. 2–3; *CJI*, vol. 3, app. pp. cccxcvi–cccxcviii.

43. *Stat. Ire.*, vol. 5, pp. 487–92, 508–10.

44. BL, Add. MS 20102, ff. 138, 152–4, 160; TNA, SP 63/394/93–4, 109, 117–18, 121, 123, 127, 129, 135–6, 139, 141–2, 145; PC 2/91, pp. 474–5, 485–9; *CJI*, vol. 4, pp. 9–10, 22–5, 27–8, 38–41, 43; app. pp. v, xi–xiii; McGrath, 'The Public Wealth', pp. 191–4.

45. Clayton to Mrs Clayton, 2 January 1732 (BL, Add. MS 20102, f. 160).

46. *Reflections on the National Debt; with Reasons for the Reducing the Legal Interest; and against a Public Loan. With Some Advice to the Electors of Members of Parliament* ([Dublin], 1731), pp. 11–13; McGrath, 'Money, Politics and Power', p. 31.

47. *Reflections*, p. 13.

48. *Reasons for Regulating the Coin, and Reducing the Interest; with a Scheme for Paying Part of the National Debt without Burthening Ireland* ([Dublin], 1731), pp. 21–2; McGrath, 'Money, Politics and Power', p. 31.
49. *CJI*, vol. 4, pp. 33, 39.
50. *Stat. Ire.*, vol. 6, pp. 5–9, 175–80, 393–8, 483–9.
51. *CJI*, vol. 4, pp. 74–5, 76–8; app. pp. xxii, xxv, xxxvii–xli, xliii, li–liii, lx–lxi, lxxiii, lxxxi, cv–cvi, cxv, cxxxix–cxl, cl; BL, Add. MS 21123, ff. 62, 66–7; TNA, SP 63/396/99–100, 103; McGrath, 'The Public Wealth', pp. 194–5.
52. *CJI*, vol. 4, pp. 341–6, 368–72; app. pp. cl–clii, clviii; NLI, MS 694, pp. 1–76; TNA, SP 63/403/39–40, 45, 49, 53–7, 61–3, 79; SP 63/404/70, 82, 98, 211–12, 223–4, 258; PC 2/97, pp. 20–5; PRONI, Wilmot papers, T3019/239, 341, 359; *Stat. Ire.*, vol. 6, pp. 605–12.
53. *CJI*, vol. 4, pp. 406, 408; app. pp. clvii–clviii, clx, clxx, ccxlviii–ccxlix; *Stat. Ire.*, vol. 6, pp. 643–50; TNA, PC 2/98, pp. 58–60, 64–7; PRONI, Wilmot papers, T3019/497, 510.
54. TNA, SP 63/408/167, 169, 171–2, 196, 221–4; PC 2/99, pp. 246–7, 249–50, 257–9, 264–5; PRONI, Wilmot papers, T3019/699, 706, 822; *CJI*, vol. 4, pp. 449–58, 462–6, 470–5; *Stat. Ire.*, vol. 6, pp. 702–10; vol. 7, pp. 6–15; McGrath, 'The Public Wealth', pp. 197–8.
55. *Stat. Ire.*, vol. 4, pp. 325–7; vol. 5, pp. 337–40, 487–92; vol. 6, pp. 605–12, 702–10.
56. *CJI*, vol. 4, pp. 453, 458; app. pp. ccxlviii–ccxlix, cclix.
57. *Stat. Ire.*, vol. 6, pp. 698–702, 810–17; vol. 7, pp. 6–15, 104–11; *CJI*, vol. 4, app. pp. clxvi, ccliv–cclvii, cclix, cclxxxii–cclxxxvii; TNA, SP 63/411/49–55, 214–16; Cullen, *An Economic History*, pp. 50–99; Dickson, *New Foundations*, pp. 102–3.
58. *Stat. Ire.*, vol. 7, pp. 6–15; O'Donovan, 'The Money Bill Dispute', pp. 55–87; Magennis, *Political System*, pp. 62–83.
59. *CJI*, vol. 5, app. p. xxxii; *Stat. Ire.*, vol. 7, pp. 6–15.
60. *Stat. Ire.*, vol. 7, pp. 104–11.
61. TCD, MS 7264, ff. 39, 44; *CJI*, vol. 5, app. p. ccl–ccli.
62. McGrath, 'Money, Politics and Power', pp. 34–6; idem, 'The Public Wealth', pp. 201–2; idem, 'The Irish Experience', pp. 178–80; O'Donovan, 'The Money Bill Dispute', pp. 55–87.
63. *CJI*, vol. 5, pp. 187–8, 190; TNA, SP 63/413/73.
64. BL, Add. MS 35592, ff. 200–1; TNA, SP 63/412/206–7; PC 2/102, pp. 378–9; *CJI*, vol. 5, pp. 91–2; *Stat. Ire.*, vol. 7, pp. 104–11; Magennis, *Political System*, pp. 66–8.
65. TNA, PC 2/103, pp. 515–16; Magennis, *Political System*, p. 82; O'Donovan, 'The Money Bill Dispute', p. 64.
66. TCD, MSS 7265, ff. 49, 55–7; 7266, ff. 28, 30, 32; PRONI, Wilmot papers, T3019/2295; BL, Add. MSS 32736, f. 473; 32737, f. 49; *CJI*, vol. 3, app. pp. clxxii–clxxiii; O'Donovan, 'The Money Bill Dispute', pp. 69, 74–9.
67. *Common Sense: In a Letter to a Friend. To Which Is Prefixed an Explanatory Preface. By the Author of Ireland in Tears* (London, 1755), p. 48.
68. *Stat. Ire.*, vol. 7, pp. 619–22, 801–7; *CJI*, vol. 7, p. 13; Magennis, *Political System*, pp. 133–43; James, *Ireland in the Empire*, pp. 259–61.
69. *Stat. Ire.*, vol. 7, pp. 809–20; *CJI*, vol. 7, pp. 95, 97–8, 108–10, 117–18, 147–9, 151–2.
70. *Stat. Ire.*, vol. 9, pp. 7–17, 272–85, 489–503.
71. *CJI*, vol. 6, pp. 150–1, 155, 172–3, 180, 191, 207–8, 228; vol. 7, pp. 64, 69, 198, 239, 255–6, 260; vol. 8, pp. 313–14.
72. *Stat. Ire.*, vol. 7, pp. 809–20; vol. 9, pp. 7–17, 272–85, 489–503. See also Table 7.5.
73. *Stat. Ire.*, vol. 10, pp. 6–22; Bartlett, 'The Augmentation', pp. 540–59.

74. *Stat. Ire.*, vol. 10, pp. 71–87, 333–41, 681–9; vol. 11, pp. 3–12, 303–11, 374–86; vol. 12, pp. 1–18.

75. *Stat. Ire.*, vol. 10, pp. 71–87, 342–56, 647–62; vol. 11, pp. 13–29, 311–33, 353–72, 407–22; vol. 12, pp. 19–50.

76. Clarendon, *Sketch*, app. p. xvi.

77. *Stat. Ire.*, vols 4–10; McGrath, 'Central Aspects', pp. 16, 19, 23, 27.

9 The Public Creditors

1. D. Stasavage, *Public Debt and the Birth of the Democratic State: France and Great Britain, 1688–1789* (Cambridge: Cambridge University Press, 2003); Brewer, *The Sinews of Power*, pp. 88–91; Roseveare, *The Financial Revolution*, pp. 3–5.

2. Colley, *Britons*, pp. 65–71.

3. Dickson, *The Financial Revolution*, p. 12.

4. Ibid., pp. 256–7, 313, 316–17; Devine, *Scottish Nation*, p. 49; T. Devine, *Scotland's Empire, 1600–1815* (London: Penguin, 2003), pp. 40–8, 65–8, 331–2.

5. *CJI*, vol. 3, pp. 73–5, 124, 127.

6. Cullen, *An Economic History*, pp. 43–4; McGrath, *Constitution*, pp. 50, 54–5, 64, 70–2.

7. *CJI*, vol. 3, app. pp. cxiii–cxiv; G. E. Cokayne, *The Complete Peerage of England, Scotland, Ireland, Great Britain and the United Kingdom, Extant, Extinct or Dormant*, rev. by V. Gibbs, G. White and R. S. Lea, 12 vols (London: St Catherine Press, 1910–59), vol. 7, p. 244; vol. 8, p. 615; vol. 9, p. 351; vol. 11, pp. 656, 669; Johnston-Liik, *Parliament*, vol. 3, pp. 194–5, 256, 266–9, 270–2, 299–300, 316–18, 474–9; vol. 4, pp. 43–4, 147, 208–9, 257–60, 279–80, 340–2, 371, 450–1; vol. 5, pp. 190–1, 240–1; vol. 6, pp. 187–9, 538–40.

8. Dickson, *The Financial Revolution*, pp. 47, 80, 93, 254, 262, 273, 344; Roseveare, *The Financial Revolution*, pp. 52–3; Brewer, *The Sinews of Power*, p. 114.

9. See Ryder, 'The Bank', pp. 557–82; Johnston, 'Bank Project', pp. 44–51; Hall, *The Bank of Ireland*, pp. 15–29; Griffin, 'Parliamentary Politics', pp. 100–12, 190–3; McGrath, 'The Irish Experience', pp. 170–3.

10. NLI, MS 2256, pp. 27–8, 31–3, 39, 41, 59–61, 63–5, 67–9; Hall, *The Bank of Ireland*, pp. 23–4; Ryder, 'The Bank', pp. 559–61.

11. *CJI*, vol. 3, pp. 267–8, 289; Griffin, 'Parliamentary Politics', pp. 102, 190–3; Johnston-Liik, *Parliament*, vols 3–6.

12. NLI, MS 2256, pp. 67–9; Hall, *The Bank of Ireland*, pp. 23–6.

13. *Stat. Ire.*, vol. 5, pp. 337–40.

14. BL, Add. MS 21123, ff. 1–4; Malcomson, *Clements*, p. 125.

15. *Stat. Ire.*, vol. 5, pp. 337–40.

16. *CJI*, vol. 4, app. p. v; BL, Add. MS 21123, ff. 2–3.

17. *CJI*, vol. 3, app. pp. cccxcvi–cccxcviii; Johnston-Liik, *Parliament*, vol. 3, pp. 179–80, 241–6, 437–8, 442–5; vol. 4, pp. 129–30, 284–6, 488–90.

18. Coghill to Southwell, 18 April 1730 (BL, Add. MS 21123, ff. 2–3).

19. *CJI*, vol. 3, app. pp. cxiii–cxiv, cccxcvi–cccxcviii; NLI, MS 2256, pp. 27–8, 31–3, 39, 41, 63–5, 67–9; Hall, *The Bank of Ireland*, pp. 23–4.

20. Johnston-Liik, *Parliament*, vol. 3, pp. 270–2, 316–18; vol. 4, pp. 371, 450–1; vol. 5, pp. 190–1, 240–1; vol. 6, pp. 21–2, 45–6, 216–17, 233–4, 267–8, 562–3.

21. NLI, MS 2256, pp. 8–9; Griffin, 'Parliamentary Politics', pp. 108–10.

22. Johnston-Liik, *Parliament*, vol. 6, pp. 21–2, 216–17.

23. Hartley Hutchinson, Richard Nuttall, Alderman William Quayle and Ann Hall.

24. Johnston-Liik, *Parliament*, vol. 4, pp. 257–60, 340–2, 417–18; L. M. Cullen, 'Land-lords, Bankers and Merchants: The Early Irish Banking World, 1700–1820', in A. E. Murphy (ed.), *Economists and the Irish Economy from the Eighteenth Century to the Present Day* (Dublin: Irish Academic Press, 1984), pp. 25–44, on pp. 32, 34.
25. McGrath, 'Revenue', pp. 228–9.
26. Another Dublin banker who acted for the government.
27. A nephew of Benjamin.
28. A partner in a private bank with Gardiner in the 1730s.
29. Became a partner in Burton's bank in 1726.
30. Johnston-Liik, *Parliament*, vol. 3, pp. 140–1, 214–15, 322–3, 377–81, 403–4; vol. 4, pp. 129–30, 284–6, 409–10, 417–18; vol. 5, pp. 62, 136–7, 337–8; vol. 6, pp. 41–2, 227–9, 276–7, 327, 379–80, 395–7, 435–6, 493–4; Cullen, 'Bankers', pp. 27, 29, 32, 34; T. W. Moody, F. X. Martin and F. J. Byrne (eds), *A New History of Ireland, IX: Maps, Genealogies, Lists* (Oxford: Oxford University Press, 1984), pp. 405 (hereafter *NHI*, vol. 9); Malcomson, *Clements*, pp. 125, 145–6.
31. William Burgh (possibly a former accountant-general), Francis Cocksedge, Captain William Duponset, George Haughton/Houghton, Captain Richard Jackson, Edward Kean, Joseph Leeson, Joseph Nagle, John Taylor, Ralph Leland, Simon Sandys and Daniel Virazell.
32. *Stat. Ire.*, vol. 5, pp. 508–10, 487–92; vol. 6, pp. 605–12, 702–10.
33. TCD, MSS 7259–7266; Malcomson, *Clements*, passim.
34. TCD, MS 7260, pp. 48–57; Malcomson, *Clements*, pp. 125–6.
35. TCD, MS 7261, pp. 46–7.
36. TCD, MSS 7261, pp. 49–55; 7262, pp. 45–50.
37. *Stat. Ire.*, vol. 7, pp. 6–15.
38. TCD, MS 7263, pp. 50–2.
39. *CJI*, vol. 5, app. p. xxxii.
40. La Touche, Mitchell, Gleadowe, Fade and Wilcocks.
41. TCD, MS 7263, pp. 52–8.
42. *Stat. Ire.*, vol. 7, pp. 104–11.
43. TCD, MS 7264, pp. 39, 44.
44. TCD, MS 7264, pp. 40–3.
45. TCD, MS 7264, pp. 49–51, 54–7.
46. PRONI, Wilmot papers, T3019/2295.
47. O'Donovan, 'The Money Bill Dispute', pp. 69, 74–9.
48. Newcastle to Murray, 10 September 1754 (BL, Add. MS 32736, f. 473).
49. Murray to Newcastle, 6 October 1754 (BL, Add. MS 32737, f. 49).
50. TCD, MS 7265, pp. 55–7.
51. TCD, MSS 7265, pp. 49, 52–3; 7266, p. 28; 7266, p. 30.
52. TCD, MS 7266, p. 32.
53. *CJI*, vol. 6, app. pp. clxxii–clxxiii; vol. 7, app. pp. xii–xiii.
54. *CJI*, vol. 3, app. pp. cxiii–cxiv; TCD, MSS 7263, p. 53; 7265, pp. 52, 55; *NHI*, vol. 9, pp. 396–7.
55. A. P. W. Malcomson, *Archbishop Charles Agar: Churchmanship and Politics in Ireland, 1760–1810* (Dublin: Four Courts Press, 2002), pp. 303, 343, 390, 456, 493–4.
56. *CJI*, vol. 3, app. pp. cccxcvi–cccxcvii; *NHI*, vol. 9, pp. 435–6.
57. TCD, MSS 7260, p. 56; 7261, p. 52; 7263, pp. 56, 58; 7264, pp. 40, 42, 49; 7265, p. 57.
58. Malcomson, *Agar*, pp. 137, 187, 404.
59. *CJI*, vol. 3, app. pp. cxiii–cxiv; TCD, MSS 7260, p. 56; 7264, pp. 40, 42, 51, 55; 7265, p. 57; *NHI*, vol. 9, p. 418; TNA, SP 63/407/6.

60. TCD, MSS 7260, p. 55; 7261, p. 46; 7263, pp. 55, 57; *NHI*, vol. 9, pp. 418, 423.
61. *CJI*, vol. 3, app. pp. cccxcvi–cccxcvii; TCD, MSS 7260, pp. 52, 54; 7261, pp. 47, 52, 54; 7263, pp. 54, 57; 7264, p. 56; 7265, pp. 52–3, 55; *NHI*, vol. 9, pp. 394, 405, 410, 426, 432; Malcomson, *Agar*, p. 404.
62. *CJI*, vol. 3, app. pp. cxiii–cxiv, cccxcvi–cccxcvii; TCD, MSS 7260–6, passim; Malcomson, *Clements*, pp. 125, 145–6; Johnston-Liik, *Parliament*, vol. 3, pp. 231–2, 403–4; vol. 4, pp. 257–60, 488–90; vol. 5, pp. 62, 136–7; vol. 6, pp. 552–3.
63. Dickson, *The Financial Revolution*, pp. 284–5, 322–4; Brewer, *The Sinews of Power*, pp. 114–15.
64. Malcomson, *Clements*, pp. 227–9; Dickson, *The Financial Revolution*, p. 331.
65. NLI, MS 2256, pp. 27–8, 31–3, 39, 41, 63–5, 67–9; TCD, MSS 7260–6, passim; Hall, *The Bank of Ireland*, pp. 23–4; Johnston-Liik, *Parliament*, vol. 3, pp. 403–4; vol. 4, pp. 257–60; vol. 5, pp. 136–7, 215–16; vol. 6, pp. 552–3.
66. Johnston-Liik, *Parliament*, vol. 3, pp. 395–9, 530; vol. 4, pp. 147, 409–10; vol. 5, p. 237; vol. 6, pp. 36–7, 529–30.
67. TCD, MS 7261, pp. 46–7.
68. TCD, MS 7259, p. 105.
69. TCD, MSS 7261, p. 46; 7262, p. 49; 7266, pp. 28, 32; *CJI*, vol. 5, pp. 233, 377.
70. TCD, MS 7266, p. 32.
71. *Complete Peerage*, vol. 2, p. 108; vol. 3, p. 118; vol. 7, p. 244; vol. 8, p. 615; vol. 9, p. 351; vol. 11, pp. 656, 669.
72. Dickson, *The Financial Revolution*, pp. 280–1.
73. *CJI*, vol. 3, app. pp. cccxcvi–cccxcvii; TCD, MSS 7260, p. 51; 7261, pp. 46, 49; 7265, p. 55; Johnston-Liik, *Parliament*, vol. 4, pp. 488–90; *NHI*, vol. 9, p. 510.
74. TCD, MSS 7260, pp. 50, 55; 7262, pp. 45–6, 48; 7265, p. 55. For Yorke see TNA, SP 63/413/27, 39, 149. For Bowes see Johnston-Liik, *Parliament*, vol. 3, pp. 231–2; *NHI*, vol. 9, pp. 510, 514, 518. For Mountney see TNA, SP 63/404/45, 49; Burns, *Parliamentary Politics*, vol. 2, p. 54.
75. TCD, MSS 7260, pp. 48–57; 7261, pp. 46–7, 49–55; 7262, pp. 43, 45–50; 7263, pp. 50, 52–8; 7264, pp. 40–3, 49–51, 54–7; 7265, pp. 52–3, 55–7; Johnston-Liik, *Parliament*, vol. 3, p. 71; vol. 5, pp. 183–8.
76. McGrath, *Constitution*, passim.
77. *Stat. Ire.*, vol. 7, pp. 619–22, 809–20; vol. 9, pp. 7–17, 272–85, 489–503; vol. 10, pp. 6–22, 71–87, 342–56, 357–66, 647–62, 662–74; vol. 11, pp. 13–29, 311–33, 353–72, 407–22; vol. 12, pp. 19–50.

Conclusion

1. *Stat. Ire.*, vol. 20, pp. 448–87; Bartlett, 'Ireland, Empire, and Union', pp. 72–88.
2. A Jackson, 'Ireland, the Union, and the Empire, 1800–1960', in Kenny (ed.), *Ireland and the British Empire*, pp. 123–53.
3. See Chapters 5–6; Denman, 'Recruitment', pp. 158–66; Bartlett, 'Army and Society', p. 175; idem, 'Counter-Insurgency', pp. 248–93; Guy, 'Military Establishment', pp. 228–30.
4. *Net Public Income*, pp. 321–55, 438–9; Murray, *Financial Relations*, p. 161.
5. *Net Public Income*, pp. 317–21, 438–9.
6. *Stat. Ire.*, vol. 10, pp. 65–87, 333–79, 647–704; vol. 11, pp. 3–52, 278–84, 303–11, 333–460, 646–52; vol. 12, pp. 1–118; *Net Public Income*, pp. 438–9; Hall, *The Bank of Ireland*, pp. 30–8.
7. *Stat. Ire.*, vol. 20, p. 448.

WORKS CITED

Manuscript Primary Sources

British Library

1660 Convention Papers: Add. MS 4781; Stowe MS 82.

Blenheim Papers: Add. MSS 61633; 61634; 61635; 61636; 61638.

Egmont Papers: Add. MS 47002 A.

Ellis Papers: Add. MSS 28879; 28880; 28883; 28888; 28889; 28890; 28891; 28892; 28893; 28946; 28947.

Hardwicke Papers: Add. MSS 35592; 35596; 35892; 35919.

Historical and other tracts: Add. MS 27382.

Holland House Papers: Add. MS 51385.

Irish Exchequer: Add. MS 31237.

Leeds Papers: Egerton MSS 790; 3435.

Letters of Sir Richard Cox: Add. MSS 38153; 38154.

Milles Collection: Add. MS 4761.

Miscellaneous: Harleian MSS 4892; 6274.

Newcastle Papers: Add. MSS 32690; 32713; 32726; 32736; 32737, 32862; 32863.

Redesdale Papers: Add. MS 36651.

Revenue of Ireland: Add. MS 18022.

Southwell Papers: Add. MSS 9715; 21122; 21123; 21136; 21138; 34774; 37674.

Sundon Papers: Add. MS 20102.

Vernon Papers: Add. MS 40771.

National Archives of Ireland

Irish Correspondence, 1697–1782: MS 2447.

Frazer MSS: MS 10.

Phillips MSS: M2455; M2456; M2461.

Revenue Accounts, 1689–95: M2465.

Wyche Papers, Series 1: 1/1/1; /3/-; /4/-.

Wyche Papers, Series 1: 2/-.

Military Accounts: 999/308/3/13.

National Library of Ireland

Bank of Ireland Papers: MS 2256.

Fingall Papers: MS 8020(3).

Inchiquin MSS, Keightley papers: Folders 2598–2601.

Irish Establishment, 1709: MS 2097.

[King, William], Some observations on the taxes paid by Ireland to support the government: MS 694.

Military Accounts: MS 174.

Proclamations: MS 1793.

Revenue Accounts, 1689–1701: MS 50.

Revenue Accounts, 1689–1700: MS 1437.

Northamptonshire Record Office

Isham MSS: I.C. 2205 [History of Parliament Trust Transcripts].

Public Record Office of Northern Ireland

Chatsworth Papers: T3158.

De Ros MSS: D638/13; /18; /25; /48; /166; /145.

Shannon Papers: D2707/A1/4; /7; /12.

Wilmot Papers: T3019.

Surrey History Centre, Woking

Midleton Papers: 1248/1; /2.

The National Archives, Kew

Ireland (Entry Books): PRO 30/26/60.

Maps and Plans: MPF 1/315.

Privy Council Registers: PC 2/79; /85; /86; /87; /90; /91; /97; /98; /99; /101; /102; /103; /106; /108 (14 vols).

State Papers, Ireland: SP 63/247; /351; /353; /365; /367; /369; /373; /374; /375; /377;
   /378; /379; /380; /381; /383; /384; /386; /387; /388; /389; /390; /391; /392; /394;
   /396; /397; /399; /403; /404; /406; /407; /408; /409; /410; /411; /412; /413; /414;
   /415; /416; /417; /418; /419; /420; /421; /422; /423; /429; /430; /452; /453 (51 vols).

State Papers Military: SP 41/6.

Treasury Board Papers: T 1/393.

War Office (Maps): WO 78/419.

Trinity College Dublin

1641 Depositions: MS 840.

Clements Papers: MSS 7259; 7260; 7261; 7262; 7263; 7264; 7265; 7266.

Miscellaneous: MS 1178.

Shrewsbury Papers: MSS 2022; 2023.

Southwell Papers: MSS 1179; 1180.

UCD Special Collections

Historic Maps Collection: W1.U.2/1–2; W1.U.4/1–4.

Printed Primary Sources
Official Publications

Accounts of Net Public Income and Expenditure of Great Britain and Ireland, 1688–1800, pp. 227–53, H.C. 1868–9 (366), xxxv, 1, 483.

An Abridgement of the Laws of Jamaica, 2 vols (Jamaica, 1793).

By the King: A Declaration. For the better Government of the Army. James R. (Dublin, 1689).

By the Lords-Justices and Council, A Proclamation (Dublin, 1690).

By the Lords-Justices of Ireland. A Proclamation (Dublin, 1691).

By the Lords Justices of Ireland, A Proclamation [Regarding Winter Quarters] (Dublin, 1691).

By the Lords Justices of Ireland, A Proclamation. Requiring All Officers and Soldiers to Observe Strict Discipline, and for Payment of Quarters (Dublin, 1692).

Calendar of Home Office Papers, 1760–69, 2 vols (London: Stationery Office, 1878–9).

Calendar of State Papers, Domestic Series, 1685–1704, 15 vols (London: Stationery Office, 1895–1972).

Calendar of State Papers, Ireland, 1669–70 and Addenda (London: Stationery Office, 1910).

Calendar of Treasury Books, 1660–1718, 32 vols (London: Stationery Office, 1904–59).

Calendar of Treasury Papers, 1557–1714, 4 vols (London: Stationery Office, 1868–79).

Journals of the House of Commons, 51 vols (London, 1803).

Journals of the House of Lords, 61 vols (London, 1767–1830).

Proclamation. By the King, James Rex (Dublin, 1605).

Proclamation by the Lord Lieutenant and Council. Ormonde, 16 October 1678 (Dublin, 1678).

Proclamation by the Lord Lieutenant and Council. Ormonde, 12 December 1678 (Dublin, 1678).

Proclamation by the Lord Lieutenant and Council. Ormonde, 26 March 1679 (Dublin, 1679).

Proclamation by the Lord Lieutenant and Council. Ormonde, 26 April 1680 (Dublin, 1680).

The Journals of the House of Commons of the Kingdom of Ireland, 1st edn, 11 vols (Dublin, 1753–63).

The Journals of the House of Commons of the Kingdom of Ireland, 3rd edn, 21 vols (Dublin, 1796–1800).

The State of the Nation, with Respect to Its Public Funded Debt, Revenue, and Disbursement; Comprised in the Reports of the Select Committee on Finance (with the Appendices to Each Report) Appointed by The House of Commons, 3 vols (London, 1799).

The Statutes at Large, 8 vols (London, 1770).

The Statutes at Large, 6 vols (London, 1758).

The Statutes at Large Passed in the Parliaments Held in Ireland, 21 vols (Dublin, 1765–1804).

Published Correspondence

Berwick, E. (ed.), *Rawdon Papers* (London, 1819).

Coxe, W. (ed.), *Private and Original Correspondence of Charles Talbot, Duke of Shrewsbury, with King William, the Leaders of the Whig Party, and Other Distinguished Statesmen* (London, 1821).

Falkiner, C. L. (ed.), 'Correspondence of Archbishop Stone and the Duke of Newcastle', *English Historical Review*, 20 (1905), pp. 508–42, 735–63.

Harcourt, W. E. (ed.), *Harcourt Papers*, 15 vols (privately printed, 1876–1903).

HMC, *Buccleuch and Queensberry MSS*, vol. 2 (London: Stationery Office, 1903).

HMC, *Downshire MSS*, vol. 1 (London: Stationery Office, 1924).

HMC, *Finch MSS*, vols 2 and 3 (London: Stationery Office, 1957, 1965).

HMC, *Le Fleming MSS* (London: Stationery Office, 1890).

HMC, *Ormond MSS*, new series, vol. 2 (London: Stationery Office, 1899).

HMC, *Portland MSS*, vol. 3 (London: Stationery Office, 1894).

HMC, *Various Collections*, vols 6, 8 (London: Stationery Office, 1913).

James, G. P. R. (ed.), *Letters Illustrative of the Reign of William III, from 1696 to 1708, Addressed to the Duke of Shrewsbury, by James Vernon, Esq. Secretary of State*, 3 vols (London, 1841).

Letters Written by his Excellency Hugh Boulter, D.D. Lord Primate of all Ireland, &c. to Several Ministers of State in England, and Some Others, 2 vols (Oxford, 1769).

Russell, Lord J. (ed.), *Correspondence of John, Fourth Duke of Bedford*, 3 vols (London: Longman, 1842–6).

Walton, J. (ed.), *The King's Business: Letters on the Administration of Ireland, 1740–1761, from the Papers of Sir Robert Wilmot* (New York: AMS Press, 1996).

Williams, H. (ed.), *The Correspondence of Jonathan Swift*, 5 vols (Oxford: Clarendon Press, 1963–5).

Pamphlets, Tracts and Other Contemporary Publications

An Account of the Revenue and National Debt of Ireland. With Some Observations on the Late Bill for Paying off the National Debt (London, 1754).

An Exact List of All Their Majesties Forces in Flanders, England, Scotland, and Ireland, For the Year 1692. And the Charges of Each Regiment (London, 1692).

A Fragment of the History of Patrick ([Dublin], 1753).

A Journal of the Life of Thomas Story: Containing, an Account of His Remarkable Convincement of, and Embracing the Principles of Truth, as Held by the People Called Quakers; and Also, of His Travels and Labours in the Service of the Gospel: With Many Other Occurrences and Observations (Newcastle-upon-Tyne, 1747).

A Letter from a Member of the House of Commons of Ireland to a Gentleman of the Long Robe in Great-Britain. Containing an Answer to Some Objections Made against the Judicatory Power of the Parliament of Ireland (Dublin, 1720).

*A Letter to the Right Honourable the Lord ********, Occasion'd by a Pamphlet, Just Publish'd, Entitled, Thoughts on the Affairs of Ireland, with an Account of the Expulsion of A—r J—s N—ll, Esq; Late Surveyor and Engineer-General, from the Hon. the H-se of C-mm-ns in that Kingdom. By M. B. Drapier* (London, 1754).

A List of Such of the Names of the Nobility, Gentry and Commonalty of England and Ireland, (amongst Whom Are Several Women and Children) Who Are All by an Act of a Pretended Parliament Assembled in Dublin in the Kingdom of Ireland, the 7th of May, 1689, before the Late King James, Attainted of High Treason (London, 1690).

A List of the General and Field Officers ... to Which Are Added, the Quarters of the Army in Ireland, in the Year 1755 ... (Dublin, 1755).

A List of the Members of the Honourable House of Commons of I—d, Who Voted on the Question Previous to the Expulsion of Arthur Jones Nevill, Esq; Late Engineer and Surveyor-General of that Kingdom (Dublin, 1753).

A Political and Military Rhapsody, on the Invasion and Defence of Great Britain and Ireland ..., 3rd edn (London, 1794).

A Second Letter to a Gentleman of the Long Robe in Great-Britain. Wherein Some of the Late Illegal Proceedings of the Barons of the Exchequer, in the Kingdom of Ireland, Are Plainly and Impartially Set Forth (Dublin, 1720).

Atwood, W., *The History and Reasons, of the Dependency of Ireland upon the Imperial Crown of the Kingdom of England. Rectifying Mr Molyneux's State of the Case of Ireland* ... (London, 1698).

A Warrant for the Regulation of Barracks (London, 1795).

[Bingham, Sir C.], *An Essay on the Use and Necessity of Establishing a Militia in Ireland, and Some Hints towards a Plan for That Purpose* (Dublin, 1767).

Bolton, Sir R., 'A Declaration Setting Forth, How, and by What Means, the Laws and Statutes of England, from Time to Time, Came to Be of Force in Ireland', in W. Harris, *Hibernica. Part II. Or, Two Treatises Relating to Ireland* (Dublin, 1770), pp. 9–45.

Brooke, H., *The Farmer's Letter to the Protestants of Ireland. Number I* (Dublin, 1745).

[—], *The Secret History and Memoirs of the Barracks of Ireland* (London, 1747).

Cary, J., *An Answer to Mr Molyneux His Case of Ireland ... And His Dangerous Notion of Ireland's Being under No Subordination to the Parliamentary Authority of England Refuted* (London, 1698).

—, *A Vindication of the Parliament of England, in Answer to a Book, Written By William Molyneux of Dublin, Esq; Intitled, The Case of Ireland* ... (London, 1698).

Chamberlen, H., *A Proposal and Considerations Relating to an Office of Credit upon Land Security: Proposed to Their Excellencies the Lords Justices: And to the Lords of the Privy Council; and the Parliament of Ireland* (London, 1697).

Clarendon, R. V., *A Sketch of the Revenue and Finances of Ireland and of the Appropriated Funds, Loans and Debt of the Nation from Their Commencement* (Dublin, 1791).

Common Sense: In a Letter to a Friend. To which is Prefixed an Explanatory Preface. By the Author of Ireland in Tears (London, 1755).

Considerations on the Present State of the Military Establishment of This Kingdom, Addressed to the Knights, Citizens, and Burgesses of Ireland, in Parliament Assembled (Dublin, 1768).

Court and no Country. A Seri-Tragi-Comi-Farcical Entertainment, (Not Acted but Once, These Twenty Years.) Wherein Are Occasionally Exhibitted, the Groans of the Barracks. Or, The History of Sir Arthur Vantrype ... ([Dublin], 1753).

Dalrymple, Sir J., *Memoirs of Great Britain and Ireland*, 3 vols (London, 1790).

Darcy, P., *An Argument Delivered By Patrick Darcy Esquire, by the Express Order of the House of Commons in the Parliament of Ireland, 9 Iunii, 1641* (Waterford, 1643).

Defoe, D., *An Argument Shewing, That a Standing Army, with Consent of Parliament, Is Not Inconsistent with a Free Government* (London, 1698).

Domville, Sir W., 'A Disquisition Touching that Great Question Whether an Act of Parliament Made in England Shall Bind the Kingdom and People of Ireland without Their Allowance and Acceptance of such Act in the Kingdom of Ireland', ed. Patrick Kelly, *Analecta Hibernica*, 40 (2007), pp. 17–70.

Eaton, R., *A Book of Rates, Inwards and Outwards* (Dublin, 1767).

Eyre, T., *A Reply to the Report of the Commissioners and Others, upon the Condition of the Dublin Barracks* (Dublin, 1760).

Hiberniae Notitia: Or, A List of the Present Officers in Church and State, and of All Payments to be Made for Civil and Military Affairs For the Kingdom of Ireland, upon the Establishment Which Commenced on the 24th Day of August 1717 ... (London, 1723).

Hogarth, W., *The March to Finchley*, 1749–50 (Oil on canvas).

—, *The Invasion, Plate 2: England*, 8 March 1756 (Etching and engraving on paper).

[Jephson, R.], *Considerations upon the Augmentation of the Army. Addressed to the Public* (Dublin, 1768).

Lawrence, R., *The Interest of Ireland in its Trade and Wealth Stated. In Two Parts* (Dublin, 1682).

Letters on the Impolicy of a Standing Army, in Time of Peace. And, on the Unconstitutional and Illegal Measure of Barracks ... (London, 1793).

Lewis, R., *The Dublin Guide: Or A Description of the City of Dublin, and the Most Remarkable Places within Fifteen Miles ...* (Dublin, 1787).

London Chronicle (Newspaper: 1762).

Lucas, C., *To the Right Honourable the Lord Mayor, the Worshipful the Board of Aldermen, The Sheriffs, Commons, Citizens, and Freeholders of Dublin, ... upon the Proposed Augmentation of the Military Establishment* (Dublin, 1768).

[Maxwell, H.], *An Essay upon an Union of Ireland with England: Most humbly Offered to the Consideration of the Queen's Most Excellent Majesty and Both Houses of Parliament* (Dublin, 1704).

Mayart, Sir S., 'Serjeant Mayart's Answer to a Book Intitled, A Declaration ...', in W. Harris, *Hibernica. Part II. Or, Two Treatises Relating to Ireland* (Dublin, 1770), pp. 47–231.

Modus tenendi Parliamenta et consilia in Hibernia. Published out of an Antient Record by the Right Reverend Father in God, Anthony, Lord Bishop of Meath. To Which is Added the Rules and Customs of the House, Gathered out of the Journal Books from the Time of Edward the Sixth. By H.S.E. C.P. (Dublin, 1692).

Molyneux, W., *The Case of Ireland's Being Bound by Acts of Parliament in England, Stated* (Dublin, 1698).

Moyle, W., *The Second Part of an Argument, Shewing, That a Standing Army Is Inconsistent with A Free Government, and Absolutely Destructive to the Constitution of the English Monarchy* (London, 1697).

O'Callaghan, J. C., *History of the Irish Brigades in the Service of France* (Glasgow: Cameron & Ferguson, 1870).

Prior, M., *A New Answer to an Argument against a Standing Army* ([London], 1697).

Reasons for an Augmentation of the Army on the Irish Establishment, Offered to the Consideration of the Public (Dublin, 1768).

Reasons for Building of Barracks; Disencumbering the Inn-Keepers and Publicans; Restoring Discipline to the Army; and A Right Understanding between the Soldiers and the People ... (London, 1756).

Reasons for Regulating the Coin, and Reducing the Interest; With a Scheme for Paying Part of the National Debt without Burthening Ireland ([Dublin], 1731).

Reflections on the National Debt; With Reasons for the Reducing the Legal Interest; And against a Public Loan. With Some Advice to the Electors of Members of Parliament ([Dublin], 1731).

Rules, Orders, Powers, and Directions, for the Good Government and Preservation of the Barracks and Redoubts, for Quartering the Army in Ireland (Dublin, 1701).

Rules, Orders, Powers, and Directions, for the Good Government and Preservation of the Barracks and Redoubts for Quartering the Army in Ireland (Dublin, 1726).

Some Impartial Observations on the Proposed Augmentation. By a Country Gentleman (Dublin, 1768).

Supplement [London] (Newspaper: 1708).

[Swift, J.], *A Letter to the Shopkeepers, Tradesmen, Farmers and Common-People of Ireland, Concerning the Brass Half-Pence Coined by Mr Woods, with a Design to Have Them Pass in This Kingdom* (Dublin, 1724).

[—], *A Letter to the Whole People of Ireland. By M.B. Drapier* (Dublin, 1724).

[—], *Seasonable Advice* ([Dublin,] 1724).

—, *The Story of the Injured Lady. Being a True Picture of Scotch Perfidy, Irish Poverty, and English Partiality* (London, 1746).

The Acts of That Short Session of Parliament Held in Dublin, May 7, 1689. Under the Late King James II (Dublin, 1756).

The Argument against a Standing Army, Discussed. By a True Lover of His Country (London, 1698).

The Cabinet: Containing, A Collection of Curious Papers, Relative to the Present Political Contests in Ireland; Some of Which Are Now First Published (London, 1754).

The Groans of Ireland. Humbly Address'd to the L—rds and C—mm—s of This Kingdom. With Some Interesting Arguments in Behalf of the Right Honourable the Earl of K—d—e ([Dublin], 1753).

The History and Antiquities of the City of Dublin, from the Earliest Accounts ... (Dublin, 1766).

The History and Proceedings of the House of Commons 1660–1743, 14 vols (London, 1742–4).

The Patriot; Or, The Irish Packet Open'd (London, [1753?]).

The Public Register: Or, Freeman's Journal (Newspaper: 1767–9).

The Quarters of the Army in Ireland in 1744 (1745, 1748–52). To Which Is Added, the Succession of Colonels to All His Majesty's Land Forces and Marines ... (Dublin, 1744–52).

The Representation of the L[ord]s J[ustice]s of Ireland, Touching the Transmission of a Privy Council Money Bill Previous to the Calling of a New Parliament in Two Letters. Addressed to His Grace the Duke of Bedford (Dublin, 1770).

Toland, J., *Reasons Most Humbly Offered to the Honourable House of Commons, Why the Bill Sent Down to Them from the Most Honourable House of Lords, Entituled, An Act for the Better Securing the Dependency of the Kingdom of Ireland upon the Crown of Great Britain, Should Not Pass into a Law* (London, 1720).

To the Nobility, Gentry and Commonalty of this Kingdom of Ireland ([Dublin], 1720).

Trenchard, J., *An Argument Shewing, That a Standing Army Is Inconsistent with A Free Government, and Absolutely Destructive to the Constitution of the English Monarchy* (London, 1697).

—, *An Argument Shewing, that a Standing Army Is Inconsistent with A Free Government, and Absolutely Destructive to the Constitution of the English Monarchy*, 2nd edn (London, 1698).

—, *A Short History of Standing Armies in England* (London, 1731).

Walsh, P., *The History and Vindication of the Loyal Formulary, or Irish Remonstrance, So Graciously Received by HM Anno 1661 against All Calumnies and Censures in Several Treatises* (London, 1674).

Secondary Sources

Books and Articles

Akenson, D. H., *The Irish Diaspora: A Primer* (Belfast: Institute of Irish Studies, 1993).

Anderson, F., *Crucible of War: The Seven Years War and the Fate of Empire in British North America 1754–1766* (London: Faber & Faber, 2000).

Anderson, V. D., 'New England in the Seventeenth Century', in N. Canny (ed.), *The Oxford History of the British Empire, vol. I: The Origins of Empire* (Oxford: Oxford University Press, 1998), pp. 193–217.

Andrews, J. H., *Shapes of Ireland: Maps and Their Makers 1564–1839* (Dublin: Geography Publications, 1997).

Appleby, J. C., 'War, Politics, and Colonisation, 1558–1625', in N. Canny (ed.), *The Oxford History of the British Empire, vol. I: The Origins of Empire* (Oxford: Oxford University Press, 1998), pp. 55–78.

Armstrong, R., 'Ormond, the Confederate Peace Talks and Protestant Royalism', in M. Ó Siochrú (ed.), *Kingdoms in Crisis: Ireland in the 1640s* (Dublin: Four Courts Press, 2001), pp. 122–40.

Baltes, S., *The Pamphlet Controversy about Wood's Halfpence (1722–25) and the Tradition of Irish Constitutional Nationalism* (Frankfurt: Peter Lang, 2003).

Barnard, T., 'The Government and Irish Dissent, 1704–1780', in K. Herlihy (ed.), *The Politics of Irish Dissent 1650–1800* (Dublin: Four Courts Press, 1997), pp. 9–27.

—, 'New Opportunities for British Settlement: Ireland, 1650–1700', in N. Canny (ed.), *The Oxford History of the British Empire, vol. I: The Origins of Empire* (Oxford: Oxford University Press, 1998), pp. 309–27.

Bartlett, T., 'The Townshend Viceroyalty, 1767–72', in T. Bartlett and D. W. Hayton (eds), *Penal Era and Golden Age: Essays in Irish History, 1690–1800* (Belfast: Ulster Historical Foundation, 1979), pp. 88–112.

—, 'The Irish House of Commons' Rejection of the "Privy Council" Money Bill in 1769: A Re-Assessment', *Studia Hibernica*, 19 (1979), pp. 63–77.

—, 'Opposition in Late Eighteenth-Century Ireland: The Case of the Townshend Viceroyalty', *Irish Historical Studies*, 22 (1980–1), pp. 313–30.

—, 'The Augmentation of the Army in Ireland 1767–1769', *English Historical Review*, 96 (1981), pp. 540–59.

—, 'Army and Society in Eighteenth-Century Ireland', in W. A. Maguire (ed.), *Kings in Conflict: The Revolutionary War in Ireland and Its Aftermath 1689–1750* (Belfast: Ulster Historical Foundation, 1990), pp. 173–82.

—, *The Fall and Rise of the Irish Nation: The Catholic Question, 1690–1830* (Dublin: Gill & Macmillan, 1992).

—, '"A Weapon of War Yet Untried": Irish Catholics and the Armed Forces of the Crown, 1760–1830', in T. G. Fraser and K. Jeffery (eds), *Men, Women and War* (Dublin: Lilliput Press, 1993), pp. 66–85.

—, 'Defence, Counter-Insurgency and Rebellion: Ireland, 1793–1803', in T. Bartlett and K. Jeffery (eds), *A Military History of Ireland* (Cambridge: Cambridge University Press, 1996), pp. 247–93.

—, 'The Irish Soldier in India, 1740–1947', in M. Holmes and D. Holmes (eds.), *Ireland and India: Connections, Comparisons, Contrasts* (Dublin: Folens, 1997), pp. 12–28.

—, 'Ireland, Empire, and Union, 1690–1801', in K. Kenny (ed.), *Ireland and the British Empire* (Oxford: Oxford University Press, 2004), pp. 61–89.

—, *'The Academy of Warre': Military Affairs in Ireland, 1600 to 1800* (Dublin: National University of Ireland, 2002).

—, *Ireland: A History* (Cambridge: Cambridge University Press, 2010).

Bartlett, T., and D. W. Hayton (eds), *Penal Era and Golden Age: Essays in Irish History, 1690–1800* (Belfast: Ulster Historical Foundation, 1979).

Bartlett, T., and K. Jeffery (eds), *A Military History of Ireland* (Cambridge: Cambridge University Press, 1996).

Beckett, J. V., 'Land Tax or Excise: The Levying of Taxation in Seventeenth- and Eighteenth-Century England', *English Historical Review*, 100 (1985), pp. 285–308.

Bell, D. A., 'Culture and Religion', in W. Doyle (ed.), *Old Regime France, 1648–1788* (Oxford: Oxford University Press, 2001), pp. 78–104.

Beresford, M., 'Francois Thurot and the French Attack at Carrickfergus, 1759–60', *Irish Sword*, 10 (1971–2), pp. 255–74.

Bergin, J., E. Magennis, L. Ní Munghaile and P. Walsh (eds), *New Perspectives on the Penal Laws: Eighteenth-Century Ireland Special Issue No. 1* (Dublin: Eighteenth-Century Ireland Society, 2011).

Black, J., *European Warfare 1660–1815* (London: University College London Press, 1994).

Bolton, G. C., *The Passing of the Irish Act of Union* (Oxford: Oxford University Press, 1966).

Bosher, J. F., 'The Franco-Catholic danger, 1660–1715', *History*, 79 (1994), pp. 5–30.

Bossenga, G., 'Society', in W. Doyle (ed.), *Old Regime France, 1648–1788* (Oxford: Oxford University Press, 2001), pp. 42–77.

Boyce, D. G., R. Eccleshall and V. Geoghegan (eds), *Political Discourse in Seventeenth- and Eighteenth-Century Ireland* (Basingstoke: Palgrave, 2001).

Boynton, L., 'Billeting: The Example of the Isle of Wight', *English Historical Review*, 74 (1959), pp. 23–40.

—, 'Martial Law and the Petition of Right', *English Historical Review*, 79 (1964), pp. 255–84.

Braddick, M., *The Nerves of State: Taxation and the financing of the English state, 1558–1714* (Manchester: Manchester University Press, 1996).

Bradley, J., *Irish Historic Towns Atlas: Kilkenny* (Dublin: Royal Irish Academy, 2000).

Bradshaw, B., 'Sword, Word and Strategy in the Reformation in Ireland', *Historical Journal*, 21 (1978), pp. 475–502.

—, *The Irish Constitutional Revolution of the Sixteenth Century* (Cambridge: Cambridge University Press, 1979).

Brady, C., *The Chief Governors: The Rise and Fall of Reform Government in Tudor Ireland, 1536–1588* (Cambridge: Cambridge University Press, 1994).

Brady, C., and J. Ohlmeyer (eds), *British Interventions in Early Modern Ireland* (Cambridge: Cambridge University Press, 2005).

Brand, P., 'The Birth and Early Development of a Colonial Judiciary: The Judges of the Lordship of Ireland, 1210–1377', in W. N. Osborough (ed.), *Explorations in Law and History* (Dublin: Four Courts Press, 1995), pp. 1–48.

Brewer, J., *The Sinews of Power: War, Money and the English State* (London: Unwin Hyman, 1989).

—, 'The Eighteenth-Century British State: Context and issues', in L. Stone (ed.), *An Imperial State at War: Britain from 1689 to 1815* (London: Routledge, 1994), pp. 52–71.

Bric, M. J., *Ireland, Philadelphia and the re-invention of America, 1760–1800* (Dublin: Four Courts Press, 2008).

Brown, M., C. I. McGrath and T. P. Power, T. P. (eds), *Converts and Conversion in Ireland, 1650–1850* (Dublin: Four Courts Press, 2005).

—, 'Introduction: Converts and Conversion in Ireland', in M. Brown, C. I. McGrath and T. P. Power (eds), *Converts and Conversion in Ireland, 1650–1850* (Dublin: Four Courts Press, 2005), pp. 11–34.

Brumwell, S., 'Wade, G. (1673–1748)', *ODNB*, at <http://www.oxforddnb.com/view/article/28377>.

Buchanan, R. H., *Irish Historic Towns Atlas: Downpatrick* (Dublin: Royal Irish Academy, 1997).

Bullion, J. L., 'The Ten Thousand in America: More Light on the Decision on the American Army, 1762–3', *William and Mary Quarterly*, 43 (1986), pp. 646–57.

—, 'Security and Economy: The Bute Administration's Plans for the American Army and Revenue, 1762–3', *William and Mary Quarterly*, 45 (1988), pp. 499–509.

Burke, J., 'Limerick in the Golden Age of Siege Warfare', in B. Whelan (ed.), *The Last of the Great Wars: Essays on the War of the Three Kings in Ireland 1688–91* (Limerick: University of Limerick Press, 1995), pp. 83–107.

Burke, W. P., *The Irish Priests in the Penal Times (1660–1760)* (Shannon: Irish University Press, 1969).

Burns, R. E., *Irish Parliamentary Politics in the Eighteenth Century*, 2 vols (Washington, DC: Catholic University of America Press, 1989–90).

Butler, D. J., 'Defence from the Dispossessed: The State-Sponsored Garrisoning of the South Tipperary Landscape, c. 1650– c. 1730', *Irish Sword*, 24 (2004), pp. 45–56.

Canny, N., *Kingdom and Colony: Ireland in the Atlantic World* (Baltimore, MD: Johns Hopkins University Press, 1988).

—. (ed.), *The Oxford History of the British Empire, vol. I: The Origins of Empire* (Oxford: Oxford University Press, 1998).

—, 'The Origins of Empire: An Introduction', in N. Canny (ed.), *The Oxford History of the British Empire, vol. I: The Origins of Empire* (Oxford: Oxford University Press, 1998), pp. 1–33.

—, *Making Ireland British 1580–1650* (Oxford: Oxford University Press, 2001).

Carter, C. E., 'The Significance of the Military Office in America, 1763–1775', *American Historical Review*, 28 (1923), pp. 475–88.

Chandaman, C. D., *The English Public Revenue 1660–1688* (Oxford: Oxford University Press, 1975).

Childs, J., *The Army, James II, and the Glorious Revolution* (Manchester: Manchester University Press, 1980).

—, *Armies and Warfare in Europe 1648–1789* (New York: Holmes & Meier, 1982).

—, 'The Williamite War, 1689–1691', in T. Bartlett and K. Jeffery (eds), *A Military History of Ireland* (Cambridge: Cambridge University Press, 1996), pp. 188–210.

Christianson, P., 'Arguments on Billeting and Martial Law in the Parliament of 1628', *Historical Journal*, 37 (1994), pp. 539–67.

Claffey, J. A., *Irish Historic Towns Atlas: Tuam* (Dublin: Royal Irish Academy, 2009).

Clarke, A., 'The History of Poynings' Law, 1615–41', *Irish Historical Studies*, 18 (1972–3), pp. 207–22.

—, 'Colonial Constitutional Attitudes in Ireland, 1640–60', *Proceedings of the Royal Irish Academy*, 90, section C (1990), pp. 357–75.

—, *Prelude to Restoration in Ireland: The End of the Commonwealth, 1659–1660* (Cambridge: Cambridge University Press, 1999).

—, 'Patrick Darcy and the Constitutional Relationship between Ireland and Britain', in J. Ohlmeyer (ed.), *Political Thought in Seventeenth-Century Ireland* (Cambridge: Cambridge University Press, 2000), pp. 35–55.

—, *The Old English in Ireland, 1625–42* (Dublin: Four Courts Press, 2000).

Clode, C. M., *The Military Forces of the Crown: Their Administration and Government*, 2 vols (London: John Murray, 1869).

Cokayne, G. E., *The Complete Peerage of England, Scotland, Ireland, Great Britain and the United Kingdom, extant, extinct or dormant*, rev. by Vicary Gibbs, Geoffrey White, and R. S. Lea, 12 vols (London: The St. Catherine Press, 1910–59).

Colley, L., *Britons: Forging the Nation 1707–1837*, 3rd edn (London: Pimlico, 2003).

—, *Captives: Britain, Empire and the World, 1600–1850* (London: Pimlico, 2003).

Connolly, S. J., *Religion, Law and Power: The Making of Protestant Ireland 1660–1760* (Oxford: Clarendon Press, 1992).

—, 'The Defence of Protestant Ireland, 1660–1760', in T. Bartlett and K. Jeffery (eds), *A Military History of Ireland* (Cambridge: Cambridge University Press, 1996), pp. 231–45.

— (ed.), *Political Ideas in Eighteenth-Century Ireland* (Dublin: Four Courts Press, 2000).

—, 'Precedent and Principle: The Patriots and their Critics', in S. J. Connolly (ed.), *Political Ideas in Eighteenth-Century Ireland* (Dublin: Four Courts Press, 2000), pp. 130–58.

—, 'The Glorious Revolution in Irish Protestant Thinking', in S. J. Connolly (ed.), *Political Ideas in Eighteenth-Century Ireland* (Dublin: Four Courts Press, 2000), pp. 27–63.

—, *Contested Island: Ireland 1460–1630* (Oxford: Oxford University Press, 2009).

—, *Divided Kingdom: Ireland 1630–1800* (Oxford: Oxford University Press, 2010).

Conway, A., *Henry VII's Relations with Scotland and Ireland 1485–1498. With a Chapter on the Acts of the Poynings Parliament 1494–95 by Edmund Curtis* (Cambridge: Cambridge University Press, 1932).

Conway, S., *War, State, and Society in Mid-Eighteenth-Century Britain and Ireland* (Oxford: Oxford University Press, 2006).

Cosgrove, A., 'Parliament and the Anglo-Irish Community: The Declaration of 1460', in A. Cosgrove and J. I McGuire (eds), *Parliament and Community* (Belfast: Ulster Historical Foundation, 1983), pp. 25–42.

— (ed.), *A New History of Ireland, II: Medieval Ireland 1169–1534* (Oxford: Oxford University Press, 1987).

Costello, K., *The Court of Admiralty of Ireland 1575–1893* (Dublin: Four Courts Press, 2011).

Coward, B., *The Stuart Age: England 1603–1714*, 3rd edn (London: Longman, 2003).

Coyle, E. A., 'Talbot's Fencibles and the Drogheda Mutiny', *Journal of the County Louth Archaeological and Historical Studies*, 24 (1997), pp. 39–50.

Crawford, J. G., *A Star Chamber Court in Ireland: The Court of Castle Chamber, 1571–1641* (Dublin: Four Courts Press, 2005).

Creighton, A., 'The Remonstrance of December 1661 and Catholic Politics in Restoration Ireland', *Irish Historical Society*, 34 (2004–5), pp. 16–41.

Cullen, L. M., 'Landlords, Bankers and Merchants: The Early Irish Banking World, 1700–1820', in A. E. Murphy (ed.), *Economists and the Irish Economy from the Eighteenth Century to the Present Day* (Dublin: Irish Academic Press, 1984), pp. 25–44.

—, 'Catholics under the Penal Laws', *Eighteenth Century Ireland*, 1 (1986), pp. 23–36.

—, *An Economic History of Ireland since 1660*, 2nd edn (London: B. T. Batsford Ltd, 1993).

—, 'The Irish Diaspora of the Seventeenth and Eighteenth Centuries', in N. Canny (ed.), *Europeans on the Move: Studies on European Migration, 1500–1800* (Oxford: Clarendon Press, 1994), pp. 113–49.

Curtis, E. and R. B. McDowell (eds), *Irish Historical Documents 1172–1922* (London: Methuen, 1943).

Davies, G., 'Swift's *The Story of the Injured Lady*', *Huntington Library Quarterly*, 6 (1943), pp. 473–89.

Davies, K. M., *Irish Historic Towns Atlas: Bray* (Dublin: Royal Irish Academy, 1998).

Davis, R., *The Rise of the Atlantic Economies* (New York: Cornell University Press, 1973).

Davis, T., *The Patriot Parliament of 1689*, ed. C. G. Duffy (London: T. Fisher Unwin, 1893).

Denman, T., '"*Hibernia officina militum*': Irish recruitment to the British regular army, 1660–1815', *Irish Sword*, 20 (1996–7), pp. 148–66.

Devine, T. M., *The Scottish Nation, 1700–2000* (London: Penguin, 2000).

—, *Scotland's Empire, 1600–1815* (London: Penguin, 2003).

Dickson, D., *New Foundations: Ireland 1660–1800* (Dublin: Helicon, 1987).

—, *Old World Colony: Cork and South Munster 1630–1830* (Cork: Cork University Press, 2005).

Dickson, P. G. M., *The Financial Revolution in England: A Study in the Development of Public Credit 1688–1756* (London: Macmillan, 1967).

Dictionary of Irish Architects 1720–1940 (electronic database, Dublin, 2011).

Dictionary of Irish Biography (Cambridge: Cambridge University Press, 2009).

Doherty, R., *The Williamite War in Ireland 1688–1691* (Dublin: Four Courts Press, 1998).

Donlan, S. P., 'Brooke, Henry', *DIB*, at <http://dib.cambridge.org/viewReadPage.do?articleId=a0990>.

Donovan, R. K., 'The Military Origins of the Roman Catholic Relief Programme of 1778', *Historical Journal*, 28 (1985), pp. 79–102.

Doran, L. (ed.), *Irish Historic Towns Atlas: New Ross* (Dublin: Royal Irish Academy, forthcoming).

Douet, J., *British Barracks 1600–1914: Their Architecture and Role in Society* (London: Stationery Office, 1998).

Downey, D. M., 'Accommodations with the Protestant State and Church: A Comparative Study of Respective Dutch and Irish Catholic Experiences', in J. Bergin, E. Magennis, L. Ní Munghaile and P. Walsh (eds), *New Perspectives on the Penal Laws: Eighteenth-Century Ireland Special Issue No. 1* (Dublin: Eighteenth-Century Ireland Society, 2011), pp. 75–92.

Doyle, W. (ed.), *Old Regime France, 1648–1788* (Oxford: Oxford University Press, 2001).

Dudley Edwards, Robin, *Church and State in Tudor Ireland: A History of Penal Laws against Irish Catholics 1534–1603* (London: Longman, 1935).

Dudley Edwards, Robin, and T. W. Moody, 'The Early Interpretation of Poynings' Law: Part 1, 1494–1615', *Irish Historical Studies*, 2 (1940–1), pp. 415–24.

Dudley Edwards, Ruth, *An Atlas of Irish History*, 3rd edn (London: Routledge, 2005).

Duffy, E., *The Stripping of the Altars: Traditional Religion in England c.1400–c.1580* (New Haven, CT: Yale University Press, 1992).

Duffy, S., *Ireland in the Middle Ages* (Dublin: Gill & Macmillan, 1997).

Edie, C. A., 'The Irish Cattle Bills: A Study in Restoration Politics', *Transactions of the American Philosophical Society*, new series, 60 (1970), pp. 1–66.

Edwards, P., 'Logistics and Supply', in J. Kenyon and J. Ohlmeyer (eds), *The Civil Wars: A Military History of England, Scotland, and Ireland 1638–1660* (Oxford: Oxford University Press, 1998), pp. 234–71.

Elton, G. R., *The Tudor Constitution: Documents and Commentary*, 2nd edn (Cambridge: Cambridge University Press, 1982).

Fagan, P., *Divided Loyalties: The Question of an Oath for Irish Catholics in the Eighteenth Century* (Dublin: Four Courts Press, 1997).

Ferguson, N., *Empire: How Britain Made Modern Europe* (London: Penguin, 2004).

Fields, W. S., and D. T. Hardy, 'The Third Amendment and the Issue of the Maintenance of Standing Armies: A Legal History', *The American Journal of Legal History*, 35 (1991), pp. 393–431.

Fitzpatrick, D., *Irish Emigration 1801–1921* (Dublin: Economic and Social History Society of Ireland, 1984).

Flaherty, M. S., 'The Empire Strikes Back: *Annesley V. Sherlock* and the Triumph of Imperial Parliamentary Supremacy', *Columbia Law Review*, 87 (1987), pp. 593–622.

Fleming, D., *Politics and Provincial People: Sligo and Limerick, 1691–1761* (Manchester: Manchester University Press, 2010).

Ford, A., 'The Church of Ireland, 1558–1624: A Puritan Church?', in A. Ford, J. I. McGuire and K. Milne (eds), *As by Law Established: The Church of Ireland since the Reformation* (Dublin: Lilliput Press, 1995), pp. 52–68.

—, *The Protestant Reformation in Ireland, 1590–1641* (Dublin: Four Courts Press, 1997).

Garnham, N., 'Ireland's Protestant Militia, 1715–76: A Military Assessment', *Irish Sword*, 20 (1996–7), pp. 131–6.

—., 'Military Desertion and Deserters in Eighteenth-Century Ireland', *Eighteenth Century Ireland*, 20 (2005), pp. 91–103.

—., 'Defending the Kingdom and Preserving the Constitution: Irish Militia Legislation 1692–1793', in D. W. Hayton, J. Kelly and J. Bergin (eds), *The Eighteenth-Century Composite State: Representative Institutions in Ireland and Europe, 1689–1800* (Basingstoke: Palgrave, 2010), pp. 107–35.

Gearty, S., M. Morris and F. O'Ferrall, *Irish Historic Towns Atlas: Longford* (Dublin: Royal Irish Academy, 2009).

Gentles, I., *The English Revolution and the Wars of the Three Kingdoms 1638–1652* (London: Longman, 2007).

Geoghegan, P. M., *The Irish Act of Union* (Dublin: Gill & Macmillan, 1999).

Gibney, J., 'Robinson, Sir William', *DIB*, at <http://dib.cambridge.org/viewReadPage.do?articleId=a7736>.

Gillespie, R., *The Transformation of the Irish Economy 1550–1700* (Dublin: Economic and Social History Society of Ireland, 1991).

—, *Seventeenth-Century Ireland: Making Ireland Modern* (Dublin: Gill and Macmillan, 2006).

Gillespie, R., and S. Royle, *Irish Historic Towns Atlas: Belfast, part 1 to 1840* (Dublin: Royal Irish Academy, 2003).

Goodwin, A., 'Wood's Halfpence', *English Historical Review*, 51 (1936), pp. 647–74.

Gray, P., and O. Purdue (eds), *The Irish Lord Lieutenancy c. 1541–1922* (Dublin: UCD Press, forthcoming 2012).

Greene, J. P., *Peripheries and Center: Constitutional Development in the Extended Polities of the British Empire and the United States, 1607–1788* (Athens, GA: University of Georgia Press, 1986).

— (ed.), *Exclusionary Empire: English Liberty Overseas, 1600–1900* (Cambridge: Cambridge University Press, 2010).

—, 'Introduction: Empire and Liberty', in J. P. Greene (ed.), *Exclusionary Empire: English Liberty Overseas, 1600–1900* (Cambridge: Cambridge University Press, 2010), pp. 1–24.

Guy, A. J., 'A Whole Army Absolutely Ruined in Ireland: Aspects of the Irish Establishment', *Annual Report of the National Army Museum* (1978–9), pp. 30–43.

—, *Oeconomy and Discipline: Officership and Administration in the British Army 1714–63* (Manchester: Manchester University Press, 1985).

—, 'The Irish Military Establishment, 1660–1776', in T. Bartlett and K. Jeffery (eds), *A Military History of Ireland* (Cambridge: Cambridge University Press, 1996), pp. 211–30.

Hall, F. G., *The Bank of Ireland, 1783–1946* (Dublin: Hodges Figgis, 1949).

Harris, B., *Politics and the Nation: Britain in the Mid-Eighteenth Century* (Oxford: Oxford University Press, 2002).

Harvey, K., *The Bellews of Mount Bellew: A Catholic Gentry Family in Eighteenth-Century Ireland* (Dublin: Four Courts Press, 1998).

Hayton, D. W., 'Constitutional Experiments and Political Expediency, 1689–1725', in S. G. Ellis and S. Barber (eds), *Conquest and Union: Fashioning a British State 1485–1725* (London: Longman, 1995), pp. 276–305.

—, 'Exclusion, Conformity, and Parliamentary Representation: The Impact of the Sacramental Test on Irish Dissenting Politics', in K. Herlihy (ed.), *The Politics of Irish Dissent 1650–1800* (Dublin: Four Courts Press, 1997), pp. 52–73.

—, 'The Stanhope/Sunderland Ministry and the Repudiation of Irish Parliamentary Independence', *English Historical Review*, 113 (1998), pp. 610–36.

—, 'Ideas of Union in Anglo-Irish Political Discourse, 1692–1720: Meaning and Use', in D. G. Boyce, R. Eccleshall and V. Geoghegan (eds), *Political Discourse in Seventeenth- and Eighteenth-Century Ireland* (Basingstoke: Palgrave 2001), pp. 142–68.

—, 'Introduction: The Long Apprenticeship', *Parliamentary History*, 20 (2001), pp. 1–26.

—, *Ruling Ireland, 1685–1742: Politics, Politicians and Parties* (Woodbridge: Boydell and Brewer, 2004).

—, 'Henry Maxwell, M.P., Author of *an Essay upon an Union of Ireland with England* (1703)', *Eighteenth Century Ireland*, 22 (2007), pp. 28–63.

Hayton, D. W., J. Kelly and J. Bergin (eds), *The Eighteenth-Century Composite State: Representative Institutions in Ireland and Europe, 1689–1800* (Basingstoke: Palgrave, 2010).

Hayton, D. W., and J. Kelly, 'The Irish Parliament in European Context: A Representative Institution in a Composite State', in D. W. Hayton, J. Kelly and J. Bergin (eds), *The Eighteenth-Century Composite State: Representative Institutions in Ireland and Europe, 1689–1800* (Basingstoke: Palgrave, 2010), pp. 3–16.

Herlihy, K. (ed.), *The Politics of Irish Dissent 1650–1800* (Dublin: Four Courts Press, 1997).

Hill, J., 'Ireland without Union: Molyneux and His Legacy', in J. Robertson (ed.), *A Union for Empire: Political Thought and the British Union of 1707* (Cambridge: Cambridge University Press, 1995), pp. 271–96.

—, '"Allegories, Fictions, and Feigned Representations": Decoding the Money Bill Dispute', *Eighteenth Century Ireland*, 21 (2006), pp. 66–88.

Holmes, G., *British Politics in the Age of Anne*, revised edn (London: Hambledon Press, 1987).

Hoppit, J., *A Land of Liberty? England 1689–1727* (Oxford: Oxford University Press, 2000).

Horn, J., 'Tobacco Colonies: The Shaping of English Society in the Seventeenth-Century Chesapeake', in N. Canny (ed.), *The Oxford History of the British Empire, vol. I: The Origins of Empire* (Oxford: Oxford University Press, 1998), pp. 170–92.

—, 'British Diaspora: Emigration from Britain, 1680–1815', in P. J. Marshall (ed.), *The Oxford History of the British Empire, vol. II: The Eighteenth Century* (Oxford: Oxford University Press, 1998), pp. 28–52.

Horwitz, H., *Parliament, Policy and Politics in the Reign of William III* (Manchester: Manchester University Press, 1977).

Houlding, J. A., Fit for Service: *The Training of the British Army, 1715–1795* (Oxford: Clarendon Press, 1981).

Houston, C. J., and W. J. Smyth, *Irish Emigration and Canadian Settlement: Patterns, Links and Letters* (Belfast: Ulster Historical Foundation, 1990).

Howe, S., *Ireland and Empire: Colonial Legacies in Irish History and Culture* (Oxford: Oxford University Press, 2000).

Ingram, T. D., *A History of the Legislative Union of Great Britain and Ireland* (London: Macmillan, 1887).

Ives, E. W., 'Fortescue, Sir John (c.1397–1479)', *ODNB*, at <http://www.oxforddnb.com/view/article/9944>.

Jackson, A., 'Ireland, the Union, and the Empire, 1800–1960', in K. Kenny (ed.), *Ireland and the British Empire* (Oxford: Oxford University Press, 2004), pp. 123–53.

Jackson, R. W., 'Queen Anne's Irish Army Establishment in 1704', *Irish Sword*, 1 (1949–53), pp. 133–5.

James, F. G., 'The Irish Lobby in the Early Eighteenth Century', *English Historical Review*, 81 (1966), pp. 543–57.

—, *Ireland in the Empire 1688–1770* (Cambridge, MA: Harvard University Press, 1973).

—, 'Historiography and the Irish Constitutional Revolution of 1782', *Éire-Ireland*, 18 (1983), pp. 6–16.

—, 'Illustrious or Notorious? The Historical Reputation of Ireland's Pre-Union Parliament', *Parliamentary History*, 6 (1987), pp. 312–25.

—, *Lords of the Ascendancy: The Irish House of Lords and Its Members, 1600–1800* (Dublin: Irish Academic Press, 1995).

Jeffery, K., 'Introduction', in K. Jeffery (ed.), *'An Irish Empire'? Aspects of Ireland and the British Empire* (Manchester: Manchester University Press, 1996), pp. 1–24.

Johnston, J., 'Berkeley and the Abortive Bank Project of 1720–21', in J. Johnston (ed.), *Bishop Berkeley's Querist in Historical Perspective* (Dundalk: Dundalgan Press, 1970), pp. 44–51.

Johnston, S. H .F., 'The Irish Establishment', *Irish Sword*, 1 (1949–53), pp. 33–6.

—, 'The Scots Army in the Reign of Anne', *Transactions of the Royal Historical Society*, 5th series, 3 (1953), pp. 1–21.

Johnston, W. J., 'The First Adventure of the Common Law', *Law Quarterly Review*, 36 (1920), pp. 9–30.

Johnston-Liik, E. M., *History of the Irish Parliament 1692–1800: Commons, Constituencies and Statutes*, 6 vols (Belfast: Ulster Historical Foundation, 2002).

Kearney, H. F., 'The Political Background to English Mercantilism, 1695–1700', *Economic History Review*, 2nd series, 11 (1958–9), pp. 484–96.

Kelly, J., 'The Origins of the Act of Union: An Examination of Unionist Opinion in Britain and Ireland, 1650–1800', *Irish Historical Studies*, 25 (1986–7), pp. 236–63.

—, *Prelude to Union: Anglo-Irish Politics in the 1780s* (Cork: Cork University Press, 1992).

—, 'Harvests and Hardship: Famine and Scarcity in Ireland in the Late 1720s', *Studia Hibernica*, 26 (1992), pp. 65–105.

—, *'That Damn'd Thing Called Honour': Duelling in Ireland 1570–1860* (Cork: Cork University Press, 1995).

—, '1780 Revisited: The Politics of the Repeal of the Sacramental Test', in K. Herlihy (ed.), *The Politics of Irish Dissent 1650–1800* (Dublin: Four Courts Press, 1997), pp. 74–92.

—, *Henry Flood: Patriots and Politics in Eighteenth-Century Ireland* (Dublin: Four Courts Press, 1998).

—, 'Monitoring the Constitution: The Operation of Poynings' Law in the 1760s', *Parliamentary History*, 20 (2001), pp. 87–106.

—, 'Public and Political opinion in Ireland and the Idea of an Anglo-Irish Union, 1650–1800', in D. G. Boyce, R. Eccleshall and V. Geoghegan (eds), *Political Discourse in Seventeenth- and Eighteenth-Century Ireland* (Basingstoke: Palgrave, 2001), pp. 110–41.

—, 'The Conversion Experience: The Case of Fr James O'Farrell, OP, 1785–7', in M. Brown, C. I. McGrath, and T. P. Power (eds), *Converts and Conversion in Ireland, 1650–1850* (Dublin: Four Courts Press, 2005), pp. 214–36.

—, 'The Making of Law in Eighteenth-Century Ireland: The Significance and Import of Poynings' Law', in N. M. Dawson (ed.), *Reflections on Law and History* (Dublin: Four Courts Press, 2006), pp. 259–77.

—, *Poynings' Law and the Making of Law in Ireland 1660–1800* (Dublin: Four Courts Press, 2007).

—, 'Sustaining a Confessional State: The Irish Parliament and Catholicism', in D. W. Hayton, J. Kelly and J. Bergin (eds), *The Eighteenth-Century Composite State: Representative Institutions in Ireland and Europe, 1689–1800* (Basingstoke: Palgrave, 2010), pp. 44–77.

—, '"Era of Liberty": The Politics of Civil and Political Rights in Eighteenth-Century Ireland', in J. P. Greene (ed.), *Exclusionary Empire: English Liberty Overseas, 1600–1900* (Cambridge: Cambridge University Press, 2010), pp. 77–111.

—, 'The Historiography of the Penal Laws', in J. Bergin, E. Magennis, L. Ní Munghaile and P. Walsh (eds), *New Perspectives on the Penal Laws: Eighteenth-Century Ireland Special Issue No. 1* (Dublin: Eighteenth-Century Ireland Society, 2011), pp. 27–54.

Kelly, P., 'The Irish Woollen Export Prohibition Act of 1699: Kearney Re-visited', *Irish Economic and Social History*, 7 (1980), pp. 22–44.

—, 'William Molyneux and the Spirit of Liberty in Eighteenth-Century Ireland', *Eighteenth Century Ireland*, 3 (1988), pp. 133–48.

—, 'Recasting a Tradition: William Molyneux and the Sources of *The Case of Ireland ... Stated* (1698)', in J. Ohlmeyer (ed.), *Political Thought in Seventeenth-Century Ireland* (Cambridge: Cambridge University Press, 2000), pp. 83–106.

—, 'The Politics of Political Economy in Mid-Eighteenth-Century Ireland', in S. J. Connolly (ed.), *Political Ideas in Eighteenth-Century Ireland* (Dublin: Four Courts Press, 2000), pp. 105–29.

—, 'Conquest *versus* Consent as the Basis of the English Title to Ireland in William Molyneux's *Case of Ireland ... Stated* (1698)', in C. Brady and J. Ohlmeyer. (eds), *British Interventions in Early Modern Ireland* (Cambridge: Cambridge University Press, 2005), pp. 334–56.

—, 'Sir Richard Bolton and the Authorship of "A Declaration setting forth, How, and by what Means, the Laws and Statutes of England, from Time to Time, Came to be of Force in Ireland", 1644', *Irish Historical Studies*, 35 (2006), pp. 1–16.

Kennedy, W., *English Taxation 1640–1799* (London: G. Bell & Sons, 1913).

Kenny, C., 'The Exclusion of Catholics from the Legal Profession in Ireland, 1537–1829', *Irish Historical Studies*, 25 (1986–7), pp. 337–57.

Kenny, K., *The American Irish: A History* (London: Longman, 2000).

— (ed.), *Ireland and the British Empire* (Oxford: Oxford University Press, 2004).

—, 'The Irish in the Empire', in K. Kenny (ed.), *Ireland and the British Empire* (Oxford: Oxford University Press, 2004), pp. 95–122.

Kenyon, J. P. (ed.), *The Stuart Constitution 1603–1688: Documents and Commentary* (Cambridge: Cambridge University Press, 1966).

Kerrigan, P. M., *Castles and Fortifications in Ireland 1485–1945* (Cork: Collins Press, 1995).

Kiernan, T. J., *A History of the Financial Administration of Ireland to 1817* (London: P. S. King & Son, 1930).

Kilroy, P., *Protestant Dissent and Controversy in Ireland 1660–1714* (Cork: Cork University Press, 1994).

Kinsella, E., 'In Pursuit of a Positive Construction: Irish Catholics and the Williamite Articles of Surrender, 1690–1701', *Eighteenth Century Ireland*, 24 (2009), pp. 11–35.

Kirkham, G., 'The Origins of Mass Emigration from Ireland', in R. Kearney (ed.), *Migrations: The Irish at Home and Abroad* (Dublin: Wolfhound, 1990), pp. 81–90.

Lammey, D., 'The Growth of the 'Patriot Opposition', in Ireland during the 1770s', *Parliamentary History*, 7 (1988), pp. 257–81.

Lawson, P., *The East India Company: A History* (London: Longman, 1987).

Leerssen, J., 'Anglo-Irish Patriotism and its European Context: Notes Towards a Reassessment', *Eighteenth Century Ireland*, 3 (1988), pp. 7–24.

—, *Mere Irish and Fíor-Ghael: Studies in the Idea of Irish Nationality, its Development and Literary Expression prior to the Nineteenth Century*, 2nd edn (Cork: Cork University Press, 1996).

—, 'Brooke, Henry', *ODNB*, at <http://www.oxforddnb.com/view/printable/3545>.

Lenman, B. P., 'Colonial Wars and Imperial Instability, 1688–1793', in P. J. Marshall (ed.), *The Oxford History of the British Empire, vol. II: The Eighteenth Century* (Oxford: Oxford University Press, 1998), pp. 151–68.

Lennon, C., *Sixteenth-Century Ireland: The Incomplete Conquest* (Dublin: Gill and Macmillan, 1994).

—, *Irish Historic Towns Atlas: Dublin Part II, 1610 to 1756* (Dublin: Royal Irish Academy, 2010).

Little, P., 'The English Parliament and the Irish Constitution, 1641–9', in M. Ó Siochrú (ed.), *Kingdoms in Crisis: Ireland in the 1640s* (Dublin: Four Courts Press, 2001), pp. 106–21.

Luttrell, N., *A Brief Historical Relation of State Affairs from September 1678 to April 1714*, 6 vols (Oxford: Oxford University Press, 1857).

Lyons, M. A., 'FitzGerald, Gerald (Gearóid Mór) 8th Earl of Kildare', *DIB*, at <http://dib.cambridge.org/viewReadPage.do?articleId=a3148>.

MacDonagh, J. C. T., 'An Eighteenth-Century Redoubt in County Donegal', *Irish Sword*, 1 (1949–53), pp. 338–40.

Magennis, E., *The Irish Political System, 1740–1765: The Golden Age of the Undertakers* (Dublin: Four Courts Press, 2000).

—, 'Coal, Corn and Canals: The Dispersal of Public Moneys, 1695–1772', *Parliamentary History*, 20 (2001), pp. 71–86.

—, 'Fitzgerald, James, 20th Earl of Kildare, 1st Duke of Leinster', *DIB*, at <http://dib.cambridge.org/viewReadPage.do?articleId=a3157>.

—, 'Select Document: "The Present State of Ireland", 1749', *Irish Historical Studies*, 36 (2009), pp. 581–97.

Maguire, W. A. (ed.), *Kings in Conflict: The Revolutionary War in Ireland and Its Aftermath 1689–1750* (Belfast: Ulster Historical Foundation, 1990).

Mahony, R., *Jonathan Swift: The Irish Identity* (New Haven, CT: Yale University Press, 1995).

Malcomson, A. P. W., *Archbishop Charles Agar: Churchmanship and Politics in Ireland, 1760–1810* (Dublin: Four Courts Press, 2002).

—, *Nathanial Clements: Government and the Governing Elite in Ireland, 1725–75* (Dublin: Four Courts Press, 2005).

Mancke, E., 'The Languages of Liberty in British North America, 1607–1776', in J. P. Greene (ed.), *Exclusionary Empire: English Liberty Overseas, 1600–1900* (Cambridge: Cambridge University Press, 2010), pp. 25–49.

Marshall. P. J. (ed.), *The Oxford History of the British Empire, vol. II: The Eighteenth Century* (Oxford: Oxford University Press, 1998).

—, 'The English in Asia to 1700', in N. Canny (ed.), *The Oxford History of the British Empire, vol. I: The Origins of Empire* (Oxford: Oxford University Press, 1998), pp. 264–85.

—, *The Making and Unmaking of Empires: Britain, India and America c.1750–1783* (Oxford: Oxford University Press, 2005).

Maynard, H., 'Butler, Sir Theobald (Toby)', *DIB*, at <http://dib.cambridge.org/viewReadPage.do?articleId=a1307>.

McBride, I., '"The Common Name of Irishman": Protestantism and patriotism in eighteenth-century Ireland', in T. Claydon and I. McBride (eds), *Protestantism and National Identity: Britain and Ireland, c.1650–c.1850* (Cambridge: Cambridge University Press, 1998), pp. 236–61.

—, *Eighteenth-Century Ireland: The Isle of Slaves* (Dublin: Gill & Macmillan, 2009).

—, 'Catholic Politics in the Penal Era: Father Sylvester Lloyd and the Delvin Address of 1727', in J. Bergin, E. Magennis, L. Ní Munghaile and P. Walsh (eds), *New Perspectives on the Penal Laws: Eighteenth-Century Ireland Special Issue No. 1* (Dublin: Eighteenth-Century Ireland Society, 2011), pp. 115–48.

McCafferty, J., *The Reconstruction of the Church of Ireland: Bishop Bramhall and the Laudian Reforms, 1633–1641* (Cambridge: Cambridge University Press, 2007).

McCavitt, J., *Sir Arthur Chichester: Lord Deputy of Ireland 1605–16* (Belfast: Institute of Irish Studies, 1998).

McGrath, C. I., 'Securing the Protestant Interest: The Origins and Purpose of the Penal Laws of 1695', *Irish Historical Studies*, 30 (1996–7), pp. 25–46.

—, *The Making of the Eighteenth-Century Irish Constitution: Government, Parliament and the Revenue, 1692–1714* (Dublin: Four Courts Press, 2000).

—, 'Central Aspects of the Eighteenth-Century Constitutional Framework in Ireland: The Government Supply Bill and Biennial Parliamentary Sessions, 1715–82', *Eighteenth Century Ireland*, 16 (2001), pp. 9–34.

—, 'Parliamentary Additional Supply: The Development and Use of Regular Short-Term Taxation in the Irish Parliament, 1692–1716', *Parliamentary History*, 20 (2001), pp. 27–54.

—, 'English Ministers, Irish Politicians, and the Making of a Parliamentary Settlement in Ireland, 1692–5', *English Historical Review*, 119 (2004), pp. 585–613.

—, 'The Provisions for Conversion in the Penal Laws, 1695–1750', in C. I. McGrath and T. P. Power (eds), *Converts and Conversion in Ireland, 1650–1850* (Dublin: Four Courts Press, 2005), pp. 35–59.

—, 'Government, Parliament and the Constitution: The Reinterpretation of Poynings' Law, 1692–1714', *Irish Historical Studies*, 35 (2006–7), pp. 160–72.

—, 'The "Union" Representation of 1703 in the Irish House of Commons: A Case of Mistaken Identity?', *Eighteenth Century Ireland*, 23 (2008), pp. 11–35.

—, 'The Irish Experience of "Financial Revolution", 1660–1760', in C. I. McGrath and C. Fauske (eds), *Money, Power and Print: Interdisciplinary Studies on the Financial Revolution in the British Isles* (Newark, NJ: University of Delaware Press, 2008), pp. 157–88.

—, 'The Parliament of Ireland to 1800', in C. Jones (ed.), *A Short History of Parliament: England, Great Britain, the United Kingdom, Ireland and Scotland* (Woodbridge: Boydell & Brewer, 2009), pp. 321–38.

—, 'Alan Brodrick and the Speakership of the House of Commons, 1703–4', in J. Kelly, J. McCafferty, and C. I. McGrath (eds), *People, Politics and Power: Essays on Irish History 1660–1850 in Honour of James I. McGuire* (Dublin: UCD Press, 2009), pp. 70–93.

—, 'Waging War: The Irish Military Establishment and the British Empire, 1688–1763', in W. Mulligan and B. Simms (eds), *The Primacy of Foreign Policy in British History, 1660–2000* (Basingstoke: Palgrave, 2010), pp. 102–18.

—, 'Money, Politics and Power: The Financial Legislation of the Irish Parliament', in D. W. Hayton, J. Kelly and J. Bergin (eds), *The Eighteenth-Century Composite State: Representative Institutions in Ireland and Europe, 1689–1800* (Basingstoke: Palgrave, 2010), pp. 21–43.

—, '"The Public Wealth Is the Sinew, the Life, of Every Public Measure": The Creation and Maintenance of a National Debt in Ireland, 1716–45', in D. Carey and C. J. Finlay (eds), *The Empire of Credit: The Financial Revolution in the British Atlantic World, 1688–1815* (Dublin: Irish Academic Press, 2011), pp. 171–208.

—, 'Late Seventeenth- and Early Eighteenth-Century Governance and the Viceroyalty', in P. Gray and O. Purdue (eds), *The Irish Lord Lieutenancy c. 1541–1922* (Dublin: UCD Press, forthcoming 2012).

McGuire, J. I., 'The Irish Parliament of 1692', in T. Bartlett and D. W. Hayton (eds), *Penal Era and Golden Age: Essays in Irish History, 1690–1800* (Belfast: Ulster Historical Foundation, 1979), pp. 1–31.

—, 'The Treaty of Limerick', in B. Whelan (ed.), *The Last of the Great Wars: Essays on the War of the Three Kings in Ireland 1688–91* (Limerick: University of Limerick Press, 1995), pp. 127–38.

—,'Dopping, Anthony', *DIB*, at <http://dib.cambridge.org/viewReadPage.do?articleId=a2714>.

McNally, P., 'Wood's Halfpence, Carteret, and the Government of Ireland, 1723–6', *Irish Historical Studies*, 30 (1996–7), pp. 354–76.

—, *Parties, Patriots and Undertakers: Parliamentary Politics in Early Hanoverian Ireland* (Dublin: Four Courts Press, 1997).

McParland, E., 'The Office of the Surveyor-General in Ireland in the Eighteenth Century', *Architectural History*, 38 (1995), pp. 91–101.

—, *Public Architecture in Ireland 1680–1760* (New Haven, CT: Yale University Press, 2001).

Meigs, S. A., *The Reformations in Ireland: Tradition and Confessionalism, 1400–1690* (Dublin: Gill & Macmillan, 1997).

Miller, J., *Popery and Politics in England, 1660–1688* (Cambridge: Cambridge University Press, 1973).

—, *Charles II* (London: Weidenfield and Nicolson, 1991).

Miller, K. A., *Emigrants and Exiles: Ireland and the Irish Exodus to North America* (Oxford: Oxford University Press, 1985).

Moody, T. W., F. X. Martin and F. J. Byrne (eds), *A New History of Ireland, III: Early Modern Ireland 1534–1691* (Oxford: Oxford University Press, 1976).

— (eds), *A New History of Ireland, IX: Maps, Genealogies, Lists* (Oxford: Oxford University Press, 1984).

Moody, T. W., and W. E. Vaughan (eds), *A New History of Ireland, IV: Eighteenth-Century Ireland, 1691–1800* (Oxford: Oxford University Press, 1986).

Morley, V., *Irish Opinion and the American Revolution, 1760–1783* (Cambridge: Cambridge University Press, 2002).

Morrill, J., 'The Causes of the Penal Laws: Paradoxes and Inevitabilities', in J. Bergin, E. Magennis, L. Ní Munghaile and P. Walsh (eds), *New Perspectives on the Penal Laws: Eighteenth-Century Ireland Special Issue No. 1* (Dublin: Eighteenth-Century Ireland Society, 2011), pp. 55–73.

Mullett, M. A., *Catholics in Britain and Ireland, 1558–1829* (Basingstoke: Macmillan, 1998).

Murphy, D., *The Irish Brigades, 1685–2006: A Gazetteer of Irish Military Service, Past and Present* (Dublin: Four Courts Press, 2007).

Murphy, E., 'O'Brien, William, 2nd Earl of Inchiquin', *DIB*, at <http://dib.cambridge.org/viewReadPage.do?articleId=a6502>.

Murray, A. E., *A History of the Commercial and Financial Relations between England and Ireland from the Period of the Restoration* (London: P. S. King & Son, 1903).

Murtagh, H., 'The War in Ireland, 1689–91', in W. A. Maguire (ed.), *Kings in Conflict: The Revolutionary War in Ireland and Its Aftermath 1689–1750* (Belfast: Ulster Historical Foundation, 1990), pp. 61–91.

—, *Irish Historic Towns Atlas: Athlone* (Dublin: Royal Irish Academy, 1994).

—, 'Irish Soldiers Abroad, 1600–1800', in T. Bartlett and K. Jeffery (eds), *A Military History of Ireland* (Cambridge: Cambridge University Press, 1996), pp. 294–314.

Norman, E., *Roman Catholicism in England* (Oxford: Oxford University Press, 1986).

Ó Ciardha, É., *Ireland and the Jacobite Cause, 1685–1766: A Fatal Attachment* (Dublin: Four Courts Press, 2002).

Ó hAnnracháin, T., *Catholic Reformation in Ireland: The Mission of Rinuccini, 1645–1649* (Oxford: Oxford University Press, 2002).

Ó Siochrú, M., *Confederate Ireland 1642–1649: A Constitutional and Political Analysis* (Dublin: Four Courts Press, 1999).

— (ed.), *Kingdoms in Crisis: Ireland in the 1640s* (Dublin: Four Courts Press, 2001).

—, 'Catholic Confederates and the Constitutional Relationship between Ireland and England, 1641–1649', in C. Brady and J. Ohlmeyer. (eds), *British Interventions in Early Modern Ireland* (Cambridge: Cambridge University Press, 2005), pp. 207–29.

O'Brien, G. (ed.), *Catholic Ireland in the Eighteenth Century: Collected Essays of Maureen Wall* (Dublin: Geography Publications, 1989).

O'Brien, P. K., 'The Political Economy of British Taxation, 1660–1815', *Economic History Review*, 2nd series, 41 (1988), pp. 1–32.

O'Brien, P. K., and P. A. Hunt, 'The Rise of a Fiscal State in England, 1485–1815', *Bulletin of the Institute of Historical Research*, 66 (1993), pp. 129–76.

O'Byrne, E. (ed.), *The Convert Rolls: The Calendar of the Convert Rolls, 1703–1838, with Fr Wallace Clare's Annotated List of Converts, 1703–18, Edited by Anne Chamney* (Dublin: Irish Manuscripts Commission, 2005).

O'Donnell, P. D., 'Dublin Military Barracks', *Dublin Historical Record*, 25 (1972), pp. 141–54.

O'Donovan, D., 'The Money Bill Dispute of 1753', in T. Bartlett and D. W. Hayton (eds), *Penal Era and Golden Age: Essays in Irish History, 1690–1800* (Belfast: Ulster Historical Foundation, 1979), pp. 55–87.

O'Flaherty, E., *Irish Historic Towns Atlas: Limerick* (Dublin: Royal Irish Academy, 2010).

O'Flanagan, P., *Irish Historic Towns Atlas: Bandon* (Dublin: Royal Irish Academy, 1988).

O'Neill, T. P., 'Discoverers and Discoveries – a Preliminary Note' (NLI, unpublished paper).

—, 'Discoverers and Discoveries: The Penal Laws and Dublin Property', *Dublin Historical Record*, 37 (1983–4), pp. 2–13.

Ohlmeyer, J. (ed.), *Political Thought in Seventeenth-Century Ireland* (Cambridge: Cambridge University Press, 2000).

—, 'A Laboratory for Empire? Early Modern Ireland and English Imperialism', in K. Kenny (ed.), *Ireland and the British Empire* (Oxford: Oxford University Press, 2004), pp. 26–60.

Osborough, W. N., 'Catholics, Land and the Popery Acts of Anne', in T. P. Power and K. Whelan (eds), *Endurance and Emergence: Catholics in Ireland in the Eighteenth Century* (Dublin: Irish Academic Press, 1990), pp. 21–56.

—, 'The Failure to Enact an Irish Bill of Rights: A Gap in Irish Constitutional History', *Irish Jurist*, 33 (1998), pp. 392–416.

Oxford Dictionary of National Biography (Oxford: Oxford University Press, 2004).

Pagden, A., 'The Struggle for Legitimacy and the Image of Empire in the Atlantic to c.1700', in N. Canny (ed.), *The Oxford History of the British Empire, vol. I: The Origins of Empire* (Oxford: Oxford University Press, 1998), pp. 34–54.

—, *Peoples and Empires: Europeans and the Rest of the World, from Antiquity to the Present* (London: Phoenix Press, 2002).

Parker, G., *The Army of Flanders and the Spanish Road 1567–1659* (Cambridge: Cambridge University Press, 1972).

—, *The Military Revolution: Military Innovation and the Rise of the West, 1500–1800* (Cambridge: Cambridge University Press, 1988).

Parry, J. H., *Trade and Dominion: The European Overseas Empires in the Eighteenth Century* (London: Phoenix Press, 2000).

Pereira, H. P. E., 'Barracks in Ireland, 1729, 1769', *Irish Sword*, 1 (1949–53), pp. 142–4.

—, 'Quarters of the Army in Ireland, 1769', *Irish Sword*, 2 (1954–6), pp. 230–1.

Phair, P. E. H., and R. Law, 'The English in Western Africa to 1700', in N. Canny (ed.), *The Oxford History of the British Empire, vol. I: The Origins of Empire* (Oxford: Oxford University Press, 1998), pp. 241–63.

Powell, M. J., 'The Reform of the Undertaker System: Anglo-Irish Politics, 1750–67', *Irish Historical Studies*, 31 (1998–9), pp. 19–36.

—, *Britain and Ireland in the Eighteenth-Century Crisis of Empire* (Basingstoke: Palgrave, 2003).

Power, T. P., 'Converts', in T. P. Power and K. Whelan (eds), *Endurance and Emergence: Catholics in Ireland in the Eighteenth Century* (Dublin: Irish Academic Press, 1990), pp. 101–27.

—, 'Conversions among the Legal Profession in Ireland in the Eighteenth Century', in D. Hogan and W. N. Osborough (eds), *Brehons, Serjeants and Attorneys* (Dublin: Irish Academic Press, 1990), pp. 153–74.

—, 'The Theology and Liturgy for Conversion from Catholicism to Anglicanism', in M. Brown, C. I. McGrath and T. P. Power (eds), *Converts and Conversion in Ireland, 1650–1850* (Dublin: Four Courts Press, 2005), pp. 60–78.

—, '"A Weighty, Serious Business": The Conversion of Catholic Clergy to Anglicanism', in M. Brown, C. I. McGrath and T. P. Power (eds), *Converts and Conversion in Ireland, 1650–1850* (Dublin: Four Courts Press, 2005), pp. 183–213.

Power, T. P., and K. Whelan (eds), *Endurance and Emergence: Catholics in Ireland in the Eighteenth Century* (Dublin: Irish Academic Press, 1990).

Quinn, D. B., 'The Early Interpretation of Poynings' Law, 1494–1534', *Irish Historical Studies*, 2 (1940–1), pp. 241–54.

Richter, M., *Medieval Ireland: The Enduring Tradition* (Dublin: Gill & Macmillan, 1988).

Robbins, C., *The Eighteenth-Century Commonwealthman* (New York: Atheneum, 1968).

Robinson, P., *Irish Historic Towns Atlas: Carrickfergus* (Dublin: Royal Irish Academy, 1986).

Rogers, H. C. B., *The British Army of the Eighteenth Century* (London: Allen & Unwin, 1977).

Rose, C., *England in the 1690s: Revolution, Religion and War* (Oxford: Blackwell, 1999).

Roseveare, H., *The Financial Revolution 1660–1760* (London: Longman, 1991).

Rudé, G., *Europe in the Eighteenth Century: Aristocracy and the Bourgeois Challenge* (London: Phoenix, 2002).

Ryder, M., 'The Bank of Ireland, 1721: Land, Credit and Dependency', *Historical Journal*, 25 (1982), pp. 557–82.

Ryrie, A., *The Age of Reformation: The Tudor and Stuart Realms 1485–1603* (London: Longman, 2009).

Schwoerer, L. G., 'The Role of King William III of England in the Standing Army Controversy – 1697–1699', *Journal of British Studies*, 5 (1966), pp. 74–94.

—, *'No Standing Armies!': The Anti-Army Ideology in Seventeenth-Century England* (Baltimore, MD: Johns Hopkins University Press, 1974).

Scouller, R. E., *The Armies of Queen Anne* (Oxford: Clarendon Press, 1966).

Shy, J. W., *Toward Lexington: The Role of the British Army in the Coming of the American Revolution* (Princeton, NJ: Princeton University Press, 1965).

Simms, A., H. Clarke and R. Gillespie, *Irish Historic Towns Atlas: Armagh* (Dublin: Royal Irish Academy, 2007).

Simms, J. G., *The Williamite Confiscation in Ireland 1690–1703* (London: Faber and Faber, 1956).

—, 'Irish Catholics and the Parliamentary Franchise, 1692–1728', *Irish Historical Studies*, 12 (1960–1), pp. 28–37.

—, 'The Making of a Penal Law (2 Anne, c. 6), 1703–4', *Irish Historical Studies*, 12 (1960–1), pp. 105–18.

—, *The Treaty of Limerick* (Dundalk: Dundalgan Press, 1965).

—, *Jacobite Ireland 1685–91* (London: Routledge, 1969).

—, 'The Bishops' Banishment Act of 1697 (9 Will. III, c. I)', *Irish Historical Studies*, 17 (1970–1), pp. 185–99.

—, *The Jacobite Parliament of 1689* (Dundalk: Dundalgan Press, 1974).

—, *Colonial Nationalism 1698–1776: Molyneux's The Case of Ireland ... stated* (Cork: Mercier Press, 1976).

— (ed.), *The Case of Ireland Stated by William Molyneux* (Dublin: Cadenus Press, 1977).

—, *William Molyneux of Dublin 1656–1698*, ed. P. H. Kelly (Dublin: Irish Academic Press, 1982).

Smyth, J., '"Like Amphibious Animals": Irish Protestants, Ancient Britons, 1691–1707', *Historical Journal*, 36 (1993), pp. 785–97.

—, 'Anglo-Irish Unionist Discourse, c.1656–1707: From Harrington to Fletcher', *Bullán*, 2 (1995), pp. 17–34.

—, '"No Remedy More Proper": Anglo-Irish Unionism before 1707', in B. Bradshaw and P. Roberts (eds), *British Consciousness and Identity: The Making of Britain, 1533–1707* (Cambridge: Cambridge University Press, 1998), pp. 301–20.

—, *The Making of the United Kingdom, 1660–1800* (London: Longman, 2001).

Spiers, E. M., 'Army Organisation and Society in the Nineteenth Century', in T. Bartlett and K. Jeffery (eds), *A Military History of Ireland* (Cambridge: Cambridge University Press, 1996), pp. 335–57.

Stasavage, D., *Public Debt and the Birth of the Democratic State: France and Great Britain, 1688–1789* (Cambridge: Cambridge University Press, 2003).

Stone, L. (ed.), *An Imperial State at War: Britain from 1689 to 1815* (London: Routledge, 1994).

—, 'Introduction', in L. Stone (ed.), *An Imperial State at War: Britain from 1689 to 1815* (London: Routledge, 1994), pp. 1–32.

Swann, J., 'Politics: Louis XIV', in W. Doyle (ed.), *Old Regime France, 1648–1788* (Oxford: Oxford University Press, 2001), pp. 195–222.

Thomas, A., *Irish Historic Towns Atlas: Derry – Londonderry* (Dublin: Royal Irish Academy, 2005).

Trevelyan, G. M., *The English Revolution 1688–1689* (Oxford: Oxford University Press, 1965).

Truxes, T. M., *Irish-American Trade, 1660–1783* (Cambridge: Cambridge University Press, 1988).

Victory, I., 'The Making of the 1720 Declaratory Act', in G. O'Brien (ed.), *Parliament, Politics and People: Essays in Eighteenth-Century Irish History* (Dublin: Irish Academic Press, 1989), pp. 9–29.

Wall, M., *The Penal Laws, 1691–1760* (Dundalk: Dundalgan Press, 1976).

—, 'The Quest for Catholic Equality, 1745–1778', in G. O'Brien (ed.), *Catholic Ireland in the Eighteenth Century: Collected Essays of Maureen Wall* (Dublin: Geography Publications, 1989), pp. 115–34.

Walsh, P., *The Making of the Irish Protestant Ascendancy: The Life of William Conolly, 1662–1729* (Woodbridge: Boydell and Brewer, 2010).

Walsh, P. A., and A. O'Brien, 'Nevill, Arthur Jones', *DIB*, at <http://dib.cambridge.org/viewReadPage.do?articleId=a6164>.

Walton, C., *History of the British Standing Army 1660–1700* (London: Harrison & Sons, 1894).

Wauchope, P., *Patrick Sarsfield and the Williamite War* (Dublin: Irish Academic Press, 1992).

Webb, S. S., *The Governors-General: The English Army and the Definition of the Empire, 1569–1681* (Williamsburg, VA: Chapel Hill, 1979).

Whelan, B. (ed.), *The Last of the Great Wars: Essays on the War of the Three Kings in Ireland 1688–91* (Limerick: University of Limerick Press, 1995).

Wilson, P., 'Warfare in the Old Regime 1648–1789', in J. Black (ed.), *European Warfare 1453–1815* (Basingstoke: Palgrave, 1999), pp. 69–95.

York, N. L., *Neither Kingdom nor Nation: The Irish Quest for Constitutional Rights, 1698–1800* (Washington, DC: Catholic University of America Press, 1994).

Unpublished Theses

Aydelotte, J. E., 'The Duke of Ormond and the English Government of Ireland, 1677–85' (PhD, Iowa University, 1975).

Doyle, T. G., 'Parliament and Politics in Williamite Ireland 1690–1703' (MA, UCD, 1992).

—, 'The Politics of Protestant Ascendancy: Politics, Religion and Society in Protestant Ireland, 1700–1710' (PhD, UCD, 1996).

Egan, S., 'Finance and the government of Ireland, 1660–85', 2 vols (PhD, TCD, 1983).

Ferguson, K. P., 'The Army in Ireland from the Restoration to the Act of Union' (PhD, TCD, 1981).

Griffin, J., 'Parliamentary Politics in Ireland during the Reign of George I' (MA, UCD, 1977).

Hayton, D. W., 'Ireland and the English Ministers 1707–16: A Study in the Formulation and Working of Government Policy in the Early 18th Century' (DPhil, Oxford, 1975).

Léoutre, M., 'Life of a Huguenot Exile: Henri de Ruvigny, Earl of Galway, 1648–1720' (PhD, UCD, 2012).

Lyons, E., 'Morristown Lattin: A Case Study of the Lattin and Mansfield Families in County Kildare, c. 1660–1860' (PhD, UCD, 2011).

McGrath, C. I., 'Securing the Protestant Interest: Parliament, Policy and Politics in Ireland in the Aftermath of the Glorious Revolution 1690–1695' (MA, UCD, 1991).

—, 'The Irish Revenue System: Government and Administration, 1689–1702' (PhD, University of London, 1997).

O'Donoghue, F., 'The Irish Parliament under Charles II' (MA, UCD, 1970).

INDEX

Page numbers in italics refer to figures and tables and those including an 'n' refer to notes.

For Product Safety Concerns and Information please contact our EU
representative GPSR@taylorandfrancis.com
Taylor & Francis Verlag GmbH, Kaufingerstraße 24, 80331 München, Germany

www.ingramcontent.com/pod-product-compliance
Ingram Content Group UK Ltd.
Pitfield, Milton Keynes, MK11 3LW, UK
UKHW021621240425
457818UK00018B/681